PARIS: A CENTURY OF CHANGE, 1878-1978

NEW HAVEN AND LONDON: YALE UNIVERSITY PRESS: 1979

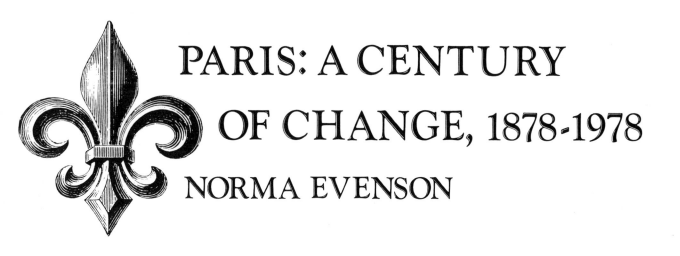

PARIS: A CENTURY OF CHANGE, 1878-1978

NORMA EVENSON

*Published with assistance from the
National Endowment for the Humanities.*

*Designed by Sally Harris
and set in VIP Garamond type.
Printed in the United States of America by
The Murray Printing Co., Westford, Mass.*

*Published in Great Britain, Europe, Africa, and
Asia (except Japan) by Yale University Press,
Ltd., London. Distributed in Australia and
New Zealand by Book & Film Services, Artarmon,
N.S.W., Australia; and in Japan by Harper & Row,
Publishers, Tokyo Office.*

Library of Congress Cataloging in Publication Data

Evenson, Norma.
  Paris: a century of change, 1878–1978

  Bibliography: p.
  Includes index.
  *1. Paris—City planning—History. 2. Urban
renewal—France—Paris. 3. City planning—France—
Case studies. I. Title.*
  HT169.F72P356   309.2'62'0944361   78-10257
  ISBN 0-300-02210-7

CONTENTS

ILLUSTRATIONS

Unless otherwise indicated, all photographs are by the author. The following abbreviations are used:

Concours	*Concours pour l'aménagement de la voie allant de la Place de l'Étoile à la Place au Rond Point de la Défense*
Concours de façades	*Les concours de façades de la ville de Paris 1898–1905*
Établissement Public—La Défense	Établissement Public pour l'Aménagement de la Région de La Défense
Études	Eugène Hénard, *Études sur les transformations de Paris*
Interphotothèque, D.F.	Interphotothèque, Documentation Française
OC	Le Corbusier, *Oeuvre complète* (S.P.A.D.E.M.)
Photo B.N. Paris	Photographie Bibliothèque Nationale Paris
Proc Amer Inst Archit	*Proceedings of the American Institute of Architects*
RATP	Régie Autonome des Transports Parisiens
Schéma directeur—Région de Paris	*Schéma directeur d'aménagement et d'urbanisme de la région de Paris*
Schéma directeur—Ville de Paris	*Schéma directeur d'aménagement et d'urbanisme de la ville de Paris*
Service Régional de l'Équipement	Service Régional de l'Équipement de la Région Parisienne

PREFACE

On a visit to Paris in 1969, I had the opportunity to become acquainted with current planning efforts and to visit some of the sites of new development in and around the city. Like many foreigners, I had known Paris primarily for its historic urban fabric, its famous monuments, and the nineteenth-century renovations directed by Georges Haussmann. A century had passed since the retirement of Haussmann, and Paris seemed once again in the midst of a massive transformation. However one might love old Paris, there was a new Paris that was difficult to ignore.

Haussmann's work is amply documented and forms a well-known chapter in the history of urbanism. Study of the subsequent development of Paris has been relatively fragmented. It seemed of interest, therefore, to undertake a history that would trace the evolution of planning efforts in Paris from the end of the Second Empire to the present.

I began my research in Paris during the summer of 1971 and continued during 1972–73, 1975–76, and the summer of 1977. Support was provided by the American Philosophical Society, the Fulbright-Hays Program, the Guggenheim Foundation, and the University of California Humanities Professorship Program.

This book is a series of essays, each of which considers a separate facet of the planning of Paris. The term *planning* has been taken to include not only the creation of master plans, but also major government policies and programs that have affected the development of the city. These include street works, transportation systems, building regulation, public housing, preservation and restoration, and urban renewal. I have been guided in selection and emphasis by the problems that have been of greatest and most persistent concern to the planners of Paris and the issues that have generated the most public controversy. Although this is not a social history, the physical developments dealt with clearly have social origins and social consequences.

The pressures for expansion and change that Paris has experienced during the past century have been felt in many cities, but the urban heritage Parisians have attempted to adapt to contemporary needs is unique. Paris is no ordinary city, but a cherished part of the cultural endowment of the Western World. There has been a temptation, not altogether resisted, to add yet another voice to the chorus currently denouncing the "destruction" of Paris. Like most lovers of Paris, I love old Paris and have reservations about the new. Yet to a historian there is a fascination in observing the forces of change. It has been my desire to illuminate the nature of certain disputes, rather than to participate in them. As this study forms a segment of the continuing history of Paris, moreover, one can draw no true "conclusions."

Throughout its evolution, Paris has never been free of controversy, nor has the city ever been immune to urban problems. In 1900, an American publication informed its readers that "the French people have created the cleanest, the healthiest and the most beautiful city in the world." Yet from the same epoch, there is abundant testimony of the filth and stench of the streets, the squalor and pestilence of the slums, the shortage of open space, and the æsthetic horrors of contemporary architecture. A turn-of-the-century architectural critic was moved to envision the existence of a sinister organization composed of architects and officials that called itself the Society of the Enemies of Paris. Meeting secretly in the basement of city hall, this malign conspiracy presumably pursued its aim of making Paris ugly. Paris has been continually perceived as a threatened environment, and cries of alarm have been raised repeatedly during the past century. The development of Paris may be used as evidence to justify almost any ideological position one wishes to take, and among the villains who have been denounced for the decline and fall of the city have been the forces of laissez-faire capitalism, excessive government control, and various foreign influences.

Protest over the direction of urban renovation in Paris has been especially abundant in recent years. The city which a century ago was a potent influence on urban planning has been the recipient of a wave of reconstruction sometimes characterized as "Americanization" and evidenced in large renewal projects, skyscrapers, multilane expressways, supermarkets, and an outward movement of population toward an automobile-based pattern of suburban settlement. While some have deplored such development as an alien infection, others have accepted it as a wide-ranging and virtually irresistible international trend.

In any event, it is difficult to evaluate the importance of a single century in the life of a city. Habitation of the Paris region goes back to Paleolithic times, and the city was an ancient settlement when the Romans arrived in 51 B.C. A hundred years, as Gertrude Stein observed, "is not so long. Anybody can know somebody who remembers somebody else and makes it go back one hundred years. If it cannot be done in two generations it can be done easily done in three. And so one hundred years is not so long." Yet, while a century in the modern world is still short in this sense, the pace of change has accelerated. A century no longer implies a period of slow accretion. Apprehension about the future of Paris seems to reflect a fear that, in the rapidity of redevelopment, all sense of continuity with the past may be lost, and the richness of old Paris obliterated and even forgotten. The current wave of rhetoric inevitably contains some exaggeration of present-day horrors as well as some romanticizing of the past.

Has Paris ceased to be Paris? It depends on one's definition. Certainly the city has changed and will continue to do so. Paris today is a populous urbanized region in which the historic central city forms a specialized and symbolically crucial part. The traditional image of Paris is vital to its attraction, yet the greatness of the city has never depended on a specific ensemble of buildings or configuration of streets. And Paris remains a great city. While one may view the skyline with less than delight, the compelling vitality of Paris, its political, economic, and cultural primacy remain undiminished. It is, in fact, the very vitality of the city which continually threatens the stability of the physical environment. Contrary to rumor, Paris is alive and well and living in Paris.

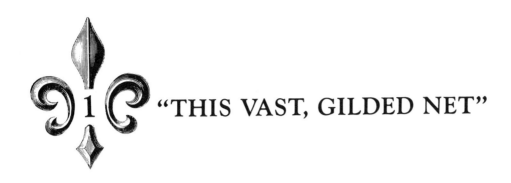

1 "THIS VAST, GILDED NET"

It was said, in the previous century, "good Americans, when they die, go to Paris."[1] Only thus, one assumes, might a life sternly disciplined by Puritan morality and relentlessly dedicated to utilitarian toil be appropriately rewarded. Certainly, the concrete imagery of broad, tree-lined boulevards, the shops, cafes, and theaters, the good food and wine of this earthly city might easily eclipse a nebulous vision of celestial pearly gates and golden stairs. Rich Americans, of course, did not have to wait until they were dead to see the City of Light.

Americans were by no means the only foreigners attracted to the French capital, and much of the richness of Paris, then as now, lay in its cosmopolitan nature. Victor Hugo once observed that "this city does not belong to a people, but to peoples . . . the human race has a right to Paris. France, with sublime detachment, understands this."[2] A century later, another Frenchman noted that "it is traditionally an honor for France to have known how to cultivate a city so open that one can consider oneself a Parisian, and be recognized as such, without the necessity of being French."[3]

Paris is an old city. In common with many other European capitals, it embodies the physical remnants of centuries of settlement. Yet Paris has never become a museum, and the heritage of the past has continually been subordinated to the dynamism and pressures for change inherent in a vital and growing city.

Gertrude Stein, who settled in Paris in 1903, once remarked, "Paris was where the twentieth century was."[4] Paris had also been where the nineteenth century was, and in terms of planning the Paris of a hundred years ago was a widely emulated model of modernity. The outward face of the city embodied the results of a massive

1. This widely repeated phrase has been credited to Thomas Gold Appleton (1812–84), a well-traveled Bostonian.
2. "Reliquat de 'Paris,'" notes prepared by Victor Hugo for his Paris guide book of 1867. Reproduced in Victor Hugo, *Paris,* edition prepared by Hubert Juin, Paris: Livre Club du Libraire, p. 309.
3. Alain Griotteray, "Exigences du destin de Paris," *Urbanisme* 84 (1964): 29.
4. Gertrude Stein, *Paris, France* (New York: Scribner, 1940), p. 11.

I

program of renovation undertaken by the emperor Napoleon III and directed by Baron Georges-Eugène Haussmann, who had served as Prefect of the Seine between 1853 and 1870.[5] While Paris still contained many old and picturesque quarters, the dominant impression of the city was that of a busy, sprawling metropolis. The recently completed boulevards throbbed with traffic, the growing volume of building emphasized an expanded urban scale, and the highly visible commercial activity underlined the character of the city as a center of luxury and wealth.

One can obtain a vivid impression of the impact of Paris on the visitor of a century ago from the account of an Italian writer, Edmondo de Amicis, who arrived at the time of the 1878 Exposition. Characterizing the city as "this vast gilded net, into which one is drawn again and again,"[6] he began his chronicle with a description of the journey by carriage from the Gare de Lyon toward the center of the city. "The first impression," he noted, "is an agreeable one. It is the large, irregular square of the Bastille, noisy and crowded, into which open four Boulevards, and ten streets, and from which one hears the deafening clamor of the immense suburb of St. Antoine. . . . It is the first quick, deep whiff of Paris life." Proceeding down the Boulevard Beaumarchais, de Amicis admired the "wide streets, the double row of trees, the cheerful-looking houses," observing that "everything is neat and fresh, and wears a youthful air. . . . Between the two rows of trees is a constant passing and repassing of carriages, great carts and wagons drawn by engines and high omnibuses, laden with people, bounding up and down on the unequal pavement, with a deafening noise. Yet the whole air is different from that of London—the green open place, the faces, the voices, and the colors give to that confusion more the air of pleasure than of work."

Upon entering the Boulevard du Temple, de Amicis noted, "the wide street grows broader still, the side ones lengthen, and the houses rise higher. The grandeur of Paris begins to appear; and so, as we proceed, everything increases in proportion and becomes more impressive. Then we begin to see the theaters, the Cirque and Olympique, the Lyrique, the Gaîté and Folies, the elegant cafes, the great shops, the fine restaurants, and the crowd assumes a more thoroughly Parisian aspect."

The Boulevard St. Martin provided "another step forward upon this road of elegance and grandeur (figure 1). The variegated chiosks become thicker, the shops more splendid, and the cafes more pretentious. The little terraces and balconies of the houses are covered with gilded cubital characters, which give to every facade the air of the frontispiece of an immense book. The theater fronts, the arches of the arcades, the edifices covered with woodwork up to the second floors, the restaurants

---

5. The work of Haussmann has been widely dealt with by historians. A readable and scholarly account in English is David Pinkney, *Napoleon III and the Rebuilding of Paris* (Princeton: Princeton University Press, 1958).

6. Edmondo de Amicis, *Studies of Paris* (translated from the Italian) (New York: Putnam, 1882).

All subsequent quotations from de Amicis are taken from chapter 1, "The First Day in Paris," pp. 1–36. To avoid excessive footnotes, the remaining quotations will not be identified.

1. The boulevard Saint Martin in 1873.

which open upon the streets in the form of little temples, and the theaters gleaming with mirrors, succeed each other uninterruptedly, each connected with the other like one unending shop. . . . The Boulevard St. Denis succeeds the Boulevard St. Martin. The great street descends, rises, narrows, receives from the large arteries of the populous neighboring quarters crowds of horses and people; and extends before us as far as the eye can reach, swarming with carriages and black with the crowd, divided into three parts by the enormous garlands of verdure, which fill it with shade and freshness. For three quarters of an hour we have been going step by step, winding in and out and just clearing interminable lines of carriages, which present the appearance of a fabulous nuptial cortege extending from one end of Paris to the other. We enter the Boulevard Bonne Nouvelle, and the bustle, hum and noise increase, as does the grandeur of the great shops which line the street with their enormous show windows. . . . It is not a street through which we are passing, but rather a succession of squares. A single, immense square decked for a fête, and overflowed by a multitude gleaming in quicksilver. Everything is open, transparent and placed in view as at an elegant, great market in the open air. . . . Meanwhile we

2. Street life on the Boulevard des Italiens, 1872.

enter the Boulevard Poissonière from the Boulevard Bonne Nouvelle and the spectacle grows more varied, extended and richer. We have already traversed the length of four thousand metres. . . .

At last, we enter the Boulevard Montmartre, which is followed by those of the Italiens, Capucines and Madeleine (figures 2 and 3). Ah! Here is the burning heart of Paris, . . . the high road to mundane triumphs, the great theatre of the ambitions and of the famous dissolutenesses, which draws to itself the gold, vice and folly of the four quarters of the globe. Here is splendor at its height. . . . Here the street becomes a square, the sidewalk a street, the shop a museum, the café a theatre, beauty elegance, splendor dazzling magnificence, and life a fever. The horses pass in troops, and the crowd in torrents. Windows, signs, advertisements, doors, façades, all rise, widen and become silvered, gilded and illumined. . . . The gigantic panes of glass, the innumerable mirrors, the bright trimmings of wood which extend half way up the edifices, reflect everything. Great inscriptions in gold run along the façades like the verses from the Koran along the walls of the mosques. The eye finds no space upon which to rest. On every side gleam names illustrious in the kingdom of fashion and pleasure, the titles of the restaurants of princes and Croesuses; and the shops, whose doors one opens with a trembling hand—everywhere an aristocratic luxury, provoking and bold, which says, Spend—Pour out—and Enjoy, and at the same time excites and chafes the desires. . . . It does not seem like passing through a public place, so great is the cleanliness and grandeur. The crowd itself moves there with a certain staid grace, as if in a great hall, gliding over the asphalt without noise, as over a carpet. . . . Even the vendors of newspapers in the chiosks here assume a certain literary air. . . . One can in fact collect with the thoughts all the scattered pictures which are to be found in our most flourishing cities; but no one, who has never seen it, will ever be able to represent the spectacle of that living stream which flows without rest between those two interminable walls of glass, amid that verdure and that gold, beside that noisy tumult of horses and wheels, and in that wide street whose end one cannot see; nor form a just idea of the figure, which the miserable valises belonging to us poor *literati* made in its midst."

3. The Boulevard des Italiens in 1905.

Following his initial immersion into Paris, de Amicis took a carriage ride "describing an immense zig-zag on the right bank of the Seine, in order to see life circulating in the minor arteries of Paris." He observed with pleasure "that verdant and splendid Boulevard, Sébastopol and Strasbourg, which seems made for the triumphal passage of an army, and that endless Rue Lafayette." He described "the immense openings" of the Boulevards Haussmann, Malesherbes, Magenta, and Prince Eugène, "into which one glances with a shudder, as into an abyss." At the Rond Point de l'Étoile, he noted "flying in all directions, like the spokes of an immense wheel, the main streets which divide into fourteen gay, triangular quarters, the tenth part of Paris." Returning to the heart of the city, he traversed "that inextricable net of small crooked streets, full of noise and crowded with memories, whose sudden, malicious turnings prepare the great unexpected views of the cross-roads full of light, and of the noted streets closed at the end by a magnificent pile, which rises above the city like a mountain of chiselled granite."

Having climbed to the top of Notre Dame, de Amicis observed the city from above. "Paris fills the horizon and seems as if it would cover all the world with the gray, immovable, measureless waves of its roofs and walls." He looked down upon the Seine, which "glistened like a silver scarf from one end of Paris to the other, striped by its thirty bridges," and noted "here and there great spots that were cemetaries, gardens and parks, and resembled green islands in that ocean." He let his eyes sweep "from Belleville to Ivry, from the Bois de Boulogne to Pantin, from Courbevoie to the Forest of Vincennes, springing from cupola to cupola, tower to tower, from colossus to colossus, from memory to memory and century to century, accompanied as if with music, by the long, deep inhalation of Paris."

Returning to the streets, de Amicis immersed himself in dinner-hour traffic, and as the first lamps were lighted, and crowds began to assemble at the theaters and restaurants, he absorbed the heady stimulation of the great city at play.

In the center of Paris, the city lights produced an extraordinary effect. In the words of the awestruck visitor: "It is not an illumination, but a fire. The Boulevards are blazing. Half closing the eyes it seems [as] if one saw on the right and left two rows of flaming furnaces. The shops cast floods of brilliant light half across the street, and encircle the crowd in a golden dust. . . . The chiosks, which extend in two interminable rows, lighted from within, with their many colored panes, resembling enormous Chinese lanterns placed on the ground, or the little transparent theatres of the Marionettes, give to the street the fantastic and childlike aspect of an Oriental fête. The numberless reflections of the glasses, the thousand luminous points shining through the branches of the trees, the inscriptions in gas gleaming on the theatre fronts, the rapid motion of the innumerable carriage lights, that seem like myriads of fireflies set in motion by the wind, the purple lamps of the omnibuses, the great flaming halls opening into the street, the shops which resemble caves of incandescent gold and silver, the hundred thousand illuminated windows, the trees that seem to be lighted, all these theatrical splendors, half-concealed by the verdure, which now and then allows one to see the distant illuminations, and presents the spectacle in successive scenes,—all this broken light, refracted, variegated, and mobile, falling in showers, gathered in torrents, and scattered in stars and diamonds, produces the first time an impression of which no idea can possibly be given. It seems like an immense display of fireworks, which suddenly being extinguished, will leave the city buried in smoke. There is not a shadow on the sidewalks, where one could find a pin. Every face is illuminated. . . . Before every café there is the parquette of a theatre, of which the Boulevard is the stage. . . . You walk on, always in the midst of a fire, amid an immovable and seated crowd, so that it seems as if you were passing from saloon to saloon in an immense open palace, or through a suite of enormous Spanish *Patios,* amid the spendors of a ball, among a million guests, without knowing when you will arrive at the exit, if there be one."

Reaching the Place de l'Opéra, the already bedazzled tourist reported "it is here that Paris makes one of its grandest impressions. You have before you the façade of the *Theatre,* enormous and bold, resplendent with colossal lamps between the elegant columns, . . . and turning around, you see three great diverging streets which dazzle you like so many luminous abysses . . . and a crowd coming and going under a shower of rosy and whitest light diffused from the great ground-glass globes, which produce the effect of wreaths and garlands of full moons."

"Yet," continued de Amicis, "this is not the greatest spectacle of the night." It remained for the Place de la Concorde to inspire "the loudest and most joyous

4. The Place de la Concorde, looking south toward the Chambre des Députés.

exclamation of surprise which Paris can draw from the lips of a stranger (figure 4). There certainly is no other square in any European city where beauty, light, art and nature aid each other so marvellously by forming a spectacle which entrances the imagination."

Reflecting on the apparent vitality and prosperity of Paris, de Amicis found it extraordinary that this city, "which one day seemed to have sunk entirely under the maledictions of God," should appear after only seven years "so grand, superb and proud, so full of blood, gold and glory." He was referring, of course, to the recent Franco-Prussian War and the crisis of the Paris Commune.

It may be recalled that Napoleon III, having ruled for twenty years during an era of stability and optimism, concluded his reign amidst national humiliation and defeat. As his personal power began to ebb late in the 1860s, the emperor, allying himself closely with conservative elements in his government, had hoped to bolster his position through a French victory at arms. A hasty and ill-advised war was declared against Prussia on July 19, 1870. Less than six weeks later, on September 2, 1870, Napoleon surrendered to William I of Prussia at Sedan, together with an army of some eighty thousand men. In spite of this stunning defeat, however, the nation continued to resist. A provisional government in Paris declared the formation of the Third Republic on September 4 and proceeded to direct the virtually hopeless military campaign against the invading Prussians.

The focus of some of the most bitter fighting was the city of Paris itself, which was besieged for four and one-half months. A ring of fortifications surrounding the city had been completed in 1845, and this defensive belt, with its bastions and earthworks, was hastily put back into service. The initial strategy of the attackers had been to reduce the city through famine. On December 27, however, the impatient Prussian commander, Count von Moltke, decided to break the siege through bombardment, and by the middle of January German artillery was close enough to strike the interior of the city. In a world as yet unused to the commonplaces of modern mechanized warfare, the shelling of a famished civilian population, together with the threatened destruction of a world-famous capital, produced a measure of albeit ineffective diplomatic protest.

By the end of January, when sickness and starvation were producing alarming death rates, the armistice was signed. Included in the terms of peace was provision for a brief, largely symbolic Prussian occupation of the capital. On March 1, 1871, occupying troops marched along the Avenue de la Grande Armée, and down the Champs Élysées to the Place de la Concorde. The invaders remained quietly in the central part of the city, and on the morning of March 3 they marched back up the Champs Élysées, cheering as they passed through the Arc de Triomphe. Although the sight of enemy troops within the monumental precincts of Paris may have been less painful physically than the starvation and shelling, it struck a vivid blow to the pride of the city. The parade of Prussian soldiers through the Place de l'Étoile was judged a desecration sufficient to prompt a symbolic purification of its pavement through fire.

An additional blow to civic pride was the chioce of Versailles as the seat of the new national government. Within the demoralized city the political vacuum was soon filled by a revolutionary municipal government called the Commune, supported by remnants of the National Guard. Failing in an effort to attack and overthrow the Versailles government, the Commune forces were in turn attacked in Paris and eventually destroyed by regular troops of the national government. National forces entered the capital on May 21 and fought their way through the city street by street until the bitter and savage conflict ended on May 28. Meanwhile, as their position became increasingly desperate, the communards avenged themselves through the destruction of the city's architectural monuments.

Even before the government attack, on May 16, 1871, the column of the Place Vendôme, crowned with its statue of Napoleon I, had been demolished. The toppling of this column, promoted by the painter Courbet, was virtually a ceremonial occasion, for which invitations were issued. Subsequent attacks on civic monuments took place in a sudden destructive frenzy while fighting filled the city.

On the night of May 23 the Tuileries Palace, which had been filled with barrels of gunpowder and smeared with tar and petrol, was set afire, and by the next day fires raged throughout the city. The blaze continued throughout the night, while the clouds of smoke hanging over Paris inspired comparisons with the eruption of Vesuvius and the fall of Babylon. Among the buildings destroyed were the Hôtel de Ville, the Cour des Comptes, a large part of the Palais Royal, the Prefecture of Police, the Légion d'Honneur, the Ministry of Finance (housed in a wing of the Louvre), and sections of the Rue de Rivoli. Other monuments, including Notre Dame Cathedral, narrowly escaped destruction.

Once the rebellion was mastered, the national army took revenge with a ferocity that grimly prophesied the future conduct of modern civilized society. Mass executions reportedly left the Seine streaked with blood, while funeral pyres of burning flesh scented the air. As often occurs in civil conflict, the wounds inflicted were deep and festering, and for those who had seen the Commune as the promise of a new social order the euphoria of hope gave way to swift and brutal despair.

And yet the very intensity of the disaster seemed to inspire a corresponding energy toward recovery. Even in defeat the French capital maintained its magnetism, and by the beginning of June 1871 Thomas Cook was organizing special tourist excursions to visit the ruins of Paris. Although the city had been burdened with a heavy war indemnity, the succeeding years marked continuous efforts at repairing the destruction left by the conflict, as well as a resumption of the Second Empire redevelopment plan.

The new column of the Place Vendôme was completed by 1875, and the Ministry of Finance, burned by the Commune, was moved into the newly repaired Rivoli wing of the Louvre. A design for the new Hôtel de Ville was selected through a competition held in 1872, which was won by the architects Théodore Ballu and E. Deperthes. The style of the Hôtel de Ville maintained the general character of the original Renaissance building, although the new structure, to be completed in 1882, also reflected a nineteenth-century taste for sumptuous decoration, high relief, and dramatic roof lines. When de Amicis visited Paris in 1878 the Hôtel de Ville was under construction, and from the top of Notre Dame he saw its skeleton, "resembling a great bird cage."

The gutted walls of the Tuileries remained standing, awaiting a final decision as to the disposition of the ruin. The remaining structure appears to have been salvageable, and various proposals were made for its restoration. Haussmann came out of retirement to urge that the old royal residence be saved, suggesting that it be used as a national museum of modern art. The radical-republican majority which dominated the Municipal Council, however, was hostile to the idea of preserving an imperial symbol. In 1882, the year in which final amnesty was granted to the communards, the city razed the Tuileries, completing the work of the Commune.

Meanwhile the civic projects begun by Haussmann had been continued under prefects Calmon and Duval, with Haussmann's old associate Jean Alphand serving as director of works, a position he held until 1891, the year of his death. On January 5, 1875, the Paris Opéra, begun in 1861, was inaugurated, and the architect, Charles Garnier, acknowledged admiring applause as he ascended its opulent staircase. In 1876 the Boulevard Henri IV was cut through and the Pont Sully constructed, making a direct connection between the Place de la Bastille and the Boulevard Saint Germain on the Left Bank. The Parc de Montsouris was opened the same year.

In 1877 President MacMahon dedicated the recently completed Avenue de l'Opéra, a monumental artery leading from the Rue de Rivoli to the Place de l'Opéra (figure 5). In contrast to most of Haussmann's boulevards, the street did not have a government-provided design for the building facades. Architectural harmony was achieved, however, through the application of building regulations controlling height, window sizes, and decorative elements. In order that the vista toward the facade of the Opéra be uninterrupted, the new avenue was to have neither trees nor sidewalk appurtenances. Almost immediately it became a center for luxury shops, drawing trade away from the nearby Palais Royal. It was observed by the 1890s that the Avenue de l'Opéra had "already gone far to assume its natural position of the first and most fashionable of Parisian streets. The arcades of the once-crowded Rue de Rivoli seem to have lost their charm for fashionable loungers, and even the Rue de la Paix must now divide its former unique attractions with the rising popularity of its more modern neighbor."[7]

Although remains of Commune destruction were still to be seen in 1878, Paris seemed at least on the surface to have regained a measure of stability and

7. *Paris As It Is* (Paris: Brentano, 1892), p. 49.

5. The Avenue de l'Opéra viewed from the Place du Théatre Français.

confidence. The Exposition, which filled the Champ de Mars and crowned the Trocadéro with its colorful new palace, had been intended as a signal of recovery. Returning from exile, the national legislature would in the succeeding year make Paris its home.

In its urban dynamism, Paris reflected trends common to many industrialized cities. The French capital was unique, however, in its intensive centralization of urban functions. This concentration was long to remain both a point of pride and a source of dismay. It endowed the city with a remarkable richness and diversity, yet it would be deemed responsible for a future pattern of almost unmanageable growth and a national dominance often condemned as detrimental to a balanced regional development.

Most conspicuous among the multiform activities of Paris was its function as the national capital, for the monumental fabric of the city was the visual symbol of a remarkably centralized system of political and administrative control.

imperialism

Although the empire of Napoleon III was to be succeeded by a series of republics, the centralization of the French government continued, and the city of Paris, like the rest of France, remained under the dominance of the national administration. Although the local government included an elected city council, extensive authority rested in the hands of appointed prefects, and much planning activity in the city was to be directed by central government agencies. It was observed in the 1960s: "If good planning were a matter of strong power, Paris would be abundantly served: administered directly by the national government since the Commune, the centralization of power has done nothing but grow, to the point that today, Parisian urbanism is made in the Élysée Palace."[8] Napoleon III was not the only chief of state to feel a personal identification with the evolution of the French capital, and such recent presidents as Pompidou and Giscard d'Estaing have, in their disparate ways, had a notable influence on the development of Paris.

In addition to being the center of government, Paris has long been the cultural focus of France. This resulted in part from a series of governmental decisions that established all major institutions of higher education in Paris. The capital has been the center of French academic and intellectual life and the site of all important libraries, archives, and museums. A combination of government and private patronage made Paris the professional center for art, music, dance, and the theater. It also became the focus for publishing and journalism, for medical institutions and scientific research.

Paris evolved into the banking and financial center of France, providing the headquarters for major business enterprises. Commercial interests have often been cited as a major influence in the development of modern Paris. The renovations of Haussmann were seen as embodying the desires of a rising bourgeoisie allied to the government establishment, and this powerful partnership was long to be regarded as the dominant force in deciding the destinies of the French capital.

The promotion of Paris as a manufacturing center was aided substantially when a goverment decision in 1842 organized the French railroads into a radial system focusing on the capital, which became the cul-de-sac destination for all major lines. According to the historian Pierre Gaxotte: "Ten other cities were situated more advantageously to shelter the metallurgical, mechanical and chemical industries. Paris had in its favor only that it was artificially favored at a decisive moment."[9] Although central Paris would continue to house a number of artisan industries, most manufacturing establishments tended to concentrate in the peripheral areas, with heavy industry developing in the suburbs.

A massive migration of workers to nineteenth-century Paris had been encouraged by the building projects of Haussmann, and it continued, inspired by the variety and abundance of employment and also by the notably high wages of the city. Surveys at

8. Edmond Preteceille, "Misères de la planification urbaine," *Architecture d'aujourd'hui*, no. 176: 16.
9. Quoted in Robert Flanc, *Le scandale de Paris* (Paris: Grasset, 1971), p. 43.

the end of the century indicate that industrial wages in Paris were virtually double those of the provinces, and this salary differential was to remain characteristic of the French capital. As modern industry evolved, Paris continued to be in the forefront—the most complete and varied industrial center in France, the focus of innovation, research, and the most highly skilled occupations.

Paris has been a magnet for the ambitious, for, no matter what one's occupation, reaching the top has usually meant residence in the capital. Observing the urban throng during his visit, Edmondo de Amicis commented: "This is the great torrent that swallows up mediocre excellence . . . One experiences a sensation of being there on that pavement scattered with crushed ambitions and dead glories, upon which rise other ambitions, and other forces try their strength without rest."

Many years later, Paul Valéry was to observe: "Paris is much more than a political capital and an industrial center, a port of first importance and a great market, an artificial paradise and a sanctuary of culture. Its uniqueness consists, first, in that all these characteristics combine there, remaining no longer separate. Eminent men with the most different specialities always end by coming together and exchanging their gifts. This precious commerce could scarcely exist except in a place where, for centuries, the elite of every type of a great people had been jealously summoned and held. Every Frenchman who distinguishes himself is destined for this concentration camp. Paris invoques, attracts, commands, and sometimes consumes them."[10]

Although Paris provided abundant rewards for the successful, there always remained a vast populace to whom it offered neither fame nor affluence. It might have been said of Edmondo de Amicis, as of many tourists, that he was seeing only the best of Paris, the tip of an urban iceberg. Needless to say, beyond the glitter of the fashionable quarters was another Paris where the lights were not as bright. There were large districts disfigured by dilapidation and squalor, where the primitive living conditions of the poor were unaffected by the apparent modernity characterizing much of the city. For many people the struggle to survive left little opportunity to savor either the physical beauty or the cultural richness of Paris.

De Amicis's acquaintance with the Paris suburbs seems to have been limited to a view from the top of Notre Dame Cathedral. He had noted that "away in the distance, on the horizon, across light violet mists, lay uncertain outlines of smoking suburbs, behind which, nothing being visible, we still fancied Paris. On another side, other enormous suburbs, crowded upon the heights like armies ready to descend, full of sadness and menace." In contrast to the order which dominated much of central Paris, the suburbs had grown haphazardly, with a mixture of industry and some of the most wretched slums of the city. Huysmans, viewing this region from the ramparts of the Parisian fortifications, reported that "along the horizon, against the sky, the round and square brick chimneys vomit clouds of boiling soot into the

---

10. Paul Valéry, *Regards sur le monde actuel* (Paris: Gallimard, 1945), p. 152.

clouds, while' below them, barely passing over the flat roofs of the workshops covered with tarpaper and tin, jets of white vapor escape, whistling, from thin iron tubes."[11] To the eyes of Huysmans, the suburban fringe of Paris, its disorderly industry intermingled with ragpickers' huts, was a setting in which nature seemed to join with the works of man to create a landscape dominated by sadness and misery.

Like most modern cities, Paris was a focus of contrasts, a juxtaposition of the best and worst in contemporary life. As for de Amicis, one cannot really blame him for neglecting a close examination of the Paris slums. He had come to Paris to visit the Exposition and to enjoy himself. He wanted to see the things for which Paris was famous, the things that were unique to the French capital. There were plenty of poor people at home.

To the receptive visitor, as well as to its citizens, Paris would retain a magnetic allure overriding the inevitable problems of urban living. Paris is a city for city lovers, and even in our day, weakened and rent, debased and distorted, the gilded net attracts and holds (figure 6).

11. J[oris] K[arl] Huysmans, *Croquis parisiens* (Paris: Mermod, 1955), p. 130. This book, first published in 1880, has been reissued several times.

6. Central Paris. The Île de la Cité appears at the bottom. On the right may be seen the monumental axis of Paris, with the Louvre, the Tuileries Gardens, and the Champs Élysées leading toward La Défense. The Eiffel Tower breaks the horizon on the left.

2 AVENUE TO AUTOROUTE

The Heritage of Haussmann

The carriage that took Edmondo de Amicis from the Gare de Lyon to the center of Paris in 1878 followed a sequence of streets known as the interior boulevards or *grands boulevards.* Although the broad, tree-lined avenue is often associated with the nineteenth-century renovations of Haussmann, the *grands boulevards* had their origin in the seventeenth century.

The development of Paris had included a series of defensive walls, including a semicircular line of fortifications on the Right Bank initiated by Charles V and augmented between the time of Charles IX and the time of Louis XIII. This fortified wall, which extended from the Bastille on the east to the future site of the Place de la Concorde, had become obsolete by the time of Louis XIV, who in 1646 authorized that the wall be razed and replaced by streets lined with planting. The result was a curving artery which eventually became the most animated thoroughfare in Paris, a center for entertainment and commerce, and a major traffic route. The Bædeker guide of 1878 recommended that the visitor acquaint himself with Paris by walking the length of the interior boulevards from the Madeleine to the Place de la Bastille.

Beyond the interior boulevards lay another ring of streets, based on the wall of the *fermiers généraux,* a barrier constructed in the eighteenth century to control the collection of taxes on goods entering the city. This system of arteries, of which the Place de la Nation and Place de l'Étoile provided the eastern and western poles, was known as the exterior boulevards. The line of the *fermiers généraux* marked the city boundary until Haussmann extended the Paris borders to the line of fortifications in 1859.

When Haussmann projected the new network of streets which formed the most conspicuous part of his program of urban renovation, he attempted to augment and extend the existing series of boulevards, incorporating them in a city-wide system of circulation (figures 7, 8, and 9). A series of diagonal streets were created to connect the interior and exterior boulevards. On the east the Boulevard Voltaire, extending

15

from the Place de la République, connected the Boulevard Saint Martin with the Place de la Nation, from which the Cours de Vincennes led eastward out of the city, passing near the Bois de Vincennes. To the west, the Boulevard Haussmann was designed to link the Boulevard Montmartre with the Avenue de Friedland leading to the Place de l'Étoile. From the Étoile, the Avenue de la Grande Armée led westward out of the city, passing by a corner of the Bois de Boulogne.

On the Left Bank, the Boulevard Saint Germain was plotted to create a curving path of circulation from east to west, connecting with the semicircular band of interior boulevards on the Right Bank. The Boulevard Saint Germain met the river at a point opposite the Place de la Concorde, and again opposite the eastern tip of the Île Saint Louis. The completion of the Pont Sully and the Boulevard Henri IV closed the circular configuration on the east, while the Pont de la Concorde and

7. The street pattern of Paris.

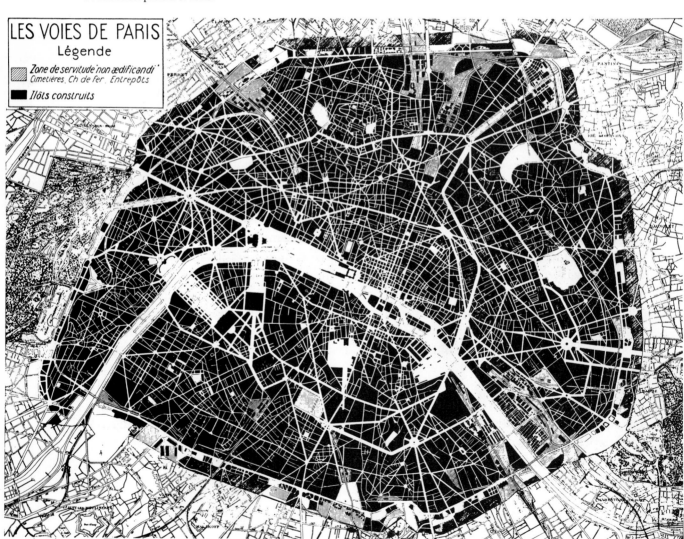

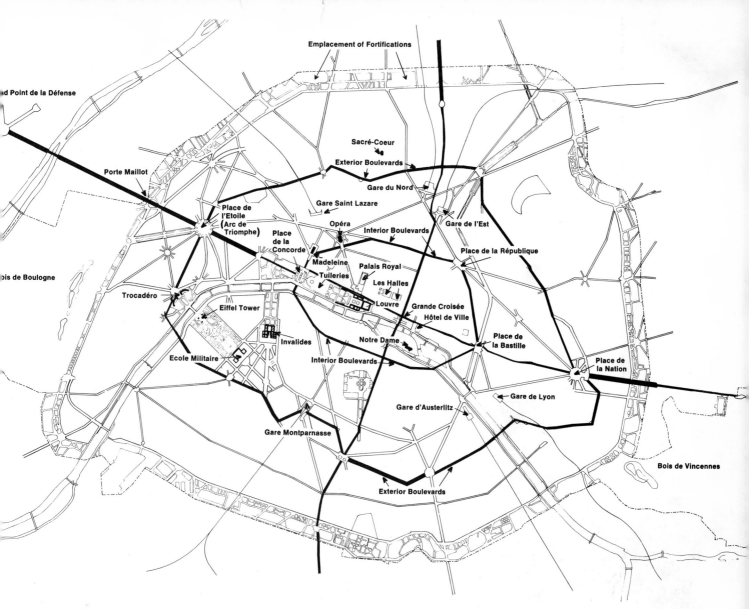

8. Major elements of the Parisian street system.

Place de la Concorde made the liaison on the western side. It may be observed that in addition to incorporating existing streets into his traffic system, Haussmann also made existing urban spaces, like the Place de la Concorde, serve as connecting points.

One of the most important elements in Haussmann's street system was the creation of a major north-south, east-west axial crossing in the center of the city, the so-called *grande croisée.* The east-west axis was established by prolonging the Rue de Rivoli to connect with the Rue Saint Antoine (figure 10). To the east, this route continued from the Place de la Bastille by means of the Rue du Faubourg Saint Antoine to the Place de la Nation, where it connected with the Cours de Vincennes.

To the west, the Rue de Rivoli was linked to the Champs Élysées, which led to the Place de l'Étoile and continued westward as the Avenue de la Grande Armée. The north-south axis extended from the Porte d'Orléans in the south, following the path of the Avenue du Général Leclerc, the Avenue Denfert-Rochereau and the Boulevard Saint Michel. The route crossed the Seine to the Île de la Cité by means of the Pont Saint Michel, traversed the island by the Boulevard du Palais, and reached the Right Bank over the Pont au Change. The intersection of the two axes was marked by the Place du Châtelet, from which the route northward followed the Boulevards Sébastopol and Strasbourg to the Gare de l'Est. From this point, a choice of routes led toward the northern gates of the city.

9. OPPOSITE. Central Paris on the Right Bank. A densely built urban fabric in which a network of narrow streets is intersected by broad avenues. Across the bottom, starting on the left, may be seen the Place de la Concorde, the Tuileries Gardens, and the Louvre. Also visible are the Madeleine, the Place Vendôme, the Opéra, and the Palais Royal. On the lower right is the partially cleared site of Les Halles, with the Plateau Beaubourg on the far right. The Gare Saint Lazare is on the upper left.

10. The Rue de Rivoli.

Observing the streets of Paris, the Bædeker guide of 1888 noted that "the general appearance of Paris is more uniform than that of most other towns of its size, . . . principally on account of the vast schemes of improvement carried out in our own days. The stranger is almost invariably struck by the imposing effect produced by the city as a whole, and by the width, straightness, and admirable condition of the principal streets. Picturesqueness has doubtless been greatly sacrificed in the wholesale removal of the older buildings, but the superior convenience and utility of those spacious thoroughfares is easily appreciated."[1]

The construction of wide vehicular streets had been accompanied by the creation of expansive sidewalks, and the continuous animation of these tree-lined promenades gave Paris much of its attraction. The sidewalks provided an outdoor living area for the city, an all-day circus and fair accessible to everyone. Much of the pedestrian space was given over to commercial kiosks, and although these appurtenances served a useful function, their proliferation gave rise to continual grumbling in the press.

Deploring the sidewalk clutter, a journalist in 1891 noted that although the total width of the boulevards might be thirty to forty meters, circulation space for pedestrians was often reduced to one or two. Sidewalk furniture included "chairs and benches of iron, advertising signs, mud-scrapers, a portable stage for concerts and other public performances, and finally kiosks, square kiosks, round kiosks, oval kiosks—like hat boxes—kiosks for all purposes, kiosks abandoned for lack of renters, kiosks of florists spilling out over the sidewalk, kiosks for bars, kiosks for the pleasure of being kiosks since they have been closed since birth . . . The pedestrian, thrust by all these kiosks and sheds toward the inner edge of the sidewalk, is thrust back toward them by the café terraces which gain ground every day, to the point where one wonders why there is an interior, and by the displays of shops, which have become actual sale counters complete with sales personnel of both sexes."[2]

The pedestrian's progress was also hampered by numerous ambulant peddlers, and the journalist complained that: "The oyster peddler tosses shells at our legs, the distributer of broadsheets bars the passage, the perambulating salesman draws a crowd ideal for pickpockets; deprived of the sidewalk, we must hop quickly into the street, where the omnibus waits to run over us, if we have, happily, escaped the carriage."[3]

A prefectural regulation of 1884 had established a perimeter of emplacements available to sidewalk commerce, with fixed rentals based on square meters occupied. The increasing number of commercial enterprises using sidewalk space thus

1. Karl Bædeker, *Paris and Environs,* 9th ed. (Leipzig: Bædeker, 1888), p. 48.
2. *La Paix*, January 17, 1891. Quoted in *Paris, la rue* (exhibition catalog) (Paris: Société des Amis de la Bibliothèque Historique, 1976), p. 71.
3. Ibid.

provided the city with revenue, and gave critics increasing evidence of the predominant commercialism of the French capital.

When the city authorized some new sidewalk structures in 1904, *Le Figaro* commented ironically: "Our boulevards lacked sheds. There was too much space between the newspaper stands, the police shelters, the benches, the public toilets, the lamp posts, the post boxes, the 'buffets parisiens,' and the decorative posts. The farseeing administration which presides over the encumberment of our sidewalks has understood its duty. It is going to install in these voids a hundred little sheds of pitchpine which is has already baptised 'chalets-abris,' and where one will sell flowers, brochures and various souvenirs of Paris."[4]

In the years following Haussmann's renovations, the boulevard became the symbol of modern Paris. City life was essentially a public life, and the street was the stage on which the urban drama was played. All the variety and vitality of Paris—its social range, its material abundance, its sense of fashion—seemed to be visible in the streets. To artists the boulevard was an abundantly stimulating subject; probably no other city sat for its portrait as often as the French capital.

Although not all of Haussmann's projected streets were completed during his time in office, the logic of his planning was often sufficient to bring about their eventual construction. Some of the streets, such as the Avenue de l'Opéra and the Boulevard Henri IV, were completed soon after his retirement; others were delayed for decades. The Boulevard Raspail, linking the exterior boulevards with the Boulevard Saint Germain, was begun in 1866 but not completed until 1913, while the Boulevard Haussmann was finished as recently as 1927.

Haussmann's planning had been premised on the importance of street circulation in the modern city, and as horse-drawn vehicles gave way to automobiles he was sometimes credited with magical foresight in creating a series of thoroughfares adaptable to motor traffic. In spite of the controversy which had attended Haussmann's radical alterations in the urban fabric, his name was to be admiringly evoked by those who considered his work essential to the functioning of Paris and who advocated action in a similar spirit. In 1952 the Union Routière de France demanded: "What would city traffic circulation be today in Paris if Haussmann had not existed? And what will it be in our cities in twenty years if we don't take the necessary measures?"[5]

With regard to the planning of Paris, the figure of Haussmann cast a long shadow. A French writer recently observed:

As an urban system, the Paris of 1950, even that of 1960, remained essentially the city which Napoleon III and his great associate, Baron Haussmann, had magisterially fashioned in seventeen years of forcefully directed work. During

4. *Le Figaro*, October 24, 1904. Quoted in *Paris, la rue*, p. 74.
5. *Urbanisme et circulation* (Paris: Union Routière de France, 1952), p. 6.

the ninety years which followed, the current of history . . . did not overwhelm Haussmann's Paris. Neither structured nor restructured it. Torrential as it was, history flowed in the bed of Haussmann's Paris. Strange. Everyday life, conditions of work, production, exchange, habits and life-styles, and circulation (our monstrous automobiles!), all these changed. The spectacle of the street is no longer the same, but it unfolds in the same streets, almost unchanged. Only a little, here and there, has the decor been superficially modernized. The urban organism has held. It has accepted the changes in social life. It has accommodated to them. . . . And then, in truth, it isn't Paris alone which remains Haussmannized. Even now in 1972! We ourselves, the Parisians, in our penchants and our æsthetic inclinations, we rest under the dominance of Haussmannism. It conditioned us. We are saturated with it. Paris as remodeled under the Second Empire has been our primary school of urbanism.[6]

The work of Haussmann exemplified the engineer's approach to city planning, in which the city is viewed essentially as a technical problem. Although the scope of his achievement was impressive, as the nineteenth century neared its close new attitudes to urban development were voiced, and the conception of urban renovation which had marked the Second Empire was challenged from several directions. In 1889 Camillo Sitte, an Austrian, published *Der Städtebau*. This work was in part an analysis of existing urban complexes and in part a presentation of proposals for contemporary planning. In his discussion of townscape, Sitte focused attention on the æsthetics of the nongeometric, accretive urban texture of many old cities. He included illustrations showing the close interweaving of many cathedrals with the surrounding urban fabric, arguing that the isolation of buildings in large open spaces frequently robs the structures of their æsthetic impact. Sitte's work did much to increase appreciation of the small-scale pedestrian environment, emphasizing the need for variety of form, broken vistas, and a sense of intimate enclosure.

In the view of many, the long straight vistas and uniform facades characterizing Haussmann's work reflected an insensitive and mechanical conception of urban design. New streets had been plotted across the map of Paris regardless of topography and existing building, and the resulting destruction had inevitably generated protest. During the course of Haussmann's demolitions, the Île de la Cité, the site of the oldest settlement of the city, was completely razed and its closely knit urban fabric replaced by new, coarsely scaled government offices. Two medieval monuments, the Notre Dame Cathedral and the church of Sainte Chapelle remained, but in totally altered surroundings. Sainte Chapelle was encased in a modern government office complex, while Notre Dame was disengaged from its surrounding building, confronted by a large square, and flanked on two sides by

6. Marcel Cornu, *La Conquête de Paris* (Paris: Mercure de France, 1972), pp. 33–34.

parkland. A large area of old building was also destroyed to make way for the expanded Louvre complex.

In his Paris renovations Haussmann had worked within the existing city, accepting both its monumental scale and its high density. Inherent in his work was an acknowledgment of the large metropolis as a normal component of modern civilization. Toward the end of the century, however, the idea of urban size itself came to be questioned, and in 1898 Ebenezer Howard published the treatise that became the basis of the Garden City movement. In Howard's view the problems of the modern city were too deep-rooted to be solved through improved utilities, new street systems, and civic embellishment. The constantly rising land values abetted by speculation, the overcrowding, social pressures, noise, and unwholesomeness of the big city could, he felt, only be countered through a program of systematic decentralization and the creation of comprehensively designed new towns. With the growth of the Garden City movement, the attention of many French urbanists turned toward England, which had become a major center of innovative planning concepts.

The Garden City movement focused attention on the city as a living environment, and its adherents were concerned less with monumental vistas than with the relation of domestic building to natural surroundings. To a group of theorists oriented toward the ideal of a low-density, limited-scale community, a city like Paris, for all its superficial splendor, might be judged unfit for human habitation.

Although Haussmann's approach to city planning was to be challenged and criticized, his concepts were by no means totally discredited. His largeness of vision and his sense of urban grandeur were not without appeal. Moreover, he epitomized the Man Who Gets Things Done, and to those who felt the need for comprehensive action he continued to provide the model of a powerful, decisive planner.

When Daniel Burnham presented his plan for Chicago in 1909, he observed in the introduction: "The task which Haussmann accomplished for Paris corresponds with the work which must be done for Chicago, in order to overcome the intolerable conditions which invariably arise from a rapid growth of population."[7] As his sponsors, the Commercial Club, were presumably practical men, Burnham made clear his conviction that embellishment of the Haussmann type *Paid,* pointing out that "the convenience and beauty of Paris bring large returns in money as well as in æsthetic satisfaction."[8]

---

7. Daniel Burnham, *A Plan for Chicago* (Chicago: Commercial Club, 1909), p. 18.
8. Ibid. To demonstrate the financial advantages of city planning, Burnham estimated that in 1907 the gold imported into France by travelers approximated $600 million, a sum equal to the highest gold reserve in the Bank of France. The visual imagery of Paris seems clearly to have influenced the presentation of the Chicago Plan, with its illustrations of broad, tree-lined boulevards and monumental plazas. A building closely resembling the Paris Opéra appeared as a focal point in one picture, while buildings not unlike the Grand Palais and the Petit Palais appeared in a museum complex.

As time passed, the street penetrations of Haussmann would seem to some modernists, altogether too modest for the needs of contemporary Paris. To the architect Le Corbusier, who never tired of making proposals for the French capital, the texture of Haussmann's city, with its closely set buildings and congested "corridor streets," could well be wiped out and replaced by a completely restructured environment in which widely spaced high-rise building would be set amid vast open space, and the boulevard replaced by the limited-access expressway. Feeling his own efforts continually frustrated, however, he was unrestrained in his admiration for the scale of Haussmann's accomplishment, praising it as "a titanic achievement. Hats off! Today Paris lives on Haussmann's work."[9]

Proposals for a New Century

Although Haussmann's planning projects would continue to furnish guidelines for the development of Paris, the pace of urban reconstruction, as the twentieth century progressed, was often hampered by financial crises and governmental indecision. Would-be Haussmanns were not lacking, but there was no Napoleon III.

Some of the most interesting proposals for Paris just after the turn of the century can be found in the work of Eugène Hénard. The son of a Parisian architect, Hénard had studied in his father's atelier at the École des Beaux Arts, and in 1882 he obtained an appointment in the Travaux de Paris, the office directing municipal public works, where he remained until his retirement in 1913. Government programs during his professional career remained relatively modest, and his association with large-scale projects was limited to the expositions of 1889 and 1900. His personal vision was large, however, and his interests embraced the planning of Paris as a whole. On his own initiative, between 1903 and 1909 he published a series of eight studies or "fascicules" dealing with planning problems of Paris. They established his reputation as an urbanist, and Hénard became internationally known, especially as an expert on traffic circulation.

Although the turn of the century had been marked by a growing concern for the social aspects of urbanism, Hénard's interests, like those of Haussmann, centered on the physical fabric of the city and its adaptation to modern needs. Hénard turned his attention to the planning of Paris at a time when the automobile, though still a novelty, seemed destined to become an increasingly important element in city circulation. Aviation too was in its infancy, but would attract increasing interest among urban designers projecting the future of cities.

Focusing his attention on the Parisian traffic system, Hénard made diagrammatic studies comparing the street system with those of Moscow, London, and Berlin

---

9. Le Corbusier, *The Radiant City* (New York: Grossman, Orion Press, 1967), p. 209. First published as *La ville radieuse* Boulogne (Seine): Éditions de l'Architecture d'Aujourd'hui, 1935.

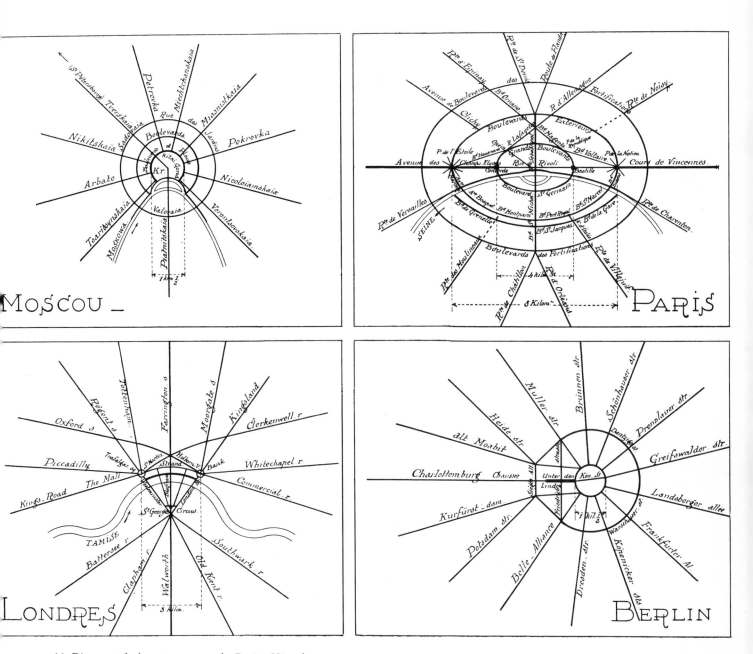

11. Diagrams of urban street systems by Eugène Hénard.

(figure 11). While in each he saw a pattern involving radial access to the central core, together with a means of peripheral distribution, he considered access to the center of Paris to be more difficult than in the other cities. As he analyzed the general form of the modern city, it consisted of two parts: the center of affairs containing business and government offices, large stores, theaters, and so forth, and an outer ring of dwelling area. He believed that the center, as the focus of circulation, naturally required a system of large traffic arteries, while the surrounding districts of housing needed this less. The existing system in Paris, however, was virtually the reverse. The center of the city was the historic core, comprising an intricate medieval street pattern and a dense fabric of building. He pointed out: "The streets of the central area are the oldest and the narrowest; the streets surrounding this area are the more recent as well as the widest, when exactly the opposite should be the condition. . . . We may see that the great boulevards and also the new streets executed by Haussmann are stopped at the belt formed by the great interior boulevards, and that the other great radiating avenues are stopped at the second belt formed by the exterior boulevards. Only the Avenue de l'Opéra and the Boulevard Sébastopol extend to a point in the center of the city."[10] The belt of the interior boulevards, with the Place de la Bastille and Place de la Concorde as eastern and western poles, formed a rough ellipse with a long diameter of four kilometers and a perimeter of ten kilometers. This enclosed area, Hénard maintained, was too large to function without additional penetrating streets.

Hénard's solution included the creation of a second *grande croisée* on the Right Bank (figures 12 and 13). The north-south axis would be established by widening and extending an existing street, the Rue de Richelieu, to create a parallel artery one kilometer west of the Boulevard Sébastopol. The east-west axis would involve the creation of a new street to be called the Avenue du Palais Royal, which would run north of and parallel to the Rue de Rivoli, incorporating the Rue Rambuteau. The new Rue de Richelieu would cross the Seine to the Left Bank by way of the Pont du Carrousel, intersecting the Boulevard Saint Germain and continuing southward. Before reaching the Boulevard Saint Germain, however, it would intersect a new east-west artery, the Avenue de l'Université, which would itself intersect the Boulevard Saint Germain to the east. The configuration formed by the intersection of the Boulevards Saint Michel and Sébastopol with the new Avenues l'Université and Palais Royal, combined with the new Rue de Richelieu, was a square kilometer, an area Hénard felt suitable to define the urban core and provide the perimeter for a series of new radiating streets.

From each corner of the square a street would radiate outward. One of these, the Avenue de l'Opéra, extending from the northwest corner, was already in existence; the others would be created: radiating from the northeast corner, a street called the Avenue du Temple, and from the southeast corner a street called the Avenue du Panthéon. The remaining radial, from the southwest corner, was designated the Avenue du Carrousel.

Hénard believed that the thirty-meter width of most of Haussmann's boulevards was insufficient for modern traffic, and he proposed a width of forty meters for his new major streets. Although some urbanists had hoped that the subway system

10. Eugène Hénard, "A Description of the Development of Paris," *Proceedings of the American Institute of Architects* 39 (1905–06): 109–10.

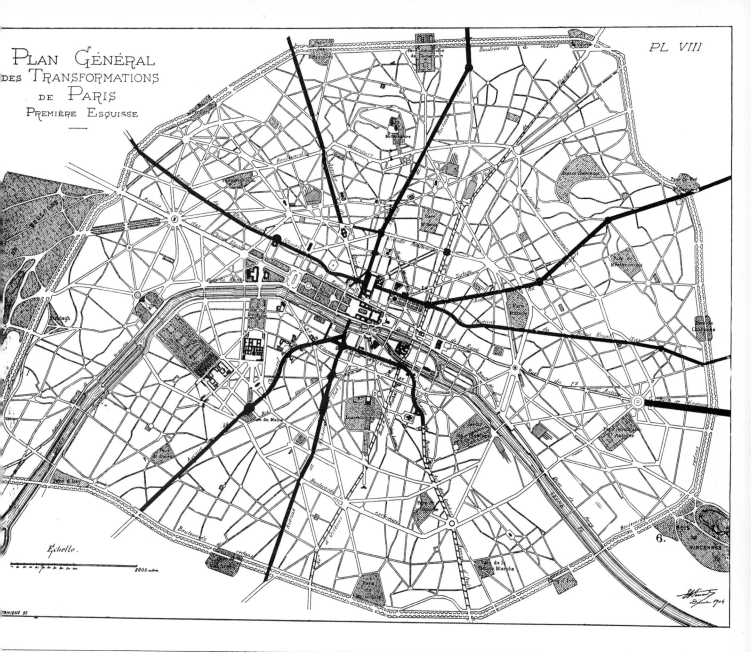

PLAN GÉNÉRAL
DES TRANSFORMATIONS
DE PARIS
PREMIÈRE ESQUISSE

Echelle.

2000 mètre

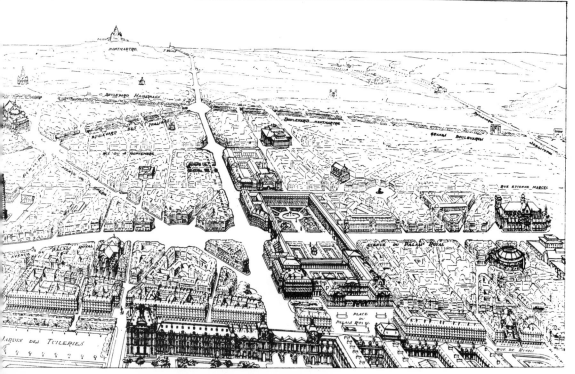

12. Transformations of Paris proposed by Eugène Hénard. New streets radiating from the center are shown in black, and existing streets to be altered are shown with hatched lines. The fortifications marking the city boundaries provide the site for a *boulevard à redans,* and several new parks have been added.

13. The new *grande croisée.* The widened Rue de Richelieu leads north-south, while a new avenue extends east-west, cutting through the Palais Royal.

inaugurated in 1900 might relieve street congestion, Hénard correctly predicted that the volume of vehicular traffic would continue to expand. He pointed out: "If the Métropolitain is far superior to the omnibus, the automobile is far superior to the Métropolitain. . . . For the automobile has just come into existence; its growth in a few years has been prodigious, and it can only increase more and more. . . . The day when industry provides automobiles which are cheap and fast; the day when the omnibuses themselves are motorized, traffic in the streets of Paris will attain such dimensions that no subway could affect the intensity."[11]

Although Hénard's proposed streets might have been useful for vehicular circulation, their construction would have been ruinously destructive of the historic fabric of the city. His new east-west axis on the Right Bank was plotted to cut directly through the Palais Royal, and would have ended forever the quiet and serenity of its sheltered courtyard. In justification of this radical transformation, Hénard pointed out that the Palais Royal had "fallen into almost complete abandon."[12]

The Place Vendôme also lay in the path of the projected Avenue du Palais Royal. Hénard permitted the street to curve below the square, however, leaving the enclosure intact. Although Haussmann had consistently designed his streets to follow straight lines, Hénard included curving segments when he felt it desirable for preservation or convenience.

Just as the new Right Bank streets would cut a destructive path through the historic core of Paris, the new Avenue de l'Université on the Left Bank was to sweep through the dense fabric of the Latin Quarter. In discussing this street, Hénard appears as indifferent to the æsthetic qualities of the existing urban texture as Haussmann when he destroyed the buildings of the Île de la Cité. "It is fortunate," he stated, "that the path does not encounter a single monument until it debouches on the Place Saint Michel."[13] (Like Haussmann, Hénard believed in saving monuments.) The new Avenue du Panthéon, as it left the Place Saint Michel, was designed to curve its forty meter swath between the churches of Saint Séverin and Saint Julien le Pauvre. The street would then ascend the Mont Sainte Geneviève, passing behind the Panthéon from which its path would completely obliterate the

---

11. Eugène Hénard, *Études sur les transformations de Paris. Fascicule 6: La Circulation dans les villes modernes. L'Automobilisme et les voies rayonnantes de Paris* (Paris: Librairies-Imprimeries Réunies, 1905), pp. 229–30.

12. Ibid., p. 137. The arcade facing the Palais Royal courtyard flourished as a center of luxury commerce from 1850 to about 1880. It began to decline as a shopping area after the Avenue de l'Opéra was completed, and the center of fashionable Paris began moving west to the new quarters developed by Haussmann. The decline of the Palais has lasted to the present time, a circumstance which has made it one of the most agreeable places in central Paris. Proposals continue to be made for its "revitalization," however. Hénard was not the only one to propose breaking through the enclosure of the Palais. In 1930, despite protests, the Paris Municipal Council approved a scheme for the westward extension of the Rue du Colonel Driant through the Palais, but by the time a definitive plan had been completed, its execution was prevented by a ban on borrowing.

13. Ibid., p. 173.

Rue Mouffetard, and eventually join that of the Avenue d'Italie. Apparently unconcerned about the demolitions necessary for his new street, Hénard maintained that because of its proximity to ancient monuments it would be "one of the most picturesque and æsthetic streets of Paris."[14]

Although his manner of tracing streets across the existing fabric of the city bore a resemblance to Haussmann's methods, Hénard included in his studies an attempt to vary the uniform street facade typical of Haussmann's boulevards. Unbroken building lines faced by uniform rows of trees tended, in Hénard's view, to produce urban monotony, and he complained: "For many long years, the great majority of Parisians have found that all is for the best in the best possible Paris, and that the Haussmann-type boulevard is the ideal of urban beauty."[15] To bring variety into the urban streetscape, Hénard proposed two types of building alignment, one termed *alignement brisé* (broken alignment) and the other *boulevard à redans* (boulevard with setbacks).

The *alignement brisé* was produced by placing each rectangular building so that a corner, rather than a single side, faced the sidewalk (figure 14). This arrangement would provide an increase in street frontage, and space for greenery in the wedge-shaped spaces where buildings met. Hénard suggested that the projecting corners be developed architecturally in such a way as to emphasize this portion of the building.

The *boulevard à redans* involved having a continuous line of building break forward and back (figure 15). The facade would run adjacent to the sidewalk for thirty-six meters. It would then be set back to a depth of twenty meters, where the building line would continue for twenty-eight meters before shifting back to the sidewalk. The series of U-shaped courtyards thus produced would be filled with greenery and could function as either public or private space visible from the street. Thus instead of an unbroken line of building masked by a continuous line of trees, the street would present an alternating view of architecture and foliage. This type of building would eliminate the interior courtyards found in most conventional building, providing for increased street frontage and ventilation.

Although there was little likelihood that any part of existing Paris would be rebuilt along the lines suggested by Hénard, he believed that his type of street could well be applied in new districts. For many years the municipal government had discussed the demolition of the ring of obsolete fortifications surrounding Paris, and Hénard proposed that his *boulevard à redans* might provide the model for a linear development of this site.

In addition to his proposals to renovate the street pattern of Paris, Hénard analyzed vehicular movement. Traffic in Paris in the year of his study, 1906, included

14. Ibid., p. 225.

15. Eugène Hénard, *Études sur les transformations de Paris. Fascicule 2: Les Alignements brisés. La Question des fortifications et le boulevard de grande-ceinture* (Paris: Librairies-Imprimeries Réunies, 1903), p. 45.

14. The *alignement brisé* proposed by Eugène Hénard as a method of varying street facades.

VUE PERSPECTIVE DU BOULEVARD A REDANS TRIANGULAIRES

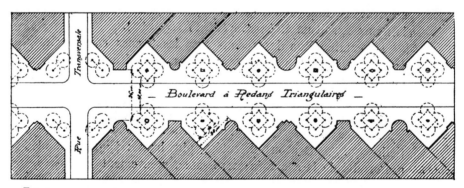

Fig. 2

PLAN D'UN FRAGMENT DE BOULEVARD

15. The *boulevard à redans,* in which foliage and building facades would alternate along the street.

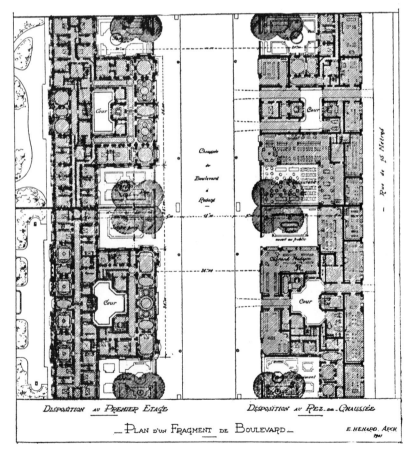

a mixture of horse-drawn conveyances, trams (either horse-drawn or mechanically powered), motor vehicles, and bicycles. Although at this time only 6.5 percent of Parisian traffic was motorized, the number of automobiles (4,077) was double that of the previous year, and there was every reason to anticipate a rapid increase to come. The volume of traffic in general had been growing, and the number of vehicles had risen 45 percent in the previous fifteen years (1891–1906).

At the time of Hénard's study no traffic regulations existed, and at complex intersections, where several large streets came together, conditions were dangerous and chaotic. One could enter such a crossroad and proceed left, right, straight across, or at a diagonal. Under such conditions it is not surprising that, in 1909, it reportedly required thirty minutes to cross the intersection at the Opéra during rush hour. To facilitate traffic flow, Hénard devised a "simple and elegant"[16] solution, the

16. Eugène Hénard, *Études sur les transformations de Paris. Fascicule 7: Les Voitures et les passants. Carrefours libres et carrefours à giration* (Paris: Librairies-Imprimeries Réunies, 1906), p. 282.

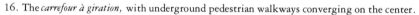

16. The *carrefour à giration,* with underground pedestrian walkways converging on the center.

carrefour à giration, or roundabout, in which all entering vehicles would turn right and proceed in the same direction before leaving the intersection (figure 16). The roundabout, as he designed it, would have a portion in the center raised to keep it free of traffic. Where streets joined the intersection, wedge-shaped dividers would direct the angle at which vehicles could enter.

The initial application of Hénard's principle was made at the Place de l'Étoile in 1907, and this twelve-branched intersection became the world's first *carrefour à giration* (figure 17). When the first traffic regulations in Paris were published five years later, Hénard's rule, requiring movement to the right in circular intersections, was included in the first article.

To facilitate pedestrian circulation across such intersections, Hénard suggested underpasses, illustrating the concept with a design for the projected crossing of his redeveloped Rue de Richelieu with the Boulevards Haussmann, Montmartre, and Italiens. Pedestrian passages would lead below the street, joining at a circular

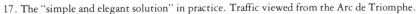

17. The "simple and elegant solution" in practice. Traffic viewed from the Arc de Triomphe.

concourse in the center of the intersection. This concourse, although below grade, would be open to the sky, and would contain such services as telephones, toilets, letter boxes, newsstands, and so forth (figure 16).

In addition to developing the *carrefour à giration*, Hénard studied the concept of the multi-level traffic interchange, which he termed the *carrefour à voies superposées*, including in fascicule 7 an illustration of such a street overpass. He believed, however, that this complicated type of intersection was suitable only for very specific topographic conditions.

Although Hénard's urban design was destined to remain largely in project form, he was influential in the creation of one of the most impressive vistas in Paris. In 1894 Hénard was one of three first-prize winners in a competition for a general plan for the Exposition of 1900, and included in his scheme was the creation of a new street and bridge making a connection between the Champs Élysées and the Invalides. Although the project generated some opposition because it meant the demolition of the Palais de l'Industrie, the scheme was incorporated into the plan of the Exposition, resulting in the Avenue Nicholas II (now the Avenue Churchill) and Pont Alexandre III (figure 18). The preservation of the axial vista toward the dome of the Invalides was achieved through Hénard's insistence that a proposed Invalides railroad terminal be placed underground.

Hénard was not alone in his conviction that the functioning of Paris necessitated an extension of traffic arteries. In the early years of the century, the Municipal Council had sponsored a series of traffic studies, all of which indicated a continuing increase in surface movement. Many streets were regarded as too narrow, and in 1909 a minimum width of fifteen meters was established for all new streets, except those where traffic would be minimal. In the same year the council had approved a loan of 900 million francs for civic improvements, with 440 million francs to be allocated to street renovation. Included in the projected program were plans for facilitating circulation in the historic core of the Right Bank through the extension and widening of a number of streets. Although new street works were viewed as necessary, there was an increasing spirit of conservatism with regard to demolition, and the Prefect of the Seine warned: "Don't let's fall into the error of Haussmann. Let's guard ourselves against the fetishism of the straight penetration."[17]

To obtain a comprehensive analysis of the needs of Paris, in 1911 the city created the Commission d'Extension de Paris, composed of officials, councillors, and urban specialists. The report of this commission, published in 1913, focused on what were considered the two most urgent needs in Paris, the development of open space in and around the city and the improvement of traffic circulation.[18] Street traffic at the

17. Quoted in Paul Léon, *Histoire de la rue* (Paris: La Taille-Douce, 1947), p. 208.

18. Volume 1 of the report, *Aperçu historique*, was written by Marcel Poëte, the director of the Bibliothèque Historique. Volume 2, *Considérations techniques*, was written by M. Petit, the chief surveyor of the city of Paris, and his assistant, M. François.

18. The Avenue Churchill (formerly the Avenue Nicholas II), looking toward the Pont Alexandre III, with the Invalides in the distance.

time was described as a chaotic mixture of horse-drawn vehicles of all types plus automobiles, motor buses, trucks, bicycle-carts, handcarts, and tramways. Although the existing street system was heavily encumbered, the report concluded that it was "so developed, so tight, so coordinated that it would be useless to demolish it and substitute a new system."[19]

The proposals of Eugène Hénard were, of course, well known, but they were considered by the commission to be unnecessarily destructive and based on an overly abstract conception of urban design. Hénard had proposed a symmetrical configuration of new streets radiating from a central node one kilometer square. Considering this concept, the commission commented:

> It has been proposed that a narrower perimeter of radiation be created. This would scarcely be suitable for a city, the expansive force of which is so great and which, in a century, will have perhaps quintupled its area. And where create this little perimeter of radiation? A very elastic question, as the center of Paris is not fixed. It is, in fact, the Place des Vosges under Henry IV, the Palais Royal during the Revolution, the Place de l'Opéra yesterday, the Rue Royale today. . . . The improvement of the street plan of Paris does not consist in finding a center or a perimeter of radiation, in duplicating the main crossing, or in creating four great radial arteries. . . . The Parisian street system can be improved, certainly, but one should guard against thinking that it is necessarily bad and that it must be remade from top to bottom. Moreover, in this matter, overly simple formulas are useless and dangerous.[20]

The center of Paris in terms of traffic volume had indeed been shifting westward. In 1881 the busiest intersection in Paris was the focus of the *grande croisée*, the crossing of the Rue de Rivoli and the Boulevard Sébastopol. Traffic surveys counted 4,702 vehicles there between three and seven in the evening. In the same year the crossing of the Boulevard des Italiens and the Rue de Richelieu had 3,829 vehicles. To the west, traffic volumes fell; the crossing of the Rue Royale and the Rue Saint Honoré was found to have a total of 2,117 vehicles, while the Avenue des Champs Élysées at the Place de la Concorde received only 1,435. In 1912 a survey of the same four intersections indicated a reversal of order. Traffic volume at the Saint Honoré–Rue Royale crossing had risen to 12,222 vehicles and at the Champs Élysées to 11,634. The two eastern intersections, however, showed much smaller augmentations, the Rivoli-Sébastopol crossing having 6,091 vehicles and the Italiens-Richelieu intersection 7,327. By 1920 the greatest volume of street traffic

19. Commission d'Extension de Paris, Préfecture du Département de la Seine. Vol. 2. *Considérations Techniques* (Paris: Chaux, 1913), p. 49.
20. Ibid., pp. 53–54. In terms of the existing city, the commission considered the already established path of the interior boulevards to be "the ideal perimeter of radiation; it encloses most of the principal public establishments, the theatres, the most highly commercialized and animated quarters, and it passes near the railroad stations" (p. 53).

was found to occur in the Place de l'Opéra, the Avenue de l'Opéra and adjoining boulevards, in the Rue Royale, the western part of the Rue de Rivoli, the Place de la Concorde, and the Avenue des Champs Élysées.

The commission report admitted that the problem of street renovation was complicated in Paris by the need to avoid "altering the æsthetic of a city which must preserve and increase throughout the world its artistic prestige."[21] It was hoped that traffic movement could be facilitated largely through street widening, and that demolitions could be kept to a minimum by rebuilding one side of a street. The most noticeable effects of the commission proposals would have been in the Right Bank center, where city officials had already been attempting street alterations. It was felt that this district required extensive improvement in circulation, especially with regard to the development of north-south arteries.

The commission report suggested that, in many cases, traffic lanes could be enlarged by diminishing sidewalk areas, observing that in London a much larger proportion of the street width was given over to vehicles than in Paris. By contrast with Paris, the London sidewalks "are free of all obstacles. Ours are encumbered with displays, café terraces, newspaper kiosks, publicity columns, public toilets, urinals, etc. . . . One must note also that the busier a street, that is to say encumbered with vehicles and pedestrians, the more it is commercialized, the more the terraces and concessions naturally multiply there, the more the sheds abound."[22]

The program of street widening attempted shortly before World War I was such that, according to a visitor, "walking about in the dense central quarters nearest the Seine, one often met with hideous gaps cut right through a block, and indicating the future course, or plowed along an existing street to make it wider."[23]

Although the war interrupted the program, extensive efforts at street construction were made during the following years. The period between 1921 and 1932 marked the completion of the Boulevard Haussmann and the Avenues Matignon and Paul Doumer. The Rue Étienne Marcel was lengthened to the Boulevard Sebastopol, and the Rue Beaubourg and Rue du Renard were enlarged.

The problems inherent in altering the existing urban fabric of Paris attracted continuing attention in the press, and the question of demolition for street construction remained controversial. Many believed, however, that vehicular circulation should have priority over other considerations, and a design competition for Paris held in 1919 included among the prize winners a scheme by the architect

21. Ibid., p. 56.

22. Ibid, pp. 58–59. The drawing up of the Commission d'Extension report coincided with a campaign to rid the sidewalks of excessive encumbrances. The Municipal Council had become concerned about the problem, and a municipal commission prepared a survey of existing sidewalk structures. Enumerated in the study were 76 automatic scales; 415 postboxes, 234 chalets-abris, 112 public toilets, 225 Morris columns (for publicity), 401 illuminated kiosks, 87 illuminated motifs, 280 shelters for small peddlers. 1,204 urinals. Sixteen "diverse concessions" were also reported.

23. Nils Hammarstrand, "The Plan of Paris," Journal of the American Institute of Architects 6 (May 1918): 291.

Paul Meyer-Lévy, which incorporated ideas from both Haussmann and Hénard and suggested a radical program of street renovation.

Responding to a hypothetical admonition, "Don't touch the center of Paris," Meyer-Lévy maintained that Parisians "confused respect for the architectural heritage with the preservation of buildings completely lacking in interest."[24] On the Left Bank he proposed an extensive network of new boulevards, including a direct connection from the Montparnasse station to the Luxembourg Gardens, and from the Luxembourg Gardens to the Invalides. Three new streets would radiate from the Pont du Carrousel, and an axial street would be cut through to focus on the facade of Saint Sulpice, destroying the enclosure of the courtyard. From the rear of the Panthéon, two streets would fan out, one leading to the river, directly on axis with the Pont Sully, and the other formed through an extension of the Avenue des Gobelins.

On the Right Bank, Hénard's conception of the Rue de Richelieu as a north-south artery was retained and a series of new intersecting streets projected, including a large boulevard linking the Opéra to Sacré-Coeur. Although his plan was never adopted for execution, Meyer-Lévy maintained that "sooner or later it will be necessary to envisage analogous solutions. A large capital needs easy circulation."[25]

The "Voie Triomphale"

Of all the streets in Paris, the most famous is the Avenue des Champs Élysées, extending from the Place de la Concorde to the Place de l'Étoile (figure 19). While many Parisian boulevards were designed to serve the utilitarian function of traffic circulation, then beautified to serve an ornamental function as well, the Champs Élysées was initially an ornamental promenade, which by the age of the automobile had become an important traffic artery.

The path of the Champs Elysées was established in 1667, when André Le Nôtre, having redesigned the Tuileries Gardens, planted an avenue of elm trees extending the central axis of the Tuileries to the Montagne de Chaillot, later to become the site of the Place de l'Étoile. With the principles of Baroque composition dominant in French design, the initial outline of the monumental axis developing at the edge of Paris would in future years inspire its own elaboration and expansion.

In 1745 a design competition was held for a commemorative plaza for Louis XV. The winning scheme, later to become the Place de la Concorde, suggested a logical addition to the Louvre-Tuileries complex, placing the new square between the garden and the Champs Élysées axis. The palace of Saint Germain to the west and

24. Paul Meyer-Lévy. "Á-propos de la réconstruction du Pont du Carrousel," *Urbanisme* 15 (June 1933): 193.
25. Ibid., p. 195.

Versailles to the southwest of Paris created an incentive for extending the Champs Élysées axis beyond the city, and in 1753 the Montagne de Chaillot was leveled off and an avenue projected westward across the Seine to a hill called the Montagne du Chante-Coq. This later became the site of the Rond Point de la Défense. The Pont de Neuilly, completing the axial connection across the river, was designed in 1772 by the engineer Perronet.

When Napoleon began the Arc de Triomphe in 1806 the Étoile marked the edge of the city, and his towering monument provided both a terminal point for the Champs Élysées as one looked westward from the Tuileries and a ceremonial entrance to the city as one approached it from the west. The hill of Chante-Coq, about seven kilometers west of the Étoile, received a commemorative statue in 1875, bearing the name La Défense and serving as a memorial to the defenders of Paris during the Franco-Prussian War. This monument, erected in the center of a circular street intersection or *rond point,* provided the western focus of the monumental axis of Paris.

Eventually the term "Voie Triomphale" came to be applied to the sequence of streets beginning with the Champs Élysées and continuing westward along the Avenue de la Grande Armée to the Porte Maillot. Beyond the Porte Maillot, which

19. The Champs Élysées looking from the Place de la Concorde toward the Arc de Triomphe.

20. The Voie Triomphale, looking westward.

marked an entrance through the fortifications at the northeast corner of the Bois de Boulogne, the axis continued along the Avenue de Neuilly and across the Pont de Neuilly, extended by the Avenue de la Défense to the Rond Point de la Défense (figure 20).

Although the Champs Élysées formed part of a monumental composition, providing the axial link between two historic focal points, the character of the street itself was secular. As the trend of upper-class residence turned westward in the nineteenth century, the street became lined with private mansions. By the turn of the century, however, it was characterized by luxury commerce and the mansions had largely given way to apartment houses and hotels. During the 1920s the Champs Élysées was the most fashionable and "modern" street of Paris, and a book published in 1930 noted that, however one might admire the other Parisian boulevards, "the buildings, the cafés, the theaters recall a time and a fashion which is no more. One senses that the newest face of Paris is no longer here; one is certain of it when one arrives at the Champs Élysées. It is here that the true Paris of 1930 appears. The large avenue permits vehicles to circulate by the hundreds, by the thousands, without traffic jams. The sidewalks are large and each one is a promenade; the trees with which they are planted give, when spring comes, the freshness of their greenery to this great perspective. Everywhere you see only beautiful new buildings with simple lines; the stores are all luxury shops; it is the kingdom of the automobile, of high fashion, of the grand hotels, of elegant restaurants, of magnificent cafés."[26]

26. André Warnod. *Visages de Paris* (Paris: Firmin-Didot, 1930), p. 329.

Although the spontaneous commercial character of the Champs Élysées had made it one of the most popular streets in the world, the concept of the Voie Triomphale encouraged the view that this axial configuration of streets and focal points should receive architectural treatment consistent with its monumental nature. One of the problem points along the route was the traffic intersection at the Porte Maillot. Here the Avenue de la Grande Armée became the Avenue de Neuilly, intersecting the Boulevard Maillot and streets leading from the Bois de Boulogne, as well as roads from the north. In 1929 an entrepreneur, Léon Rosenthal, organized an architectural competition for the development of this heavily used entrance to the city, proposing that land which had previously been used for an amusement park be developed as a new commercial center. Included in the resulting projects were designs by the modern architects Mallet-Stevens, Auguste Perret, and Le Corbusier (figure 21).

21. *Top*: Mallet-Stevens. *Center*: Perret. *Bottom*: Le Corbusier.

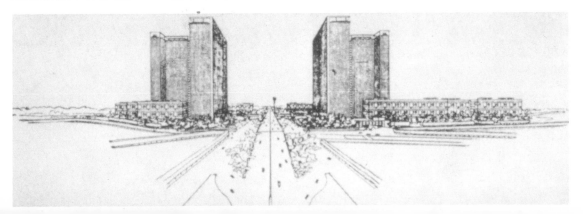

The proposals of these three were similar in their overall symmetry and desire to employ high-rise building. The design of Perret defined the Porte with uniform horizontal buildings punctuated at their outer extremities by towers. These two tall blocks were intended to frame the view toward the Arc de Triomphe. The designs of Mallet-Stevens and Le Corbusier concentrated symmetrical high-rise structures at the center, on either side of the Avenue de la Grande Armée. In the plan of Mallet-Stevens the street would be flanked by twin towers connected by a giant round arch, while the scheme of Le Corbusier, also marking the entrance of the street with towers, bridged the avenue with a raised pedestrian plaza. Meanwhile, city officials concluded that planning for the Porte Maillot should be related to a plan for the Voie Triomphale as a whole.

To investigate the possibilities of such a scheme, in 1931 the city of Paris sponsored a design competition for the redevelopment of the street axis extending from the Place de l'Étoile to the Rond Point de la Défense. Although the competition was announced as primarily a *concours d'idées,* unlikely to lead to immediate realization, the program stressed the desire for practical proposals. It was pointed out that it would be highly unrealistic for entrants to propose a complete reconstruction of the existing line of streets. Preference in awarding the prizes was to be given to projects which limited new architectural ensembles to the Place Maillot, the Pont de Neuilly and its surroundings, and the Rond Point de la Défense.

The program stated that although the proposals should be appropriate to the needs of modern circulation, the æsthetic aspects of the designs need not be made subordinate to practical concerns. It was stipulated that "the mass of the Arc de Triomphe must continue to dominate the perspective of the principal street." In evaluating the schemes, the judges would "not tolerate any construction the height of which would be likely to mar the effect of this glorious monument."[27]

The winner of the first prize, an architect named Bigot, redesigned the Porte Maillot to include a semicircular plaza dedicated to Clemenceau. Although some of the contestants developed the plaza symmetrically across the axis, the circulation of traffic was generally to the south. Bigot acknowledged this by placing the semicircular plaza on the south side of the Avenue de la Grande Armée. The Pont de Neuilly was projected as a monument to marshalls of the army and flanked by two giant pylons carrying equestrian statues (figure 22). Providing the climax of the composition, at the Rond Point de la Défense, would be a gigantic personification of victory in the form of a winged female figure (figure 23). It might be noted that the Rond Point de la Défense, with a diameter measuring 234 meters, displayed approximately the same dimensions as the Place de l'Étoile, which measures 256 meters. Given the size of the plaza and its position as the terminus of the

27. Ville de Paris et Département de la Seine. *Concours pour l'aménagement de la voie allant de la Place de l'Étoile à la Place au Ront-Point de la Défense* (Paris: Éditions d'Art Charles Moreau, 1931).

22. Bigot's design for the Pont de Neuilly, to be rechristened the Pont des Maréchaux.

23. Statue of victory proposed by Bigot for the Rond Point de la Défense.

24. Project of Molinié, Nicod, and Barbaud for the Porte Maillot.

monumental axis, most of the entrants sought to achieve a scale of development comparable to that of the Étoile. The jury approved of Bigot's scheme, noting that he had avoided "all repetition of well-known motifs: arches and obelisks," and that he had "wished to create, against the sky of greater Paris, a new silhouette marking a stage in the extension of the capital and characterizing our epoch, as the Arc de Triomphe is the indelible mark of the past century." The great pylons of the Pont de Neuilly (to be renamed the Pont des Maréchaux), would "form, in the perspective of the avenue, a powerful frame for the principal motif."[28]

While the scheme of Bigot focused on the Rond Point de la Défense, the second prize-winning plan, submitted by the architects Molinié, Nicod, and Barbaud, emphasized the development of the Place Maillot (figure 24). The design embodied a symmetrical composition which created a gigantic polygonal plaza extending across

28. Ibid., p. 16.

the line of the axis. On the eastern side, the plaza was to be bordered by the columned facades of identical building masses, framing the vista toward the Arc de Triomphe as Gabriel's palaces flank the opening toward the Madeleine at the Place de la Concorde. The projected plaza was further embellished with symmetrically placed fountains and obelisks, and in its sweeping scale recalled somewhat the visionary schemes of the eighteenth-century architect Boullée.

The design of the third-prize winner, a joint project by Bruneau and Sallez, developed the Porte Maillot in a manner similar to Bigot, with a semicircular plaza to the south. On the north an ornamental mall, the "Avenue des Maréchaux," extended to the Place de la Porte des Ternes.

Although the winners of the first three prize-winning designs had observed the restrictions of the competition program, many of the entries presented far-reaching proposals. The design awarded first honorable mention, submitted by André Granet, proposed that the Avenue de la Défense be lined with a symmetrical row of tall buildings. Another scheme, a group project submitted by Boutterin, Grenard, and Reynard, included the complete reconstruction of both the Avenue de Neuilly and Avenue de la Défense. Even more ambitious, and somewhat prophetic, was the proposal of Beau and Meyer-Heine, which envisioned the redevelopment of the district of Courbevoie lying west of La Défense as a center of skyscrapers. Although most of the plans restricted renovation to areas beyond the city boundaries, the scheme of Guilbert and Son suggested extensive demolition and reconstruction within Paris itself to extend as far east as the Place de la Concorde. Other plans proposed extending the monumental axis as far west as Saint Germain.

Although the principles of classical composition generally dominated the design proposals, many of the entrants included modern high-rise building in their schemes. The competition program had specified that nothing be of such a height as to detract from the dominance of the Arc de Triomphe. Many of the contestants, however, evidently believed that towers might well be used at the Place Maillot and at La Défense (figures 25 and 26). Some of the projects employed tall buildings to mark focal points, others to embellish a street axis, while some suggested the creation of entire districts of towers.

Although the competition had involved both problems of monumental design and practical matters of traffic circulation, most entrants concentrated on æsthetics. This was particularly evident with regard to the Porte Maillot. The decision reported:

> The commission wished this Place to be the object of an urban and architectural renovation that would satisfy the necessities of circulation and be worthy of our capital. Frankly speaking, not one contestant solved the problem. Perhaps it is impossible to solve. It seems, once again, urbanists must realize that a traffic intersection cannot be a decorative plaza.[29]

29. Ibid., p. 13.

25. Proposal of Viret and Marmorat for the Porte Maillot.

26. Design for the Porte Maillot by Masson, Detourbet, and Tambute.

It is not altogether surprising that the competition inspired such grandiose and essentially ornamental projects. The concept of the Voie Triomphale, after all, involved the extension and embellishment of one of the most renowned urban compositions in existence. Leading from the Louvre to the Arc de Triomphe, the monumental axis of Paris embodied a majestic sequence of architecture, formal landscaping, and plazas evoking major events of French history since the Renaissance. It was only natural that in approaching such a project designers would wish to equal in their own compositions the scale and grandeur of the past. Thus the Porte Maillot might be envisioned as another Place de la Concorde, and the Rond Point de la Défense as a focal point to rival the Place de l'Étoile.

In the context of the 1930s, the Voie Triomphale projects formed part of a trend toward traditional monumental design. In the same year as the Parisian competition, the Palace of the Soviets in Moscow had been projected as a grandly scaled classical structure providing the focal point for an expansive axial composition. During the same epoch, Washington, D.C., was being rebuilt according to the tenets of classical design, while in Italy and Germany official architecture reflected a self-conscious desire to symbolize the prevailing regimes with traditional forms.

Although the economic crisis of the 1930s halted any attempt to realize the Voie Triomphale plan, the monumental axis of Paris inspired Adolf Hitler to envision a similar composition for Berlin, but on a greatly expanded scale. The German capital was to receive a new monumental avenue seventy feet wider than the Champs Élysées and two and one-half times its length. In addition to providing the site for a vast domed hall, the new street was to be ornamented by a great triumphal arch three hundred and eighty-six feet high, intended to overshadow by comparison the relatively modest one-hundred-and-sixty-foot height of Napoleon's arch.

Hitler's desire to rival the French capital was a lasting obsession. Returning from his brief Parisian visit following the French defeat in 1940, he reportedly remarked to his chief architect, Albert Speer: "Wasn't Paris beautiful? But Berlin must be made far more beautiful. In the past I often considered whether we would not have to destroy Paris, but when we are finished in Berlin, Paris will only be a shadow. So why should we destroy it?"[30]

For Paris, the 1931 Voie Triomphale competition was to mark the end of a tradition. As the economic crisis gave way to the greater crisis of war and occupation, succeeded at last by a period of growth and prosperity, the vocabulary of French urban design underwent a substantial change. Although the old monumental axis of Paris retained its historic value, the desire to emulate its forms seemed to

---

30. Quoted by Albert Speer in *Inside the Third Reich* (New York: Avon, 1970), p. 172. Although the necessities of war prevented the Berlin scheme from being carried out, a model was constructed and frequently exhibited by Hitler to visitors. According to Speer, the urbanistic scheme would remain "Hitler's favorite project" (p. 132). As defeat drew near, Hitler, having failed in his plan to rival Paris, unsuccessfully commanded the destruction of the French capital.

27. The Porte Maillot. Redevelopment of the site began in 1965. The Boulevard Périphérique is visible in the foreground, passing under the axis of the Avenue de la Grande Armée and Avenue de Neuilly. Adjacent to the intersection is the Centre International de Paris, constructed between 1971 and 1974. It includes the high-rise Hôtel Concorde Lafayette and the Palais des Congrès, an ovoid structure containing an ensemble of meeting halls. The architects were Guillaume Gillet, Henri Guibout, and Serge Maloletenkov.

28. The Voie Triomphale. The principal elements reading left to right are: La Défense, the Avenue de Neuilly, the Porte Maillot, the Avenue de la Grande Armée, the Étoile, the Avenue des Champs Élysées, the Place de la Concorde, the Tuileries Gardens, and the Louvre.

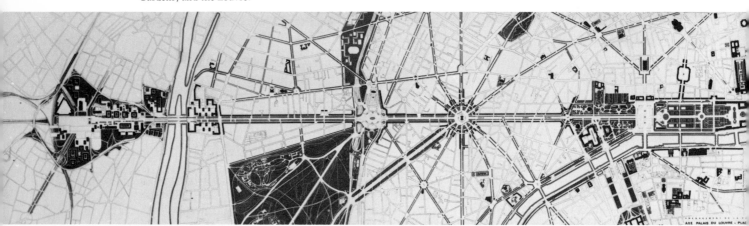

have disappeared. In the postwar redevelopment of the Porte Maillot and Rond Point de la Défense, symmetrical colonnades, ornamental fountains, giant pylons, and commemorative statues were to be notably absent.

The Porte Maillot would come to serve primarily as a multilevel interchange for motor traffic, with its architectural embellishment limited to a skyscraper hotel and conference center placed at one side of the major axis (figure 27). As to the old Rond Point de la Défense, it was to be totally obliterated as the surrounding district became subject to a massive program of high-rise commercial development (figure 28).[31]

Contemporary Paris makes no concession to the traditional image of monumentality. The sense of permanence and continuity, the desire to commemorate such concepts as Victory in giant winged stone figures has been supplanted by the matter-of-fact, the utilitarian, and the profitable. The jury of 1931 had insisted that "a traffic intersection cannot be a decorative plaza." Yet in a city where the circulation of traffic has so consistently prevailed over the ornamental, one may view the Voie Triomphale designs with a certain nostalgia. Formalist and hierarchic, they embody a sense of urban order which seems irretrievably lost.

The Street and the Automobile

When Edmondo de Amicis left the Gare de Lyon in 1878, he found himself suddenly immersed in Parisian traffic which, judging from his description, was fully as congested, chaotic, and dangerous as in our own time. In spite of the width of the street, circulation was clogged, and, he noted: "Out carriage is obliged to stop every moment to wait until the long line which precedes it is in motion. The omnibuses, of every shape, which seem like perambulating houses, pursue each other madly. The people cross each other, running in every direction, as if playing ball across the street, and on the sidewalks, they pass in two unbroken files."[32] Describing his first exposure to dinner-hour traffic, de Amicis reported: "The commotion is simply indescribable. Carriages pass six in a row, fifty in a line, in great groups, or thick

31. The redevelopment of La Défense emphasized a westward expansion of the commercial center of Paris, rather than a westward extension of the monumental axis. Of some interest as an alternative to the outward extension of the Champs Élysées axis was a proposal made by the architect Claude le Cœur in 1948. He suggested that the monumental aspect of the city be augmented through the creation of what he termed the "Pour Champs Élysées"; according to this plan the monumental axis of Paris would be centered on the *grande croisée*. The spaciousness and verdure of the Champs Élysées axis would be reflected in a redevelopment of the north-south axis of the boulevards Saint Michel and Sébastopol, and in an eastern extension of the Rivoli–Saint Antoine axis toward the Place de la Nation. Such a scheme would, of course, have involved massive demolitions along the paths previously hacked out by Haussmann. A presentation of this scheme may be found in *Urbanisme* 23, nos. 37–38: 1954, 80–95.

32. Edmondo de Amicis, *Studies of Paris* (New York: Putnam, 1882), p. 6.

masses, . . . making a dull, monotonous sound, resembling that of an enormous unending railway train which is passing by."[33]

In addition to the noise and confusion, Parisian traffic presented a "hell for horses," and to sensitive observers the street was a theater of cruelty. In 1906 it was noted: "Our boulevards are still dishonored by the pitiable nags who, with dragging backs, pull the carriages." Describing the scene near a freight station, a writer observed that "there the unfortunate percherons almost strangle themselves straining their muscles, when fatigue halts them. Then they are made to move with blows of whips, kicks, and clubbing. It's a tumult of curses and whip cracks. The poor beasts foam, fall: there are scenes of indescribable barbarism."[34]

In addition to providing ample scope for brutality to animals, the age of horse-drawn traffic made the boulevards a continuous repository for manure, and the beauty of many streets was accompanied, according to contemporary observations, by some rather persistent smells.

In a book entitled *Les Odeurs de Paris,* published in 1881, it was noted that "the public street is the great receptacle for a mass of debris and decomposing matter: it is the principal ground where offensive and toxic smells originate and propagate; it is the common reservoir, par excellence, where one gets the majority of diseases engendered by an unwholesome locale."[35]

It was the horses, of course, who, "by their always increasing numbers, and the quantity of their excrement, are the principal contributors to the infection of the public street. Who has not observed, near the stands of omnibuses and carriages, the repugnant dung heaps which persist in a permanent state?"[36] The author had no suggestions to make, however, except to urge more frequent street cleaning. Looking ahead, in 1885, an engineer expressed the hope, "but perhaps it is only a dream, that the horses will be freed one day, and that they will be replaced in large part, in the cities, by mechanical devices, stronger, more docile, more agreeable, and more economical."[37]

Such mechanical devices, needless to say, were not long in coming, giving rise almost at once to complaints about their speed, noise, smell, and general destructiveness. It was observed in 1909 that "the inconveniences, the dangers which circulation presents, are aggravated. . . . It is because, since the beginning of the twentieth century, a veritable revolution has taken place through the entry on the scene of more and more automobiles. . . . It was one thing, previously, to protect oneself from a carriage when the horse had a consistent and relatively slow speed; it's another thing now to shelter yourself from these dreadful vehicles which suddenly

33. Ibid., p. 25.
34. Jacques Lux, "Les Laideurs de Paris," *La Chronique,* August 17, 1906, p. 224.
35. Jean Chrétien, *Les Odeurs de Paris*, (Paris: Baudry), p. 9.
36. Ibid., p. 11.
37. Jules Garnier, *Projet comparé d'un chemin de fer aérien* (Paris: Capiomont et Renault, 1885), p. 58.

appear around the turn of a street, describing curves and zigzags in passing one another, and really terrifying people who thought themselves possessed of sangfroid."[38]

Another writer commented gloomily: "It's finished, the tranquility of our streets, and the charm of promenading either on foot or in a carriage. . . Paris belongs to the machines." Added to the alarming speed of the new automobiles, was the frightening bulk of the motor bus, "deformed, enormous, a masterpiece of ugliness. You can't imagine anything worse, and yet, one sees in the streets of Paris a machine more horrible yet: it is the truck. One can recognize it from a distance, from its formidable gasping, from its black plume of smoke, from the trembling of the ground and the shaking of the buildings. It's a terrifying mass, which poisons the atmosphere and troubles pedestrians, building occupants, and vehicles within a three-hundred-meter circumference."[39]

Although horse-drawn traffic had not been without problems, efforts to ameliorate conditions had been limited to the creation of new streets. Vehicles of different speeds employed the same roadway, with circulation hampered through frequent intersections and confused through a lack of traffic regulations. Pedestrians were generally unassisted in their efforts to thread their own patterns of movement among the vehicles.

As the twentieth century advanced, however, and mechanized transport became dominant, theorists of the modern movement began to envision a total reordering of the urban fabric. The speed and power of the automobile seemed to demand a pattern of uninterrupted movement, separated from pedestrians and building lines. In the thinking of the modernists, the heterogeneous mixture of activities and structures which had dominated most existing cities was incompatible with efficiency, and a new urban form was conceived in which civic elements would be sorted out and separated. In France, the most influential of these visionaries was Le Corbusier, who in 1922 had produced his well-publicized City for Three Million People. This exhibition project presented an imaginary new city in which the traditional street had been replaced by the limited-access expressway. Building lines were freed from traffic lanes, and pedestrian circulation developed within ample park areas. As Le Corbusier continued to rework his concept of a renovated urban form, he frequently juxtaposed his new vision against the existing fabric of Paris. The dense pattern of building, the constricted block sizes, the shadowed courtyards, the clogged "corridor streets" were continually contrasted with an open texture of superblocks, widely spaced high-rise building, and broad motor freeways.

Observing the street pattern of Paris, Le Corbusier noted that: "It is into this tight network, locked in, infinitely fragmented, that modern speeds, twenty and thirty

38. Fernand Bournon, *La Voie publique et son décor* (Paris: H. Laurens, 1909), p. 71.
39. Lux, "Les Laideurs de Paris," pp. 223–24.

times increased, are thrust. It's useless to describe the crisis, the disorder: you can't move, you waste time, gasoline, and vehicles. You mark time in place."[40]

In 1925 Le Corbusier exhibited the first specific application of his ideas to Paris in a project called the Voisin Plan. His proposal included a complete reconstruction of the center of the Right Bank, involving the demolition of all existing structures in an area of 240 hectares extending from the Rue du Louvre to the Place de la République, and from the Gare de l'Est to the Rue de Rivoli. A new district of geometrically spaced skyscrapers would be created along the axis of the Boulevard Sébastopol, with an area of redevelopment extending westward along the Champs Élysées axis. Essential to the proposal was the creation of a new east-west artery in the form of a limited-access expressway paralleling the existing Rue de Rivoli-Champs Élysées route (figures 29 and 30). He was to refer to this motorway as the "east-west backbone of Paris, crossing the entire city: opening up, making way. . . . In this way the 'Voie Triomphale' would be rescued from compromise, ambiguity, absurdity, and all of the traffic hastily thrust into the *cul-de-sac* of the Place de la Concorde would be re-absorbed."[41] This proposal was to be redeveloped by the architect for many years. A version presented in 1939 to the sixth meeting of the Congrès Internationaux d'Architecture Moderne (CIAM) included the addition of a north-south expressway system intersecting the east-west route in the center of Paris. Beyond the city, these routes would connect with the regional highway system.

Because of its vast scale and the massive urban revovations that would accompany it, the circulation scheme of Le Corbusier was among the most destructive proposed for Paris. Like most advocates of urban renewal, he claimed that he was revitalizing a slum, pointing out: "All the ancient buildings are preserved. The historic past of Paris (from the Étoile to the Hôtel de Ville) is outside of the plan."[42] In examining his proposal one may see that such monuments as the Palais Royal, the Place Vendôme, and the Madeleine are retained, but in surroundings altered out of recognition. Although a few existing arteries such as the Rue Royale, the Rue Castiglione, and the Rue de la Paix were to be retained, the entire street and block pattern of the redevelopment area would be changed into a large grid. The open spaces of the Palais Royal and Place Vendôme would be surrounded by open spaces, while the Opéra would sit, disengaged, on the north side of the giant expressway.

40. Le Corbusier, *Destin de Paris* (Paris: Editions Fernand Sorlot, 1941), pp. 28–29.

41. Le Corbusier, *The Radiant City*, p. 213. *La Ville Radieuse* was first published in 1935. It was reissued in 1964, with an English translation appearing in 1967. This later edition includes on page 206 an addition to the caption of a drawing of Le Corbusier's proposed Paris expressway. The addition reads: "At the center of this drawing appears, *for the first time in the world,* the 'multi-level' traffic intersection. This drawing is forty years old!!!" Le Corbusier had evidently forgotten the drawing of a multilevel traffic intersection published by Hénard in 1906. (He was familiar with Hénard's work, however, and included references to it in his books.)

42. Le Corbusier, *Oeuvre complète* 1910–1929 (Zurich: Girsberger, 1929), p. 111. Reprinted, George Wittenborn, New York, 1964.

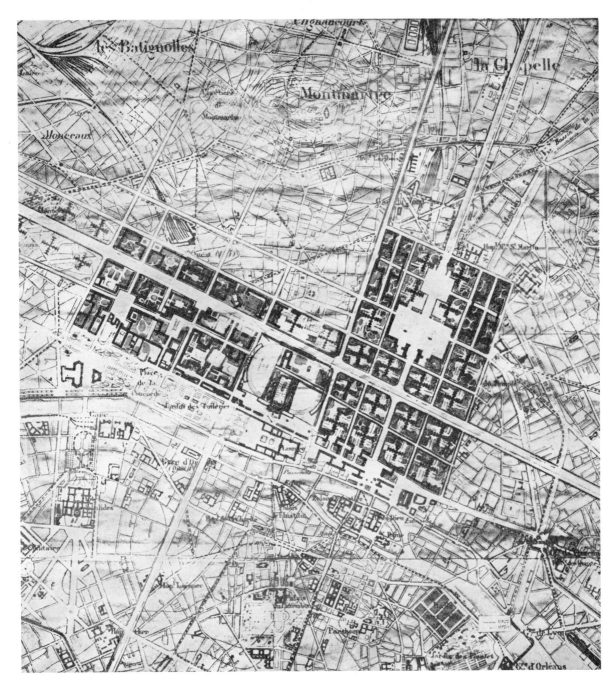

29. The Voisin Plan. To compare with the existing urban
fabric, see figure 9.

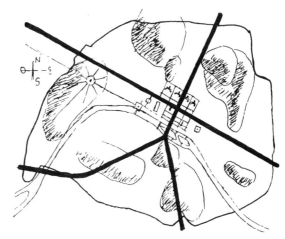

30. Le Corbusier's *grande croisée*. To compare with Hénard's
proposals, see figure 12.

Even people who respected Le Corbusier's talent and admired the imagination of his visionary urban designs might well have been appalled to see the center of Paris rebuilt according to his principles. Le Corbusier, however, seemed unable to understand why people didn't like his plan, and he continued to elaborate it throughout his career. Toward the end of his life, he reported: "Since 1922 (for the past 42 years) I have continued to work, in general and in detail, on the problem of Paris. Everything has been made public. The City council has never contacted me. It calls me 'Barbarian'!"[43]

When Le Corbusier produced his Voisin Plan, the number of automobiles in the Paris region was approximately 150,000. By 1930 the number had increased to 300,000, and on the eve of the Second World War it had reached 500,000. Following the interruption of the war and occupation, the volume of automobile

43. Le Corbusier, *The Radiant City* (1967 ed.), p. 207.

31. Vehicular circulation in Paris in 1957. The map shows areas of greatest traffic volume recorded during weekday afternoons.

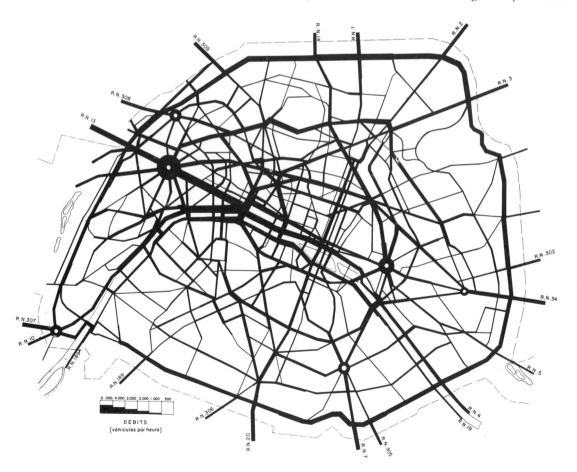

traffic began to climb dramatically (figures 31 and 32). There were over 1 million automobiles in Paris by 1960 and over 2 million by 1965. In 1970 the figure had reached 2.5 million. Meanwhile, since the beginning of the century, the street surface of Paris had increased by only 10 percent.[44]

During the 1950s and 60s, persistent efforts were made to expand traffic lanes at the expense of the adjoining sidewalks. Included in this program was the widening of the Boulevard Montparnasse, in which traffic lanes were increased from 13.50 meters to 21 meters, the Avenue des Ternes (16.50 meters to 22 meters), the Boulevard Malesherbes (14 meters to 22 meters), part of the Boulevard Haussmann (14 meters to 22 meters), and the Boulevard de Magenta (15 to 20 meters). The reduction of sidewalks, in addition to removing circulation space for pedestrians,

44. Statistics from the *Bulletin d'information de la région parisienne*, No. 2, p. 30 (published by the Institut d'Aménagement et d'Urbanisme de la Région Parisienne).

32. Traffic in the Place de la Concorde.

notably diminished the number of trees in Paris (figures 33 and 34). Sidewalks that had previously carried a double row were reduced to one, and other sidewalks lost all their trees. Along with the greenery, many of the old sidewalk structures disappeared. For years there had been complaints that the sidewalks were excessively cluttered. Now there were few sidewalks, in the old sense, left in Paris. The outdoor living room, the linear park-bazaar-cafe-circus-promenade, was giving way to a minimal utilitarian strip of raised pavement.

The modern world presumably supplied compensations for the decline of the street. What did they expect of the average Parisian sidewalk, the little people of the Second Empire, for whom, above all, it was developed? They wished to find there the essential things which they lacked in their own sad lodgings. . . . Today the great majority of Parisians enjoy sufficient comfort to find at home

33. Looking east from the Boulevard Saint Denis toward the Boulevard Saint Martin at the turn of the century. The Porte Saint Martin is at the left, largely obscured by trees.

the varied services which the street used to furnish. . . . As to the slight incidents of the street, they seem pale next to the televised news. What does the Parisian of today wish to find in the street? In a city where private gardens disappear at great speed, where the meters of habitable surface are each day more restricted for each occupant, would it be a little fresh air, a foretaste of the country, trees and flowers which evoke the garden of their dreams around a charming pavilion? Vain utopia! The noise and the gasoline fumes will have discouraged the stroller who would like to relax and breathe on a bench! Perhaps the pedestrian aspires more deeply to recover a little of that human warmth which he found previously on the sidewalks of Haussman. The timid attempts at 'pedestrian streets,' will they be enough to satisfy this?[45]

45. Marie de Thézy (Librarian of the Bibliothèque Historique de la Ville de Paris), *Paris, la rue*, p. 79.

34. Looking west from the Boulevard Saint Martin toward the Boulevard Saint Denis in 1973. The Porte Saint Martin is at right.

35. Automobiles parked on the sidewalk of the Avenue Montaigne during the 1950s.

Not only was an increasing amount of street surface, in the postwar years, given over to motor traffic, but under the tolerant eyes of the police it became commonplace for the already reduced sidewalks to be invaded by parked cars (figure 35).

Meanwhile, many officials were convinced that mere street widenings were inadequate to cope with vehicular traffic, and that more radical measures would be required to provide for the apparently insatiable needs of motor cars. Although Parisian urbanists had previously concluded that the dense fabric of the city did not lend itself to large-scale street alterations, the postwar boom inspired some urbanists to contemplate a rapid program of renovation. Paris was to be adapted to the future, and just as the tall building became, to some eyes, a symbol of economic power, so the automobile was seen as an inevitable accompaniment to prosperity and progress. According to the Prefect of the Seine, Paul Delouvrier, "If Paris wants to espouse her century, it is high time that urbanists espouse the automobile."[46] There was no stronger enthusiast for this concept than the president of France, Georges

46. Premier Ministre. Délégation Générale au District de la Région de Paris. *Avant-Projet de programme duodécennal pour la région de Paris* (Paris: Imprimerie Municipale, 1963), p. 90.

Pompidou, who insisted: "Paris must adapt itself to the automobile. We must renounce an outmoded æsthetic."[47]

As city officials began the long series of studies and proposals leading toward a master plan for Paris, the need to improve traffic circulation maintained a high priority. A proposal submitted to the Paris Municipal Council in 1951 attempted to project a traffic system for the succeeding hundred years. The old problem of circulation across the center of Paris was taken up again, and it was suggested that three north-south arteries be created, one of which would involve widening the Rue Saint Denis to fifty or sixty meters, and building a tunnel to connect the Rue Rambuteau to the Boulevard Saint Germain. This plan was considered too costly and destructive to be undertaken, however, and studies continued.

A somewhat different solution was proposed by the president of the Municipal Council, Bernard Lafay, in 1954. He acknowledged the problem of circulation through central Paris, but he did not believe that massive demolitions or street widenings should take place in this part of the city. Rather he sought to ease the flow of traffic by having vehicles bypass the center on a new motor expressway to be built in an oval loop around the historic core. This inner motorway would be connected by radial motorways to an outer loop which was to ring the city at its edge. Lafay believed that such a system would disencumber the center of many vehicles by absorbing a large volume of north-south and east-west traffic. Although the new motor route would have involved extensive demolitions in the districts through which it passed, Lafay was content that he had left the center of the city untouched.

As planning continued, Lafay's ideas exerted an influence. The concept of a peripheral motorway to be built around the city boundary was easily adopted, as it could be constructed on unbuilt land which had previously been part of the system of fortifications. The development of the traffic system was complicated by the fact that planning for the city of Paris coincided with the working out of a plan for the Paris region. Obviously the regional traffic pattern would need to be coordinated with that of the city. In 1956 the Plan d'Aménagement de la Région incorporated the principle of Lafay's radial system, in which regional highways connected with a peripheral loop. An internal loop, or *rocade,* was included, which would more or less follow the route of the exterior boulevards, and the radial routes were to extend into Paris as far as this circuit.

Various proposals were made for the form of this internal expressway. Some suggested that it be designed as a double-level structure, with underground sections in the Sixteenth Arrondissement. Others envisioned it as a single-level expressway eight lanes wide. Consideration of the motor route revealed a number of difficulties, in addition to the expense, technical problems, and physical destructiveness it presented. How, for example, could a large number of vehicles be ejected from this

47. Quoted in Pierre Lavadon, *Nouvelle histoire de Paris: histoire de l'urbanisme à Paris* (Paris: Hachette, 1975), p. 536.

rapid motorway into the adjacent streets? Studies for linking the expressway to the existing urban fabric provided no satisfactory solution.

The idea of the interior *rocade* was rejected by the Municipal Council in 1959. It was decided instead to facilitate traffic movement through a renovation of the exterior boulevards. However, studies of a north-south transversal at the Place de la Bastille continued, together with consideration of the question of radial streets. Included in the conception of radials was the Boulevard Vercingetorix, designed to lead southward from Montparnasse. Construction of this street began in 1976.

While discussions of the *rocade* were underway, construction began on the expressway surrounding Paris. Although the city did not acquire the fortifications until 1919 and did not complete acquisition of the surrounding zone until the end of the Second World War, the eventual addition of this area to the city had long been contemplated by urbanists. In 1903 Eugène Hénard had suggested using the site for an ornamental boulevard lined with building, and other schemes had included the concept of a landscaped avenue.

In 1956, however, when the new road was incorporated into the Paris regional plan, it took the form of a multi-lane, limited-access expressway (figures 36 and 37). Thirty-five and a half kilometers in length, the road was designed to have thirty-three exit points. The first section, approximately five kilometers long, extended from the Porte de la Plaine to the Porte d'Italie, and it was linked to the main highway leading south. The final section, connecting the Porte d'Asnières and the Porte Dauphine, was put into service in 1973.

By the time this new artery, named the Boulevard Périphérique, was completed, Parisians had had ample time to experience the blessings of the automotive age. Although a government journal proudly referred to it as "a gigantic operation of road building, which has formed the principal and the most spectacular renovation realized in Paris in several decades,"[48] a newspaper, in 1972, described the Boulevard Périphérique, then carrying over 170,000 vehicles daily, as an "inferno" and a "ring of death,"[49] producing an accident per kilometer per day.

While the Boulevard Périphérique serves to facilitate traffic movement around the edge of Paris, it does not help internal circulation. Vehicles leaving the expressway are discharged directly into the heavily congested street system, and during rush hours the areas adjacent to the boulevard contain masses of stalled traffic.

At the time that the Boulevard Périphérique was begun, city officials were seeking a way of developing an east-west route through the city, and they decided to transform the river quais into motor expressways. The first segment of this system

48. Atelier Parisien d'Urbanisme (APUR), *Paris projet*, no. 10–11, p. 74. This journal, published by the Atelier Parisien d'Urbanisme, a service of the Paris Prefecture, provides a continuous documentation of government planning proposals.

49. *France Soir*, November 22, 1972, pp. 1–2.

36. The Boulevard Périphérique looking north at the Bagnolet interchange. To the left may be seen the site of the old fortifications. The outer edge, previously part of the zone *non aedificandi,* was developed following the Second World War and includes widely spaced high-rise housing. The inner band represents the emplacement of the fort itself and was urbanized during the 1920s and 1930s as a district of relatively dense apartment housing.

37. The Boulevard Périphérique looking south near the Porte Maillot. The buildings bordering the motorway on the left were constructed on the site of the fortifications. The high-rise hotel at left marks the site of the Porte Maillot. The Bois de Boulogne is in the distance.

was begun on the Left Bank in 1956, where a river-bank expressway extending from the Pont de l'Alma to the Pont Royal was completed in 1960. Further work on the Left Bank was then suspended, and a scheme was conceived for an extensive motorway along the quais of the Right Bank. This motor route, approved by the city in 1964, was intended to permit drivers to traverse Paris in fifteen minutes. It was projected from Auteuil on the west to the Pont National on the east, a distance of thirteen kilometers. Connections to the Boulevard Périphérique were provided at each end. There had been some objections to the new expressway from the Departmental Commission on Sites, and some members of the Municipal Council wanted part of the road to be placed underground—the section running from the Place de la Concorde on the east to the Pont Sully, marking the western tip of the Île Saint Louis. In this way the expressway would have been invisible as it passed through the historic heart of the city. As it was eventually built, however, the Right Bank expressway dips into a tunnel only as it approaches the Louvre and emerges above ground as it reaches the Pont Neuf.

Although the Right Bank expressway, completed in 1967, provided Paris with a new east-west traffic artery without the need of building demolitions, it was soon evident that the city had lost one of its most cherished promenades (figure 38). The

38. The Voie Georges Pompidou passes the Quai de la Mégisserie on the Right Bank opposite the Île de la Cité. In the foreground a lone fisherman defies the traffic.

calm, tree-lined quais, the photogenic refuge of fishermen and lovers, had been sacrificed for the rapid movement of automobiles.

The president of the Union Routière de France, not surprisingly, had only praise for the waterfront roadway. He admitted in a speech in 1968 that "when the construction of the route along the river bank was decided, a veritable chorus of protest was heard." He insisted, however, that driving along the completed roadway "is a veritable joy. One travels at a moderate speed, advancing rapidly enough, but above all you see, in a few minutes of travel, one of the most moving scenic compositions in the world. The beauty of Paris is thus made available for the benefit of a far greater number of Parisians than before. Is this regression or progress? I respond without hesitation, it is progress."[50]

"Progress," however, was not without its critics, and as Parisians contemplated what had previously been one of the most beautiful river fronts in the world given over to noise, speed, and exhaust fumes, the Municipal Council began to consider the completion of the Left Bank expressway. The principal problem in extending the route lay with the section adjacent to the Latin Quarter. This was one of the most famous strolling grounds of Paris (figure 39). At street level were the booksellers, carrying on an activity traditional to the quarter since the sixteenth century, while the river quais provided a heavily used recreation area. On the Île de la Cité, close to the shoreline, was the most beloved architectural monument in Paris, Notre Dame Cathedral. In an atmosphere of increasing public criticism, the council attempted to develop an acceptable proposal for extending the expressway.

In 1972 the Paris Prefecture exhibited three proposals for the development of the Left Bank in the Latin Quarter. The schemes were painstakingly presented and involved complicated designs. All made an attempt to conceal the expressway where it lay opposite Notre Dame Cathedral, by using tunnels or camouflaged roadways. Although some concessions were made to pedestrians, and some access to the water included, all the proposals involved a radical renovation of the existing riverfront. Few people looking at the exhibition models were convinced that the new Left Bank would be as agreeable as the old. The Municipal Council continued to study the project, but was unable to come to a decision.[51]

Meanwhile a presidential election was held, and in 1974 Valéry Giscard d'Estaing came into office. In contrast to his predecessor, Georges Pompidou, who had enthusiastically promoted the modernization of Paris in the form of high-rise building, urban renewal, and motor routes, Giscard d'Estaing advocated a more conservative approach to the physical development of the city. Included in his program was the suspension of the Left Bank freeway, which was accomplished by withholding national government funds from the project.

50. Georges Gallienne. *Paris 2000 ou Paris 1900?* Conférence des Ambassadeurs, October 1968, pp. 15–16.
51. Studies for this route were published in *Paris projet*, no. 9, pp. 6–63.

"He Who Hesitates Is Sometimes Saved."
                              James Thurber, *Fables for Our Time*

While one could hardly maintain that in Paris the irresistible force of the automobile met the immovable object of the city and gave way, there was evidence by the 1970s that some degree of balance might be reached between the demands of circulation and the physical character of the city. The Prefect of Police in 1968 stated, "I proceed on the assumption that we do not want to . . . or that we cannot . . . remake Paris from top to bottom to adapt it to the priority of automobile circulation."[52] Such an announcement was doubtless welcome news to the many Parisians who apprehensively viewed the increasing inroads by motor traffic on the French capital.

The assumption that the needs of street circulation took precedence over almost all other urban considerations had long been dominant in Parisian planning. It had characterized Haussmann's thinking and had strongly influenced the work of his successors. The persistence of this attitude, as well as its eventual modification, may be seen in a project which continued to be studied for almost a century: the extension of the Rue de Rennes.

One of the generating forces in Haussmann's scheme had been the need to create access to railroad terminals. On the Left Bank, the Rue de Rennes had been projected to lead toward the city center from the Gare Montparnasse (figure 40). As built, the street extended only from the station to the church of Saint Germain des Prés, where it intersected the Boulevard Saint Germain. Haussmann had intended, however, that the Rue de Rennes would continue directly to the river, cutting a wide swath through the ancient fabric of the Saint Germain Quarter (figure 41). The demolitions necessary to prolong the street would have been no deterrent; Haussmann's street penetrations had been similarly destructive elsewhere. A problem arose, however, as the projected Rue de Rennes approached the river, for directly in its path lay the Institut de France, a seventeenth-century building by Louis de Vau, long regarded as one of the masterpieces of French baroque classicism. Even Haussmann would not have dared to mar its renowned riverfront facade; he therefore designed the new street to be bifurcated at the rear of the Institut. One branch of the street would cut through the rear wings of the Institut before debouching on the Quai de Conti, while the other branch would make a connection with the river on the west side of the building. The Institut would thus sit disengaged from its surroundings on a wedge-shaped plot. Additional street penetrations through the quarter were projected to the west in the form of two new streets leading in a fan-shaped configuration from the Pont du Carrousel. One of these would intersect the Rue de Rennes at the church of Saint Germain des Prés.

The extension of the Rue de Rennes was not attempted in Haussmann's time, in part because of the opposition of the Institut, in part because other aspects of his

52. Maurice Grimaud, *La Circulation à Paris*, Conférence des Ambassadeurs, March 1968, p. 20.

39. OPPOSITE. The Quai de Montebello opposite Notre Dame Cathedral.

40. The Rue de Rennes looking south toward the Tour Maine-Montparnasse.

program were given higher priority. The idea, however, would remain embedded in the thinking of Parisian planners, and for almost a century the necessity of establishing this north-south artery through the heart of the Latin Quarter was never questioned by city officials.

When Eugène Hénard began his studies of Paris, his first fascicule, published in 1903, was devoted to the Rennes project, which he described as "an old legacy, not the happiest, of the imperial administration."[53] Although he did not doubt the importance of extending the Rue de Rennes, he found a number of flaws in the current municipal scheme. He considered the penetration of the street through the rear wings of the Institut to be unnecessary, and he suggested that the street meet the quai directly to the west of the building.

Hénard also objected strenuously to Haussmann's suggestion that a new bridge be

53. Eugène Hénard. *Études sur les transformations de Paris. Fascicule 1: Projet de prolongement de la rue de Rennes avec pont-en-X sur la Seine* (Paris: Librairies-Imprimeries Réunies, 1903), p. 5.

41. The Rue Bonaparte looking north toward the river. This quarter lay in the path of the proposed extension of the Rue de Rennes.

built across the western point of the Île de la Cité to join the Rue de Rennes with the Rue du Louvre. Such a structure, he maintained, would destroy one of the most beautiful vistas in Paris, the view of the river dividing at the wooded tip of the island. In addition, the quiet and charm of the small park would have been permanently blighted. He therefore suggested a bridge connection in an alternate form.

By shifting the position of the Rue de Rennes, Hénard placed the opening of the street to the west of the Rue du Louvre. To make a direct connection between the two would involve the construction of a bridge crossing the river at an oblique angle. It would also necessitate the destruction of the Pont des Arts, a pedestrian bridge making an axial link between the Institut de France and the Louvre facade. The destruction of the Pont des Arts did not disturb Hénard, as he deemed the structure "of little interest in itself";[54] but he was aware that the angle of the proposed new

54. Ibid., p. 19.

bridge would mar the frontal relationship of the two classical facades. In order to restore symmetry to the composition, Hénard proposed adding a second bridge, also constructed at an angle and designed to cross the first bridge at a point directly between the two building facades (figures 42 and 43). It is not surprising that this eccentric and not overly practical scheme, which Hénard christened the Pont-en-X, was disregarded by city officials.

Although an attempt to revive the Haussmann plan in 1910 was halted by a campaign of protest, the city continued developing the scheme, and it was included in the proposals of the Commission d'Extension de Paris in 1913. In the same year the Service du Plan de Paris produced a slight modification of the plan, retaining the major elements of Haussmann's projections, but giving the extended Rue de Rennes a curving configuration. (Evidently the Service believed that the Haussmann plan would be more agreeable if its straight lines were softened, although the new scheme involved the same amount of demolition). Haussmann's conceptions were also embodied in the Paris plan which Meyer-Lévy produced in 1919. Meyer-Lévy, however, proposed much more extensive demolitions in the Saint Germain Quarter than had been imagined by Haussmann, and he projected three, rather than two, new boulevards focusing on the Pont du Carrousel.

While action was postponed, the city government continued to produce variations on the Haussmann plan and in 1937 presented a scheme which rivaled that of Meyer-Lévy in destructiveness. As in Haussmann's plan, two streets would extend from the Pont du Carrousel, one of which would connect with Saint Germain des Prés. It would open into a large square to be created north of the church, from which the Rue de Rennes would extend to the river. To the east of Saint Germain des Prés, the Rue de Seine would be widened to create an opposing diagonal to the Rue de Rennes. The two streets would meet at a large plaza south of the Institut, then divide toward the river. Adding further demolitions to those required in constructing the new streets, the block of building between the Rue Guénégaud and the Rue de Nevers leading toward the Pont Neuf would be razed to create a linear open space between the two streets (figure 44).

The historian Pierre Lavedon remarked in 1943 that "the extension of the Rue de Rennes has been the mania of all the Parisian prefects since Haussmann." Comparing the original Haussmann scheme with the 1937 plan, he observed: "Their similarity is striking. One can disconcern the same destructive rage, ferocious and gratuitous against a healthy, peaceful, evocative quarter." The initial plan, however, had been considerably "aggravated by our modern surveyors, next to whom Haussmann appears almost a figure of moderation."[55]

Not everyone, of course, was in agreement about the need to protect the Saint Germain Quarter. An architect, contemplating the district in the 1930s, set aside the

55. Pierre Lavedon, "Les grandes *enterprises* d'aménagement de Paris avant Haussmann," in Bernard Champigneulle, ed., *Destinée de Paris* (Paris: Chêne, 1943), p. 68.

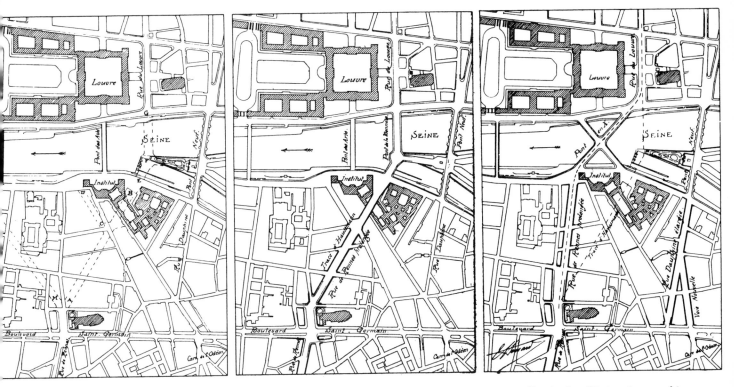

42. Proposed extensions of the Rue de Rennes. At left, the existing street pattern. At center, the plan proposed by the city of Paris at the turn of the century. At right, the project published by Eugène Hénard in 1903.

43. Hénard's proposal for a Pont-en-X crossing the Seine between the Louvre on the left and the Institut de France at right.

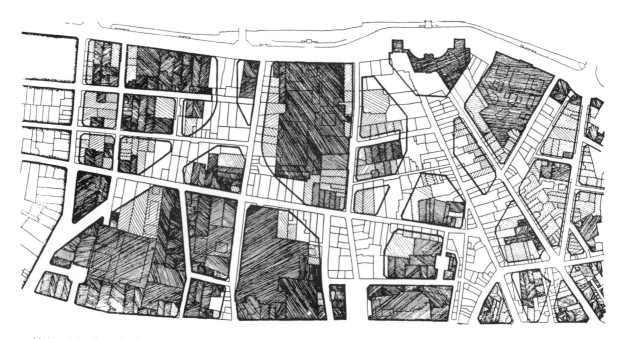

44. The Saint Germain Quarter. Redevelopment projected during the 1930s. Land parcels shown in white would be completely expropriated, those marked with diagonal lines would be partially expropriated, and those with shading in black would be retained.

pleas of preservationists with the comment: "What crimes, history, one commits in your name! One ought, at least, to distinguish among the memories it leaves us. There are some it is better to forget. It is impossible to traverse the narrow streets which go from the Quai de Conti to the old abbey of Saint Germain des Prés, without seeing again the horrible days of the revolution of which they were the theater, where the walls themselves have retained the cries of the victims of September, and where the blood, according to contemporaries, flowed like a river." Not only did the district, he insisted, embody evil memories of the past, but it also left much to be desired in the present. A consultation of the municipal records indicated: "Where the disorders were unchained, prostitution and disease has elected its domicile. History and a concern for human dignity, never in conflict, order us, imperiously, to abolish, together with this past, the present-day misery."[56]

The 1930s, however, marked the beginning of an increasingly conservative approach toward the Latin Quarter, and a 1939 proposal by the architect André Gutton suggested the use of tunnels to carry northbound traffic from Saint Germain des Prés. The onset of the Second World War, needless to say, eliminated the

56. André Ménabréa, "Les Enseignements du vieux Pont Neuf," *Urbanisme*, nos. 8-9, (November-December 1932): 226.

possibility of extensive public works in Paris. It also removed the problem of automobile traffic, for during the Occupation street transportation to most Parisians meant a bicycle. At this time, although planning projects continued, a preservationist spirit grew.

In 1944 André Gutton was engaged by the Institut de France to develop a program for remodeling the Institut building, and his proposal, together with a plan for the redevelopment of the Saint Germain Quarter produced by a member of the Institut, Charles Nicod, was exhibited by UNESCO in 1946. Street patterns were developed to move vehicles around rather than through the Saint Germain Quarter, and, although the plan would have involved some demolition, it was essentially respectful of the existing fabric. Moreover, in contrast to many of the designs from the time of Haussmann, the scheme had been produced not simply by laying a ruler across a city map but through a careful study of the district itself. Like its predecessors, however, this plan was not put into effect.

Curiously, from the time of Haussmann until the end of the Second World War, it was taken for granted by planners that Paris could not function without expanded north-south street circulation through the Saint Germain Quarter. Yet in the 1960s, with traffic volumes greater than ever, and with pressures to accommodate the automobile constantly increasing, the Saint Germain district suddenly appeared, for the first time in a century, to be safe from Haussmannizing. A project produced for the area in 1960 indicated the supression of some streets and the development of pedestrian ways, while the future state of the quarter was described in 1963 as "a street system of pedestrians without vehicles, streets with bookstores, art galleries, antique shots, and decorators." It was suggested that isolating the quarter from automobile traffic would "permit man to make his reappearance in the city in place of the machine."[57] By this time, the rapidly changing face of modern Paris had made the old districts all the more precious, and the historic and aesthetic value of the Latin Quarter at last seemed sufficient to counterbalance the need for expanded traffic circulation (figure 45).

From the time it was built, the Rue de Rennes had continued one block beyond the Boulevard Saint Germain, and for many years the church of Saint Germain des Prés had fronted on this segment of the uncompleted street. In 1976, however, the long-contemplated extension of the street seemed permanently abandoned. The sidewalk was enlarged, and the newly expanded pedestrian area rechristened the Place de Rennes.

By the 1970s the pedestrian, long ignored by Parisian planners, was achieving a few modest concessions. The construction of underground parking garages at the Place Vendôme in 1972, and in front of Notre Dame Cathedral in 1973, was accompanied by the creation of pedestrian areas at surface level (figure 46). On the

57. André Gutton, "L'aménagement de l'Institut de France et le Quartier de Saint Germain des Prés," *La vie urbaine*, no. 2 (April–June 1963): 144.

45. The Latin Quarter. Intersection of the Rue de Seine and the Rue de l'Échaude.

Left Bank, vehicular access to some of the narrow streets near the river was restricted (figure 47), and the Place Saint André des Arts expanded to provide café space. With the long-contemplated extension of the Left Bank expressway definitely abandoned, the river quais extending from the Pont de l'Archevêché to the Pont d'Austerlitz were redeveloped as a waterfront park (completed in 1977). On the Right Bank, the creation of pedestrian streets accompanied the renovation of the Plateau Beaubourg.

Assuming the desirability of increased traffic circulation and the undesirability of altering the existing street fabric, Parisian planners have, from time to time, considered the possibility of tunneling underground. Eugéne Hénard, in developing

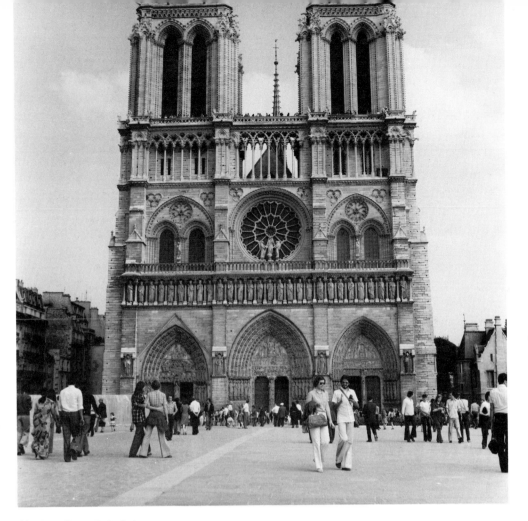

46. Notre Dame Cathedral.

47. Pedestrians in the Latin Quarter.

a project for future cities in 1910, included the concept of a double-level street. An underground artery, equal in width, was to underlie the surface street, providing passage for the removal of trash and access to utility lines, sewers, and so forth. Although the scheme was not projected specifically for Paris, he considered it applicable to any modern city.

Proposals for underground automobile circulation in Paris have included projects to alleviate circulation problems at specific points and full-scale plans for a city-wide system of subsurface streets. Even the path of the Seine has been envisioned as the site of underground construction. In 1968, the architect Paul Maymont suggested building a multilevel structure under the bed of the river to provide parking, auto routes, rail lines, and building sites.

The earliest attempt at a coordinated underground system of auto routes was made by Émile Massard in 1928, who proposed linking several heavily used points on the Right Bank with the Quai des Tuileries. In 1933, a young engineer and architect, Édouard Utudjian, fascinated by the idea of subterranean construction, formed the GECUS (Groupe d'Études et de Coordination de l'Urbanisme Souterrain), which continued to promote the conception of an underground traffic system. For the 1937 Exposition, this group worked out a plan for a city-wide underground street system, taking into consideration all existing underground constructions. The plan included a basically symmetrical configuration of straight streets, with two concentric, lozenge-shaped portions ringing the center and a series of diagonals to provide connections inward to the center of the city and outward to regional routes. A system of underground parking garages was included.

With traffic problems increasing, city officials have continued to investigate the possibilities of underground circulation. A plan produced by GECUS in 1970 maintained the concept of a geometric configuration, comprising a central rectangular ring and a series of radiating diagonals. This system would, like the 1937 plan, include an underground *grande croisée* intersecting at the center and linking up with the regional highways at the outskirts. Connection between the underground system and the surface would be made through "buffer garages," ramps, and elevators.

Should Parisian officials, at some time in the future, seriously contemplate a system of underground streets, the task will be complicated by the growing number of subsurface constructions. Discussing this problem, Édouard Utudjian deplored the "subterranean chaos, where all the elements mutually disregard one another."[58] (Underground parking garages, for example, have been constructed without regard for future patterns of subsurface circulation.) By 1970 city officials were beginning to consider the creation of an "Underground Master Plan" for Paris, by which all subsurface development could be coordinated.

58. *Paris projet*, no. 3, p. 35.

Meanwhile, of course, traffic conditions in Paris have continued to worsen, and there is really no remedy. In peak hours the streets are gorged with cars that barely move. One of the most frequent complaints of city residents concerns traffic noise, and the volume of sound at the Place de l'Opéra and has been found to be comparable to that of Niagara Falls. The percussion of iron-shod hoofs on paving stones, which de Amicis likened to the noise of an unending railway train, has been replaced by a maddening whine and roar. A small victory for noise abatement occurred in 1954, however, when a law was effected prohibiting the use of horns in Paris. To the astonishment of the world and, perhaps even more, to the amazement of the Parisians, the law has been more or less obeyed.

It has been suggested by some urbanists that if it is sufficently difficult to operate an automobile in a city, people will, albeit reluctantly, find other means of movement. Paris, in the view of some planners, may be approaching a vehicular saturation point, and in 1971 a government bulletin noted that "the number of vehicles which can be found simultaneously in the capital has leveled off in the past two years."[59]

In 1976, the catalog of an exhibition of Parisian street furniture began by stating, "The traditional Parisian street is dead, or almost."[60] The announcement was perhaps exaggerated, for in spite of erosion by the demands of motor traffic, in spite of noise and fumes and the loss of trees, the Parisian street scene has not been totally deprived of its richness. One may hope that in the face of continuing proposals for street renovation and textbook schemes for expressways and pedestrian malls, the old-fashioned city street, with its incompatible mixture of housing, commerce, pedestrians, and vehicles, may yet survive.

59. Institut d'Aménagement et d'Urbanisme de la Région Parisienne. *Bulletin d'information de la région parisienne*, no. 2, pp. 30–31.
60. *Paris, la rue*, p. 7.

3 THE DAILY JOURNEY

Omnibus to Autobus

Discussing the transport problem in 1972, the Prefect of the Region of Paris, Maurice Doublet, observed: "Urban transport has unchained a veritable religious war. From the problem of circulation, certain elevated spirits deduce the end of our civilization. From difficulties in the functioning of public transport, some hotheads conclude that we need a change in political administration. Some preach a crusade of the city against the vehicle, while others, with arguments equally unanswerable, exalt a crusade in reverse. One opposes the private right against the public. In a word, we are very French, we are very Parisian."[1]

Pointing out that transportation problems were common to all large cities, Doublet admitted that "France has succeeded in concentrating the maximum of difficulties on the minimum of terrain: the Parisian agglomeration." He observed that the subject had long provided Parisisans with a topic of conversation, and he quoted a de Maupassant description of a nineteenth-century dinner party.

> Everyone was discussing the great project of the Métropolitain. The subject wasn't exhausted until the end of dessert, each one having a quantity of things to say regarding the slowness of communication in Paris, the inconvenience of the tramways, the tedium of the omnibus, and the crudity of the coachmen.[2]

Among the conveyances cited by de Maupassant, the most long-lived was the horse-drawn omnibus, which had provided Paris with its first comprehensive public transportation system. It was the philosopher Pascal who had developed the idea that Paris should have a system of carriages, available to the public, which would traverse the city following fixed routes and a fixed schedule. Permission for the establishment of such a service was granted by Louis XIV in 1661, and in the

---

1. Maurice Doublet, *Les transports dans la région parisienne* (Paris: Conférence des Ambassadeurs, November 1972), p. 5.
2. Ibid.

following year a line was put into service between the Luxembourg and the Rue Saint Antoine. The new system of transportation was highly popular, too popular apparently, for a parliamentary edict subsequently denied access to the carriages to "soldiers, pages, lackeys, and other people in livery . . . for the great convenience of people of merit."[3] In spite of public protests, the regulation remained in force, denying the transport system a large part of its clientele. A rise in fares to six sols further reduced patronage, and the system disappeared in 1675.

A scheduled service of public carriages did not reappear in Paris until 1828, when a society called the Entreprise des Omnibus opened a system comprising twelve lines and employing carriages called diligences, which seated from twelve to eighteen passengers. The system was highly successful, and there were soon several competing companies. During the time of Haussmann the omnibus system was reorganized, and a monopoly was given to the Compagnie Générale des Omnibus (CGO), which received a thirty-year contract in 1855. In 1860, following the annexation of the outlying districts, the company was given a fifty-year contract, and by 1873 it was providing the city with thirty-two routes carrying 111 million passengers per year.

Describing Parisian traffic in 1878, Edmondo de Amicis likened the omnibuses to "perambulating houses" (figure 48). By this time the omnibus had taken the form of a rectangular closed carriage with a line of windows on each side. Passengers sat side by side facing inward on two long benches. The rooftop, called the *impériale,* carried passengers in two rows of open seating facing outwards, and the presence of an exterior stairway, according to a contemporary guidebook had recently made this area "accessible to ladies" (figure 49).[4] The interior seating constituted the first-class area of the omnibus, and the cheaper *impériale,* the second class. By 1878 two types of omnibuses were in service, the "old" omnibus, pulled by two horses and seating twenty-eight people, and a larger, more recent vehicle, the "new" omnibus, pulled by three horses and seating forty.

Although the onmibus followed a fixed route, there was no system of fixed boarding points, and prospective passengers could signal to the driver to stop anywhere along the street. Passengers might also board at offices of the onmibus company, where a system of tickets provided a queuing order. The omnibus system seems to have been chronically overloaded, and the offices were reportedly surrounded by "harassed crowds who lose, in fruitless waiting, time borrowed, if not from work, at least from daily repose. In the rain, in the burning sun, a resigned crowd awaits with mute patience for the omnibus to pass, always full when it's needed, and, at the door where the distribution of numbers is made, there is soon a battle in which coarseness too often triumphs, and where brutality flaunts itself, where the relatively strong, with temporary authority, overcome the weak, drenched

3. Quotation from Pierre Merlin, *Les transports parisiens* (Paris: Masson et Cie, 1967), p. 22.
4. Karl Bædeker, *Paris and Environs,* 6th ed. (Leipzig: Bædeker, 1878), p. 25.

48. Horse-drawn omnibus.

49. Omnibus staircase leading to the *impériale*.

50. Intersection of the Quai des Grands Augustins and the Pont Saint Michel in 1878. A horse-drawn tramline serves traffic crossing the bridge, while omnibuses provide transport along the quais.

to the bones or burned to the marrow. These daily battles, unworthy of a population in which education progresses, these ardent competitions to occupy a place in a vehicle of public transport, are unfortunately forced on women, old people, children, invalids, on all those whom we respect the most and who most deserve our concern."[5] Once aboard, the journey was by no means comfortable, and Huysmans once described the omnibus passengers as "unfortunates who roll jolting amid a noise of metal, of shaking windows, of snorting horses and clanging bells."[6]

Although the horse-drawn omnibus existed as late as 1913, it had long been supplanted as a major means of transport. Competition for the omnibus in surface travel first appeared in the form of the horse-drawn tram (figure 50). As this type of transport had originated in New York City in 1832, it became known in France as

5. Max de Nansouty, quoted by Roger H. Guerrand in *Mémoires du Métro* (Paris: La Table Ronde, 1960), pp. 32–33.
6. J. K. Huysmans, *Croquis parisiens* (1886), p. 58.

the *chemin de fer américain,* or simply *l'américain.* The first American tramway was unsuccessful, however, for the rails protruded above street level, causing a number of accidents sufficient to bring about the suppression of the system. Subsequently, a French engineer, Loubat, developed a tramway in which the rails were level with the street, and, having been refused a concession in Paris, successfully developed a line in New York in 1852. Encouraged by this, city officials allowed him to attempt his system in Paris the following year, and in 1855 Loubat put the first public tramline in Paris into service. At this time the omnibus system was being reorganized under a monopoly, and in 1856 Loubat was persuaded to transfer his concession to the Compagnie Générale des Omnibus.

By the 1870's the tramways had become an important part of the transportation system, and, as the advantages of this type of vehicle became apparent, the omnibus began to decline in popularity. Although the form of the tram was similar to the omnibus, including the use of the *impériale,* passengers experienced the comfort of gliding over smooth rails, instead of bouncing over paving stones. Two horses could pull a tram with forty seats with an average speed of nine kilometers per hour as compared with seven for the omnibus. Tracks were laid down the center of streets, and because of the bulk of the trams the system of necessity followed the major boulevards.

Like the omnibus, the tram initially had no fixed stops (these were introduced in 1910). To board, one signaled the coachman to stop, and to alight one told a conductor, who signaled by pulling a cord passing under the knees of the coachman. In many instances, however, the speed was sufficiently slow that one could board while the tram was in motion.

The Baedeker guide to Paris in 1878 suggested that visitors could get a good idea of the general appearance of the city by riding on the top of an omnibus or tram. In general, the public transportation systems were considered to be "admirably arranged, and, if properly used, enable the visitor to save so much time and money, that it will repay him to study the various routes and correspondences."[7] Omnibuses and trams, it was noted, operated from 7 A.M. until midnight, with vehicles passing approximately every five minutes.

In 1873 the city approved a plan for a tramway system comprising a circular path within the city linked to radial routes extending into the suburbs. The Compagnie Générale des Omnibus was given the concession for the circular route, while the suburban extensions were given to two new companies: Tramways Nord and Tramways Sud. Although the CGO line in the center was profitable, the two suburban companies eventually went bankrupt, to be replaced in 1890 by the Compagnie des Tramways de Paris et du Département de la Seine (TPDS) and the Compagnie Générale Parisienne des Tramways (CGPT).

7. Bædeker, *Paris and Environs,* 6th ed., p. 25.

51. Mechanically powered tram at the Place de la Bastille.

The tramway system became an important factor in linking the city with the suburbs, and it served to support the trend toward working-class residence in the outskirts. By 1884 suburban extensions of the tramlines went as far as Versailles, Créteil, Saint Denis, Gennevilliers, Vitry, and Fontenay-aux-Roses. It would appear, in fact, that as working hours were gradually reduced the time saved was increasingly devoted to commuting.

Although the last horse-drawn tram would not disappear until 1913 (along with the horse-drawn onmibus), various forms of mechanical traction began to appear as early as the 1870's, when limited use was made of small steam locomotives. By the 1880's notable improvements had been made in mechanical equipment, and a variety of engines were employed on Parisian lines, including Rowan steam-powered cars, Francq hot-water engines, and compressed-air Mekarski engines. Electric traction using battery power was introduced in 1892, followed in 1896 by the first tramway with live contacts. The use of overhead wires began in the suburbs in 1897, and inside city limits the following year. At the same time the underground conduit was introduced (figure 51).

Although the city had granted a monopoly to the CGO to operate the omnibus system, a large number of concessions had been granted to private tramway companies, with no attempt either to coordinate routes or to unify equipment and power systems. By 1910 twelve companies operated more than a hundred tram lines in Paris and the suburbs, and included in this system was a variety of rolling stock and mechanical systems that made Paris virtually an open-air museum of traction equipment. At this time, for example, the CGO was operating thirty lines, and its systems included horse-drawn equipment, Purrey steam cars, compressed-air Mekarski cars, and both overhead-wire and battery-powered electrical traction. The Paris-Arpajon Company used steam traction in outlying districts, overhead electric trolley systems in the inner suburbs, and battery cars inside the city.

The designs of the cars included both single units and double-deck units with an enclosed upper level. When Eugène Hénard made his traffic study in 1906, the largest single vehicle on the Paris streets was the three-horse omnibus, which was 2.5 meters wide and 8.7 meters long. The average tramcar was about the same size, ranging in width from 2 to 2.10 meters and in length from 7.82 to 10.40 meters. The tramcars, however, were frequently linked together in pairs or even larger units (figure 52). At the time of Hénard's study, the longest tram circulating in the interior of Paris belonged to the Arpajon line and consisted of a five-car ensemble 35 meters long. Hénard termed it "a veritable street railroad."[8]

The years immediately preceding the First World War saw increasing modernization of the tramway system, with electrification increasing on most lines.

8. Eugène Hénard, *Études sur les transformations de Paris. Fascicule 7: Les voitures et les passants. Carrefours libres et carrefours à giration* (Paris: Librairies-Imprimeries Réunies, 1906), p. 249.

52. Steam-powered trams with linked passenger cars at the Place de l'Étoile.

Following the war, however, most transport systems were reduced and in bad repair, and the tramway companies were operating with mounting deficits which could not be offset by increased fares or government subsidies.

The growing importance of public transportation to the functioning of Paris made officials recognize the need for greater government control over the transport system, and in 1921 all private concessions were repurchased. At this time surface transport was unified under a new organization, the Société des Transports en Commun de la Région Parisienne (STCRP), and placed directly under the control of the Département de la Seine.

Although at this time the tramway system was dominant, the balance would soon begin to shift in favor of motor buses. The lumbering trams were considered to take up too much street space and were blamed for causing traffic jams, especially at intersections. As the automobile became dominant in urban traffic, the motor bus began to appear as a rapid, comfortable, and versatile means of transport, and the inflexible and slow-paced tram inadequate and out-of-date. In 1929 the decision was made to replace the tramways with buses, and in 1937 the last electric tramcar, on the route from Vincennes to Saint Cloud, made its final run. At the time of the 1937 Exposition, a transport official, praising the modernity of the Parisian transportation system, pointed out proudly that Paris was the only major European capital to have achieved the abolition of the tramway.

The motor bus was first introduced in Paris in 1905, the initial line running from Montparnasse to Saint Germain des Prés. This early vehicle, designed somewhat like an omnibus, had an *impériale* on top and attained a speed of fourteen kilometers per hour (twice that of the omnibus and equal to that of the electric tram) (figures 53 and 54).

Not everyone welcomed this new form of transport, however, and in 1907 a Parisian journalist condemned the motor bus as "a machine that will kill all Paris." At the time of his first exposure he had been sitting peacefully on the terrace of a café on the Rue Montmartre. "Suddenly a terrifying noise was heard, resembling thunder. My glass struck my teeth painfully, and part of the liquid spilled on me: a motor bus was passing." He appealed to his readers: "All of you who, for various reasons, still find some charm in life, raise with me, raise a cry of alarm. The Omnibus Company, tainter of our blood, threatens to depopulate Paris. There was a time when the tramways were content to jostle carriages filled with baggage, or to run over startled pedestrians venturing across their tracks. As in olden days Athens sacrificed to a fabulous monster, Paris has regularly paid her tribute of human lives. But this is no longer sufficient to satisfy the company. It hurls its engines against our own houses. They overturn our carriages. They rip open our facades. One day you will see them gather from your balcony your wife and little children. Oh progress! What crimes are committed in your name!"[9]

9. Quoted in Jacques Castlemen, *En remontant des grands boulevards* (Paris: Le Livre Contemporain, 1960), pp. 291–92.

53. Motor bus with *impériale*.

54. Mixed horse-drawn and motorized traffic
at the "Carrefour Drouot," the intersection of
the Boulevard Montmartre, the Rue de
Richelieu, the Boulevard des Italiens, the
Boulevard Haussmann, and the Rue Drouot.
(It was for this intersection that Hénard projected his *carrefour à giration*. See figure 16.)

By the time buses had completely replaced tramways, the Paris region had 226 lines, with routes covering a total distance of 1,900, kilometers. The bus itself by 1911 had assumed what, for years, would be its classic form, a single-deck closed vehicle with an open rear platform which replaced the *impériale* as the second-class area. Although, in the period following the Second World War, the city began to replace the open-platform model, it did not disappear completely until 1971 (figure 55).[10]

When the decision was made in 1929 to replace the trams with buses, motor vehicles had appeared to provide a rapid and efficient service. In the years following the Second World War, however, increasing street congestion tended to make the bus

10. In the mid-1970s limited use was made of an experimental bus with an open rear platform. This platform, however, was not usable for boarding purposes.

55. The *grands boulevards* in the 1920s. A motor bus passes the Porte Saint Denis.

one of the least reliable forms of transport. A traffic specialist observed in 1970 that the bus had become "the first victim of the traffic jams; it is desperately slow" (figure 56).[11] The annual passenger load fell from 450 million in 1950 to 300 million in 1965, and dropped to 180 million in 1970. Between 1965 and 1970, buses lost about 10 percent of their passengers every year, and it became increasingly clear that most travelers preferred either the convenience of a private car or the speed and regularity of the Métro. By 1972 traffic studies indicated that buses were used in Paris primarily for short trips during off-hours.[12]

By the mid-1960s the bus system was operating with what appeared to be a permanent deficit, and city transport officials were uncertain what methods might be employed to improve patronage. A slight increase in the speed of circulation resulted

11. François Knecht, *Circulation et stationnement dans la région parisienne* (Paris: Conférence des Ambassadeurs, October 13, 1970).
12. An analysis of the problems of bus transport in Paris may be found in "Pour les autobus dans Paris," *Paris projet*, no 8 (1972): 60–79.

56. Bus stop in the 1950s.

from the establishment in 1968 of street lanes reserved for buses in the central part of the city. By 1974 approximately seventy kilometers of such bus corridors existed, and some officials considered the possibility of reserving certain streets for the exclusive use of public transport.

In any event, contrary to turn-of-the-century predictions the bus did not kill Paris. It seemed more likely that Paris would kill the bus.

Suburban Rail Lines

While the tramways and bus lines served to link the inner suburbs with Paris, large-scale commuting from the outer suburbs came to depend on the development of a system of suburban railroad lines. Railway connections to Paris had been established initially to provide service to distant provinces rather than to the immediate surroundings, although a few lines serving the adjacent area were begun in the nineteenth century. In 1837 a line was opened between Paris and Saint Germain en Laye, followed shortly after by two lines to Versailles. These routes were supplemented by rail connections to Sceaux (1846), Bourg-la-Reine and Orsay (1857), and Boissy–Saint Léger (1859). There was little regular commuting at this time, however, as working hours seldom permitted lengthy travel between home and work.

Toward the end of the century, a shortening of the working day, together with systematic reductions in fares, encouraged increasing use of rail travel. Special fares for commuters were introduced, together with monthly and weekly subscriptions and special rates for students and apprentices. Service was improved and equipment modernized, with electrification appearing on the Invalides line in 1900. The electrification of all lines was completed by 1967 (figure 57).

Rail commuting increased dramatically following the First World War. At this time the eight-hour day became almost universal, which permitted a greater dedication of the day to travel. Improvements in rail service, together with the energetic promotion by land speculators of suburban allotments, served at this time to expand the periphery of suburban settlement. Rail commuting continued to grow during the 1920s, the number of travelers reaching 363 million during 1931. In 1938, following the economic crisis, the railroads were nationalized, and all private lines succeeded by the Société Nationale des Chemins de Fer Français (SNCF).

In addition to the initiation of a series of rail lines radiating outward from the center of Paris, the nineteenth century marked the creation of two circular lines serving Paris and its suburbs. The railroads had been introduced into Paris in such a way that they did not traverse the city, but arrived at a series of cul-de-sac terminals ringing the center. In order to provide a connection between the lines for the transfer of goods, it was decided to construct a circular railroad inside the line of fortifications surrounding the city. This line, controlled by the Compagnie de la Petite Ceinture, was begun in

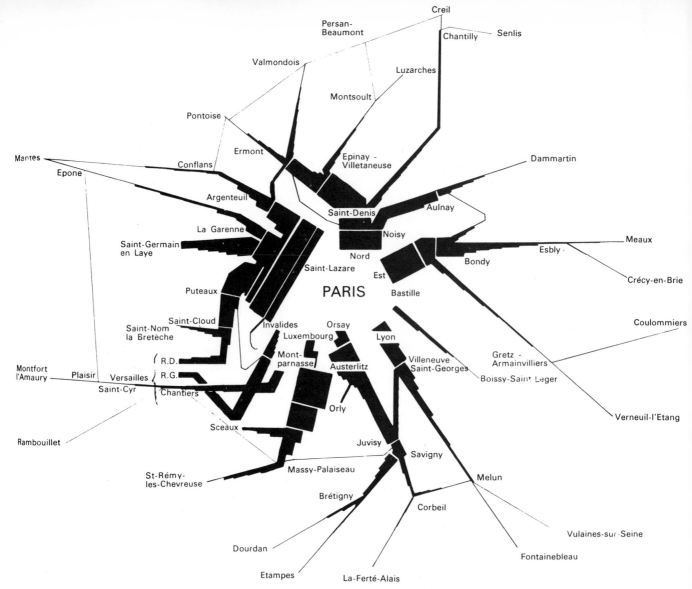

57. Diagram of suburban rail lines, showing relative volumes of traffic served by Paris terminals in 1963. By far the heaviest volume is at the Gare Saint Lazare.

1851, and, although it had been initiated primarily for the transport of merchandise, it also served to carry passengers.

The Chemin de Fer de la Petite Ceinture followed a twenty-three-mile circuit, and in 1878 the Baedeker guide suggested that it might be useful for tourists visiting such outlying spots as the Bois de Boulogne and the Parc Buttes-Chaumont. It was noted, however, that except on the west the trains ran either between walls, or in cuttings and tunnels, and so were less than ideal for sightseeing. Prospective passengers were also warned that riding on the open *impériale* was drafty and exposed one to dust and smoke.

In addition to the Petite Ceinture running within the walls, there was a Chemin de Fer de la Grande Ceinture, a railroad circuit surrounding Paris in the suburbs. This line, begun in 1875, served, as did the inner circle, to connect the major railroad lines.

River Transport

As transport systems in Paris evolved, one heavily used conveyance was destined to disappear completely. This was the riverboat (figures 58 and 59). In the middle ages, when bridge connections across the Seine were few, boats provided an essential

58. River traffic shown near the Gare d'Orsay.

59. River steamer docking at a floating pier.

means of communication between the riverbanks, and with the beginning of public omnibus transport on shore in 1662, a lively competition developed between land and water systems, As in the case of the horse-drawn carriages, the system of riverboats operated under government-sponsored private concessions.

The type of vessel in use by the late nineteenth century was a small steamer, nicknamed the Bateau Mouche, because the first models were constructed in this district of Lyons. In 1867 a Lyonnaise company, the Compagnie des Bateaux Mouches, put the vessel into service in Paris, to be followed in 1872 by another Lyonnaise company, the Société des Hirondelles Parisiennes. The two companies merged briefly, then separated in 1879, dividing routes so that the Compagnie des Bateaux Mouches served the interior of Paris, and the Hirondelles Parisiennes the suburbs. Service existed between Auteuil and Charenton, and between Auteuil and the Pont de Suresnes. In 1886 the two companies merged with a third, the Compagnie des Bateaux-Express, to form the Compagnie Générale des Bateaux Parisiens. Employing a fleet of 105 boats, this new company began a passenger service for an average of twenty-five million people per year, serving a total of forty-two million the year of the 1900 Exposition.

The Baedeker guides recommended the riverboats as a means of obtaining a good view of the city, but noted that, "being small, they are apt to be crowded and uncomfortable."[13] River traffic was greatly influenced by the weather, and in the winter fog and ice could interrupt service.

The number of passengers began to decline after 1900, possibly because of the competition of the new Métro, and by 1913 the annual total had dropped to thirteen million. With the advent of the First World War, the government took over transport systems and stopped the river service altogether.

Following the war, the Municipal Council attempted to create a municipally operated system of riverboats. Transportation habits had evidently changed, however, and it was difficult to lure people back to traveling by water. In 1923 the service carried only five million passengers and suffered a one and one-half million franc deficit. Traffic remained dependent on the weather, and as a result winter traffic was eventually suspended. In an effort to cut the deficits, service was increasingly restricted, resulting not unnaturally in further decreases in patronage. Finally in 1934 all service was discontinued.

Following the Second World War, however, the city began to consider the question of river transportation for tourists, and by 1949 the Prefecture of the Seine had received numerous requests for authorization of such service. The first tourist service began in 1950, and by 1973 the number of passengers was estimated at two million annually.

Although no attempt was made to provide a system of regular transport, the tourist boats were requested to provide an emergency transport service during a Métropoli-

13. Bædeker, *Paris and Environs*, 6th ed., p. 29.

tain strike between October 8 and 14, 1971. During this period, river service was provided between the Pont de Suresnes, the center of Paris, and the Pont de Charenton. This brief period of circulation evidently stimulated city officials to renew consideration of river transport.

In 1973 a government publication discussing the question observed: "The Seine is without any doubt the most beautiful avenue in Paris. The automobile driver immobilized in a bottleneck on the quais must often find himself daydreaming as he sees the barges crossing majestically, free from traffic lights and gasoline fumes. The image of the utilization of the Grand Canal in Venice by a flotilla of "vaporetti" comes to mind."[14] In considering the requirements of a river craft suitable for mass transport, it was felt that the new vessel should be able to attain a speed of thirty kilometers per hour, as compared to the eighteen-kilometer per-hour speed of the tourist boats, but without any increase in water turbulence. It was also felt that the new vessels would require better passenger access than the tourist boats, to facilitate the rapid boarding and disembarking of large crowds. Some type of hovercraft was considered as a possibility.

It was believed, however, that the feasibility of a water-transport system was not primarily dependent on technical problems, but on the ability of such a system to attract a profitable clientele. As there was a relatively light concentration of employment centers close to the riverbanks, there might be difficulties in establishing good liaison with other transport systems. In addition, the sinuous pattern of the river would tend to make travel time more lengthy than that of other systems.

A possible routing for a water transport system was worked out by a government study group in 1973. The suburban poles would be the Pont de Suresnes to the west and the Pont de Charenton to the east. Stops within Paris were projected for places not well served by other means of public transport, places particularly likely to benefit from an east-west connection, and important transportation nodes. Included in the proposed itinerary were the Pont de Grenelle, the Pont de l'Alma, Cité-Châtelet, and the Pont d'Austerlitz. The study group believed, however, that use of the route would be insufficient to insure a viable service, and concluded that "one cannot, under present circumstances, foresee the reestablishment of a line of public transportation on the water."[15]

The Métro: The Long Debate

Although nineteenth-century Paris was served by a variety of transportation systems, facilities always seemed strained to the limit, and as the population grew conventional surface transport appeared increasingly inadequate to meet the needs

14. "La Seine pour un transport en commun?", *Paris projet*, no. 9, 1973, p. 77.
15. "La recherche d'une clientele," *Paris projet*, no. 9, 1973, p. 99.

of a modern metropolis. The idea of rapid rail transport was achieving wide acceptance as the solution to the problem of mass movement in cities. London opened the first section of its underground railway in 1863, while New York inaugurated an elevated railway in 1868. In Paris proposals had been made as early as 1845 for an underground railway serving to transport goods, and by the 1870s city officials were giving serious consideration to such a system for public transportation. The term *réseau métropolitain*—metropolitan network—was employed by the municipal council in 1871 to describe the proposed rail system, which soon became popularly known as the *Métro*. After studying several proposals, the council decided in 1872 on the routing of an underground *chemin de fer métropolitain de Paris*. The line was to follow the *grande croisée* of Paris, with an east-west axis extending from the Place de la Bastille to the Bois de Boulogne via the Étoile, and a north-south route along the Sébastopol–Saint Michel axis. No request for a concession was produced, however, and the project remained dormant.

In 1875 the Prefect of the Seine presented a proposal of a totally different nature. He suggested the creation of a central railroad station underneath the Palais Royal, which would be linked by tunnels to the five major railroad stations. The concession for operating the system was to be given to the railroad companies. Although the Prefect's plan would have improved the service of the national railroads by providing access to the center of the city, the Municipal Council objected to it strenuously on the grounds that it was not designed to meet local transportation needs.

These two projects exemplified the issues in what was to become a twenty-year dispute between the city of Paris and the national government. The minister of public works and the prefect of the Seine maintained that the proposed transportation system was a project of national interest and thus subject to national control. The Municipal Council, however, insisted on a local system serving the needs of the city and opposed the domination of Parisian affairs by the large railroad companies.[16]

In 1876 the Municipal Council sent a group of its members to England to study the London underground system. They returned convinced that Paris could develop a similar system independent of any national subsidy, and by 1883 a scheme employing six basic lines was proposed. The minister of public works, however, continued his opposition to local control of the system, and in 1886 he presented to the Chamber of Deputies a repetition of the proposal for linking the major railroads. Although this plan was rejected by the Chamber, the minister continued his campaign to prevent implementation of the Municipal Council scheme.

The prospect of a new transportation system seems to have had a stimulating effect on French engineers and, as the debate continued, a remarkable variety of

16. The position of the national government was based on the view that the railroads were of strategic importance to national defense and thus subject to the control of the central authorities. Exceptions to this rule existed, however, for transportation systems judged to be of purely local importance, and it was the contention of the Paris government that the Métropolitain system should be categorized as local.

audacious schemes were proposed. Some designers favored the government plan to link railroad terminals, while others sought to reinforce established patterns of local circulation. Many saw the value of improved transport in making the suburban areas easily accessible, enabling the Parisian working classes to obtain more salubrious and economical housing than was available in the center of the city. Others warned that the city was thus in danger of being depopulated, that commerce in the center would be ruined, and that "grass would grow in certain quarters".[17]

As the realization of the system approached, in 1895 a municipal councillor pessimistically predicted that, "with our Métropolitain, all the life of the boulevards, the greater arteries, will disappear. The merchants, the manufacturers, the workers coming out of their offices and workshops will have but one objective: to run to catch the train. . . . There won't be any more intelligent beings. There will be only animals. In sum, with the face of Paris destroyed, the stores ruined, the small shopkeepers closing their boutiques, intellectual life no longer existing, . . . there will no longer be a Paris."[18] Possibly the most sweeping statement of opposition to the proposed transport system came in 1889 from a member of the National Assembly, Madier de Montjau, who insisted, "The Métro is anti-national, anti-municipal, anti-patriotic, and detrimental to the glory of Paris."[19]

Although the city, from the beginning, had been giving its most serious consideration to a system of underground transport on the London model, many argued that an elevated system based on the New York prototype was preferable to a "sewer train."[20] The opponents of the underground system maintained that construction costs would be prohibitive in a city as densely built as Paris. The work would disrupt the city and would involve damage to property, expropriations, and costly indemnities. It was pointed out that the subsurface of Paris was already encumbered with sewers, water mains, gas pipes, and cellars, and that the routing would thus be difficult to establish. Underground construction would be dangerous, involving accidents and illness for workers. The work site would frequently be flooded. There would be danger, moreover, in attempting to uncover the pestilential Parisian soil. "What infernal exhalations would not be desengaged from this earth, saturated from time immemorial with organic products in decomposition, and which will be unexpectedly exposed to the light of day! Isn't it to be feared that epidemics will be unleashed in Paris, following these numerous excavations of putrefying earth?"[21] It was predicted that even after construction the underground system would continue to cause damage, as buildings would be affected by the vibration of the passing trains.

17. Arsène-Olivier de Landreville, *Les grands travaux de Paris: le Métropolitain de Paris* (Paris: Baudry, 1887), p. 25.
18. Quoted in Georges Verpræt, *Paris: capitale souterraine* (Paris: Plon, 1964), pp. 216–17.
19. Quoted in Guerrand, *Mémoires du Métro*, p. 3.
20. "Le sous-sol de Paris: l'héritage de l'histoire," *Paris projet*, no. 3 , 1970, p. 30.
21. Quoted in Guerrand, *Mémoires du Métro*, p. 30.

The most frequently repeated argument against an underground transport system was the presumed antipathy of the public. It was observed:

Parisiens know very well the unpleasantness which these long tunnels would have for them. . . . There is, first of all, the permanent subterranean humidity and cold. It will be for pedestrians overheated from walking, a superb occasion to attract chills, pleurisy, bronchitis, and other maladies. . . . Then add the draft perpetually maintained in the underground by the gaping openings of the stations and by the ventilation chimneys. . . . Another inconvenience, not dangerous, it is true, but very disagreeable, will be the atmosphere one will breathe. We certainly hope that locomotives will be excluded from the Métropolitain, except for compressed air machines, or perhaps electric machines. One would thus avoid polluting the air with the smoke of the engines, but there remains the inevitable smoke of the smokers, incessantly maintained in the underground by the passage of trains filled with travelers and following each other every five minutes. There will remain, in addition, that empyemic odor which impregnates the subsoil of Paris, and which it will be very difficult to remove completely from the tunnel; finally, there will also be the vitiation of the air by the breathing of the travelers. . . . There is another disadvantage which will be singularly annoying to Parisians: it is the inherent darkness of the tunnels. One may comfortably light the interior of the cars, the stairs, and the platforms of the stations, but one will still be riding in a dark tunnel, and the Parisian, who lives so much by his eyes, will find it hard to console himself for being obliged to cross Paris without seeing anything.[22]

The term "Nécropolitain" was suggested by one opponent "to describe a railroad requiring the public to descend . . . into veritable catacombs."[23] It was observed, moreover, that while travelers might be obliged to spend only a brief time underground, there would be a large number of employees doomed to spend their lives in this purgatory.

A French engineer who had tried the London underground reported: "I came out of there absolutely oppressed, and in such a state of fatigue that I had to breathe hard the moment I was able to gain the surface."[24] To some Frenchmen, the apparent success of such a dismal form of transport could only be attributed to the dismal nature of London itself. Another engineer commented in 1884: "Indeed, what difference does it make to an inhabitant of London to be underground surrounded by vapor, smoke, and darkness; he is in the same condition aboveground. But take

---

22. The foregoing statements, reflecting the opinions of an engineer, Joly, were presented to support the proposal of an elevated system designed by Charles Tellier and published as *Le véritable Métropolitain de Paris* (Paris: Schlæber, 1885), pp. 23–25.

23. Louis Heuzé, *Chemin de fer transversal à air libre dans une rue spéciale, passage couvert pour piétons* (Paris: A. Lévy, 1878), p. 5.

24. Tellier, *Le véritable Métropolitain*, p. 22.

the Parisian who loves the day, the sun, gaiety and color around him, and propose
that he alter his route to seek, in darkness, a means of transport which will be a
foretaste of the tomb, and he will refuse, preferring the *impériale* of an omnibus."[25]

The advocates of elevated systems maintained that the necessary structures could
be built more cheaply than a series of tunnels, and without disrupting the city.
Above all, they emphasized the joys of traveling in sunlight and breathing pure air,
protected from the dust and smells of the street. The view of Paris obtainable from
such a system might make it an outstanding tourist attraction, for, it was observed:
"It isn't everything to travel quickly, one wants also to travel agreeably. The proof is
that as soon as the weather is good the *impériales* of omnibuses are absolutely
invaded.[26]

Assuming that the system would be elevated, the question remained of where to
put it. In the view of some, the logical route would follow established patterns of
movement along the existing boulevards, where the system could be constructed
without building demolitions. Several such systems were proposed during the
1870s, with a technically advanced system, designed for electric power, developed
by Jean Chrétien in 1881. Trains were to be carried on a metal viaduct running down

25. Quoted in Jules Garnier, *Avant projet d'un chemin de fer aérien* (Paris: Chaix, 1884), p. 42.
26. Tellier, *Le véritable Métropolitain*, p. 29.

60. Elevated railway proposed by Jean Chrétien in 1881.

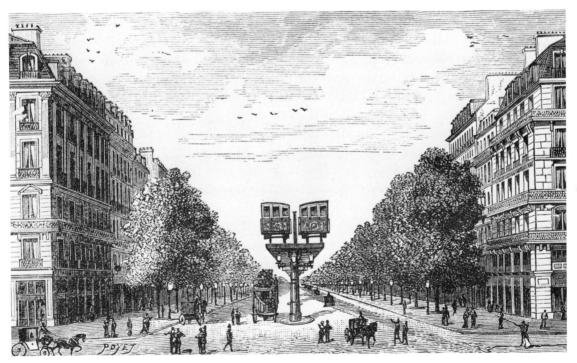

61. Chrétien's proposed viaduct at the Place de l'Opéra.

the center of the major boulevards at a height of five to six meters (figure 60). The route would lead from the Étoile to Nation, using the Avenue de Friedland and the Boulevards Haussmann and Voltaire, and from the Madeleine to Bastille using the inner boulevards.

The question of aesthetics was always present in discussions of elevated systems, and Chrétien was well aware that some people might object to the passage of his viaduct directly in front of the Opéra (figure 61). He admitted that "one could fear that this viaduct, however elegant it might be, would detract from the Place de l'Opéra, or that it would, in a disagreeable fashion, block the view of this monument." In response to such objections, he pointed out that "our modern art is not necessarily ugly. It is possible, it is even easy, to give this part of the projected work a character, either monumental or decorative, which would render it worthy to be placed on this spot without disfiguring it." He observed, moreover, that many people "believe that the Place de l'Opéra would gain by being a bit *more furnished* than it is."[27]

As a final argument Chrétien pointed out that a transport system was, in any event, more useful to Paris than the Opéra. The maintenance of the elaborate theater "costs four to five million a year, for a questionable result, from some points of view."[28] The majority of Parisians, he maintained, had no interest in the Opéra

27. Jean Chrétien, *Chemin de fer électrique des boulevards à Paris* (Paris: Baudry, 1881), pp. 53–57. Other publications describing Chrétien's elevated system are: *Chemin de fer électrique aérien sur les boulevards Voltaire, de Magenta, Richard-Lenoir, de la Contrescarpe et le Pont d'Austerlitz. Demande de concession* (Paris: Hennuyer, 1882) and *Tramway électrique aérien* (Paris: Capiomont et Renault, 1882).

28. Ibid.

and never went there. His rail-transport system, in contrast, could be regarded as a service to the working classes.

The aesthetic aspect of the elevated railway was also discussed by Jules Garnier, who published his own proposal in 1884. The basic routing of his system would, like that of Chrétien, include a line from the Étoile to Nation, following the major boulevards. As proposed by Garnier, the elevated structure would employ a two-deck single-track metal viaduct following the line of the streets at a minimum height of 4.5 meters. Although the system was to allow for the passage of standard railroad trains, the traction system for the local trains was to use compressed air, with electricity anticipated for the future. As to the appearance of the viaduct, Garnier believed that "the beautiful is the expression of the useful."[29] Should any malcontents be insufficiently receptive to the beauty of metal construction, the best designers, decorators, and sculptors of France could be engaged to provide embellishment for the structure.

The movement of the passing trains would not, in Garnier's opinion, detract from the quality of the boulevards, and the noise would simply mingle with the existing street clamor. He was familiar with the New York elevated system and claimed that there the noise was "scarcely more intense and no more disagreeable than that produced in our streets by heavy wagons, large omnibuses, and tramcars."[30] Thinking positively, Garnier insisted that the railroad was the triumph of the age, too noble an achievement to be hidden underground. "The railroad should be our glory."[31]

In spite of the continuous insistence of the promoters of elevated transport that the track systems would not mar the appearance of streets, it was undeniable that the bulky elevated roadbeds would block light from the ground below. In order to create a system which could follow existing streets with a minimum of disruption, some designers proposed the establishment of a monorail system. One of the earliest of such schemes was published in 1884 by a civil engineer, A. Angély (figure 62). The trains were to consist of three-car units suspended below a single rail, to be powered by cable, electricity, or steam. Although the supporting structure was to follow the center line of existing streets, Angély insisted that because of its relatively small bulk it could "be built on the existing roadway without hampering circulation, and without detriment to either the perspective or the decoration of our public streets."[32] (The slender dimension of the monorail track was to inspire some designers to suggest its placement, not on the street, but along the adjacent

29. Jules Garnier, *Avant-Projet d'un chemin de fer aérien* (Paris: Chaix, 1884), p, 38.
30. Jules Garnier, *Project comparé d'un chemin de fer aérien* (Paris: Capiomont et Renault, 1885), p. 42.
31. Ibid., p. 62.
32. Angéley, *Chemin de fer à voie suspendue* (Paris: Chaix, 1884), p. 13. For descriptions of additional monorail proposals, see Panafieu and Fabre, *Chemin de fer métropolitain de Paris: reseau aérien à rail unique* (Paris: Imprimerie Bernard, 1886), Charles Latigue, *Projet de voies aériennes dans Paris* (Paris: 1887), and Latigue, *Monorail ou chemin de fer à rail unique surélevé* (Paris: Bayle, 1888). Interest in monorail systems revived in the twentieth century, and in 1960 an experimental monorail system was attempted in the surburban region of Châteauneuf-sur-Loire.

62. Monorail system proposed by Angély in 1884.

63. Tellier scheme, 1885.

sidewalks.) Angély maintained that monorail installations would be cheaper than conventional tracks, and that such a system would produce less noise and vibration than ordinary rail lines. Stations were to be established inside nearby buildings, with access to the trains by means of light metal bridges.

In most proposals elevated systems were designed to follow major streets. The desire to avoid disfiguring the Parisian boulevards, however, led some to seek alternate routes, and the river quais were considered a potential site for rail lines. In 1885 a remarkable scheme published by Charles Tellier suggested using the river itself for the new Métropolitain (figure 63). His project involved the construction of a four-track rail line to run on a viaduct elevated six meters above the surface of the Seine, following the river from the suburb of Alfortville on the east to Billancourt on the west. The system, it was noted, could be constructed without disturbing streets, buildings, or river navigation, and the structure would be sufficiently high to pass over existing river bridges.

Tellier anticipated some possible objections on æsthetic grounds. It was true that the proposed viaduct would block the view across the river. He pointed out, however, that as many of the river quais carried rows of trees, the vista was already somewhat veiled by foliage. Moreover, he maintained, if people in the past had worried excessively about change, Paris would never have developed the requisites of a modern city.

Extensive consideration, however, was given to the intersection of the viaduct with the Pont de la Concorde. Tellier was well aware that the Place de la Concorde was "the most beautiful in the world; it is absolutely necessary that nothing should alter the purity of its lines. It is necessary, moreover, that the eye, in meeting the horizon, should alight only on structures in harmony with the Madeleine and the buildings that frame it. It is necessary, finally, that the members of the Chamber of Deputies conserve the view which they presently have from their palace."[33] He proposed placing on the viaduct a station that would be "absolutely monumental, worthy, in a word, of all that the art of the engineer and the knowledge of our artists can conceive as grand," believing that thereby he would not only maintain architectural harmony but at the same time embellish the Concorde site.[34]

The opening under the station would be at least fifty meters wide and six meters high, permitting the "peristyle of the Chamber of Deputies to be disengaged."[35] Each side of the station would carry a classical portico, to insure harmony with the surroundings, and there was presumably sufficient space between the monuments to insure that none would be effaced by the new structure. Tellier described the station as "a noble building, highly adorned, which through the monumental staircases

33. Charles Tellier, *Le véritable Métropolitain* (1885), p. 16. A second, slightly modified edition was published by Michelet in 1891.
34. *Le véritable Métropolitain* (1891), p. 27.
35. *Le véritable Métropolitain* (1885), p. 17.

curving between the balustrades, the candelabra, the elegant decorations, will be seen from each side of the Seine to be related to the banks."[36] On top of the building would be a statue of France carrying a torch, which would illuminate the Place de la Concorde and the Rue Royale as far as the Madeleine. Totally enamored of his new station, Tellier boasted that even though the Métropolitain was essentially a utilitarian work, it would lead to "one of the most beautiful and most grandiose creations that it has been given to man to realize."[37]

The designers who proposed elevated systems to follow the existing boulevards did so on the assumption that this was the only plausible routing. For those who did not quail at the prospect of massive demolitions, however, it seemed quite possible to establish the new rail line independent of the street system.

One such scheme was published in 1877 by Louis Heuzé. (figure 64). He maintained that placing elevated trains on the boulevards would destroy the beauty of the streets and take up space on roadways already heavily encumbered. He therefore proposed to create an elevated rail system following a path separate from the street system. Trains would be carried by a metal viaduct seven meters high and thirteen meters wide, with the ground surface under the viaduct providing a covered pedestrian way lined with shops. Heuzé considered his scheme "so advantageous from every point of view that we believe this type of penetration destined to substitute for the boulevards we still lack."[38] Realizing that there might be certain disadvantages for tenants whose buildings directly overlooked the viaduct, he indicated that the route would be bordered, not by luxury buildings, but by offices, warehouses, workshops, and stores.

As the new system would be running largely between building lines, the æsthetic aspect of the existing streets would presumably be unmarred. Heuzé indicated that, as plotted, the viaduct would cross only five large streets: the Rue de Rennes, the Boulevard Saint Germain, the river quais, the Rue de Rivoli, and the Boulevard de Poissonnière. At each of these intersections, special artistic treatment could be given to the viaduct.

Although Heuzé's system was designed to supplement the existing street pattern with a network of rail lines and pedestrian ways, another engineer, Paul Haag, proposed in 1883 that an elevated rail system be combined with a new system of street penetrations. While this would have involved extensive expropriations, Haag believed that land values would be enhanced along the new arteries. The routing would employ a series of loops, with a central circuit including both Right and Left

36. Ibid.
37. Ibid., p. 18.
38. Quoted in Émile Gerards, *Paris souterrain* (Paris: Garnier, 1909), p. 563. Louis Heuzé's publications of his plans are as follows: *Les chemins de fer dans Paris projetés en tunnels: contre-projet* (Paris: Broise et Courtier, 1877); *Paris, chemin de fer transversal à air libre* (Paris: Lapirot and Boullay, 1878–82); *Paris, chemin de fer transversal à air libre dans une rue spéciale, passage couvert pour piétons* (Paris: A. Lévy, 1878 and 1879); and *Paris, chemin de fer métropolitain en élevation à air libre dans une voie privée, avec passage couvert pour piétons* (Paris: Lapirot and Boullay, n. d.).

64. Elevated railway proposed by Heuzé in 1877.

Banks. The most important penetration would be a so-called *artère centrale* cutting through the Right Bank center. Like most advocates of urban renovation, Haag maintained that he would not be destroying anything of real value. The path of his street network would not touch a single historic monument, and he doubted that "this new street would make us regret the filthy, narrow, and characterless streets which it must replace."[39] At the time Haag introduced his scheme, the æsthetic aspects of the elevated railway caused him little concern, although he took care to refute the accusation that the system would frighten horses. He was later to stress, however, that he would not wish to see Paris with "its physiognomy altered, its

39. Paul Hagg, *Le Métropolitain Haag à l'exposition de 1889* (Paris: Chaix, 1890), pp. 58–59.

65. Arsène-Olivier's elevated system, 1868. The thirty-meter-high viaduct is shown passing by the Tour Saint Jacques on the Rue de Rivoli.

boulevards dishonored by a superstructure like the New York elevated."[40] In contrast to those who professed to see beauty in large metal structures, Haag insisted that the supporting viaduct for his system be built of masonry.

Another proposal for keeping the elevated system off the existing boulevards was made in the 1880's by the engineers Dupuis, Vibart, and Varrailhon. According to their plan, the trains would run on a metal viaduct which would penetrate directly through existing buildings at an elevated level. Demolitions would be thus kept to a minimum, as only that part of a building would be destroyed which was necessary for the vaulted railway tunnel. The rest of the building would remain "inhabited and habitable."[41]

Of all the proposed elevated systems, the most spectacular was that suggested by the engineer Arsène-Olivier, who first published his scheme in 1868 and continued to elaborate it for the next ten years (figure 65). Among the many advantages of his plan, he believed, was its suitability to the Parisian character.

"The true Parisian," he maintained, "is judicious under the appearance of lightness; patriotic, brave, generous, active, intelligent, creative, ingenious, an artist

40. Paul Haag, *Les transports en commun et les Métropolitains dans les grandes villes étrangères et à Paris* (Paris: Baudry, 1897), p. 37. Other presentations of Haag's ideas include: *Le Métropolitain de Paris et l'élargissement de la rue Montmartre* (Paris: A. Lemerre, 1883), *Note sur le chemin de fer métropolitain dans Paris* (Paris: Capiomont et Renault, 1885), and *Le chemin de fer métropolitain de Paris* (Paris: Chaix, 1890).

41. Quoted in Georges Verpræt, *Paris: capitale souterraine* (Paris: Plon, 1964), p. 218.

in every sense of the word; all that is contrary to good taste shocks him, offends and irritates his nerves. . . . The Parisian is avid for liberty, for air, for light, fleeing dark things by instinct and reason; with him, the heart, the spirit, the soul commands."[42] For such an elevated being, presumably, only an elevated railway would suffice.

The uniqueness of Arsène-Olivier's system lay in its degree of elevation, for the tracks were to be supported by a metal viaduct at a height of thirty meters. The entire structure, he claimed, would clear most existing buildings of the city, and the routing could thus be designed freely. Although the initial plan assumed that the tracks would follow major boulevards, later proposals suggested that the city be covered by a grid of transport independent of the street patterns.

Ascent to the tracks would be made through existing buildings, which would be expropriated and converted into stations containing elevators. The elevator was not yet in wide use, but Arsène-Olivier assured his readers that it was "a very convenient and agreeable device."[43]

As to the visual aspect of the towering structure, Arsène-Olivier pointed out that in places where the supports were behind buildings, pedestrians in the street would see only the upper galleries, "crowning the houses, with which they would harmonize." Where the supports could be seen from the street, suitable decoration would be employed. Electric lights might be attached to the supports to provide street illumination, and the surface could also be used for "non-irritating" advertising. In 1887 Arsène-Olivier pointed to the forthcoming 1889 Exposition as a demonstration of the artistic possibilities of metal construction combined with colorful enamel decoration. The giant metal trusses of his transport system could be similarly decorated, exemplifying "polychrome architecture in all its radiance." "Whatever form we give it," Arséne-Olivier insisted, "the purpose of the Métropolitain . . . is to complete Paris. . . . Let us make it one of the last masterpieces of this century."[44]

Although there were sufficient proponents of elevated transport in 1887 to form a "Ligue Parisienne du Métropolitain Aérien," there was also sufficient opposition to form a "Société des Amis des Monuments Parisiens," which provided an energetic and effective campaign to prevent the "destruction of France by France."[45] Created in

42. Arsène-Oliver de Landreville, *Les grands travaux de Paris: le Métropolitain* (Paris: Baudry, 1887), p. 16. Other presentations of Arsène-Olivier's ideas may be found in *Chemins de fer dans Paris et dans les grandes villes* (Paris: Auguste Lemoine, 1868, 1872) and *Les grands travaux de Paris de la paix: Paris nouveau* (Paris: Baudry et Cie, 1887). The latter work includes suggestions for the whole of Paris, including a plan for the creation of a new government center with a parliament building on the site of the old Tuileries Palace. It may be noted that Olivier's concept of an elevated structure, clearing existing buildings and carrying a line of transport, would later be echœd in the work of Le Corbusier, who in 1929 proposed building in Rio de Janeiro an elevated structure with a thirty-meter clearance, which would have a level of apartments surmounted by a motor expressway. He claimed it could be built without disrupting the city below in any way.

43. Ibid., p. 39.

44. Ibid., pp. 52, 54, 57.

45. Verpræt, *Paris: capitale souterraine*, p. 217.

1885 by Charles Normand, this organization had the designer of the Paris Opéra, Charles Garnier, as president and Victor Hugo as honorary president. The Société, which included a large number of art historians and archæologists among its members, not only opposed the creation of elevated rail systems, but also sought to insure that an underground system would not endanger monuments and sites.

Just as the elevated concept attracted a number of farfetched schemes, the idea of a subterranean system inspired some rather bizarre proposals. In 1880 J. Mareschal suggested an underground railway where the vehicles would run down inclined tracks, powered by gravity, to be lifted up at each station by elevators. Another scheme included a system of tunnels to be used for passenger trains by day and as sewers by night. A system of ventilators would remove the smell each morning.

66. Underground railway proposed by J. B. Berlier in 1887.

One of the most thoroughly developed underground schemes was produced by the civil engineer J. B. Berlier, who began outlining his proposals in 1887 (figure 66). He envisaged an underground system of metal tubes carrying electrically powered trains, and the method of tunneling he proposed would presumably permit construction without disrupting the surface. Reviewing the arguments concerning underground and elevated systems, he deemed it "inadmissible to install on the Rue de Rivoli and on the *grands boulevards* an elevated line which would be odious from the aesthetic point of view and would never be supported by the owners and tenants of the adjoining buildings."[46] Berlier maintained that a tunnel, "abundantly ventilated and luxuriously illuminated," would be more agreeable than riding in an omnibus, and that Parisian workers would appreciate a means of rapid travel, even if it had to be below the surface.

Although the long period of controversy over the Métro had inspired many ingenious and imaginative proposals for elevated railways, city officials continued to give their most serious consideration to an underground system. The Municipal Council was particularly impressed by Berlier's scheme, and in 1892 they agreed to grant his request for a concession to build. He was unable to raise sufficient funds, however, and the enterprise lapsed.

The Métro: Realization

The factor that finally brought about the construction of the much-debated Métro in Paris was the approach of the 1900 Exposition. The prestige of France was embodied in the image of the French capital as a modern city reflecting the advanced standards of French science and technology. At the time of the 1889 Exposition, existing transportation had proved barely adequate to handle the large crowds of visitors, and it seemed clear that to accommodate the even greater influx expected in 1900 Paris would need a new system of rapid transport. Rather than prolong the dispute between city and state, the minister of public works, Louis Barthou, yielded power to the city of Paris in 1895 to develop and control the new Métropolitain.

While planning the system, however, city officials still feared an eventual encroachment by the major railroads. To forestall any possible use of the track network by national lines, the city proposed using a track gauge of 1.30 meters instead of the standard gauge of 1.44 meters. As finally approved, however, the track width conformed to existing standards, and the exclusion of national rolling stock was effected by constructing smaller tunnels than those normally used for the

46. J. B. Berlier, *Les tramways tubulaires souterrains de Paris, 1887–1890* (Paris: Berlier, 1890), p. 7. Other presentations of the Berlier scheme are: *Paris, tramways souterrains* (Paris: Cusset, 1887), *Tramways tubulaires souterrains de Paris: ligne de la Place de la Concorde au Bois de Boulogne* (Paris: Cusset, 1890), and *Tramways tubulaires souterrains de Paris* (Paris: Dupont, 1891).

railroads. (The Métro system was to employ a car 2.40 meters in width, as compared to 3.20 meters for the national railroads.)

Although the city would construct the infrastructure of the system, it was decided that the operation would be directed by a private concessionaire who would be responsible for building the necessary superstructures. The concession was to last twenty-five years, during which time the city would receive a portion of the fares collected. At the expiration of the concession, the entire system was to revert to the city. From among several applicants for the concession, the city selected the Compagnie Générale de Traction, which subsequently formed the Compagnie du Métropolitain de Paris (CMP).

The creation of the Métro, described as "the most important work Paris has experienced since its foundation,"[47] was directed by Fulgence Bienvenüe, a government engineer. Included in his previous accomplishments were the construction of the Avenue de la République, the creation of the Belleville cable railway, and the development of the park of Buttes-Chaumont. His involvement with the Métro became a lifetime vocation, and he remained in charge of its development from 1895 until his retirement in 1932. Fond of the classics, he once observed: "By the enchanted lightning of Jupiter, the race of Prometheus is transported to the depths."[48]

In contrast to the London Underground, which was constructed in tubes lying far below the surface, the Paris Métro system was built close to ground level. The top of the elliptical vault housing the tracks generally lies about a meter below the street, and the depth of the tunnel averages about eight meters. This eight-meter level is the depth at which most underground constructions—sewers, water pipes, electric conduits, etc.—are located. For passengers, entrance into the Métro requires a descent of about six meters, with a ticket level located halfway.

The general method of construction involved an excavation of the upper portion of the tunnel, which was then covered with a masonry vault. The rest of the tunnel would then be excavated, and the side walls and floor completed in concrete. In order to avoid damage to private property and the payment of indemnities, all lines of the Métropolitain system were projected to follow the path of wide streets. In this way, the system reflected already established patterns of movement through the city.

Because of the need to have the system in operation for the 1900 Exposition, construction activity, employing two thousand workers, continued day and night after its beginning on October 19, 1898. Needless to say, the city was greatly disrupted, and Jules Romains reported: "You heard everyone complain that Paris was odiously encumbered. The *chantiers* of the Métro, which rose up everywhere like fortresses of clay and planks armed with an artillery of derricks, succeeded in strangling the streets and blocking the intersections" (figure 67).[49]

47. Roger Guerrand, *Le Métro* (Paris: Éditions du Temps, 1962), p. 16.
48. Quoted in Verpræt, *Paris: capital souterraine,* p. 212.
49. Quoted in Roger H. Guerrand, *Mémoires du Métro* (Paris: La Table Ronde, 1960), p. 60.

67. Scaffolding for the Métro extending from the Place Saint André des Arts along the Rue Danton.

The first segment of the Métro to be constructed followed the east-west axis of the *grande croisée*, extending between the Porte de Vincennes and the Porte Maillot, a distance of eleven kilometers. Partially completed, the line was inaugurated on July 19, 1900. In the same year two short sections were added, one running from the Étoile to Trocadéro, and the other from the Étoile to the Porte Dauphine. In spite of predictions that Parisians would never consent to ride underground, the Métro seems to have been accepted immediately. It was reported in *Le Galois,* following the opening, that "the success of this new means of transport has been very big. It is due primarily to its rapidity. . . . Travelers yesterday were enthusiastic."[50] The 1900 Bædeker guide stated that the Métro "now takes precedence of all other modes of

50. The story was dated July 20, 1900. Quoted in Verpræt, *Paris: capitale souterraine,* p. 215.

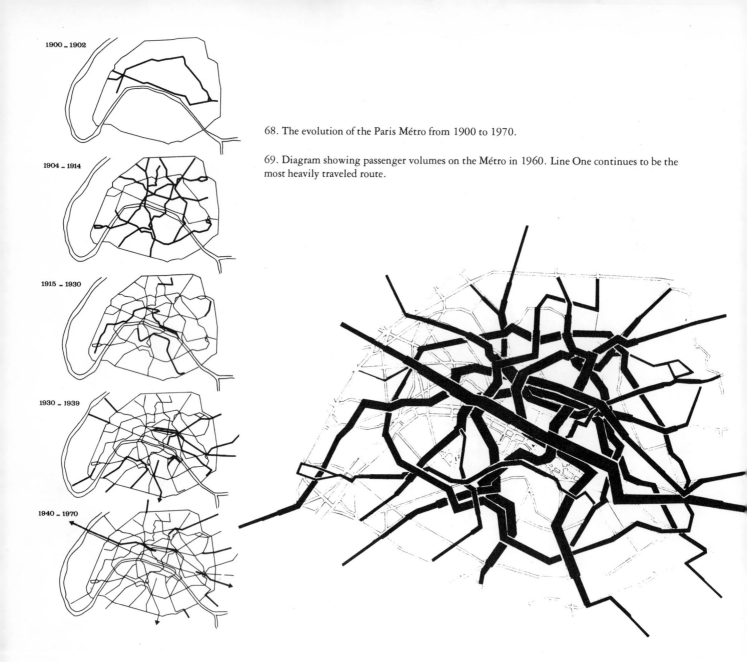

68. The evolution of the Paris Métro from 1900 to 1970.

69. Diagram showing passenger volumes on the Métro in 1960. Line One continues to be the most heavily traveled route.

1900 – 1902

1904 – 1914

1915 – 1930

1930 – 1939

1940 – 1970

locomotion in the interior of the city." Readers were informed, however, that as in London the stations were below the level of the street, "and the atmosphere is similarly oppressive to susceptible people."[51]

The initial concession for the Métro had involved the construction of six lines (figures 68 and 69). Following the completion of Line One, the second line of the system, extending from the Porte Dauphine to the Place de la Nation via the Étoile and the exterior boulevards, was built between 1901 and 1903. This line was carried on viaducts for about one third of its length. Between 1904 and 1905 a third line, extending from the Porte de Champerret to the Place Gambetta, via Opéra and the

51. Bædeker, *Paris and Environs,* 14th ed. (Leipzig: Bædeker, 1900), p. 28.

Rue Réaumur, was opened, to be followed in 1906 by Line Five, extending from the Étoile to the Place d'Italie by way of the southern exterior boulevards. The circuit begun by this line was completed in 1909 when Line Six was opened between the Place de la Nation and the Place d'Italie. Line Four, a north-south line extending from the Porte de Clignancourt to the Porte d'Orléans, was completed between 1908 and 1910, and it marked the first use by the Métro of a tunnel passing below the bed of the Seine. A "complementary network" was added to the system before 1914. This included two additional lines: Line Seven, extending from the Porte de la Villette to the Opéra, and Line Eight, running from the Place Balard to the Porte de Charenton.

It may be recalled that an engineer, J. B. Berlier, had been granted a concession for the Métro in 1892 but had been unable to raise sufficient funds. He was eventually awarded compensation of five hundred thousand francs by the city. In 1905, supported by a company called the Société du Chemin de Fer Électrique Nord-Sud de Paris, he obtained a concession for a separate underground line running from the Gare Montparnasse to Montmartre. Although his previous proposals had involved metal tubular tunnels, the construction of this line followed prevailing methods. The "Nord-Sud" line was merged with the CMP in 1930.

The length of the Métro system had been expanded from ten kilometers in 1900 to eighty in 1914, the increase in track being accompanied by a corresponding increase in the number of passengers. In its opening year, between July and December 1900, the Métro carried 17,660,286 people. The following year the figure reached 55,882,027, and had grown to 149 million in 1905. By 1914, 400 million passengers were carried annually.

Although some Parisian officials had hoped that the construction of the underground system would relive traffic pressure on the streets, the opposite seemed to be the case. A government report in 1910 suggested that the availability of rapid, cheap transport seemed to set off a demand for more transport, and that since the construction of the Métro Parisians had become accustomed to moving about with much more frequency. The construction of underground transport, it was believed, had not replaced surface movement but instead encouraged it.

In addition to the network of underground constructions, the Métro system also provided for the creation of a series of stations and entrances which, in their ingenious exploitation of Art Nouveau, created virtually a "Métro style." The Société des Amis des Monuments Parisiens, in the course of its campaign to prevent the establishment of an elevated transport system, had expressed the wish that no Métro station be allowed to extend above the sidewalk, and that they should preferably be installed in shops. Others, however, anticipated that the new transport system could be accompanied by distinguished artistic efforts. In 1886 Charles Garnier had written to the minister of public works: "The Métro, in the view of most Parisians, should reject absolutely all industrial character to become completely a work of art. Paris must not transform itself into a factory; it must remain a museum. Don't be afraid to abandon lattice girders and thin metal framework; gather to you stone and marble, summon bronze sculptures and triumphal columns."[52]

The first Métro stations embodied designs by the architect Hector Guimard. His apartment house, the Castel Béranger, which reflected an imaginative application of the currently fashionable Art Nouveau style, had just won a prize for facade composition. As the Métro itself represented a new form of transport, it may have seemed appropriate that it be accompanied by innovative design. The contribution of Guimard was in many cases limited to the embellishment of stairways leading from the sidewalks to the subterranean stations (figure 70). Metal railing employing the sinuous foliate forms typical of Art Nouveau would surround the opening, with tall, fancifully curving lampposts illuminating the entrance. The elevated signboard, in harmony with the ensemble, embodied decorative Art Nouveau lettering. In some instances, the staircase would be covered with a glass roof.

At some of the more important Métro stations, such as the Portes of Vincennes, Nation, Maillot, and Dauphine, glass pavilions marked the entrances, with perhaps the finest of these structures appearing at the Place de la Bastille (figure 71). Lightly framed in metal, with projecting glass canopies, these stations were likened to "dragonflies spreading their wings" or "fragments of the skeleton of an ichthyosaur."[53]

Because of their novelty the Guimard stations were somewhat controversial, and as Art Nouveau began to decline in popularity, strong opposition to them developed. One of the focal points of debate was the station entrance opposite the Opéra. Although the Opéra facade had been adversely criticized when it was built, by the turn of the century it had acquired the status of a historic monument, and Guimard's design was rejected in 1904 on the grounds that it did not harmonize with the neobaroque styling of Garnier's elaborate Second Empire confection. Support for Guimard was organized by the Société du Nouveau Paris, while the architect himself demanded in *La Presse:* "Will we henceforth have to harmonize the station of Père Lachaise with the cemetery, and construct it in the form of a tomb? Will we harmonize that of the Place Mazas with the Morgue? Must one place a dancer kicking her leg in front of the station at the Place Blanche, to harmonize it with the Moulin-Rouge?"[54]

The designer selected for the Opéra station was Joseph-Marie Cassien-Bernard, the architect of the Pont Alexandre III, who provided the entrance with a classical

52. Guerrand, *Mémoires du Métro,* pp. 82–83.

53. Ibid., p. 84.

54. Ibid., p. 87. The Société du Nouveau Paris was founded in 1902 to provide a counterinfluence to preservationist groups. The first president was Frantz Jourdain, an architect whose most conspicuous work in Paris was the Samaritaine department store. The Société encouraged the modernization of Paris, maintaining that excessive reverence for the past on the part of a few was standing in the way of progressive change beneficial to the populace as a whole. The stated aims of the Société included the beautification of Paris and the improvement of services.

70. Métro station entrance by Guimard, Place des Abbesses.

71. Métro station, Place de la Bastille, now demolished.

stone balustrade. Highly approving the result, *Le Figaro* pointed out: "We refused to dishonor the Place de l'Opéra with the contorted ramps and bumpy lampposts which, with their enormous frog's eyes, announce the other Métro stations. . . . Now that the first step has been taken, we hope to see disappear the ornaments of 'art nouveau' which decorate the stations of the Place de Palais Royal and the Tuileries, and that we will profit by the occasion to tear down the two pavilions of the Place de l'Étoile, which don't content themselves with being ugly, but which are useless as well."[55]

From this time on, classical stone balustrades were the only type of Métro entrance considered suitable for monumental sites, and they were employed at the Place de la République, the Gare Montparnasse and Gare de l'Est, the Madeleine, and the Place de la Concorde. Such entrances eventually replaced the Guimard pavilions at the Étoile. Although metal would continue to be used for many Métro installations, directness and simplicity would govern the design.

During the period following the Second World War, many of the Guimard Métro pavilions were destroyed as stations were modernized, and in 1962 the elegant and

55. Ibid., pp. 87–88.

72. Bourse station, 1905. The cars were wooden.

fanciful "pagoda" at the Place de la Bastille was razed. By this time the Guimard structures, no longer an eccentric novelty, were viewed by many as a valuable part of the artistic heritage of Paris, and in 1965 several of the Métro station entrances were classified as protected monuments.

Although there was some degree of variety in the design of Métro entrances, the underground stations were basically the same, with the surfaces of the walls and arched ceilings faced in white tiles. It was once observed that "each station is a sort of temple of ceramics" (figure 72).[56] Following the Second World War, however, a program of station renovation began, in which the first project was the Franklin Roosevelt station. The redecoration, begun in 1952 and directed by an industrial designer, Paul Arzens, was characterized by the use of bright color, increased lighting, and new lettering styles. Show cases and illuminated panels were also introduced. The renovation of stations has enjoyed continuing popularity, with perhaps the greatest artistic success occurring, appropriately enough, at the Louvre station, where the decor, inaugurated in 1968, includes reproductions from the museum collection (figure 73).

56. Pierre Lavedon, *La nouvelle histoire de Paris: histoire de l'urbanisme à Paris* (Paris: Hachette, 1975), p. 228.

73. Louvre station.

When the Métro was first constructed, no line extended outside the Paris boundary, thus reinforcing the conception of a purely local system. Between 1931 and 1939, however, a few modest penetrations were made into the neighboring suburbs. At the same time, the constant growth of the suburban region prompted consideration of an additional Métro system designed to join with suburban transport lines. As a first step in the establishment of such a network, the Ligne de Sceaux, a suburban rail line extending south of Paris, was made part of the Métro system in 1938. This line had been electrified the previous year.

By 1937 the Métro system included 150 kilometers of track, and in 1938 it carried 761 million people. The depression seems to have reduced passenger use somewhat, as this figure had reached 888 million in 1930. Because of the relative density of Paris, the number of passengers per kilometer of line was high, in 1935 reaching 5,800,000, as compared with 1,680,000 in London, 4,960,000 in New York, and 2,740,000 in Berlin.

The greatest pressure on the Métro system, however, was to come with the German occupation of Paris during the Second World War and in the period immediately following. During the war years the absence of gasoline rendered almost all motor vehicles inoperable, and virtually the entire burden of public transport was handled by the Métro. Crowded into increasingly antiquated and badly maintained facilities, travelers in the Métro reached over 1 billion in 1941, 1 billion 230 million in 1942, and 1 billion 320 million in 1943. The highest number of travelers was recorded during 1946, when passenger traffic reached 1 billion 598 million. Although the Métro had been crowded during the war years, it was one of the few places in Paris that was warm, and a French official reminiscing about this time observed that, "having all become poor and deprived of heat, we dreamed of prolonging our trips to avoid shivering in our offices and homes."[57]

During this period a reorganization of the transport system was begun. In 1942 it was decided to unify surface and underground transport, using a system of common fares and coordinated lines. To effect this, the Compagnie du Métropolitain de Paris and the Société des Transports en Commun de la Région Parisienne, which controlled the bus lines, were merged. Following the war, the Régie Autonome des Transports Parisiens (RATP) was created in 1948 to direct the unified system of public transportation. This organization was replaced in 1959 by the Syndicat des Transports Parisiens.

Although for a time government policies seemed to neglect public transport in favor of automobile facilities, it soon became apparent that no system of private transport could adequately serve the Paris region. The Métro system became subject, therefore, to a continuous program of modernization. New rolling stock was introduced, and during the 1960s station platforms were prolonged from

57. Ibid., p. 236. The statement was made by Martial Massioni, president of the Conseil Général de la Seine, in 1950.

seventy-five to ninety meters to accommodate longer trains. One of the most notable improvements came with the introduction of rubber tires for the cars. The tires were introduced experimentally in 1952, then employed on Line Eleven between Mairie des Lilas and Châtelet in 1956. In 1963 they were introduced on Line One, running from Vincennes to Neuilly. This line, the first portion of the Métro to be built, continues to be the most heavily traveled. Rubber tires were added to other lines during the 1960s and 1970s.

During the long period of controversy before the construction of the Métro, opponents of the underground system had made pessimistic predictions about the quality of the air in the tunnels. Once the system was built, it was maintained by André Berthelot, the first administrator of the Compagnie du Métropolitain, that the underground was among the healthiest places in Paris. He pointed out that "the absence of dust is, indeed, almost complete in the underground. . . . The air of the Métro is incomparably less charged with bacteria in the morning at the beginning of service than in the majority of public places and streets."[58] According to a contrasting view, however, the Métro was "a badly ventilated cellar, recalling, from time to time, a sewer collector. One is hit in the throat, in descending the stairs, by an unending series of odors, of unbreathable emanations, a mixture of sweat, of tar, of carbonic acid, of metallic dust, etc., . . . and all of a warm heaviness like that of a day when a storm is about to break."[59]

It had also been predicted, while the Métro was being contemplated, that Parisians would be repelled by the idea of traveling underground. Not only would the prospect of being denied light and air drive people away, but there was also the presumed threat of human passions unleashed in subterranean darkness. This assumption seems to have been inspired by the railroad tunnel of Batignolles, which took one minute to traverse. It had been suggested that "only those condemned to death, and women who are sitting face to face with a ruffian in darkness, know how long a minute can be."[60]

Once the Métro was in operation, however, with the almost frightening adaptability that characterizes the inhabitants of large cities, the Parisians simply accepted underground travel as a normal part of life. In 1960 it was found that one Parisian in four traveled daily in the Métro, and it was estimated that by the age of retirement the average Parisian would have spent two years of his life underground.

To a number of Parisian novelists, the Métro seems to have provided an ideal academy for the study of humanity. According to one writer: "The taxi is sometimes a necessity. The bus, a convenience. The Métro is something else altogether: it's the Museum of Man, the true one, the museum of living man, of man naked. In a bus, people sit so they can see the street. They look through the windows; the spectacle distracts them: they remain masked, inscrutable. Underground, by contrast, they

58. Guerrand, *Mémoires du Métro,* p. 115.
59. Ibid., p. 116.
60. Verpræt, *Paris: capitale souterraine,* p. 217.

become discomposed very fast. . . . Here there is nothing to occupy their eyes, to distract them from themselves. With empty eyes, each one sinks within himself: he becomes a statue of himself, or more precisely his own mirror. . . . The dream, the truth and falsehood of his life, floats in his gaze. It's there for you to read."[61]

The sociologist André Siegfried, describing his own feelings in the Métro, reported: "In this ensemble, the individual disappears, becomes anonymous, a simple number in a crowd of which he is an integral part. I find there, I confess, a sort of mystical sensation, freed for a few minutes from my identity, breathing and reacting with the mass, enjoying its vitality and strength."[62]

While there is no denying that the Métro provides a good theater for people-watching and an excellent opportunity to achieve intimate physical contact with one's fellows, it is possible that even a novelist or sociologist would lose enthusiasm for the experience if compelled to ride every day during rush hour.

Although the Métro is an important part of the Parisian transport system, it is only one aspect of a complex pattern of regional transportation. In 1972 over 12 million daily displacements took place in the Paris region, the largest concentration of movement naturally taking place in the commute between home and work. It was reported in 1971 that 850,000 people commuted daily to Paris from the suburbs, while 200,000 went from Paris to jobs outside. At the same time, 900,000 suburbanites traveled to employment in the suburbs and 700,000 inhabitants of Paris traveled to employment within the city. Inside Paris there were 7 million daily displacements, using public transport, with the greatest concentration during the evening rush hour. During a single hour at this time, more than 700,000 people were found to be using public transport, with 300,000 in the Métro and 230,000 passing through the railroad stations.[63]

The constant increase of commuting from the suburbs to Paris prompted consideration of an additional Métro system as early as 1929. Travelers arriving on the suburban railroad lines were compelled to transfer to the Métro or the bus system to reach the center of the city. An additional system was considered necessary, therefore, to link the suburbs directly to employment centers. The incorporation of the Ligne de Sceaux with the Métro in 1938 provided the first step in the creation of such a network.

It was not until the 1960s, however, that construction of the new rail system, called the Réseau Express Régional (RER), was begun (figure 74). In outlining the proposed system in 1961, the Transport Commission explained why the problem could not be solved by further extensions of the Paris Métro. The Métro was considered to be already saturated and, with its numerous stops, unable to provide an efficient service

61. Guerrand, *Mémoires du Métro*, pp. 206–07.
62. Verpræt, *Paris: capitale souterraine*, p. 226.
63. Statistics from Maurice Doublet, *Les transports dans la région parisienne*, pp. 15–19, and Pierre Merlin, *Vivre à Paris 1980* (Paris: Hachette, 1971), p. 164.

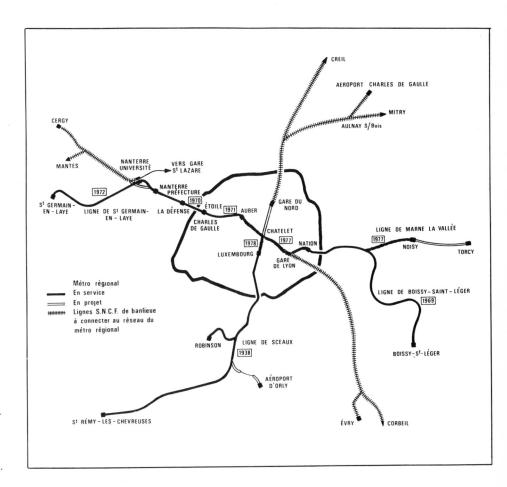

74. Routing of the Réseau Régional (RER), showing connections with the suburban railroad lines. The RER lines are shown in black, and suburban railroads with hatched lines.

to outlying areas. The commuter railroads were also considered to be overloaded and unable to penetrate the city center. The RER, it was suggested, would not only supplement existing transport systems, but open up new suburban areas for settlement.

The tunnels of the RER were designed to traverse Paris at a depth of ten to thirty meters, passing under existing Métro lines, but permitting transfer to the Métro at certain important stations (figures 75 and 76). Trains were designed with the same height as railroad stock and intended to reach a speed of seventy to ninety kilometers per hour.

The first section of the RER to be developed was an east-west line extending from Boissy–Saint Léger to Saint Germain en Laye. Construction began with the suburban sections, with the portion on the east linking Boissy–Saint Léger to Nation operating in 1969. On the west the line was first developed to provide a connection between the Étoile and a new business center at La Défense. This portion was opened in 1970, with an extension into the city to the Métro station of Auber added in 1971, and an extension westward to Saint Germain en Laye opened in 1972. By December 1977, the first RER

STATIONS "PLACE DE L'ETOILE" remblais

LIGNE N 1   LIGNE N 6   passage souterrain pour voitures

RESEAU URBAIN

LIGNE N 2

7.80 m

Collecteur — Marceau

LIGNE REGIONALE "EST-OUEST"

STATION "PLACE DE L'ETOILE"

20.87 m

30.13 m

INCLUDE FOR MÉTRO CONSTRUC.

75. Subterranean section at the Place de l'Étoile, showing the relation of existing Métro lines to the new RER station.

76. RER station at the Étoile.

system was complete. The east-west section, called Line A, now extended through the city, with connections to the Métro added at Châtelet–Les Halles and the Gare de Lyon. An eastern branch reached Noisy le Grand–Mont d'Est. A second line, Line B, incorporated the Ligne de Sceaux, leading southward from Châtelet–Les Halles to Saint Rémy–Les Chevreuse, with a branch to Robinson.

At this time, it was anticipated that by 1985 Line B would have been extended north to Charles de Gaulle airport at Roissy and to Mitry-Claye. Line A was intended to receive an eastern extension to Torcy (paralleling the axis of the new town of Marne la Vallée) and a western branch to the new town of Cergy-Pontoise. Additional RER lines were projected to serve such destinations as Montigny-Beauchamp and Argenteuil in the north, Versailles and the new town of Saint Quentin en Yvelines to the west, and Massy-Palaiseau, Dourdan, and Étampes to the south. An additional line was foreseen to extend to the new town of Melun.

"Métro, Boulot, Métro, Dodo" [64]

As the region of Paris expanded during the period following the Second World War, the transportation system became subject to continual analysis. Patterns of movement, choice of transport, length and time of journey were dissected statistically, and the cost of commuting painstakingly evaluated in terms of money and time. As a technical problem, transportation in the Paris region has made constantly increasing demands on public resources, and as improvements in transport have often been accompanied by increases in the amount of travel, the capacities of the system seem always strained to the limit.

In addition to the financial and technical burdens of mass commuting, there is also the less easily evaluated human cost (figures 77 and 78). A traffic expert pointed out in 1970 that "the Parisian, or the suburbanite, spends two hours a day in transport, both the equivalent of one-quarter of his work time and the equivalent of the time he devotes to leisure activity of all sorts. He perceives, he resents these two hours as a nuisance, as a burden much worse than his eight hours of work." [65] Reductions in working hours were thus seen to have been offset by the increasing burden of travel, leading a physician to opine that "today, for certain classes of workers, the seventy-two-hour work week corresponds to that of the worker of 1830, who lived at the gate of the factory." [66]

The hardships of suburban commuting were invoked by Le Corbusier in 1935 to bolster his own conceptions of centralized urban form. In *The Radiant City,* he de-

---

64. *Boulot* is a slang word for a job; *dodo* is baby talk for sleep. The phrase "Métro, boulot, Métro, dodo" has been popularly used in Paris to sum up the routine of daily life: "Subway, work, subway, sleep."
65. François Knecht, *Circulation et stationnement dans la région parisienne,* p. 10.
66. Brigitte Gros, *4 Heures de transport par jour (4 Hours of Travel Per Day)* (Paris: Denoël, 1970), p. 82.

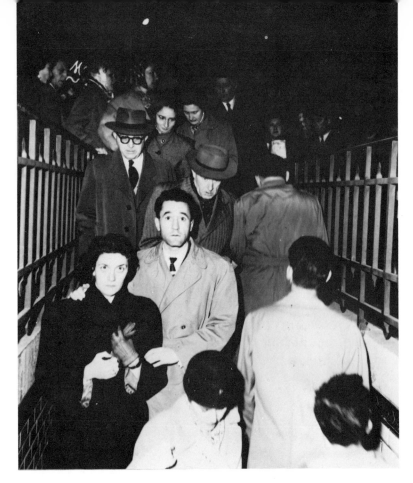

77. The descent into the inferno.

78. Rush hour at the Place de l'Opéra. By the age of retirement, the average Parisian
has spent two years of his life underground.

scribed a conversation reportedly taking place between himself and his secretary. When he asks her, "Can't you manage to arrive on time, at 8:30?," she points out, "I live in the suburbs, the stations are crowded, and if I miss my train I'm late. Look," she continues, "you can't possibly imagine what it's like, all the trains are packed solid, morning, noon and night. And sometimes the men aren't too pleasant, we're all squashed together like in the subway and you have to look out! I catch the 7:45 and I have to walk nearly half an hour along muddy roads to get it. When it rains it's terrible and when it's windy it's worse, and in the winter it's still dark." Each day she rises at five, and does not return home before eight-thirty or nine in the evening.

The architect observes, "I am beginning to be deeply interested in this daily round that reveals such a series of anxieties." Not only is the travel exhausting but, according to the secretary, life in the suburbs is lonely, dreary and isolated. She concludes unhappily: "I've been coming into Paris every day for ten years . . . I've spent the best years of my life in the train. Ten years! . . . My youth and all of life's dangers have passed me by in the train."[67]

Thirty-five years later, Brigitte Gros, the Conseiller Général of the suburban community of Aubergenville, attempted to illuminate the daily problems of rail commuting in a book called *4 Heures de transport par jour.* Although the town itself appeared serene and pleasant on the surface, the daily journey to Paris was a purgatory. According to an aging worker: "The bus, the train, the Métro, this is what makes our life a slavery. Understand me, madame, I'm fifty-five years old, and every day of my life I spend four hours in public transport! It's simply inhuman."[68] A survey of the town indicated that the average commuter left home at 6:30 A.M., returning around 7:30 P.M., thirteen hours later. The total journey to and from work averaged about three hours each day, and 80 percent of the travelers were compelled to combine use of the bus, the train, and the Métro.

In order to experience firsthand the difficulties of her commuting constituents, Madame Gros tried an experimental journey in an evening commuter train, nicknamed the "cattle train," number 651 from the Saint Lazare station. As she described the journey: "The train was packed with suburbanites, exhausted by their day of work. Standing, pressing one against the other without the power to move a centimeter, shaken by the deafening vibrations, they submitted in silence to their daily nightmare. From time to time, the lights were extinguished and the carriage plunged into total darkness. The badly regulated heat continued full blast: the temperature was suffocating, the air unbreathable. With damp clothes, everyone was bathed in a dead and oppressive atmosphere. From station to station, the train was

67. *The Radiant City* (New York: Grossman, Orion Press, 1967), pp. 11–12. First published as *La ville radieuse* (Boulogne [Seine]: Éditions de l'Architecture d'Aujourd'hui, 1935). It may be recalled that Le Corbusier's visionary project of 1922, the City for Three Million People, had included a series of *cité-jardin* dormitory suburbs. By the 1930s his visionary projects attempted to contain the entire urban population within the central city.

68. Gros, *4 Heures de transport,* p. 8.

immobilized to permit the passage of express trains; it seemed as though the torture would never be over."[69]

In the view of many urbanists, problems of transport would be better solved by reducing travel than through increasingly costly and elaborate transportation systems. Yet, although the pedestrian-centered environment in which most citizens can live close to their work remains an ideal, the planning of the Paris region has incorporated the assumption that massive commuting will continue to characterize the Parisian way of life. In the view of some, much of the attraction of any major city lies in its wide range of employment, housing, recreation, and cultural facilities, and the ability to move about through the entire urban area is essential to maintaining freedom and variety of choice.

The present-day planning of the Paris region involves the creation of a series of so-called "new towns" designed to contain both housing and employment. Although the development of such centers could reduce some commuting, they were not projected as self-contained or isolated communities but were instead designed to be linked to central Paris by rapid rail lines. The evident presupposition was that the inhabitants of such towns would in many cases travel to Paris to work. In the planning of central Paris, moreover, new poles of commercial activity have been developed adjacent to suburban railroad terminals, on the assumption that they will draw many of their employees from outside the city.

While the present regional plan reflects an attempt to develop a more coherent and unified pattern of urbanization for greater Paris, it offers no substantial alteration in existing commuting trends. Although public transport may become more rapid, convenient, and comfortable, the burden of a lengthy daily journey seems destined to remain part of the lives of many Parisians.

69. Ibid., p. 11. Pierre Merlin makes a similar effort to dramatize the plight of the suburban commuter in *Vivre à Paris 1980*, pp. 147–50. He provides a step-by-step description of a typical suburban wageearner's daily journey. A young man who lives in a housing complex at Grigny rises at 6:45 A.M. in order to take a 7:45 bus to the Gare de Juvisy. The bus ride takes ten minutes. He boards a crowded train for Paris at 8:04 and rides standing up for twenty minutes, arriving at the Gare de Lyon. Leaving the train, he continues his journey by Métro, standing in a car packed to a density of about eight persons per square meter. After a ride of over fifteen minutes, he ascends to the street, where the walk to his office takes slightly over eight minutes. When he arrives home that evening at 7:10 P.M., he will have spent approximately two and a half hours of his day traveling, in highly uncomfortable conditions.

4 A COLLECTIVE AND COMPLEX ART

The Bequest of Eclecticism

A book discussing Parisian architecture in 1913 opens with an episode in which the author encounters an American tourist near the Arc de Triomphe. Expressing his admiration for the French capital, the American exclaims: "Proud as we are of our country, we would search there in vain for a city to compare with Paris. Our agglomerations have something chaotic about them; the buildings there are gigantic, but without any concern for order or proportion. In Paris, by contrast, and this is what creates its superior beauty, its unique beauty, the streets are designed according to an intelligent plan, and the buildings are controlled in their dimensions, their facades aligned and soberly decorated, giving a remarkable impression of unity. Paris is essentially a city of harmony." The Parisian points out gloomily, however, that this harmony is in the process of destruction, directing the attention of the tourist toward "two enormous buildings which regard insolently from the windows of their upper floors the elegant and discreet buildings which form a respectable circle around the Arc de Triomphe. Consider these skyscrapers . . . The incomparable harmony of this place is already destroyed. And look around you as you walk through Paris. The crimes against the beauty of our city multiply with a horrible rapidity. There isn't a single plaza or street where the harmony has not been altered. Paris, even in the most beautiful quarters, is covered with warts and tumors."[1]

Such sentiments have frequently been expressed in Paris during the past hundred years. In any city the human fabric constantly changes. It is the relatively stable architectural environment that gives the city its physical identity. Paris is Paris

1. Charles Lortsch, *La beauté de Paris et la loi* (Paris: Recuel Sirey, 1913), pp. 12–13. This book is the published version of a doctoral dissertation in law submitted in 1912 and inspired by the architectural results of a 1902 change in building regulations. The book strongly condemns the new regulations and provides an assemblage of critical opinion supporting the author's position. A similar doctoral dissertation, also in law, had been produced in 1911 by Charles Magny, who also deplored the new regulations and sought to promote their modification.

because it looks like Paris, and although it is frequently observed that a vital city cannot be a museum, architectural innovation has often met with an instinctive opposition. Paris has been regarded not merely as a city containing artifacts, but, by some, as a single artifact which must be maintained intact.

A member of the Chamber of Deputies once observed: "A work of art dœs not always involve a canvas or a block of marble. A great city can be a work of art, a collective and complex art, but a superior art. Among all the great cities, which are like petrified civilizations, Paris has radiated, until now, the greatest splendor. It is like a synthesis of our national life, of our civilization evolving through eighteen centuries of our history."[2]

Buildings, of course, are only things. Yet they are important things. They are a projection of the human mind and spirit; they are a part of human experience. They can be loved; they have a kind of life, and when they are destroyed it is a kind of death. The beauty of a building depends on the eye of the beholder, and tastes change. The "ugly" building may survive to become "interesting" or "amusing," and finally "beautiful." What was once deemed "monotonous and mechanical" may later be seen as "harmonious and orderly," and the "excessive and vulgar" become "imaginative and vital." Every building was once new, and an initially radical form may eventually be regarded as an exemplar of tradition. What has been consistent in Parisian architectural criticism, however, has been the conviction that the beauty of Paris is unique, fragile, and threatened. There is a sense of watchfulness which has made architecture a focus of continual controversy. It has sometimes been said that Paris is essentially a classical city and that departures from classical form are out of place in the urban fabric. One writer has even suggested that the beauty of Notre Dame in Paris rests on its being "the most calm, the most serene of our old cathedrals; . . . it has great uninterrupted horizontal lines on its facade, and its massive strong towers don't stretch desperately toward the sky."[3]

Although the beginning of the nineteenth century was dominated by the classical revival, Parisian architecture came to reflect the prevailing variety of historical styles. Embodied in nineteenth century taste was a receptivity to virtually the entire existing range of architectural form. Technical innovations such as metal framing, moreover, added to the flexibility of even traditionally styled buildings, and when used openly could produce exciting new æsthetic experiences. Although classicism was to remain a strong element in French design, the full gamut of revival styles appeared in Paris.

While historicism would continue dominant in architecture, in the second half of the century emphasis would shift from strict revivalism to eclecticism, an approach that enabled the architect to draw from a variety of sources, adapting styles to

2. The deputy Chastenet, quoted in Charles Magny, *Les moyens juridiques de sauvegarder les aspects esthétiques de la ville de Paris* (Paris: Bernard Tignol, 1911), p. 3.
3. Albert Guérard, *L'avenir de Paris* (Paris: Payot, 1930), p. 84.

modern purposes with flexibility. The term *eclecticism* was borrowed from the French philosopher Victor Cousin, who in a series of lectures delivered at the Sorbonne in the 1840s had used the word to describe a system of thought comprising views assembled from a variety of systems. Although eclectic building may look traditional to our own eyes, it was recognized in its day as innovative and often shocked conservative critics. Departures from classicism were bad enough, but many new buildings seemed to have escaped clear stylistic classification altogether. To those who advocated the development of a new architectural style, however, eclecticism provided a possible transition between revivalism and a completely nontraditional form of building. Some observers saw the formal and stylistic variety of nineteenth-century building as detrimental to the unity of Paris. The Académie des Beaux-Arts had protested, for example, when the Gothic-revival church of Sainte Clothilde was built. Surveying nineteenth-century building in 1889, the architect Lucien Magne noted that "some critics, of a morose disposition, are irritated not to find today the unity of style which characterized periods when art was confined in guilds."[4] The modern age, he maintained, was an age of freedom and individualism, and, for contemporary design, originality was of prime importance. Eclectic architecture was not to be analyzed in terms of "correctness," but rather with an eye to the skill and inventiveness the architect had used to manipulate the design elements.

Typifying the eclectic approach to design was Charles Garnier's Opéra, begun in 1861 and dedicated in 1875 (figure 79). Although in its classical detailing, elaborate decoration, and monumental scale the Opéra might well have been considered "neobaroque," it could not be easily related to existing styles. Upon viewing the plans, the Empress Eugénie is reputed to have asked what style it was: Louis XIV, Louis XV, Louis XVI? The architect replied, "It is Napoleon III."[5]

Although the Opéra embodied a mixture of design elements, the *partie* was essentially classical. A far more eccentric mélange would be found in another major landmark, the Basilica of Sacré-Cœur. In 1870 the archbishop of Paris had expressed a wish to build a church on the summit of Montmartre, and in 1873, following the war and the Commune, the National Assembly voted support for the project as a testimony of repentance and a symbol of hope. The design was selected through a competition among seventy-eight entrants, most of whom provided designs characterized by stylistic mixture. The winner, Paul Abadie, who had previously been involved in the architectural restoration of the cathedrals of Angoulême and Périgueux, called his design "Romano-Byzantine." (It had apparently received some general inspiration from Saint Front and Saint Étienne in Périgueux, as well as from Saint Mark's in Venice) (figure 80). In plan Sacré-Cœur involved a Greek cross, with

4. Lucien Magne, *L'architecture française du siécle* (Paris: Firmin-Didot, 1889), p. 102.
5. Quoted in Henry Russel Hitchcock, *Architecture: Nineteenth and Twentieth Centuries* (Baltimore: Penguin Books, 1958), p. 138.

a semicircular apse bordered by six chapels, the whole being surmounted by an elongated dome flanked by four smaller domes. As the orientation of the church was to be toward the city, the choir, traditionally placed on the east, was shifted to the north.

Sacré-Cœur was finished by 1914, with dedication postponed until 1919. Although the completion of the church coincided with the emergence of the modern movement in architecture and a decline in fashion of historical eclecticism, Sacré-Cœur has maintained continuous popularity, attracting both religious and

79. The Paris Opéra.

80. Sacré-Coeur.

touristic pilgrims. Crowning one of the most conspicuous sites in the city with its distended bulbous domes and glistening white surface, the church makes no concessions to the existing character of Paris, yet through its very uniqueness it has become inextricably bound up with the image of the city.

One observer, having noted that "from outside and close up, the effect is disappointing," went on to write: "When you perceive it suddenly from the corner of the boulevard, floating unreally above Notre Dame de Lorette, or when, from the Left Bank, it springs up phantasmic and distant, guarding the city like a citadel of prayer, confess that Paris would no longer be our Paris without this strange monster which dominates it."[6]

Another eclectic confection of the 1870s that became a popular landmark was the Trocadéro Palace, erected for the 1878 Exposition and not destroyed until 1936 (figure 81). The site was an important one, an elevation opposite the Champ de Mars on an axis with the École Militaire. The design of the palace, which included a theater for 4,500 people, was produced by an architect, G. J. A. Davioud, and an engineer, J. D. Bourdais, in a style which has been characterized as Romano-Spanish-Moorish. The theater itself was contained in a round hall framed in metal, with an exterior of colorful ceramic brick. The entrance facade was flanked by minarets, and the side curving toward the river was surrounded by a two-story classical colonnade. Curving classical arcades framed the top of the hill at either side.

6. Guérard, *L'avenir de Paris,* p. 84.

81. The Trocadéro Palace.

With its bizarre mixture of forms and startling color, the Trocadéro Palace was highly controversial. Although a publication entitled *Marvels of the Exposition of 1878* stated that "modern architecture has found its Parthenon," many newspapers were critical, and again the question was asked which had been posed with regard to Garnier's Opéra: What style is it? Byzantine? Arab? Roman? Greek? Florentine? The architect Paul Sédille concluded that, "It is neither this nor that, and in spite of all that it is modern."[7]

To some, the curving form and protruding towers brought to mind a donkey's hat, while to others the open colonnade was reminiscent of a Mississippi steamboat, with the minarets representing smokestacks. Edmondo de Amicis described the Trocadéro Palace as an "enormous architectural braggart . . . that crowns the horizon, and crushes all the surrounding heights."[8]

7. Quoted in Louis Hautecœur, *Paris,* vol. 2, *De 1715 à nos jours* (Paris: F. Nathan, 1972), p. 557.
8. Edmondo de Amicis, *Studies of Paris* (New York: Putnam, 1882), p. 38. It may be noted that the colorful exterior of the Trocadéro Palace has been considered responsible for inspiring the fashion for ceramic decoration in architecture that characterized the last years of the century.

In the lively intellectual and artistic life of Paris, architecture was a subject of continual debate. Much of the discussion involved the points of view epitomized in the two centers of architectural education, the École des Beaux Arts and the École Polytechnique. The École des Beaux Arts, which had existed under the monarchy, was reorganized by Napoleon in 1806 to contain the schools of painting and sculpture as well as the previously independent school of architecture. The training of architects in the École des Beaux Arts emphasized architecture as a fine art and focused on the æsthetic aspects of design. The École Polytechnique, modeled on the school of military engineering, had been founded during the Revolution as a preparatory school for military and civil engineers. Architectural courses were included in the program, providing a training that associated architectural design with structural concerns.

Although the École des Beaux Arts represented a variety of personalities and viewpoints and showed some evolution in educational philosophy, it would remain in the eyes of many critics and architects the symbolic center of retrograde formalism. In spite of a reform in the École in 1863, it was observed in 1889: "The study of forms, independent of construction, is today still one of the errors in teaching; but this error cannot survive for long. . . . Architecture is no longer a closed art, of which the abstract formulas are accessible only to a small number of initiates; it has regained the place it ought to occupy in contemporary society, and this society will demand works appropriate to its ideas and its needs."[9]

To those theorists who espoused the cause of "rationalism," it was the responsibility of the architect to come to terms with modern technology, and, as the modern movement began to develop, the faults of nineteenth-century architecture were often attributed to an artificial separation of architecture from engineering. As viewed by certain propagandists, the engineer was to emerge a hero, the true master builder of the age. Substantiating such a view of history, however, has required a high degree of selectivity in assembling the evidence. Not every work of engineering was a success, nor was every work of conventional architecture a failure. To support the image of the progressive-minded engineer creating a masterpiece in the face of conservative opposition, there was, of course, Gustave Eiffel and the tower he created for the 1889 Exposition.

The international expositions, in addition to providing a showcase for industrial products and techniques, had also presented a natural opportunity for experimental structures. Metal framing had proved to be particularly useful for the creation of large, quickly assembled, easily demountable pavilions, and beginning with the famous London Crystal Palace of 1851 the expositions were the site of notable essays in metal construction.

The 1855 Exposition in Paris had bequeathed to the city the Palais de l'Industrie by Jean Viel, which exhibited a classical exterior but contained within a

---

9. Magne, *L'architecture française*, p. 96.

metal-framed hall with an unbroken span of forty-eight meters. This building, situated on the Champs Élysées, remained in use as an exhibition building until 1897, when it had to be demolished to make way for the Avenue Nicholas II. The 1867 Exposition had been laid out on the Champ de Mars, a site which would be used for succeeding major expositions. Exhibition space was provided in an immense, ellipitical, metal-framed structure which created a series of concentric halls and covered an area of sixteen hectares. At the center was a Galerie des Machines designed by Krantz and a young engineer, Gustave Eiffel. The 1878 Exposition, for which the Trocadéro Palace was created, contained a Galerie des Machines by Henri de Dion in the form of an elongated metal-framed pavilion.

The most daring and memorable exposition structures, however, were those erected in 1889. As the fair was intended to commemorate the French Revolution, it was perhaps appropriate that it should exhibit audacious revolutionary structures. Included in this Exposition, as in previous fairs, was a building designed to exhibit heavy machinery, a Galerie des Machines. This building, which provided four and one-half hectares of unbroken floor space, was designed by an architect, Louis Dutert, and an engineer, Victor Contamin. It was 420 meters long and 43 meters high, containing an open span of 115 meters, the widest yet achieved. An aesthetic triumph as well as a technical feat, the Galerie des Machines was judged by the architect Frantz Jourdain to be "a work of art as beautiful, as pure, as original, as elevated as a Greek temple or a cathedral."[10] Although it had been hoped by its many admirers that the Galerie des Machines could be preserved, it was demolished in 1910.

Also intended as a temporary structure was the Eiffel Tower (figures 82 and 83). The idea of constructing a three-hundred-meter tower had intrigued engineers for some time, and the 1889 Exposition, with its symbolic importance for French prestige, seemed a suitable occasion to dazzle the world with a triumph of French engineering. Gustave Eiffel, whose project was selected through a competition, had already achieved eminence as an engineer and had considerable experience in bridge construction.

Among the opponents of the tower were scientists who predicted that it was a technical impossibility and also the now-famous group of artists who, having seen the proposal for the three-hundred-meter metal tower, published a protest in *Le Temps* on February 14, 1887. This Committee of Three Hundred (one for each proposed meter of the tower) provided certain historians of the modern movement with a classic example of unenlightened reaction. Included in its membership were Bouguereau, Charles Gounod, Massenet, Alexandre Dumas, Sully Prudhomme, J. L. E. Meissonier, J. A. E. Vaudremer, and Charles Garnier. In form, the protest was a letter addressed to the Parisian director of works, Jean Alphand, including the following text:

10. Quoted in Michel Ragon, *Histoire mondiale de l'architecture et de l'urbanisme modernes,* vol. 1, *Idéologies et pionniers* (1800–1910) (Paris: Casterman, 1971), p. 174.

Dear Sir and Compatriot:

We come, writers, painters, sculptors, architects, passionate lovers of the beauty, until now intact, of Paris, to protest with all our force, with all our indignation, in the name of unappreciated French taste, in the name of menaced French art and history, against the erection, in the very heart of our capital, of the useless and monstrous Eiffel Tower, which public hostility, often endowed with good sense and a spirit of justice, has already baptized the "tower of Babel."

Without falling into an excess of chauvinism, we have the right to proclaim aloud that Paris is a city without rival in the world. Beside its streets, its spacious boulevards, along its admirable quays, amidst its magnificent promenades, rise up the most noble monuments that human genius has created. The soul of France, creator of masterpieces, radiates from this august flowering of stone. Italy, Germany, Flanders, so justly proud of their artistic heritage, possess nothing comparable to ours, and from all the corners of the universe, Paris attracts curiosity and admiration. Are we going to let all this be profaned? Is Paris going to be associated with the grotesque, mercantile imaginings of a constructor of machines, to be irreparably defaced and dishonored? For the Eiffel Tower, which American commercialism itself would not want, is, without any doubt, the dishonor of Paris. Everyone knows it, everyone says it, everyone is deeply afflicted by it, and we are only a feeble echo of universal opinion, so legitimately alarmed. And lastly, when foreigners come to visit our Exposition, they will cry, astonished: "What! Is this horror what the French have found to give us an idea of their much-vaunted taste?" And they will have reason to ridicule us, because the Paris of Gothic sublimity, the Paris of Jean Goujon, of Germain Pilon, of Puget, of Rude, of Barye, etc., will have become the Paris of Monsieur Eiffel.

It suffices to understand what we put forth, to imagine, for an instant, a ridiculously tall tower dominating Paris, like a gigantic black factory chimney, overpowering with its barbaric mass Notre Dame, Sainte Chapelle, the Tour Saint Jacques, the Louvre, the dome of the Invalides, the Arc de Triomphe, all our humiliated monuments, all our belittled architecture, which will be obliterated in this stupefying dream. And for twenty years we will see spreading out over the entire city, still vibrating with the genius of so many centuries, we will see, spreading like a blot of ink, the odious shadow of the odious column of tin.

Le Temps accompanied the publication of the artists' letter with an interview in which Eiffel responded to their fevered opposition. He observed, to begin with, that the protest had been made too late to affect the progress of the tower. The money had already been appropriated by the national government for its construction. At the close of the Exposition the tower would be ceded to the city of Paris, which had already awarded Eiffel a twenty-year concession to exploit the structure. Following this period, the city could "do with it what it pleased." Not only had all contracts been completed for the tower, but the masonry foundations were in place and the iron ordered. Arguing against the creation of the tower was, therefore, futile.

Just as the protest was too late to halt construction, Eiffel believed that it was too early to make judgments about the æsthetic impact of the completed structure. He admitted: "I think, myself, that the tower will be beautiful. Because we are engineers, do people think that beauty does not preoccupy us in our constructions, and that, at the same time that we make them solid and durable, we don't try to make them elegant? Don't the true conditions of strength conform to secret conditions of harmony? The first principle of architectural æsthetics is that the essential lines of a monument are determined by its perfect accord with its purpose. Of what factor have I had to be aware, above all, in my tower? Of wind resistance. Well, I maintain that the curves of the four edges of the monument, which my calculations have furnished me, will give an impression of beauty, for they will reveal to the eyes the daring of my conception."

He went on to note that there was an attraction in size itself. "Do you think it is for their artistic value that the pyramids have so powerfully struck the imagination of men? What are they, after all, but artificial mountains?" The æsthetic impact of the pyramids, he claimed, lay in, "the immensity of the effort and the grandeur of the result. My tower will be the highest structure that has ever been built by men. Won't it be just as grand in its fashion? Why should that which is admirable in Egypt become hideous and ridiculous in Paris?" He denied that the tower would in any way diminish the architectural integrity of the historic monuments of Paris, most of them in remote parts of the city. In addition, he pointed out that such large structures as the Arc de Triomphe and the Opéra did not appear to detract from their surroundings.

On the positive side, the tower would serve as "striking proof of the progress realized in this century by the art of the engineers. It is only in our time, in these last years, that one could make such exact calculations and work in iron with enough precision to dream of such a gigantic enterprise. Is it not to the glory of Paris that this résumé of contemporary science should be erected within its walls?"[11]

The Eiffel Tower, needless to say, proved to be an enormous popular success, and it remained the major attraction of the 1889 Exposition. It continued to be assumed, however, that it would be dismantled once the twenty-year concession had expired. An American book on Paris published in 1892 considered the Eiffel Tower "the realization and the crowning work of the century fast passing away. It comprises the inherent defects of an age little distinguished for the creative in art; we miss the

11. *Le Temps*, February 14, 1887. Both the artists' letter and the report of the Eiffel interview appear under a column heading, "Au Jour le Jour," pp. 2–3. One of the unfortunate aftereffects of the protest is that in recent years it has been used to deflect criticism of any proposed tall structure in Paris.

82, 83. The Eiffel Tower.

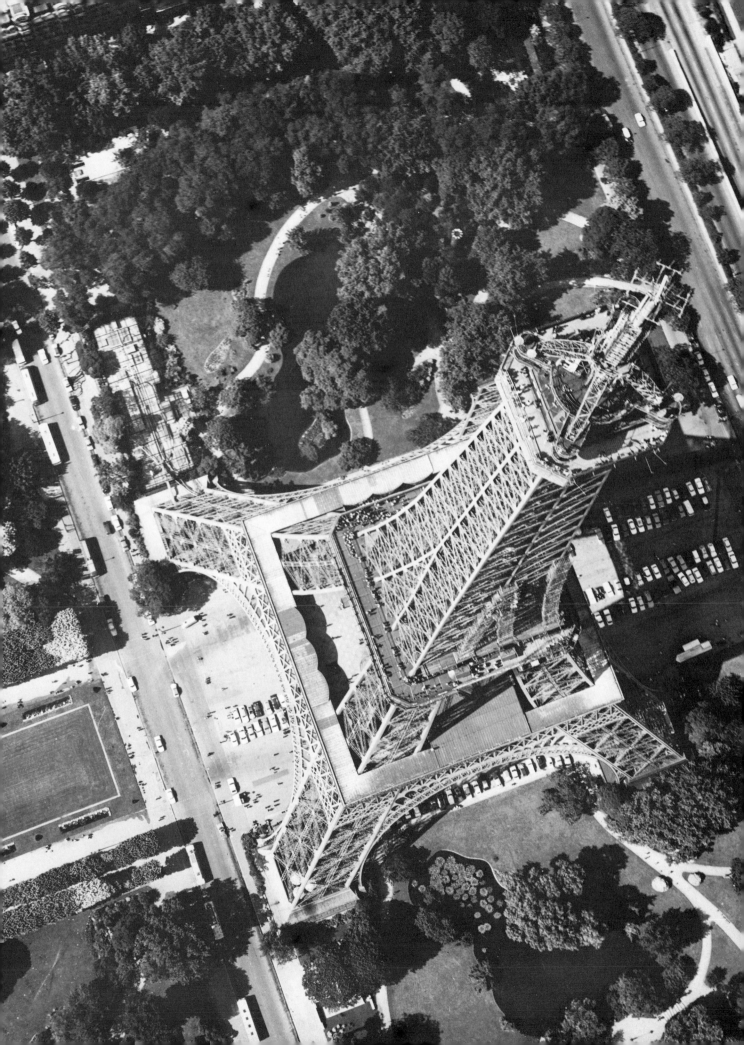

sculptured marble and delicate chiseling of older, if not more famous monuments; but we realize also, better than we have ever realized before, the vast knowledge and power of this utilitarian period." All in all, the Eiffel Tower could be deemed "the veritable Eighth Wonder of the World, which, long after it has been demolished, will live in French history and nourish patriotic confidence and pride."[12]

The survival of the Eiffel Tower following the expiration of the initial concession was partially dependent on the fact that it could be used for radio transmission. The first overseas broadcast from Paris was beamed from the tower to Casablanca in 1907. But in the meatime it had become such a beloved landmark that, even had it served no utilitarian function, its preservation might well have been assured. The dire predictions of the Committee of Three Hundred as to the blighting effect of the tower had, of course, proved totally false, and a French scholar once remarked: "The Eiffel Tower is a miracle. It is majestic in spite of its lightness, gracious above all, rather than crushing. It is so aerial, so different, that it humiliates nothing that surrounds it and dœs not spoil perspectives."[13]

The Exposition of 1889 had been marked by spectacular achievements in engineering. The next exposition, held in 1900, embodied what has been viewed as a somewhat retrograde return to the ideals of "grand art." Although metal framing was used in many structures, the audacity and inventiveness of 1889 were missing, and the predominant architectural style of the fair was an ornate classicism.

12. *Paris As It Is* (New York: Brentano, 1892), p. 20.
13. Guérard, *L'avenir de Paris,* p. 82.

84. The Pont Alexandre III.

85. The Grand Palais.

The site, which included the Champ de Mars, extended along the riverbanks to fill the esplanade of the Invalides. Included in the permanent heritage of the fair was the axial link between the Invalides and the Champs Élysées, created by the newly constructed Avenue Nicholas II and Pont Alexandre III. The design of the Pont Alexandre III involved the engineers Résal and Alby and the architects Cassien-Bernard and Cousin (figure 84). Spanning the river in a graceful curve, the bridge embodied a single metal arch 107.50 meters in length. The decoration, which included stone pylons decorated with statues, elaborate candelabra, and metal garlands on the span, was designed by Georges Recipon. Although some modern critics have deplored the sumptuous decoration of the Pont Alexandre III, the ensemble was highly admired when it opened. An American observer stated, without reservation: "The statues and bas-reliefs represent fine art in the highest achievement of modern times, while every feature in the construction of the work stands as an epitome of the perfection of 19th century progress. It is the greatest and most beautiful work of its class in the world and, finished at the end of the century, it will stand as a model for the inspiration of aspiring architects during the entire course of the new cycle of one hundred years."[14]

Flanking the Avenue Nicholas II were two exhibition buildings, the Grand Palais and Petit Palais, which were intended to remain as permanent structures. Both

14. Jose de Olivares, *Parisian Dream City.* This title applies to a series of illustrated volumes dealing with the 1900 Exposition and published in St. Louis by N. D. Thompson. They appear under the general title Educational Art Series. The quotation appears in volume 13, no. 72, May 24, 1900 (pages unnumbered).

buildings juxtaposed metal skeletons and skylit interiors with exteriors of classical masonry (figure 85). The chief architect was Charles Girault, who was assisted in the Grand Palais design by A.E.T. Thomas, Henri Delgane, and Albert Louvet. According to one contemporary opinion, the Grand Palais created "a uniform impression of grandeur and immensity. Architecturally it is regarded as almost faultless, and the prediction has been made that for some generations to come it will serve as a model for buildings of that class."[15] Like many predictions, this one failed to account for changing tastes, and a history published in 1975 described the Grand Palais as "heavily pompous, loaded with a profusion of statues and sculptural groups which have one sole merit, that of better enabling one to appreciate the sobriety of true classicism, that of the nearby Invalides, for example."[16]

Although opinion may be divided about the merit of the two palaces, there has been virtual unanimity with regard to the perspective created toward the Invalides. The view across the Pont Alexandre III has been called "one of the last great moments in Parisian urbanism."[17]

At the beginning of the nineteenth century, Paris had been dominated architecturally by the classical tradition. It was this heritage that had bequeathed to the city its monumental scale, together with a series of irreproachable architectural ensembles. The Place de la Concorde, with its adjoining palaces, the Institut de France, the École Militaire, the Invalides, the Place Vendôme might be seen as exemplifying an abstract perfection of balance, order, and harmony. As the century advanced, however, a series of new major landmarks appeared, almost like human presences: awkward, vulgar, daring, imperfect, and capable of inspiring love. If the seventeenth and eighteenth centuries had given Paris its most respected tradition, the nineteenth century provided the most beloved landmarks. Among these, only the Arc de Triomphe might be said to relate harmoniously to the monumental classicism of the city. Notre Dame Cathedral, a decaying remnant of the Gothic tradition, was renovated into a nineteenth century evocation of the Middle Ages. The Paris Opéra, the Church of Sacré-Cœur, and the Trocadéro Palace embodied ostentatious eclectic mixtures, while the Eiffel Tower provided a dramatic focal point unrelated to traditional style. Paradoxically, it seems to have been the very uniqueness of the nineteenth-century monuments that has made them symbols of Paris. The seventeenth-century facade of the Louvre may be architecturally superior to Sacré-Cœur, but one is far less likely to find its proportions reproduced on dish towels, jigsaw puzzles, calendars, lampshades, and ashtrays.

According to a French scholar: "Paris has singular indulgences; it can give the right of the city to laughable aliens, disquieting misfits. After several seasons, . . . these adopted children have become Parisian to the marrow of their bones. We have the

15. Ibid.
16. Alain Pons, 2000 ans de Paris (Paris: Arthaud, 1975), p. 167.
17. Ibid., p. 170.

Trocadéro, the Eiffel Tower, and Sacré-Cœur: initially three intruders, who, far from effacing themselves, have installed themselves on the most conspicuous sites of the capital."[18]

The Century Turns

As the nineteenth century drew to a close, the complex architectural fabric of Paris could be seen to reflect a long history of urban development. From the Middle Ages a few monuments still survived, and in the old center of the city some of the medieval street pattern remained. While much of Paris had been renovated, there were still quarters that embodied the texture of the seventeenth and eighteenth centuries. Thus, in spite of the destructiveness of the preceding century, Paris had not been totally deprived of its past. Yet the evolution had been rapid, and the volume of new construction was such that even today much of Paris seems dominated by a nineteenth-century image.

The scale of urbanism had changed, and juxtaposed with the remnants of the old urban fabric was a new dimension. Just as the street pattern had been altered to provide for the circulation of modern traffic, the building pattern had changed to accommodate a new range of activities. To those who felt a strong nostalgia for the old Paris, the sense of balance had been irretrievably destroyed. It was observed that "in the city of the past, the churches and palaces dominated the houses of the nobles, the bourgeoisie, and the artisans. The height of the buildings was like a sign of supremacy, and the physiognomy of the city reflected in a clear and elegant manner the hierarchy of society. Today the only sovereign is the people."[19] The king had given way to the merchant prince, and modern Paris increasingly reflected the needs of industry and commerce. The activity of the city centered on the production, distribution, and consumption of goods at a scale undreamed of before the industrial age, and included in the new range of building types were factories, warehouses, markets, hotels, theaters, department stores, railroad stations, and apartment houses.

One of the most conspicuous new building types in Paris was the railroad station. In the utilitarian provision of shelter for the tracks, the stations presented opportunities for technical innovation in metal and glass construction. As symbolic gateways to the city, they also served a monumental purpose, and frequently they exhibited ornate masonry exteriors. Toward the end of the century, an increase in rail traffic prompted the rebuilding of several stations in Paris. The Gare de Lyon was given a new building by Marius Toudoire between 1897 and 1900 which reflected a prevailing taste for picturesque massing. The station embodied a masonry

18. Guérard, *L'avenir de Paris,* p. 82.
19. André Hallays, quoted in Lortsch, *La beauté de Paris,* pp. 103–04.

block with a high roof and arched portals, the ensemble accented by a looming clock tower (figure 86).

At about the same time a completely new station, the Gare d'Orsay, by Victor Laloux, was being built along the banks of the Seine on the site of the old Cours des Comptes, destroyed during the Commune (figure 58). It was to provide a central station for the Orléans lines, which had been prolonged two miles from the Gare de Lyon in a tunnel built along the riverbank. As electric engines were to be employed, it was no longer necessary to separate the main station from the track housing; thus the building comprised a single volume, with an interior metal vault and an external facade of elaborate stone masonry. Although some modern critics were later to deride its massive and ornamental exterior, the Gare d'Orsay, which had been

86. The Gare de Lyon.

87. Printemps Department Store. At left is a corner of the building designed by Paul Sédille in 1882; at right, an addition designed by René Binet in 1909.

completed in 1900 to accommodate exposition traffic, was initially much admired and became one of the attractions of the fair.

Another building type which, like the railroad station, had come into existence during the nineteenth century and embodied an architectural mélange, was the department store or *grand magasin*. This type of large merchandising establishment was essentially a Parisian invention, and it was in Paris that it achieved its first architectural flowering. The department store was, in a sense, like an exposition building—a large hall displaying manufactured goods, which in this instance were for sale. Like an exposition building, the department store often made extensive use of metal framing, and in its classic form embodied a large sky-lit rotunda in which decorative metal staircases provided access to upper levels. An open use of metal in the interior would usually be juxtaposed with a sumptuous masonry exterior and an abundant use of colorful ornament. The department store was a "people's palace," an easily accessible center of luxury and display, where the elaborate decor provided an atmosphere conducive to enjoyment and spending.

Gustave Eiffel and Louis Charles Boileau were involved in the design of the Bon Marché in 1876, while Paul Sédille designed a new building for the Printemps Department Store following a fire in 1881 (figure 87). Some of the most spectacular department store design coincided with the introduction of Art Nouveau, which found dramatic expression in the Galeries Lafayette building of 1898 and the Samaritaine designed by Frantz Jourdain in 1905. According to Lewis Mumford: "If the vitality of an institution can be measured by its architecture, one can say that the department store was one of the most vital institutions of the epoch from 1880 to 1914."[20]

In addition to inspiring a new range of building types, the needs of commerce had turned many building facades into display panels for advertising. During his entry into Paris in 1878, Edmondo de Amicis had noted "the ostentation of the *Réclame* which climbs up from the first floors to the second, to the third, to the cornices, and so to the roofs."[21] Even historic importance was no protection from the constant encroachment of advertising on building facades, and the classical purity of the seventeenth-century Place des Victoires had become conspicuously defaced with signs.

By the late nineteenth century, the predominant building type in Paris, the building that provided the city with its most characteristic image, was the *maison de rapport,* constructed for profit and providing either living quarters or space for commerce. To some critics, the aim of providing the maximum amount of rentable floor space had taken precedence over æsthetic concerns, and it was observed that the architect had completely changed character; "previously he was a builder and an artist, today he is above all a business man."[22] In contrast to earlier times, "the owner dœsn't live in his building. Unknown to the passerby, he is not exposed to reprobation for having defaced the public street. He seeks to adapt his building to the conventions of all the birds of passage who will stay there several months or several years. He chooses a banal model."[23]

The desire for profit had also prompted owners to seek the maximum possible ground coverage and height. Although building regulations attempted to assure reasonable standards of ventilation and light, Paris became one of the most densely built cities in Europe, and even in fashionable districts one often received the impression of being buried in a stone quarry.

In terms of architectural style, the turn of the century saw a continuation of eclectic variety. The emergence in the 1890s of Art Nouveau, or *style moderne,* expanded this variety to include a predilection for slender, curving forms. While Art Nouveau could be found undiluted in such works as Guimard's Métro stations, it

20. Quoted in "La formation des grands magasins de Paris," *Paris projet,* no. 8, p. 93.
21. Edmondo de Amicis, *Studies of Paris,* p. 8.
22. Max Doumic, *L'architecture d'aujourd'hui* (Paris: Perrin, 1897), p. 13.
23. Paul Léon, "Maisons et rues de Paris," *Revue de Paris,* August 15, 1910, p. 858.

also provided fashionable trimming for essentially traditional building forms, where it might be seen in the design of metal balconies and entrances or in carved decorative stonework.

Although Art Nouveau introduced new forms, its decorativeness and plasticity were essentially in accord with established nineteenth-century tastes. Originality and inventiveness had been highly esteemed in eclectic design, and while Art Nouveau by no means supplanted existing styles, it supplemented them by augmenting the design vocabulary.

In 1897, when an extension of the Rue Réaumur was opened, the Municipal Council sought to encourage a high level of design for the street's new buildings by sponsoring a competition that would award prizes for the best facades (figures 88 and 89). The following year the competition was extended to include all of Paris, and

88. The Rue Réaumur looking east.

89. One-eighteen Rue Réaumur, a facade competition winner designed by de Montamal.

from 1898 until the eve of the First World War, six prizes were awarded annually.[24] The long, uniform facades bequeathed by Haussmann's renovations were judged monotonous by current tastes, and the jury deliberately selected a number of designs in which the facades were "sufficiently plastic to break, with their decorative overhangs, the assemblage of diminishing horizontal lines that sadden our streets."[25]

The predominant building type to be seen in the winners of the facade competitions was the *maison de rapport,* which had assumed virtually its classic form during the time of Haussmann. Such a building would generally be of stone, rising to a height of six or seven stories, and ornamented with metal balconies and window guards. The upper limit of the facade would be marked by a cornice, above which would rise a light attic story, usually framed by a metal-faced mansard roof, while the street level would often contain shops. Buildings would be uniformly aligned along the street with interior rooms opening onto courtyards. The same basic building

24. The proprietors of the six prizewinning buildings were exempted from half the amount of a street tax pertaining to new construction. In addition, each owner received a bronze medal, and each architect a gold medal worth one thousand francs. The jury consisted of five members of the Municipal Council, the director of the Services Municipaux d'Architecture, the chief architect of the city, and two architects chosen by the contestants.

25. *Les concours de façades de la ville de Paris 1898–1905* (Paris: Librairie de la Construction Moderne, 1905), p. 2.

90. The Castel Béranger at 15 Rue La Fontaine by Guimard.

91. Apartment house at 270 Boulevard Raspail by Bruneau.

type could be used for residence or commerce, or, as in many cases, for both. The competition juries recognized that the rental building, "which invades all the large streets, constitutes of necessity a monotonous program."[26] Floor layouts were likely to be identical, and whatever variety the building possessed would result from the ability of the architect to compose a varied facade.

The winning designs of the facade competitions embraced a variety of styles, and although some of the prize winners might appear to our eyes as eclectic pastiches, overloaded with neobaroque decoration, the juries seemed receptive to a wide range of design. It might be noted that included among the first year's winners was the Castel Béranger by Hector Guimard, now deemed an innovative monument of Art Nouveau (figure 90). In 1899 a prize was given to a brick and stone apartment house on the Boulevard Raspail, which the jury praised as "sober in ornaments," with a facade which was "well-studied" and "perfectly in harmony with the quarter" (figure 91). For a more central location, however, the same jury chose a sumptuously ornate masonry building which dramatized its corner site with an elaborate entrance pavilion. The opulent facade displayed an intricate appliqué of overhangs, window

26. Ibid., p. 20.

92. *Immeuble de la New York* at Number 1 Rue Le Peletier by Georges Morin-Goustiaux.

93. Apartment house at Number 11 Rue Edmond-Valentin by Sinell.

94, 95. Twenty-nine Avenue Rapp by Jules Lavirotte.

projections, and iron and stone decoration. Far from finding the design excessive, the jury claimed that "this luxury gives pleasure. . . . The eye is agreeably charmed by all these statues, these ornaments, these grills" (figure 92).[27] The jury was also pleased by a highly ornamented apartment building in the fashionable Sixteenth Arrondissement. They deemed it "fine, supple, elegant," observing that such buildings "make our beautiful Paris the supreme capital of good taste and artistic elegance" (figure 93).[28]

In general the prize-winning facades reflected prevailing building types and conventional designs. In 1901, however, a prize was given to the architect Jules Lavirotte for a highly bizarre residence (figures 94 and 95). Employing a

27. Ibid., p. 10.
28. Ibid., p. 11.

surrealistically carved stone entrance, the facade embodied an ornate confection of stone, brick, iron, and polychrome ceramic. The jury observed that Lavirotte had "employed much ingenuity, from the viewpoint of construction as in the decoration,"[29] for the building was the first to use a type of reinforced ceramic brick, invented by Alexandre Bigot and widely used before the First World War. Lavirotte was to win two additional facade competitions. In 1905 he was awarded a prize for the brick and ceramic facade of a house that later became the Ceramic Hotel, and in 1907 for a more sedate masonry house. On this occasion the jury indicated that Lavirotte, "with a rare courage, is deeply engaged in the study of this modern architecture, which some admire with exaggeration, and which others criticize with a prejudice unfortunate for our art."[30]

Only one industrial building was to win a facade competition, a factory of the Métropolitain system, designed by Paul-Émile Friesé and completed in 1903. The symmetrical entrance facade of brick embodied a large central arch flanked by corner pavilions. The detailing revealed Islamic references, and the overall composition was somewhat like a large mosque in which the minarets had been replaced by chimneys. In the view of the jury, "this factory entrance is almost monumental."[31]

Beauty and the Law

As to the success of the facade competitions in improving the streetscape of Paris, one may only speculate. In any event, municipal officials had much more effective means for architectural control than the awarding of prizes. Building in the French capital has long been governed by a series of regulations which have determined heights, ground coverage, and surface detailing. The artistic freedom of the architect has thus been limited by law. At the same time, the law has been responsive to changing architectural concepts.

Among the long-lived regulations in Paris was a royal edict of 1607 which, in reaction to the medieval heritage of multiple overhangs, attempted to contain building form within a flat facade, in accord with classical ideals. It was declared that there should be, "no overhang, advance, or encorbellment over the street." Each facade was required to "continue straight to the ground floor."[32] This rule remained in force until it was modified in 1823 by Louis XVIII to allow building projections. Poor construction of such embellishments, however, led to multiplying accidents, "due to the fall of entablatures, cornices, and plaster projections."[33] As a result,

29. Ibid., p. 15.
30. *Les concours de Façades de la ville de Paris 1906–1912* (Paris: Librairie de la Construction Moderne, 1912), p. 7.
31. Ibid., p. 19.
32. Paul Léon, "Maisons et rues de Paris," pp. 848–49.
33. Ibid., p. 849.

facades were again closely regulated. Pilasters could not be more than nine to ten centimeters in depth. Balconies could be constructed only with official permission and could not extend more than eighty centimeters. They were restricted, moreover, to the facade area six meters above ground level. Encorbellment remained forbidden.

The large volume of construction instigated by Haussmann kept within these regulations, and the new straight streets he built were accentuated by the equally strict geometry of identically ordered facades (figure 96). While such streets may have seemed harmonious when first built, by the latter part of the century they were considered dull and regimented. The Bædeker guide of 1888, while crediting such avenues with convenience and utility, noted that "most of them . . . exhibit an almost wearisome uniformity of style."[34] Another observer expressed the opinion that "our great Parisian streets, like the Boulevard Magenta, produce a fatiguing impression of monotony with their building facades strictly uniform and rigorously aligned, with a frigid and self-effacing decoration, without improvisation or movement."[35]

34. Karl Bædeker, *Paris and Environs,* 9th ed. (Leipzig: Bædeker, 1888), p. 48.
35. Lortsch, *La beauté de Paris,* p. 97.

96. Building of the Haussmann era. The Avenue George V, opened in 1858.

Although a new regulation with regard to facade design was put into effect in 1882, it made no radical changes in existing restrictions. Encorbellment remained prohibited. The allowable dimensions of balconies remained the same, although they were permitted at a height of 5.75 meters above ground instead of 6 meters. Exact dimensions were fixed for every decorative element, including columns and pilasters, friezes, cornices, consoles, and capitals. It was required, moreover, that each facade be aligned with that of the adjoining building. Increasingly, such restrictions conflicted with the new ideals of artistic freedom and the growing predilection for picturesque form.

In 1898 the architect Louis Charles Boileau pointed out that "artists and men of taste complain of the lack of variety in the buildings erected in our new streets, and of their decorative insignificance."[36] He went on to praise the superior picturesqueness of such cities as Brussels, London, and Vienna. The "narrow and timid" regulations of 1882, in the view of a municipal councillor, "have led to a dryness and virtual absence of decoration, and this rigid rectilinearity has ended in a flat uniformity, and what one could call an architectural militarism." Urging a greater freedom of design, the supervising architect of the Paris government, Louis Bonnier, maintained that "the French artistic spirit, which sleeps sometimes, but awakens always, makes us see that after all æsthetics are for people, not a luxury, but a need and a right, as important as hygiene."

Responding finally to pressure for a modification of building controls, the Municipal Council instituted a series of studies during the 1890s, resulting in a new set of regulations which became law in 1902. The director of works, reporting to the prefect in 1896, had stressed a desire for "projections more accentuated, more plastic, which could give to our buildings a less banal physiognomy, and thus contribute to the beautification of the city."[37]

Among the innovations contained in the new law was a regulation of building facades based, not on specific dimensions for each element of design, but on an overall spatial envelope, or *gabarit*. Within this *gabarit*, the architect was to have a new freedom in composing the facade, with the permissible degree of overhang related to the width of the street.[38]

36. Magny, *Les moyens juridiques,* pp. 65, 83–84, 62–63.

37. Ibid., p. 65.

38. On streets 30 meters or more in width, the facade was divided for design purposes into two levels, with the lower level extending from the ground to a height of 3 meters. For streets below 30 meters, the lower level extended to a height of 6 meters, minus $1/10$ of the street width. Regulations permitted a greater degree of plasticity on the upper portion of facades. For this area, the maximum projection on streets of less than 10 meters in width was to be $8/100$ of the street width. For streets 10 meters and above, it was to be 60 centimeters plus $2/100$ of the street width, with a maximum of 1.20 meters on streets 10 meters or more in width. For the lower part of the facade, the overhang could not exceed $1/4$ of that permitted for the upper part, with a maximum of 20 centimeters.

In addition, for streets 16 meters and more in width, the maximum projection of each balcony could be augmented by $1/4$, on the condition that the horizontal extension of balconies not cover more than a quarter of the surface permitted on each floor.

In comparison with the law of 1882, the 1902 law permitted an increase in the maximum projection on the upper facades from 80 centimeters to 1.20 meters. Such overhangs could also descend from 5.75 meters to 3 meters above ground on large streets, and the overall amount of projecting surface could now cover one-third of the upper facade. Alignment with adjacent facades was no longer necessary, although a separation of 50 centimeters between overhangs on adjacent buildings was required. In order to give increased emphasis to building entrances, an overhang of 60 centimeters was to be allowed, in contrast to 14 permitted in the 1882 regulations. In addition to the increased plasticity permitted on the facade, the upper silhouette of a building could now be dramatized through vertical extensions of decorative elements past the line of the cornice.

The supervising architect of Paris, explaining the new regulations in a speech at the École Nationale des Beaux-Arts, maintained that a new freedom had been given to "the fantasy of architects" and that this "would permit an extreme diversity of composition." He was sure that a more creative design would develop, for "one would no longer be able to employ the clichés that have been used continually in Parisian building, ready-made plans, ready-made facades, ready-made studies! It will be necessary to study, to work, to take pains, to do the work of an architect!"[39]

The modifications in building regulations effected in 1902 also involved the question of height (figure 97). In 1783 a royal ordinance had stated that "the excessive height of buildings is prejudicial to the wholesomeness of the air in a city as large and as heavily populated as Paris."[40] At this time an attempt was made to regulate building height according to street width. The regulations were modified in 1859, continuing to relate height to street width and extending control to courtyard frontages. Depending on the street, maximum building height could range from 11.70 meters to 20 meters.

The 20-meter maximum was maintained in the regulations of 1864, which permitted such a height on streets 20 meters wide or over, providing that the number of stories above the ground floor, excluding the attic level, was limited to five. Counting floor levels as Americans count them, this would give the building seven stories, representing the maximum practical height in an era before elevators came into wide use. Subsequent legislation in 1872 included regulation of courtyard sizes. A building 20 meters tall required a courtyard of 40 square meters, and no building could contain *courettes* (air shafts) of less than 4 square meters.

In 1880 the prefect of the Seine set up a special committee, chaired by Jean Alphand, to revise building codes. The resulting height regulations, decreed in 1884, established maximum heights corresponding to four categories of street width, and ranging from a permitted height of 12 meters on streets of 7.80 meters and below to a maximum of 20 meters on streets 20 meters or more in width. As

39. Louis Bonnier, *Les règlements de voirie* (Paris: Schmid, 1903), pp. 82, 32.
40. Léon, "Maisons et rues de Paris," p. 854.

97. OPPOSITE. The evolution of Parisian building profiles. *Upper left*: 1784. The attic story is contained within a sloping wall of forty-five degrees. *Upper right*: Regulations as modified in 1859 maintain the same building profile as before, although maximum heights are increased. *Lower left*: Following the 1884 regulations, the profile of the attic story is determined by the arc of a circle, permitting a greater total height. *Lower right*: Following the 1902 regulations, the profile of the attic story is established by the arc of a circle extended by a roof inclined at an angle of forty-five degrees. The result is an increase in height.

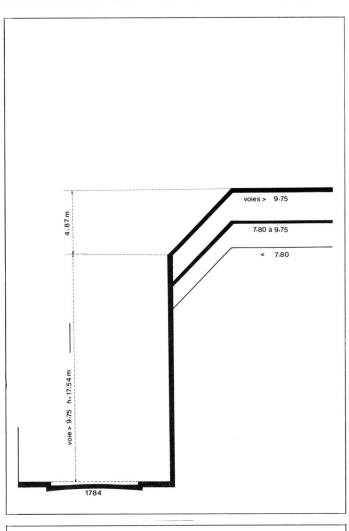

voies > 9.75

7.80 à 9.75

< 7.80

4.87 m

voie > 9.75 h=17,54 m

1784

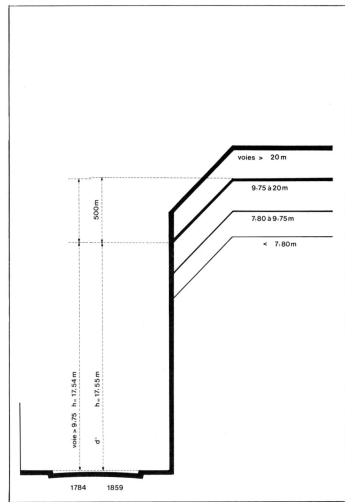

voies > 20 m

9.75 à 20 m

7.80 à 9.75 m

< 7.80 m

5.00 m

voie > 9.75 h = 17,54 m

d° h = 17,55 m

1784   1859

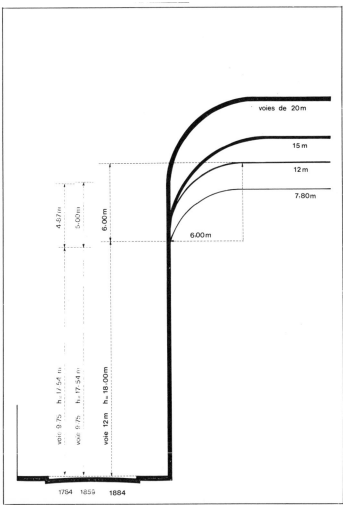

voies de 20 m

15 m

12 m

7.80 m

4.87 m

5.00 m

6.00 m

6.00 m

voie 9.75 h = 17.54 m

voie 9.75 h = 17.54 m

voie 12 m h = 18.00 m

1784   1859   1884

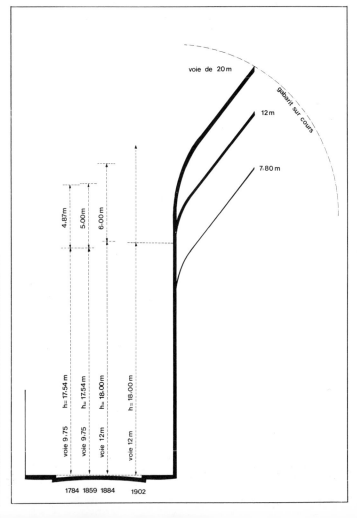

voie de 20 m

12 m

7.80 m

gabarit sur cours

4.87 m

5.00 m

6.00 m

voie 9.75 h = 17.54 m

voie 9.75 h = 17.54 m

voie 12 m h = 18.00 m

voie 12 m h = 18.00 m

1784 1859 1884   1902

official street widths were measured between building lines, it was possible, on narrow streets, to obtain a wider measurement, and thus greater height, by setting the building back from the street. Most building, however, continued to be built up to the limit of the lot line. Although the maximum height of the cornice line remained at 20 meters, an increase in the height of the attic story above the cornice was made possible. Previously this story had been contained within the envelope of a wall sloping away from the street at a forty-five degree angle plus a horizontal roof, with the attic adding 4 to 5 meters to the height above the cornice. The 1884 regulations, however, specified that the profile of the attic story be determined by the arc of a circle, of which the radius would be equal to one-half of the street, with the maximum radius of such a circle established at 8.50 meters. The effect on building of the new code was to increase the overall possible height on wide streets from 25 to 28 meters.

The regulation was further modified in 1902. At this time a detailed table of maximum cornice heights was drawn up, providing for twenty categories of street width, ranging from 1 meter to 20 meters and over. The new limits provided for a lowering of heights on narrow streets in comparison with previous laws. For major streets, however, although the maximum height from ground to cornice remained at 20 meters, a new profile for the attic story permitted a greater upward extension than before. The arc of the circle determining the form of the attic could now have a maximum radius of 10 meters, and this curving plane could then be prolonged by an inclined roof at an angle of forty-five degrees. As a result, buildings conforming to the 20-meter height limit could, with the addition of a high attic, attain a total height of over 30 meters. Instead of a single attic level, two, or even three, floors could be constructed above the cornice line. It was observed that "in this new zone which is conceded to him, the architect can execute a high monumental crown in the form he prefers. An undefined field is open to his spirit of invention."[41]

Although the intent of the 1902 regulation had been to enhance design freedom, and thus presumably to embellish the Parisian street, the results were highly controversial. A critic was soon to denounce "the horrors which shock us today in the streets of Paris, resulting, for the most part, from this misguided decree of 1902, which has permitted the most abusive elevations and bizarre designs. . . . This regulation, which was formulated in very good faith by men wishing to give builders more liberty and to ameliorate the hygiene of the city, has had unexpected consequences."[42] The additional height permitted to buildings had been welcomed by speculators wishing to add the last possible centimeter of profitable area to their structures, without regard for the harmony of the city. At the same time, the increased plasticity of surface allowed had, in the view of many, encouraged ugliness and vulgarity.

Although Second Empire building had previously been deplored for its

41. Ibid. p. 858.
42. Lortsch, *La beauté de Paris,* p. x.

monotony, it was now seen as exemplifying an admirable simplicity, unity, and harmony. It was observed in 1913: "To the eyes of the stroller in Paris, buildings can be classed in two categories: old buildings, characterized by a great uniformity of type, a perfect sobriety of lines and of decoration, by the measured proportions of their attics, which shelter only one floor; and new buildings, startling in their whiteness, which clash with the first through the discordance of their appearance, the profusion of their decorative motifs, the protuberance of certain parts of their facades, the immoderate height of their attics, which give refuge to two and three floors—in short, by their character of bad taste, and the enormity of their disproportion."[43]

Included in the offensive decoration of the new buildings was "a profusion of flowers and vaguely allegorical figures, a heap of sculptural details which clash strangely with the sober elegance of older facades. A style which pretends to be a grand style, but which is only a style swollen and overloaded, a style of decadents and parvenus—but, in fact, is it not the modern style?" Building facades had become "vast undulating surfaces" which could no longer be said to possess architectural

43. Ibid., p. 33.

98. The Hôtel Lutetia, designed by Louis-Charles Boileau and Henri-Alexis Tauzin.

99. Apartment houses on the Avenue Rapp.

100. The Avenue de l'Opéra. Royal Palace Hotel as re-modeled by Constant Lemaire in 1910.

lines, and "architectural decoration, strictly speaking, has almost disappeared." Particularly derided was the Hôtel Lutetia, completed in 1910, which, "with its decorative pastry, resembles an enormous soft cheese with bizarre blisters" (figure 98).[44]

While objecting to the amount and type of decoration permitted by the new regulations, many observers found it illogical that such projections should be concentrated on the upper part of the building. "Some of these structures," it was pointed out, "give the impression of being built upside down. All the important decorative work overflows on the upper parts, while toward the ground the facade empties and simplifies. It looks as though we wanted to express defiance not only of good taste and good sense, but also of the laws of equilibrium." (figures 99 and 100).[45]

All in all, the greatest controversy resulted from the new increase in building height. In permitting upward extensions, the regulations reflected current economic pressures. Land values were constantly increasing, prompting builders to obtain the maximum possible floor space. The single-family house was fast disappearing, and almost all new housing in Paris took the form of apartments. It was noted that:

44. Ibid., pp. 88, 92.
45. Ibid.

"Traffic in Paris is becoming more and more heavy; the noise, smells, and dust have thrown into disfavor apartments on the lower floors of buildings, previously sought-after. The individual house is abandoned in favor of sumptuous apartments on a single floor. Hygiene, of which we are very conscious today, favors upper floors, which give more sun, more air, more view, etc."[46] New building techniques, such as concrete and metal framing, made tall structures feasible, and the increasing use of the elevator made all floors equally accessible.

Objections to height were based on æsthetic grounds, for the augmented profiles of new buildings were seen to create disharmonious street facades throughout the city and to threaten the appearance of many historic sites. Increases in height were found, not only in new construction, but also in additions to existing building. "On a facade of stone," it was observed, "was superimposed a second building of zinc, containing no less than three stories and surmounted by a terrace."[47] New attic stories were added to buildings on the Rue de la Paix, the Rue Royale, the Avenue de l'Opéra, and the Rue Castiglione. The Rue de Rivoli, whose arcaded facade reflected rigid architectural controls on the lower portions, was reconstructed above the cornice line (figure 101). It was noted: "One still dœsn't dare touch the arcades,

46. Ibid., p. 51. The quotation is from a 1909 report to the prefect.
47. Paul Léon, "La beauté de Paris," *Revue de Paris,* November 15, 1909, pp. 280–302, p. 299.

101. The Rue de Rivoli, designed by Charles Percier and F. L. Fontaine in 1802. New attic stories were added after 1902.

but the roofs have had two or three floors added. . . . We are in the process of changing all the architectural lines in inflating these buildings with unbelievable coiffures."[48]

Architectural perspectives were suddenly changed as new buildings emerged above existing rooflines (figure 102). Critics were particularly incensed by

48. Lortsch, *La beauté de Paris,* p. 130.

102. Building on the Rue Mondétour, with a post-1902 profile.

developments in the vicinity of the Arc de Triomphe. When the Place de L'Étoile was developed during the Second Empire, the buildings surrounding the Arc were designed to present a unified, modestly scaled facade toward the plaza. On the surrounding streets of Presbourg and Tilsitt, however, two new hotels, the Astoria and the Mercédès, now loomed over the buildings facing the Étoile. For some, the unity, harmony, and equilibrium of the monumental plaza had been irrevocably destroyed by "these great buildings *á l'américaine,* these skyscrapers which insolently stretch up to dominate a place that isn't made for them."[49]

If such buildings could be erected near the Arc de Triomphe, there was nothing to prevent them from springing up to mar urban harmony elsewhere. One could, for example, erect a "skyscraper" behind the facades of Gabriel to loom over the Place de la Concorde. According to a pessimistic prophesy published in 1913, "within twenty years, enormous structures will be built along the Rue de Rivoli, on the Place de l'Étoile, on the Place de l'Hôtel de Ville, on the Rue de Vaugirard, on the Rue du Cloître Notre Dame, and we shall see the humiliated, miserable appearance that will be offered by the Louvre, the Arc de Triomphe, the Hôtel de Ville, the Luxembourg Palace, Notre Dame . . . and nothing will remain of the formerly famous beauty of Paris."[50]

The shift in architectural balance which had characterized nineteenth-century urbanism, seemed, with the advent of tall buildings, to be suddenly accelerated. It was observed that "our public monuments are exposed one after another to the most deplorable depreciations. Up until now, we have given them a harmonious frame, which has increased their value. The surrounding buildings kept their distance and their proportions remained modest, deferent. A hierarchy was observed between public and private building. Today, the latter increase like an assault on the former. . .Reason is alarmed by such a reversal of things. Will Paris become a Babel?. . .Our old principles of public art are abandoned. We are wiping out vistas, perspectives, the immediate neighborhoods of monuments, and regularity in architectural alignment."[51]

Although the 1902 building regulations provided the focus of controversy, much of the discussion of Parisian architecture in the years immediately preceding the First World War involved wider æsthetic concerns. There was apprehension among conservative critics regarding the future of Paris, and criticism of architecture at this time seems to have encompassed not only those structures built after 1902, but the whole range of modern building. Architecture seemed to be in a state of general decline, and the reasons, in the view of some, involved sinister foreign influences.

49. Ibid., p. 108. The author of the statement is the deputy Chastenet, and it is included in the record of the Chamber of Deputies, June 24, 1909 (Journal Officiel, p. 1620). It might be noted that the Hôtel Mercédès had been built through a variance of the 1884 building code. In 1926 the city compelled the Hôtel Astoria to demolish the offending upper stories.
50. Ibid., p. 104. The critic André Hallays is quoted.
51. Ibid., pp. 102–03.

According to the critic André Hallays: "The profound cause of this great artistic degradation is the universal expositions and the invasion of exotic styles." The Eiffel Tower was in part to blame also. "Yes, the sense of proportion today is abolished; but why should it not disappear in a city where, for more than twenty years, palace and church have been dominated by a useless hunk of metal three hundred meters high? Yes, they are ugly, all these 'palaces,' American in height, Germanic in ugliness and Annamite in decoration; but remember that the first models of them appeared on the Esplanade of the Invalides in 1900."[52]

Although classicism might, strictly speaking, be considered a foreign importation, it had been so thoroughly adopted in France as to be deemed the only legitimate French tradition. True French taste exemplified order, discipline, proportion. It was maintained that: "For two hundred years, France has been the great artistic educator of Europe; a situation which, for our country, has been a source of glory and fortune. Is it still the case? We have to recognize that it no longer remains, that our prestige is seriously damaged. Have foreign peoples made more progress, have they achieved superior productions? Not the least in the world. It is we who, little by little, seem to have lost our strength of artistic production, we who, little by little have lost our confidence, by adopting, stupidly, through snobbery, the taste of nations with a mediocre or barbaric artistic temperament. In America these gigantic structures may have their utility, their reason for being. Here they would be a heresy and, in our dear and beautiful city, an injury to our national artistic sense, based on measure and harmony. Let us remain French."[53]

The threatened beauty of Paris was, moreover, viewed not merely as a concern of æsthetes but as a matter involving national prosperity. The national Chamber of Deputies was reminded in 1909: "Not only does Paris symbolize France in the eyes of foreigners, but also, from a more down-to-earth viewpoint, because of the attraction it exercises on them, our capital could be considered as a veritable national industry, for those foreigners leave here considerable sums every year, and this money is not without utility in regulating our commercial balance. As a consequence, in default of our self-respect, our self-interest demands that we not disillusion them." Parisians were warned that "when Paris resembles Chicago and New York, the Americans, whom we want so much to attract, won't come here anymore."[54]

Strong pressures arose to have the 1902 regulations abolished, and government studies for revision began in 1908. Included in the lively discussion over the law had been an examination of the whole question of artistic freedom. A lawyer actively opposed to the law had argued that in a city like Paris special æsthetic controls were needed. He insisted that "in Paris, the city of beauty, which is to say of order and

52. Ibid., p. xii.
53. Ibid., p. 91. The quotation is from a letter from Cormon to Massard.
54. Ibid., p. 21 (the deputy Chastenet is being quoted), p. 9 (Albert Guillaume is being quoted).

harmony, in Paris, the city of good taste, elegance, and distinction, we cannot allow to be constructed, absolutely by chance and whim, the fantasies, perhaps fortunate and perhaps also monstrous, of architects and owners. It involves more than the interest of Paris. It involves the interest of France, and I would say even of the civilized world."[55]

Just as controls existed regarding sanitation and hygiene, the appearance of the street could be protected. It was pointed out that legislation existed to control establishments producing offensive smells. Might one's eyes not be protected from offensive sights? Legislation prohibited the public display of pornography. Why not prohibit architectural pornography as well?

One of the most persistent conservative critics was André Hallays, who declared bitterly: "In one of the basements of City Hall is the headquarters of a society, secret but powerful, composed of architects and officials. Its aim is to make the capital ugly. It is called the Society of the Enemies of Paris. For several years it has redoubled its activity and has had countless victories; it exhorts shopkeepers to cover the most noble facades with signs; it uses timid architects to elaborate bizarre plans and extravagant elevations; it discovers and designates the places where insane constructions will be best placed to outrage an admirable monument or ruin a beautiful perspective; it has a legal bureau to instruct builders in evading regulations, and also to provide the administration with arguments to justify all legal variances."[56]

The Modern Movement

Some people maintain that the nineteenth-century ended in 1914. Certainly the First World War seems to mark a dramatic break between two eras. A certain style of life, a social order, a sense of stability and confidence seems to have vanished forever. Viewed nostalgically from the hectic postwar period, the Belle Époque might well appear a serene and opulent age. In terms of the new artistic revolution, moreover, turn-of-the-century modernism might appear conservative, and buildings which had alarmed prewar critics with their departures from tradition could now be considered lovably old-fashioned.

Those critics who saw their mission as the protection of Paris had reason to continue the battle, but the ground had shifted somewhat. Sinister foreign influences, still presumed to be heavily Germanic, continued their assault on French culture. But their weapons were no longer caryatids, consoles, swags, and foliate decoration. Before the war, "modernism" in architecture was often taken to refer to Art Nouveau and to the formal and stylistic elaboration of late eclecticism. Postwar

55. Ibid., p. 202.
56. Ibid., p. 259.

modernists, however, rejected both eclecticism and Art Nouveau with a puritanism unmatched by any prewar conservative. "The triumph of molded pastry," it was observed, "has been succeeded by a Jansenist passion for walls of unbroken nakedness" (figure 103).[57] A new architectural æsthetic, eventually to be termed the "International Style," favored a stark simplicity of geometric form and smooth, undecorated surfaces. Whatever criticism might be brought against the proponents of the new avant-garde, they could not be accused of vulgarity, and old ideals of "originality" were rejected in favor of a new "rationality."

Accepting the assumption of certain prewar critics that Paris was essentially a classical city requiring discipline, harmony, and order, the new modernism, with its simplicity of form, its regularity and self-effacing lack of ornament, had a certain potential for harmonizing with the traditional image of the city. Some modern architects, while expressing contempt for nineteenth-century historicism, were respectful of the ordered achievements of the preindustrial epoch. Le Corbusier, a tireless propagandist for the modern movement, attempted to demonstrate that his

57. André Warnod, *Visages de Paris* (Paris: Firmin-Didot. 1930), p. 336.

103. Changing taste. Apartment houses in the Sixteenth Arrondissement.

104. One-twenty-four Rue Réaumur, 1903.

105. La Samaritaine, facade on the Rue de l'Arbre Sec, 1905.

principle of "regulating lines" was equally applicable to the Petit Palais of Gabriel and his own villa at Garches, while in his works on urbanism he consistently praised such baroque-classical ensembles as the Place Vendôme, the Invalides, and the École Militaire. In presenting his expansively scaled proposals for Paris, he persistently maintained that they would not be out of harmony with urbanistic achievements of the past.

Although the simplified geometry of the International Style became the hallmark of modernism during the 1920s, a tendency toward formal simplification could be seen in a limited way in Paris by the turn of the century. While such technical innovations as metal framing were frequently juxtaposed with elaborate masonry exteriors, there were also buildings in which the composition embodied a direct revelation of structure. In striking contrast to the opulent masonry decoration typifying the Rue Réaumur, was an office building at number 124, attributed to Georges Chedanne (figure 104). Constructed in 1903, it openly exploited its slender metal supports and extensive areas of glass. Frantz Jourdain's Samaritaine Department Store, while noted for its colorful Art Nouveau decoration, also embodied a basically simple facade expressing the framing elements and window panels. (figure 105). Notable also as a forerunner of evolving taste was an apartment building by Henri Sauvage which, in 1912, cladded its geometricized exterior in a smooth surface of white ceramic brick (figure 106). The architecture of the post office and telephone service during this period was also distinguished by its simplicity of form and detailing.

Among the most consistent of the Parisian modernists was Auguste Perret, who, early in the century, had begun to employ reinforced concrete in a manner that emphasized the rectilinear structural elements. His now-famous apartment house on the Rue Franklin, completed in 1903, was unconventional not only in its external exposure of the concrete frame, but in the central inset of the facade, which increased window frontage and broke the building line of the street (figure 107). In general, such formal experimentation would not be typical of Perret's work. His dominant predilection in form expressed a sober classicism, and the symmetry, simplicity, and orderliness of his buildings enabled them to fit unobtrusively within the existing urban fabric. Before the First World War, his contributions to the

106. Twenty-six Rue Vavin, by Henri Sauvage, 1912.

107. Twenty-five Rue Franklin, by Auguste Perret, 1903.

Parisian townscape included a garage on the Rue de Ponthieu, completed in 1905, and noted for its glass facade and slender concrete framing elements, and the Théâtre des Champs Élysées of 1911, for which he produced the definitive plan.[58]

Although the formal qualities of the International Style provided an antidote to the heaviness and ornateness of much turn-of-the-century design, its purest expressions were perhaps too spartan to be truly popular. In spite of a rhetoric paying homage to democracy and mass society, the International Style in its purest form was, like classicism, essentially an aristocratic taste. Its starkness promised little comfort, and it was frequently derided as cold, factory-like, and fit to be inhabited only by robots. Somewhat alarming also was the new urban scale advocated by certain modernists. Not only were traditional architectural forms to be supplanted, but the familar urban fabric was to be totally renovated.

58. The building history of the Théâtre des Champs Élysées is somewhat complicated and includes the contributions of Joseph-Antoine Bouvard and Henri Van de Velde. The existing facade as built appears to have been largely the conception of Bourdelle. For a discussion of the attributions, see Michel Ragon, *Histoire mondiale de l'architecture et de l'urbanisme modernes,* vol. 2 (Paris: Casterman, 1972), pp. 83–84.

108. *Zig-zag moderne* at 118 Avenue des Champs Élysées, by Jean Desbouis, 1929.

An opportunity for a concentrated expression of modern design came in 1925 in the Exposition des Arts Décoratifs. This exposition, which had been planned for 1916, then postponed by the First World War, occupied the Invalides esplanade and nearby river quais. Although the displays included Le Corbusier's Pavilion de L'Esprit Nouveau, as well as his Voisin Plan for Paris, the more rigorous aspects of modern design, as typified by the Bauhaus, seemed notably absent. A French historian has observed: "To conciliate modernism and tradition was the grand formula of the exposition, so thoroughly applied that it succeeded in massacring tradition and retaining of modernism only its artifices." Certainly, little of the exposition fit within the limits of International Style orthodoxy, and much of its imagery embodied a visual richness of decorative surfaces and luxurious materials. Many of the exhibitors were commercial firms seeking a type of design that would be modern yet appeal to the senses, and the fair embodied, in the view of some critics, an effort to fuse the decorativeness of Art Nouveau with new geometric predilections, providing a "style nouille géométrisé."[59]

For many years, the Exposition des Arts Decoratifs received little attention from serious historians, except for the Pavilion de l'Esprit Nouveau. Recently, however, a more tolerant and inclusive view of design has recognized the fair as a source for a popular and widely disseminated style, the "Art Déco," or "Moderne." Although Paris was to receive a number of buildings considered to be monuments of the International Style, the general architectural scene reflected a more diluted modernism (figure 108). The Art Déco, with its sensuous materials and visually arresting zig zag decoration, provided an agreeable way of being up to date, and it was adopted quickly in shops, theaters, restaurants, and department stores, just as Art Nouveau had been previously.

The International Style, in its purest form, had little impact on the center of Paris. Le Corbusier's Parisian commissions, for example, were mainly for single-family houses on suburban or peripheral sites (figure 109). His Swiss Pavilion was in the

59. Ibid., pp. 81, 82.

109. The Maison Jeanneret, one of a pair of houses designed by Le Corbusier in 1923 and sited in a secluded cul-de-sac, the Square du Docteur Blanche.

110. An ensemble of houses forming the Rue Mallet-Stevens, designed in 1927 by Robert Mallet-Stevens.

outlying university complex, and his Salvation Army Hostel near the outer edge of the Thirteenth Arrondissement. The only structure which might be said to fit within the Parisian pattern of building, and to reflect a prevailing building type, was a small apartment house in the Sixteenth Arrondissement containing his own apartment. In addition to works by Le Corbusier, the city also received characteristic examples of International Style design in the work of Robert Mallet-Stevens and André Lurçat (figure 110). Their work, like that of Le Corbusier, was to appear largely outside the center of Paris, either in residential quarters or suburbs.

In general, the modern movement reflected a consistent evolution in taste. Overt historicism gave way to an acceptance of new forms, characterized by simple geometry and relatively plain surfaces. Some references to classical symmetry and balance might persist, but traditional ornamentation would be stripped away.

On the occasion of the 1937 International Exposition, the magazine *Architecture d'aujourd'hui,* published a map presenting "the most characteristic constructions in the modern spirit" in Paris. The list included sixty-three buildings inside Paris and sixty-one in the suburbs. Within the city, such construction was generally to be found in the western districts, beyond the historic core, and the most active architects of the modern idiom appear to have been Michel Roux-Spitz and the firm of Auguste and Gustave Perret.

The Exposition of 1937, like previous major expositions, included some buildings intended to become a permanent part of the urban fabric. The 1878 Exposition had bequeathed to the city the Trocadéro Palace; the 1937 Exposition was to provide its replacement. Although the old palace had been a prominent landmark, it had apparently outlived its day. It was observed that: "The restoration of the Trocadéro will at least have the merit of liberating one of the most beautiful sites of Paris, in demolishing the central building which defaces and obstructs it at the same time."[60]

Following the presentation of a series of projects in 1934, the Exposition Commission decided in 1935 to give charge of the Trocadéro design to three architects, Jacques Carlu, Louis-Hippolyte Boileau, and Léon Azéma. The major fault of the old palace, in addition to its unfashionable eclectic styling, was considered to be its placement in the center of the site. The new structure was designed to embody a central opening, creating a clear vista toward the river. It was noted that, in doing so, "obeying the modern tendency . . . which asks that the architect realize today not a 'monument' like the Opéra—or like the Trocadéro of Davioud—but an 'ensemble,' with a frame and a large ærial perspective, the creators of the new Trocadéro have adopted a *partie* which, showing sufficient respect for the French monumental tradition, conforms also to the law of modern urbanism" (figure 111).[61]

60. G. H. Pingusson, "Paris, l'héritier de l'Exposition 1937," *Architecture d'aujourd'hui,* nos. 5–6, June 1937, p. 122.
61. Pierre Ladoué, "Le nouveau Trocadéro," *L'architecture,* vol. 50, March 15, 1937, p. 73. The executed design for the Trocadéro incorporated certain aspects of previous proposals. In 1932 a design by Debat-Ponsan

111. The Trocadéro Palace. See figure 81 for the old Trocadéro Palace.

The resulting ensemble employed the type of stripped classicism that characterized much official architecture of the 1930s. Such building, while avoiding overt reproduction of classical motifs and orders, maintained classical principles of overall composition. Such elements as columns and porticœs were often retained, but in simplified form. Reminiscing about the old Trocadéro Palace, a historian observed: "Its silhouette is engraved in our memories. From its birth in 1878, reservations have been held on its beauty, and its bizarre profile with that round belly flanked by skinny minarets. It had, however, a great power of seduction."[62]

envisioned the development of the Trocadéro emplacement with a central open space flanked by pavilions and terraces. The following year the Perret brothers published a scheme in *L'illustration* for the same site, embodying a monumental classical ensemble of stone and concrete.

62. Yvan Christ and others, *La belle histoire de Paris* (Paris: O. Perrin, 1964), p. 182.

112. The Trocadéro Palace.

Although the bland and self-effacing forms of the new Trocadéro might be more tasteful than those of its eclectic predecessor, it apparently lacked the capacity to seduce. One critic condemned the building as "mean and cold," and expressed the opinion that, far from enveloping the hill, it "seems to elevate, from a flat surface, the wall of some giant public lavatory" (figure 112).[63]

A similar use of simplified classicism could be found in the National Museum of Modern Art, also completed for the 1937 Exposition, and designed by Dondel, Aubert, Viard, and Dastugue (figures 113 and 114). In this symmetrical composition, two galleries, each carrying a columned portico, were linked by an open colonnade. Hitler's architect, Albert Speer, was in Paris to design the German pavilion at the exposition. Observing the Museum of Modern Art and similar structures, he remarked: "It surprised me that France also favored neo-classicism for her public buildings." He concluded, however, that the style was "characteristic of the era, and left its impress on Washington, London, and Paris as well as Rome, Moscow, and our plans for Berlin."[64]

Although the modern movement had often brought sweeping proposals for a total renovation of the physical environment, by the end of the 1930s the city of Paris had been far from revolutionized. Many buildings reflected a change in style, without

63. Pierre d'Espezel, "Illustration et défense du paysage Parisien," *Destinée du Paris* (Paris: Chêne, 1943), p. 133.
64. Albert Speer, *Inside the Third Reich* (New York: Macmillan, 1970), p. 81.

113, 114. The National Museum of Modern Art.

having any drastic impact on the existing urban fabric. This was largely because construction was still bound by building regulations which had remained essentially unchanged since 1902. It may be recalled that the 1902 regulations had produced considerable opposition. In response the city had begun studies for revision in 1907, adopting a slightly modified text in 1914. Following the war, in 1923, a government commission resumed study of the regulations, submitting a report in 1930. The two major questions still involved overhangs and height. While the 1902 provisions had been blamed for permitting decorative excesses, changing tastes had by the 1920s inspired a simplification of building surface. The commission believed that control was still necessary, however, "although today the ornamentation of facades is almost abandoned, even despised, which is, without doubt, only a passing fashion."[65]

While the problem of surface ornament had more or less solved itself, the question of building height had increased in importance. Although conservative critics had been alarmed by the thirty-meter "skyscrapers" which appeared after 1902, such heights were minimal in terms of what was technically possible and also in terms of the concepts of modern architecture. Many modern designers believed that tall building was the normal building form for a modern city, and such structures appeared frequently in the visionary designs of French architects. In the United States, skyscrapers had already transformed many urban centers, becoming, to some citizens at least, a source of national pride.

An American describing Paris in 1900 had opined that: "In the central sections, the height and general architectural appearance of the houses are so much alike as to be monotonous." The reason for low heights, he believed, lay in the imperfection of French elevators. "They move so slowly that an impatient person would prefer to climb the stairs rather than waste the time required to crawl at a snail's pace from story to story in one of these ancient 'lifts'. A nervous Frenchman would go into spasms if he were suddenly shot skyward from the ground to the 20th story in one of our improved modern electric elevators."[66]

It was perhaps inevitable that French architects interested in advanced technology and concerned with the scale of modern urbanism would envision skyscrapers for Paris. One of the earliest of these was the pioneer of concrete construction, Auguste Perret, who outlined his ideas to a journalist in 1905. His recently completed apartment house on the Rue Franklin had ten stories and was a relatively tall structure for its day. He dreamed, however, of constructing someday "a building of twenty stories." "As in the United States?," he was asked. "Exactly," he responded, "and be persuaded that the æsthetic of Paris would not suffer from it. Imagine our capital surrounded by a belt of enormous buildings." "Which would prevent the air from circulating?" "Not at all. It would suffice to space them suitably. One could even place some of these buildings in certain vast intersections." In addition to the

65. Commission des Perspectives Monumentales, *Rapport de la Sous-Commission Chargée de la Révision du Décret du 13 Août 1902* (1930), p. 79.
66. Jose de Olivares, *Parisian Dream City*, no. 84, August 16, 1900. Pages unnumbered.

belt of tall buildings, Perret wanted to erect a structure of about twenty stories at the Porte Maillot, which would serve as a "Hôtel des Sportsmen." He believed that "it would be a dream for those who drive automobiles to find, at the entrance to Paris, a suitable hotel, in which would be united every modern comfort."[67]

Although Perret did not develop this concept further, it provided the inspiration for an article published in *L'illustration* in 1922. Accompanying the text was a drawing by Jacques Lambert, purportedly based on sketches of Perret, but embodying a rather theatrical aggrandizement of his concepts. Perret's idea for a twenty-story building at the Porte Maillot was translated into a symmetrical procession of sixty-story skyscrapers linked by arches and lining a gigantically scaled boulevard (figure 115). This ensemble, designed to extend all the way from Paris to Saint Germain en Laye, would "transform the forest of Saint Germain into an annex of the Bois de Boulogne and lead Parisians there, without a discontinuity of greenery, in an architectural perspective without parallel."[68]

In considering the question of high-rise buildings, the author of the article, who termed skyscrapers "the cathedrals of the modern city," discussed some of the controversial aspects of tall buildings. He deplored the disorder with which American skyscrapers had been fitted into the existing urban fabric, pointing out that at the end of the working day hordes of employees descended into narrow streets, which "literally refuse to absorb that giant crowd." The American skyscraper represented a "daring technical solution pushed to a lopsided extreme," which should, he believed, "be a warning to European cities which would be tempted to imitate America. We must not imitate, but be aware of the American experience. . . . The state of the question is this: America, in spite of recognized inconveniences, persists in the erection of the skyscraper. Germany is orienting itself toward the question of building tall. England, traditionalist, hesitates. What is Paris going to do?"[69]

The tall building in Paris was deemed technically feasible and, when embodied in projects on the scale suggested by Perret, considered to be æsthetically valid. It was observed that the military zone surrounding Paris, recently annexed to the city, provided an opportunity for urbanization on a vast scale, and there was no reason why this area could not contain one hundred *maisons-tours,* each capable of housing three thousand people. Such a type of housing could provide a high level of modern utilities and common services, as well as a dwelling in which "man would have an immense horizon and a perspective far more exciting than that of some Boulevard Raspail."[70]

67. "Une maison de dix étages," *La Patrie,* June 20, 1905.
68. Jean Labadié, "Les cathédrals de la cité Moderne," *L'Illustration, August* 12, 1922, p. 134. It may be noted that the drawing by Lambert was recently published in *Architecture d'aujourd'hui,* no. 178, March–April 1975, with a mistaken attribution to Perret.
69. Ibid., pp. 131, 134.
70. Ibid., p. 135.

115. Skyscrapers projected to lead from Paris to Saint Germain en Laye, 1922.

Although Perret's initial conception of the skyscraper had proposed its placement only at the edge of Paris, he attempted to insert a towering structure within the inner fabric of the city through his entry in a 1926 competition for a church dedicated to Joan of Arc. The location was to be in the Eighteenth Arrondissement, on the site of the old church of Saint Denys de la Chapelle. Auguste and Gustave Perret proposed a concrete-framed structure embodying a central spire two hundred meters tall, or two-thirds the height of the Eiffel Tower. (The prize was awarded to a building in the Byzantine style.)

The most persistent advocate of high-rise building for Paris was, of course, Le Corbusier. In 1922 he had exhibited his visionary City for Three Million People, containing widely spaced, geometrically ordered skyscrapers, and in the 1925 Voisin Plan applied the same concept to a complete reconstruction of the center of Paris (figure 116). The project was to be reworked for many years. To Le Corbusier's eyes

116. Le Corbusier's Voisin Plan, 1925.

the scheme had many advantages, among them that of replacing a district "for the most part overcrowded and covered with middle-class houses now used as offices"[71] with a profitable new business center.

Far from detracting from the image of Paris, the scale of the new high-rise complex was, according to Le Corbusier, a contemporary embodiment of the grand scale of French tradition. "If the Voisin plan is studied, there can be seen to the west and southwest the great openings made by Louis XIV, Louis XV, and Napoleon: the Invalides, the Tuileries, the Place de la Concorde, the Champ de Mars and the Étoile. . . . Set in juxtaposition, the new business city does not seem an anomaly, but rather gives the impression of being in the same tradition and following the normal laws of progress."[72] Included in his many representations of the project was a series of drawings showing the evolution of major additions to the urban fabric of Paris. The city had received Notre Dame, the Louvre, the Invalides, Sacré-Cœur, and the Eiffel Tower, and had remained Paris. "Paris was transformed on its own ground, without evasion. Each current of thought is inscribed in its stones, throughout the centuries. In this way the living image of Paris was formed. Paris must continue."[73]

The virtue of the skyscraper, according to such enthusiasts as Le Corbusier, lay in its ability to concentrate activity on a small ground area. Through wide spacing, such building could presumably provide for a large population, while leaving ample ground available for parks. High-rise building was continually justified as a device for opening up the urban fabric, and Le Corbusier once illustrated his skyscrapers with the caption: "How to have air, light and greenery all around us again."[74]

Although Le Corbusier was the most energetic advocate of skyscrapers for Paris, other architects shared his conviction that this form of building would be desirable. Among the designers who supported high-rise structures was Henri Sauvage, who in 1929 envisioned a massive ensemble with setbacks, to be constructed along the banks of the Seine in the Fifteenth Arrondissement. (Although the Sauvage scheme was never attempted, this riverfront site was to become the focus of a high-rise redevelopment project beginning in 1961.) Other proposals made during the 1920s for tall building in Paris included a series of projects executed for the periodical *Vu* by the architect S. A. Laprade, who suggested the creation of regularly spaced towers along the Champs Élysées.

Making its report in 1930, the government commission charged with a reconsideration of building regulations in Paris decided, in spite of technical possibilities, economic pressures on land use, and the predilections of modern architects, to retain the old height restrictions. Basing its decision on urban

71. Le Corbusier, *The City of Tomorrow* (London: Architectural Press, 1947) pp. 277–78. First published in France as *Urbanisme* (Paris: Éditions Crés et Cie, 1925).

72. Ibid., pp. 282–83.

73. Le Corbusier, *The Radiant City* (New York: Grossman, Orion Press, 1967), p. 103. First published in France as *La ville radieuse* (Boulogne [Seine]: Éditions de l'Architecture d'Aujourd'hui, 1935).

74. Ibid., p. 101.

æsthetics, the commission reported: "In its general physiognomy, the city of Paris must conserve its own character, its discipline, its quality of order and measure. And so, without exception, buildings of excessive height, like those which provide the attraction of certain foreign cities, should be forbidden. . . . Reason dictates that Paris should be held to the same order of height as before."[75]

The Tower Triumphs

Although the refusal of city officials to modify existing building regulations reflected a conservative æsthetic bias, the decision also accorded with economic conditions. Population remained relatively stable, and the financial crisis of the 1930s did not encourage ambitious programs of construction. There was little pressure, therefore, to alter prevailing codes.

It was in the period of rapid expansion following the Second World War that the urbanistic concepts of the modernists began to be realized. Le Corbusier, in his theoretical works, had constantly chastised Parisian officials for their timidity. When he published *The Radiant City* in 1935, he complained: "Paris fills me with despair. That once admirable city has nothing left inside it but the soul of an archæologist. No more power of command. No head. No powers of action."[76] By the mid-1960s Paris was a source of despair to many, but not because of stagnation. Municipal planners were acting boldly at last, and the scale of urban transformation expanded and accelerated. Reflected in the new areas of redevelopment were design concepts embodying many of the ideas of the 1920s and 1930s. Such modernists as Le Corbusier had advocated the freeing of building lines from the street pattern, avoiding what was termed the "corridor street." Towers and slabs were to be freely disposed amid large spaces and separated by areas of greenery. When building regulations were reconsidered during the 1960s, the influence of such thinking was clearly in evidence.

In Paris, a new comprehensive building code was put into effect in 1961 and subsequently incorporated into the Plan d'Urbanisme Directeur of 1967. The presentation report of this plan adopted the terminology of the modern movement, making specific reference to "the doctrines known as the Athens Charter, which introduced *urbanisme of the ensemble,* where individual works form part of large development plans," and where projects are oriented toward "structures of great height, with deliberately simple lines, with a concern for orientation and unity of composition. . . . With these orthogonal patterns, these towers destined to mitigate by their vertical accents the monotony of great horizontals, such compositions deliberately break with the conformity of neighboring areas." In its conclusion the

75. Commission des Perspectives Monumentales, *Rapport de la Sous-Commission,* p. 44.
76. Le Corbusier, *The Radiant City,* p. 177.

report stated that *"the aspect of the city will change.* One will no longer go about between parallel walls, in these corridors, the streets, but in spaces alternating with buildings and greenery."[77]

The type of large-scale design implied in the report was to be realized in Parisian centers of urban renewal. Such areas included the Hauts de Belleville, Montparnasse, Saint Blaise, La Chapelle, Riquet, the Place d'Italie, and the Front de Seine. In these districts, old quarters were completely razed and rebuilt. Considered as "new sites," freed from existing regulations, such redevelopment areas were characterized by freestanding high-rise building (figures 117 and 118).

77. Atelier Parisien d'Urbanisme (APUR), "Une volonté de remodelage du cadre urbain de Paris: le règlement de 1967," *Paris projet* 13–14, 1975, p. 37.

117. The district of Riquet.

In addition to providing a new freedom for building design and placement in renovated districts, planning officials modified building regulations for the entire city. Previous codes had presupposed an alignment of buildings along the street and had regulated height according to street width. The 1967 regulations embodied a control based on a *cœfficient d'utilisation du sol* (CUS), which determined building volume in relation to the occupation of the plot. Restrictions remained with regard to height, although the maximum limits were increased to 31 meters in the central districts defined by the exterior boulevards, and 37 meters in the outlying arrondissements. Outside the city, heights might reach a maximum of 45 to 50 meters, with certain areas virtually free of control. The profile of the upper levels was also modified with regard to the 1902 regulations. The employment of a

118. Redevelopment project in Riquet.

segment of a circle to define part of the roofline was abandoned in favor of a terraced setback with a forty-five-degree angle (figures 119 and 120).[78]

Building height continued to be related to street width, and for narrow streets maximum heights were reduced. As street widths were measured from building line to building line, however, owners could attain increases in height by setting buildings back from the street. The overall result was an increase in new building which not only ruptured the existing urban fabric in terms of height, but which also

78. Although building regulations had remained essentially unchanged since 1902, modifications had begun in 1948. At this time, a series of exceptions to the law were made official, permitting an increase in height for buildings along unusually wide streets or facing open space. On December 20, 1958, a ruling allowed buildings on streets over 27 meters to reach a height of 31 meters, including the mansard roof. In the outer arrondissements, a limit of 37 meters was permitted. In addition, exceptions to the regulations were often made for individual buildings, such as the Cité Morland, built to house the Perfecture of Paris, and the Science Faculty of the University, constructed in 1965.

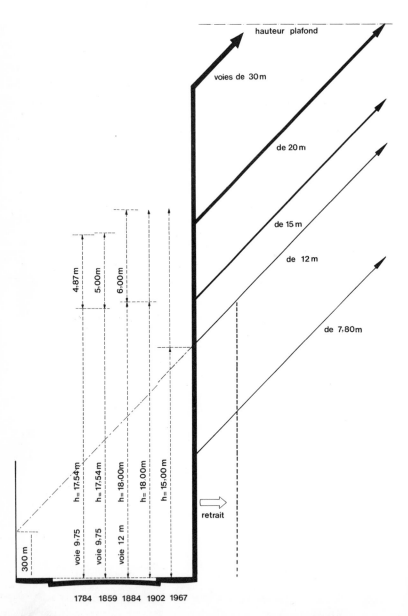

119. Building profile established by the 1967 regulations.

120. Building on the Avenue d'Iéna reflecting the 1967 regulations.

destroyed the existing street alignment. In consequence, complaints similar to those which had arisen following the 1902 regulations were heard, and similar arguments marshaled with a view to preserving the urban harmony of the city.

The question of regulation was again discussed, and a revised code was adopted by the Municipal Council in 1974. A government publication, analyzing the faults of the 1967 law, observed that the aim of its creators had been "to ærate the city, to increase the importance of the spaces opened up. The preference of the authors went naturally to the free placement of buildings away from the street, that is to say, in the heart of the block or in the center of realigned plots."[79] One of the major flaws noted in this regulation was a uniformity of control which did not take into consideration the existing character of many districts. The new regulations were embodied in the Plan d'Occupation des Sols, which attempted to prevent the destruction of the established townscape. An effort was made to control not only building form but building type. Further construction of offices in the city center was discouraged and the construction of housing encouraged. Rules of ground coverage were framed to maintain the existing character of many districts, and also to discourage speculation in the vicinity of public projects.

With regard to height, it was noted: "This question of building height has been at the center of the reconsideration of urbanism in the capital, in the press as in public opinion. It has too often been reduced to the problem of towers." As for the overall fabric of Paris, it was thought that the effect of the existing towers was "probably less serious than the destruction of the Parisian fabric, not in the form of a clean break, but by a multitude of blows and dents which it has been given, in the greatest disorder, by buildings of twelve to fifteen stories."[80]

Although variances of building codes would continue to exist for special cases, such as major redevelopment projects and certain important buildings, new construction would generally be much more strictly controlled to maintain the traditional Parisian texture. Regulations reflected the principle that "every building to be built along a public street must be built according to the alignment."[81] Setbacks might be authorized in certain cases, but an increase in height would not be permitted. It was observed that a continuity of street facade was characteristic of most of Paris and thus important to the image of the city (figure 121).

Building heights under the new regulations were lowered to conform to prevailing patterns in different parts of the city. In the historic center, the cornice height limit was placed at 25 meters, two stories below the 1967 maximum. This district was defined to extend south to the Boulevard Montparnasse and west to the Champ de Mars. To the east it included the Saint Antoine district and the Canal Saint Martin, and to the north it extended to surround Montmartre. Certain outlying

79. *Paris projet* 13–14, 1975, p. 45.
80. Ibid., p. 69.
81. Ibid., p. 79.

121. Old and new buildings on the Avenue d'Iéna. While departing notably in style from its neighbor, the new building maintains the same facade line and cornice height.

quarters with a characteristically low-rise character were also included within the 25-meter maximum limit. For districts beyond the center, a maximum height of 31 meters was imposed, with a height of 37 meters permitted only in outlying arrondissements where many 12- to-15-story buildings already existed. Some quarters, such as Montmartre and the historic quarter of the Marais, were to be subject to special regulations, reducing the maximum height in some cases to 12 meters, or 4 stories. As a result of the new regulations, two-thirds of the city could not receive new construction notably above existing levels. In addition to the general building regulations, special controls were to be instituted in order to protect important views, architectural perspectives, and the surroundings of monuments.

In terms of style, postwar modern building in Paris, like similar building during the 1920s and 1930s, reflected an international idiom. Light structural framing was frequently cladded in smooth curtain walls, employing generous amounts of glass. Just as many prewar modern buildings were inserted unobtrusively within the existing urban fabric, many postwar structures have succeeded in harmonizing with neighboring buildings, maintaining existing cornice lines and street facades. An apartment house completed in 1962 on the Avenue de La Bourdonnais, for example, was one of the few completely glass-walled buildings in Paris, yet, with its simple detailing and modest scale, it was deemed "a total success in a precarious context."[82]

In addition to those buildings intended to harmonize with the prevailing streetscape, there were other postwar structures which, because of their notable function or site, were meant as landmarks and designed to be in striking contrast with their surroundings. Included among these was the Maison de l'ORTF, the headquarters of French National Radio and Television, built between 1956 and 1963. This large complex, designed by Henry Bernard, took the form of a circular ring sheathed in glistening metal and surrounding a central tower (figure 122).

82. I. Schein, *Paris construit* (Paris: Éditions Vincent, Fréal et Cie, 1970), p. 50.

122. Maison de l'ORTF.

123. UNESCO headquarters.

The headquarters of UNESCO, completed in 1958, employed the talents of Marcel Breuer, Bernard Zehrfuss, and Pier Luigi Nervi (figure 123). Neither the form nor the style of the curved-wall structure related to its urban surroundings, but the size and isolation of the site lent an air of self-containment to the complex, and underlined its uniqueness. Another building to employ a curving glass wall was Oscar Niemeyer's Communist party headquarters, completed in 1972. In this case, although the building contrasted sharply with the existing urban fabric, its modest scale tended to mitigate the conflict with its neighbors.

Among the most ambitious and visually striking buildings of recent years is the Georges Pompidou National Center of Art and Culture, dedicated in 1976 (figures 124 and 125). Pompidou, who had wished to identify his administration with the promotion of cultural life, sponsored the project in 1969. The site was the Plateau Beaubourg, an open area near the old market site of Les Halles, and the program included a library, a museum of modern art, and design-research facilities. In 1971 a design was selected through an international competition, the prizewinning entry embodying the joint efforts of Renzo Piano and Richard Rogers.

124. Georges Pompidou National Center of Art and Culture. West facade.

125. Pompidou center. East facade.

Attempting to provide a large amount of flexible interior space, the architects designed the building as a forty-two-meter-high rectilinear frame, exposing the supporting structure, as well as the service elements, on the exterior. Both in its scale and style, the museum provided a dramatic contrast to the dense pattern of surrounding building. Although the city by this time contained other structures which departed sharply from the prevailing urban fabric, such as the ORTF building and the UNESCO headquarters, the Pompidou center marked the first attempt to insert such a building into the historic center of the city.

The creation of the Beaubourg Center coincided with the destruction of the old market complex of Les Halles, an ensemble of metal and glass pavilions which, at its inception in 1854, had embodied both technical and æsthetic innovation. Like the Pompidou center, Les Halles had stood in marked contrast to its surroundings, yet it had become such a beloved part of the image of Paris that many urged its preservation as a historic monument.

Although one cannot predict how future generations will judge the Pompidou center, it appeared to enjoy a remarkable popularity during its first years, attracting crowds far beyond anticipation. The glass-enclosed exterior escalator provides visitors with an exciting visual experience, while the sloping plaza in front of the building presents a festive and animated public gathering place. Judging from public response to the Pompidou center, Parisians have no inherent prejudice against innovative design. The focus of dispute about new building has centered primarily on scale rather than style, and especially on height. In postwar Paris, the skyscraper became a lightning rod, attracting opposition from all quarters, and providing a conspicuous symbol of widely deplored aspects of modern life (figures 126 and 127).

It may be recalled that in 1925 the Voisin Plan of Le Corbusier had envisioned the redevelopment of the center of Paris into a skyscraper office district. Although this conception may have appeared an improbable fantasy at the time, by the mid-1960s Parisians had reason to fear that such a massive transformation of this ancient quarter might well be realized. In 1963 the city decided to move the wholesale food market outside Paris, leaving its former site available for redevelopment. In 1967 the Municipal Council asked six different architectural offices to make proposals for the rebuilding of the market site, anticipating that the schemes might produce guidelines for detailed development. Although the architects had been requested to limit building height to a maximum of thirty meters, the resulting projects included some megalomaniacally scaled ensembles of high-rise building and received a generally hostile press. Public opposition to the destruction of the old market pavilions was already developing, and it was given additional force through the apprehension that they might be replaced by skyscrapers. Although public protest failed to save the market buildings, city officials were prompted to make substantial modifications in the redevelopment proposal.

126. The Science Faculty of the University of Paris conspicuously breaks the skyline of the Left Bank. The foliage on the right marks the Île de la Cité, site of Notre Dame Cathedral.

127. Science Faculty. This complex was built in 1965 on the site of the old wine market. The architects were R. Seassal, V. Cassan, R. A. Coulon, and E. Albert.

A highly publicized dispute over the height question came about in 1972, inspired by the new commercial complex of La Défense. This district, lying beyond the city boundaries of Paris and including parts of Nanterre, Puteaux, and Courbevoie, had been subject to a large-scale redevelopment program beginning in 1956. The postwar period had been characterized by a rapid increase in office building in Paris, and many were disturbed by the growing dominance of this building type. La Défense had been promoted as a means of providing the commercial interests of Paris with extensive modern office space without a drastic transformation of the center of the city. As the scheme was planned, the government would control the project and build the complex infrastructure of transport lines, auto routes, and

128. Looking west along the Avenue des Champs Élysées toward the skyscrapers of La Défense.

underground parking. Individual buildings, which included offices and apartment housing, would be privately designed and constructed.

The principal approach to La Défense from Paris is along the axis extending from the Louvre through the Tuileries, Place de la Concorde, Champs Élysées, and Arc de Triomphe (figure 128). As the culmination of this axis, La Défense was long considered part of the monumental composition of Paris, and thus a highly important site. Although the plan approved by the government in 1964 included provision for a focal point in the form of a 200-meter skyscraper, the bulk of the office space was to be provided by an ensemble of about thirty towers, 42 by 24 meters in plan and 25 stories (about 75 to 100 meters) in height. This building size, providing about 25,000 square meters of floor space, was deemed appropriate to the size of the largest French business enterprises. The overall plan was deemed such that "in the Parisian landscape, the towers of La Défense, averaging 25 stories, will appear like a homogeneous mass, and not chaotic like the New York skyscrapers."[83]

In general the design of La Défense office buildings reflected prevailing styles and provided a fashion show of curtain-wall cladding materials. Although some critics complained of a general mediocrity of design in La Défense, the complex did not become a center of strong controversy until 1972, when the effects of a change in building regulations began to be observed (figures 129 and 130).

By the late 1960s, government officials became convinced that the high costs of the infrastructure of La Défense needed to be offset by greater revenues from private builders, and the site was replanned at this time to provide for a higher density of occupation. Apparently developers preferred large buildings. In 1968 the Union des Assurances de Paris (UAP) requested the right to construct a tower with 68,000 square meters of floor space on a site intended for two buildings of 30,000 square meters. It was also requested that the plan of the building take the form of a three-branched star. Both departures from the plan were granted. As an encouragement to further development, the government decided to permit an overall increase in height, expanding the previous limit of about 25 stories to 45 stories or more. Residential units, originally restricted to 8 stories, could now match the office towers.

By the summer of 1972, the press was filled with discussion of La Défense. What had originally been a relatively orderly, if banal, plan seemed to have been replaced by a "laisser-faire à l'américaine," and the district to be dominated by a "Manhattan-style, with its architectural landscape expressing the rivalry of commercial firms." It was observed: "French business firms have, in their turn, discovered the symbolic power of modern architecture in the city, as American companies discovered long ago."[84] With the decision to supersede the original plan

---

83. *Techniques et architecture*, September 1965 (special issue on La Défense), p. 86.
84. "La Polémique sur les immeubles-tours à Paris et sur le Quartier de la Défense," *Urbanisme*, no. 132 (1972): p. xxx.

for La Défense, a number of additions were proposed for the complex. The architect Émile Aillaud proposed to close the axis of the composition with two curving buildings covered with mirror glass, intended to reflect the image of Paris back toward the city. They were to be accompanied by three towers, rectangular, triangular, and circular in plan.

The controversy over La Défense was inspired less by the æsthetic qualities of the project itself than by its effect on the monumental axis of Paris, for apprehension grew that the existing perspective from the Louvre toward the Arc de Triomphe would soon be marred by the bulky profiles of the rising office towers.

Not everyone, of course, was in agreement about the blighting effect of the towers. In September 1972 the former prefect of the Paris region, Paul Delouvrier, wrote an article in *Le Monde* defending the character of the district. He did not believe that "from the Concorde to the Étoile the towers which rise up to the right and left of the Arc present anything detrimental to the purity of the perspective. Let

129. La Défense viewed near the Pont de Neuilly. *Left to right*: the Tour Nobel, 32 stories; the Groupe des Assurances Nationales (GAN) building, 42 stories; and the Union des Assurances de Paris (UAP) building, 41 stories.

the sky show behind the Étoile a new quarter of Paris, a modern Paris of big business. . . . I myself find nothing to criticize." To those who retained doubts, he offered the comfort that "it is eight kilometers from Carrousel to La Défense, and five kilometers from the Étoile to the new quarter: with the sky of Paris often murky even in good weather, the towers will frequently blur in the distance."[85]

At the height of the controversy, the president of France, Georges Pompidou, entered the fray with a lengthy interview, published in *Le Monde* on October 17, 1972. To begin with Pompidou minimized the importance of the derogation of building regulations in La Défense. French building regulations, he noted, were "extraordinarily strict and complicated," with the result that "practically nothing of importance can be built without some variance of one or another of these codes."

The creation of La Défense was "linked to a general effort to make France a great

85. "Faut-il raser l'Arc de Triomphe?" *Le Monde,* Sept. 16, 1972, p. 13.

130. Air view of La Défense.

economic power and Paris a great center of business. But this also permitted the conception of a thoroughly exceptional ensemble of modern architecture." The augmentation in building heights had been necessary, he maintained, for the economic success of La Défense, and there was no proof that the original plan would have been better than what was presently under construction.

The question of perspective was discussed in detail. There had never been, Pompidou claimed, "a perspective from Carrousel and the Tuileries to La Défense. There was a perspective from *Carrousel to the Arc de Triomphe.* Beyond this there was a void, an avenue, very wide but without either architectural or æsthetic finality. No one has ever stood under the Arc de Triomphe to contemplate the Avenue de la Grande Armée, the Avenue de Neuilly and the pitiable buildings which covered the present site of La Défense. From Carrousel to the Tuileries, one contemplates the Champs Élysées and the perspective closed by the Arc de Triomphe. This is the truth."

As to La Défense, the nature of the project led inevitably to the construction of a large number of towers. Although some had suggested that future towers should be constructed farther to either side of the monumental axis, Pompidou did not believe that this would help. He maintained that there was "a good chance that the result obtained would be better if the Arc de Triomphe detaches itself from a *forest of towers.* Nothing is worse than five or six towers trying unsuccessfully to conceal themselves. Either one renounces towers, and there will no longer be any architecture in an ensemble of such importance . . . or one multiplies them."

Continuing his æsthetic analysis, the president observed that: "The problem remains of the opening toward the sky through the vault of the Arc. This is the questionable aspect of the Aillaud project. In itself this project is very beautiful, in my opinion. But I recognize that, from the Tuileries, it blocks the vault of the Arc de Triomphe. . . . Only I maintain that if one wants to have, from the Arc de Triomphe and toward La Défense, a true perspective, it will be necessary that this perspective, in some manner or other, be terminated. There is no perspective unless it ends in *something.* If it ends in a void, it is an avenue, more or less long, more or less wide, an immense Boulevard Malesherbes, everything except a perspective. . . . As for me, I would envision . . . at La Défense either a sculptural work, very tall and very narrow, or an immense jet of water, which would mark the terminus, create a perspective and be seen from Carrousel through the vault of the Arc, but without blocking or barring it, and leaving a large opening toward the sky."

With regard to architecture in general, Pompidou insisted that it was "a fact that the modern architecture of the big city leads to the tower. The French prejudice, and particularly that of Parisians, against height is, to my eyes, completely retrograde." He reminded his compatriots that "one can't be mired in the past. Paris is not a dead city, it's not a museum to maintain. . . . We are the guardians of civilization. The difficulty is to be at the same time the creators." Although the physical changes in Paris blessed by

Pompidou's administration had inspired controversy and criticism, he maintained stoutly: "I love art, I love Paris, I love France. I am struck by the conservative character of French taste, particularly of those who call themselves the elite, I am scandalized by the policies of the public powers in matters of art for a century, and that is why I seek to counteract it, with a mitigated success."[86]

Pompidou was not, of course, alone in viewing the tower as a natural accompaniment to modern urbanism. Such an attitude had characterized the thinking of many modern architects, and proposals for inserting such structures into the Parisian fabric continued to be made. Le Corbusier pursued his suggestions for central Paris in 1961 by proposing a high-rise slab to house a cultural center on the Quai d'Orsay. In 1960 Édouard Albert had proposed a highly sculptural *tour tridimensionnelle* of steel and glass to be placed on the Place de la Résistance, near the Pont de l'Alma. In 1970, Jean Faugeron projected a new building for the National Ministry of Education in the form of a two-hundred-meter pyramidal skyscraper to be built on the site of the Santé prison.

In 1965 Pierre Bourget, an urbanist, prepared a study for the location of skyscrapers in Paris. He felt that although heights were controlled within the city as a whole, a few well-placed towers could serve as "focal points, for which there would no longer be a question of a common scale with the quarter in which they were placed. They would play in the silhouette of the city a role analogous to that of the campaniles and clock towers in ancient cities." The places he suggested for such structures included the Point de Jour, marking a riverside site near the Boulevard Périphérique in the Sixteenth Arrondissement, and a site in Ranelagh near the Bois de Boulogne. He also proposed such a tower for the Quai de Bercy in the Eleventh Arrondissement. The most central of the sites was along the Champs Élysées in what he deemed a "dead space" between the Rond Point and the Place Clemenceau. Envisioning a seventy-five-meter tower, polygonal in plan, he observed that "the nearby Grand Palais forms a sufficiently heavy volume to be a good accompaniment to a vertical."[87]

Included in the proposed tower locations was one that had long been considered a logical site for a high-rise building, the Porte Maillot. It may be recalled that as early as 1905 Perret had wished to construct a twenty-story building there. Le Corbusier and others had made skyscraper designs for this site in 1930, and the 1931 Voie Triomphale competition included some suggestions for tall structures at this point (figures 21, 25, and 26). Bourget wished to mark this important entrance into Paris with a 150-meter tower, slightly removed from the axis of the Avenue de Neuilly, to contain offices and a luxury hotel.

---

86. Georges Pompidou, "Le président de la République définit ses conceptions dans les domaines de l'art et de l'architecture," *Le Monde,* October 17, 1972.

87. Pierre Bourget, "Essai sur l'implantation d'immeubles tours de prestige," *Urbanisme,* no. 117 (1970): 28, 29.

131. Looking south from Notre Dame Cathedral. With the exception of the Science Faculty tower on the left, high-rise building appears only at a distance.

As it was eventually developed, the Porte Maillot became the site for an ensemble that included a large meeting hall, an exposition center, and a high-rise hotel. The design, completed in 1968 by G. Gillet, H. Guibout, and S. Maloletenkov, incorporated the concept that the tower be placed at a distance from the Avenue de Neuilly, in order to leave the axial vista clear (figure 27).

In view of the constant demands for office space in Paris, the repeated proposals of architects for skyscrapers, the advancement of French building technology, the growth of economic affluence, and the symbolic appeal the skyscraper seems to have had for businessmen, it is not surprising that Paris eventually became the site of the tallest building in Europe. Although the peripheral areas of the city were increasingly characterized by high-rise redevelopment projects, their visual impact tended to be local (figure 131). With the creation of the Maine-Montparnasse tower, however, the skyline was broken by a 210-meter, 56-story building, sufficiently tall to be visible from many points in the city.

The emplacement of the building resulted from a proposal, originating in the 1930s, for demolishing the old Maine and Montparnasse railroad stations and replacing them with a single new station. The project was resumed after the Second World War, and the decision taken to employ the eight-acre site, which would be freed through the regrouping of railroad facilities, as a *pole d'animation* for the Left Bank. The site was well served by transport facilities, and it appeared to city officials as a logical place for the development of a business center. The resulting project, begun in 1958, included a new station complex containing both offices and apartments, a tall office tower, and a shopping center (figure 132). The station ensemble, characterized by long curtain-walled slabs, was completed in 1964 and embodied architectural designs by Beaudouin, Lopez, de Hoyn de Marien, Arretche, and Dubuisson.

The Maine-Montparnasse tower, on which work began in 1969, represented an international collaboration. As in many large redevelopment areas in Paris, the

132. The Maine-Montparnasse tower and station complex.

project was controlled by a *société d'économie mixte,* an organization including both government and private interests. The overall construction was in the hands of an American developer, Collins, Tuttle, and Company of New York. Explaining his presence in France, the president of the firm, Wylie Tuttle, observed, "Paris needs a skyscraper and the competition here isn't as strong."[88] Very important to the organization of the project was a French *constructeur-promoteur,* Jean-Claude Aaron, who established the financing of the enterprise through a syndicate of forty organizations, including banks, insurance companies, and pension funds. The architectural design, convex in plan and embodying a concrete service core and an external glass curtain-wall, represented the collaboration of four French architects, Eugene Beaudouin, Urbain Cassan, Louis de Hoyn de Marien, and Jean Saubot. A. Epstein and Sons of Chicago served as consulting architects, and Carl A. Morse, Inc., of New York as consulting engineers.

When the center was in its early stages, government planners gave assurance that "the architectural composition of modern inspiration has been minutely studied so that it can be inserted without any fault of taste into the Parisian landscape."[89] As it approached completion, however, the tower attracted increasingly hostile criticism. A renowned and much-loved quarter of Paris seemed threatened with a total transformation. The practicality of such a massive concentration of office space (one and one-half times the total space on the Champs Élysées) was questioned, and the looming bulk of the tower was attacked as an assault on the visual harmony of Paris (figures 133 and 134). American participation in the project seemed to underline what many dreaded as an increasing Americanization of the city.

The promoters of the Montparnasse tower, however, consistently maintained that once completed it would become a source of pride and an attraction equal to the beloved Eiffel Tower. Detractors were reminded that the Eiffel Tower had itself been strongly opposed by conservative taste. Whatever its benefits for Paris, the new tower was apparently highly beneficial to its builders, and Wylie Tuttle reported in 1971 that it had been "an immense financial success . . . far exceeding our profit expectations.[90]

A government survey of the evolution of Paris between 1954 and 1974 indicated, not unexpectedly, an overall increase in building height in the city. In 1954 the average building was six stories, or about twenty meters in height; in succeeding years, the average had reached nine floors. The survey noted also a marked increase in buildings of over thirteen floors, reporting about three hundred by the end of 1974. Most of these were concentrated in new redeveloped districts (figures 135,

88. *France Soir,* October 16 1972.
89. Préfecture de la Seine, *Plan d'urbanisme directeur de Paris* (Paris: Imprimerie Municipal, 1960), p. 84. The decision that the projected commercial complex should include a tower was made by the Municipal Council, who specified that it should not exceed two hundred meters. The architects were selected by the private promoters.
90. *Architectural Forum,* June 1971, p. 20.

133. Pedestrian plaza adjacent to the
Maine-Montparnasse tower.

134. The Maine-Montparnasse tower, completed in 1973, viewed from the Avenue du
Maine.

136, and 137). Eighty-five were in the Thirteenth Arrondissement, the site of extensive rebuilding near the Place d'Italie, while fifty-five were counted in the Fifteenth Arrondissement, in which could be found the Montparnasse tower and the Front de Seine renewal area. The Nineteenth and Twentieth Arrondissements had received a total of sixty such structures. Thus these four arrondissements contained two-thirds of all buildings of over thriteen stories built since 1954.[91]

As the urban transformations of the 1960s began to inspire serious concern about the quality of the Parisian environment, journalistic debate increasingly focused on the question of tall building. "Must we resign ourselves to see Paris transform itself to such a degree that our capital is no more than a caricature of Chicago, Sydney, or Tokyo?"[92] It was observed by one writer that: "It is above all the *beaux quartiers* which are ravaged by demolition, at the expense of superb buildings of cut stone which could last five centuries, but which have the fault of having only six stories. In replacing them by a slapdash concrete cube, the promoter will have gained several floors of 'luxury' apartments, or several hundred square meters of offices, which he will be able to rent or sell very dearly because of the *beau quartier*, and because of the law, which imposes no price limit on rents in new construction. And if the demolished building has a historic or artistic interest, so much the worse for the art lovers."[93]

Another writer noted that "a certain hostility to the 'American' forms of urbanism, and above all to tall building, is incontestably unique to Paris, to Parisians, and above all to the Parisian press. . . . The capital . . . espouses willingly the 'anti-skyscraper theories' of the intellectuals and æsthetes, venerable academicians and young opponents of growth." "This raging conformism," it was elsewhere reported, "pleases a public of every stamp, since the most left-wing readers will transform themselves willingly into conservative preservationists when it concerns architecture."[94]

In addition to its other defects, the skyscraper was deemed an economically extravagant form of building. "And so, why the towers? And why the Concorde airplane, and why the Apollo rocket? They are even more unprofitable, less necessary. And yet they exist. Because they are inevitable. Because when man has the ability to make something of this sort, he makes it. It is an old story. As old as the tower of Babel, which was already ninety meters tall."[95]

According to *Time* magazine, a young American tourist, viewing Paris from atop the Arc de Triomphe in 1972, was heard to remark: "This isn't quite what I expected, but I guess you can't stop progress."[96] And yet, it appeared, following the election of

91. 20 *Ans de transformations de Paris,* 1954–1974. (Paris: Association Universitaire de Recherches Géographiques et Cartographiques, 1974 (pages unnumbered).
92. "La Polémique," Quotation from *Le parisien libéré,* September 20, 1972. p. xviii.
93. Ibid.
94. Ibid. Quotations from *Paris-Match,* September 26, 1972; *Le Monde,* September 14, 1972.
95. "La Polémique." Quotation from *Paris-Match,* May 27, 1972.
96. "Building a New Paris," *Time,* July 10, 1972.

135. High-rise apartments in the Place d'Italie redevelopment district.

136. Hotel Nikko in the Front de Seine redevelopment area.

137. The Front de Seine area. In the foreground is the Pont Mirabeau, designed by Louis Résal in 1895.

President Giscard d'Estaing in 1974, that "progress" could be stopped, or slowed down, at least momentarily. In contrast to his predecessor, who viewed vast new building complexes and motor expressways as tangible evidence of power and prosperity, Giscard d'Estaing took a far more conservative view of the physical fabric of Paris. He halted extension of the Left Bank motor route and announced his support for public transport. Expressing a desire that all planning operations respect the character of existing quarters, he also stressed the need for increased park space within the city. As to tall building, his policies produced exultant headlines on the front page of *France Soir:* "Les Tours à Paris: C'est Fini." Although nothing could be done to abolish the large complexes of high-rise building already in existence, new construction could be halted. "The city must remain familiar to all," stated the president, declaring a moritorium on office construction in the city and subjecting the design of all current planning projects to reconsideration.[97] Several skyscraper projects, such as a 176 meter tower at the Place d'Italie, were announced as discontinued.

Giscard d'Estaing's new policies were generally popular, judging from reactions in the press. His plan to restrict untrammeled growth in Paris coincided, moreover, with a downward shift in the economy and what promised to be a chronic energy shortage. A growing disenchantment with the results of postwar growth gave increasing support to the concept of a Paris in which the physical form, at least, would still provide a measure of stability and permanence.

Public conservatism, however, has never daunted the visionary architect, and as opinion was coalescing against radical change, the more ambitious proposals of certain designers continued to envisage structures of ever greater scale. Beginning in 1958, the architect Yona Friedman proposed to construct over the existing fabric of Paris a series of giant elevated space frames containing housing. In contrast to Friedman, who proposed building above the existing city, Paul Maymont suggested in 1968 a type of architecture that would incorporate building with "crater-amphitheaters," large, open excavations permitting habitation to extend far below the surface of the city.

Although the more farfetched conceptions of the visionaries seem unlikely to be realized, it is equally improbable that the desires of the most ardent conservatives will be satisfied in modern Paris. For if the city may be considered a "collective and complex art," it is a fluid art form, destined to evolve through time. The control of architecture cannot provide a permanent mold; rather it embodies an attempt to guide the speed and character of change. In spite of some contemporary misgivings that any new building will be worse than the old one it replaces, the city must somehow evolve. Just as old buildings assure us of the creative vitality of our ancestors, new building must reflect our own, albeit uneasy, confidence in our ability to bequeath something to the future.

97. *France Soir,* October 11, 1975.

 A PLACE TO LIVE

There is, especially among citizens of English-speaking countries, a phrase that recurs frequently when the French are being discussed: "A Frenchman never invites you to his home." This is in no way taken to reflect unfavorably on the social desirability of the speaker but is understood to mean that the Frenchman doesn't have a home. Not a proper home, at any rate. As everyone knows, Frenchmen live in hotels, and they meet their friends in cafés and restaurants. Or else they live in apartments, which as everyone also knows are not a suitable place for family life. Not a really decent sort of family life at any rate. It may be pointed out as well that the French language does not even have a word for home. There is the word, *maison,* which means house, but which can also refer to an apartment house, or simply a building. There is the word *foyer,* which has some of the connotations of *home*; but which isn't quite the same thing, somehow.

Like many myths, the image of the badly housed Frenchman is not totally without basis. The belief, moreover, that the single-family house consistently favored in Anglo-Saxon societies is the ideal dwelling type has been accepted by many Frenchmen. A French historian declared during the period of Haussmann's renovations:

Parisian apartments combine extreme expense with extreme inconvenience. You don't live there, you perch there, you camp there between sky and earth, subjected to all the servitudes imposed by the proprietor, the concierge, and the neighbors, always in a hurry to get out, whether it is to seek a little air, calm, and repose in the street—yes, really, repose; or to vary your torment by changing your dwelling. Have you never thought of the influence that this type of habitation must of necessity exercise on the physical and moral temperament of the Parisians? Do you believe that all this has no effect on the anxious character, the nervous irritability which has made our people the most volatile and capricious in the world? . . . I am convinced that the English *home,* so peaceful

138. Apartment houses bordering the Champ de Mars in the Seventh Arrondissement. The two-block strip adjacent to the park was sold for private development in 1910.

and comfortable, so isolated from all the tumults of the outside world, . . . plays a great role in the prosperous political and social history of that nation.[1]

For most Parisians, however, the housing question has centered less on the debate over apartments versus houses than on the basic problem of finding a place to live. The glittering surface of nineteenth-century Paris, its architectural grandeur, broad avenues, ordered greenery, and display of material opulence, cœxisted with deplorable slums. Primitive dwelling conditions, of course, persisted despite modernization in many industrial cities. The drama of the Parisian slums, however, was heightened by the magnificence of the city, by the striking juxtaposition of elegance and squalor.

The urban renovations of Haussmann were responsible for a large volume of new middle-class housing, which served to lure the prosperous classes away from the increasingly outmoded older quarters of the city. For those whose affluence encouraged rising dwelling standards, newly developing districts in the west of Paris provided modern apartment buildings with commodious, large-windowed, high-ceilinged rooms. As apartments were usually laid out, the principal chambers faced the street, with service areas and less-used rooms opening on to courtyards or air shafts. Modern utilities were bringing a new level of comfort and convenience to middle-class dwellings, with central heating, plumbing, and gas becoming common.

1. Victor Fournel, *Paris nouveau et Paris futur* (Paris: Lecoffre, 1865), pp. 15, 71–72.

By the end of the century, electric lighting was replacing gas, elevators provided vertical transport in many residential buildings, and kitchen equipment was becoming increasingly specialized and elaborate. Although ground coverage in the new districts was relatively high, with courtyards often dark and constricted, the wide, tree-lined streets gave a sense of spaciousness and order, and the term *"beaux quartiers"* came to be applied to such areas (figures 138, 139, and 140.)

The work of Haussmann has been credited with accentuating the physical separation of social classes between eastern and western Paris (figure 141). Descriptions of pre-Haussmann dwellings have often made reference to a juxtaposition of economic levels occurring within the same building, with the more prosperous tenants occupying the lower floors and the poorest inhabitants the attic. A measure of social interaction and even social assistance is said to have accompanied this mixture of class. The new construction directed by Haussmann, however, provided primarily for middle-class occupants, with the upper story reserved for servants.

Just as Haussmann seemed relatively insensitive to the physical destructiveness of much of his work, he also seems to have been unconcerned about the social costs. As buildings were destroyed to make way for the new network of avenues, the former

139. Apartment facade on the Rue de Lyon, Twelfth Arrondissement.

140. Side wall of an apartment house in the Sixteenth Arrondissement.

occupants were reduced to the status of refugees, seeking housing in a city of constantly rising rents. A typical instance is included in a book, *Les quartiers pauvres de Paris,* published in 1868, in which a working-class woman recounts the difficulties her family experienced during Haussmann's renovations. Residents of the Halles quarter, they were dispossessed by demolitions, and when they attempted to return to the district found that rents had doubled in the old streets, while the new construction was designed to exclude working-class occupants. The family was forced to move out of the center of Paris to the suburban district of Belleville, where the family could find suitable housing, although the journey to work was considerably lengthened. They had not been long settled, however, when the Paris boundaries were extended outward, rents were raised prohibitively, and they were compelled to move still farther out.

The habitations of the poor were often makeshift quarters in buildings that had been abandoned by the affluent classes. The central and eastern districts of the city contained many old houses which originally had been occupied by a single family and which had comprised spacious rooms, courtyards, stables, and often gardens. In the social transformation of the old districts of Paris, such buildings would be continually subdivided, with rooms partitioned into tiny chambers, and often divided vertically to insert additional floor levels (figure 142). Ceilings as low as 1.7 to 2 meters could be found, and a typical room might be 1.5 meters wide and 2 meters long. Haphazard staircases, often no more than ladders, together with dark, labyrinthian passages, would provide access throughout the structure. Attics, cellars, and stables might be converted to housing, while courtyards would be built over and occupied by commercial workshops and sheds. Heat was usually lacking, and water often available only in the street or courtyard. Sanitation was virtually nonexistent.

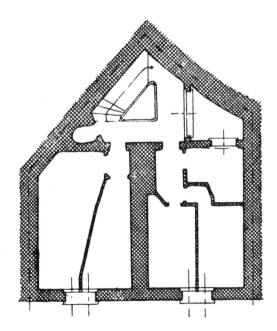

141. OPPOSITE. The Rue Mouffetard, a working-class district in the Fifth Arrondissement, photographed in 1910.

142. Plan of a slum building, showing the subdivision of rooms.

In many cases the building would be leased to a *locataire principal,* or principal tenant, who would manage the subletting. It was once observed of such a tenant: "He looks naturally for all the possible ways of augmenting his revenue; the upkeep of the building means nothing to him, that the staircases are filthy, that the pipes for wastewater have holes, that the floorboards have separated, this concerns the owner, not him."[2]

The dilapidation of the dwellings was attributable, in the opinion of some, not only to the negligence of landlords, but also to the attitude of tenants. It was observed of the Frenchman that, "in general, he is careless and takes no precaution whatever to prevent the deterioration of the dwelling he occupies; . . . So what if you damage the wallpaper and the walls, if you dirty the paint, if you gouge the plaster, the landlord is there to repair them, it's his affair."[3]

A large proportion of working-class people in Paris lived in furnished accommodations, termed *meublé* or *garnis,* often because they were too poor to afford any furnishings of their own (figure 143). By 1901, 185,674 people were living in a total of 12,175 *meublés.* Some had single rooms and others slept in dormitories. It was also possible to rent a *demi-lit,* a bed which served two or three successive occupants, for which the rental might vary according to the cleanliness of the sheets.

A report on housing conditions made by a physician during the 1870s pointed out: "Everywhere one notices that a great number of buildings containing *garnis* are in the most deplorable state from the standpoint of hygiene; the humidity is constant, ventilation and lighting insufficient, the dirtiness sordid; the lodgings are often poorly protected against harsh weather; the courts and air shafts are infected by the accumulation of decaying garbage and the stagnation of rainwater and household waste, which remains and putrefies there; the privies, when they exist, are insufficient in number; their filthiness is revolting."[4] Overcrowding of lodgings was widespread, and a physician's report of 1882 observed: "Of one room they have made two. They have placed twenty beds in rooms which formerly only had ten. They have built sheds in courts already too narrow, resulting in the most dangerous encumberments."[5]

The poorest dwellings of all were in the squatter settlements, haphazardly erected on vacant land, which became "covered with parasitic constructions sheltering colonies of poor people pushed toward the periphery by the demolitions and the increase in rents; this taking of possession is made in haste, in deplorable conditions;

2. Lucien Ferrand, *Habitation à bon marché* (Paris: Rousseau, 1906), p. 26.
3. Ibid., p. 28.
4. Roger H. Guerrand, *Les origines du logement social en France* (Paris: Éditions Ouvrières, 1966), pp. 207–08. The quotation is from O. Du Mesnil, "Les garnis insalubres de la ville de Paris, Rapport à la commission des logements insalubres," *Annales d'hygiène publique et de médecine légale,* January-June 1878, pp. 193–232.
5. Ibid., p. 208. The quotation is from the *Rapport général sur les travaux de la Commission des Logements Insalubres pendant les années 1877 à 1883,* p. 45.

143. The courtyard of the Hôtel Brémant, a working-class residence in the Eleventh Arrondissement, shown in 1886.

144. "La Fosse aux Lions," a shanty settlement in the Thirteenth Arrondissement, shown in 1863.

. . . Pathways without pavement, transformed into muddy sewers, impassable after the first rain; flimsy, insanitary constructions, this is what you find everywhere" (figure 144).[6] One such settlement was described as "a sort of open-air sewer. All the human beings who reside there present a character of complete physical degeneration: the children are pale, anemic, scrofulous, and the men and women prematurely old."[7]

6. Ibid., pp. 207–08. The quotation is from the *Rapport général sur les travaux du Conseil d'Hygiène Publique et de Salubrité du Département de la Seine depuis 1887 jusqu'à 1889 inclusivement* (1894), chap. 5 "Travaux des commissions d'hygiène instituées dans le Ressort de la Préfecture de Police," pp. 279–300.

7. Ibid., p. 206. The quotation is from the *Rapport général sur les travaux de la Commission des Logements Insalubres pendant les Années 1877 à 1883,* annexe 5, "Rapport sur la Cité des Kroumirs," pp. 164–71; Conseil d'Hygiène et de Salubrité du Département de la Seine, *Rapport sur l'insalubrité de la Cité et de la Cité des Kroumirs* (1882), A.N. AD XIX, S. 24.

One of the most long-lived squatter areas of Paris existed just outside the barrier of fortifications marking the city limits. As a military device, the fortifications were considered obsolete by the end to the Franco-Prussian War, and during the 1880s the city considered proposals for the demolition of the forts and the redevelopment of the site. Legal provision for removal of the defensive line, however, was delayed until 1919, and the gradual demolition of the masonry defenses, together with the reconstruction of the area, took decades. Surrounding the fortified wall was a ring of land, the "zone *non aedificandi,*" on which only low, temporary structures were permitted. Removed from normal urban use, this area became a district of shanties, nicknamed the *zone,* which with its impoverished inhabitants, the *zoniers,* dramatically set off the sumptuousness of Paris with a frame of filth and squalor (figure 145). By 1926, the population of the zone was estimated at 42,000, and the final removal of the *zoniers* was not attempted until the 1940s.

A book on Paris published in 1930 described this neighborhood of ragpickers as follows:

145. Housing on the zone, photographed during the 1940s.

You would think yourself in a village bombed during the war; large holes break the walls, and houses are bereft of doors and windows; the road enters the house and becomes part of it. An atrocious swamp of trash, of blackened rags, old papers, bones, of debris of all sorts, fills the rooms as well as the courts. Heaps of trash take the place of furnishings; a lopsided table and a bed of rusted iron with overlapping old rags and bones; the leprous walls are naked except when the artistic taste of the inhabitants has inspired them to decorate their lodgings with pictures found in a trashcan. . . . The houses are constructed in a hundred different fashions, cabins made of everything and nothing, ends of wood and bits of iron, with roofs of tarpaper or corrugated tin, a chimney hole, a roof like a jack-in-the-box. Here is a little "castle" surrounded by a garden, and the sunflower which grows there, a magnificent golden sun, is taller than the house that shelters the gardener. Farther away, a ragpicker raises chickens and rabbits, which one can see restless in their wire cages. Another, a more ambitious entrepreneur, gives all his attention to pigs (figure 146).[8]

8. André Warnod, *Visages de Paris* (Paris: Firmin-Didot, 1930), pp. 273–76.

146. Residents of the zone, photographed during the 1920s.

The Road to Reform

The insanitary conditions of the Paris slums were consistently reflected in disease and mortality statistics. A cholera epidemic which caused 989 deaths in 1884 was almost entirely limited to slum quarters. A second cholera epidemic occurring in 1892 was accompanied by 906 deaths in Paris, the districts most affected being the Eleventh, the Eighteenth, and the Nineteenth Arrondissements, all working-class areas. A similar pattern of localization was observed for a typhoid epidemic which occurred in Paris in 1882. In the view of some observers, it was primarily the fear that disease might spread from slum quarters to middle-class districts, that motivated general public and government concern for improving housing conditions.

Government efforts to introduce hygienic improvements in housing often met with opposition from landlords invoking the rights of property owners. In the view of extreme conservatives, almost any regulation of property was a step toward dreaded socialism, and Haussmann's ordinance of 1852 requiring the periodic cleaning of building facades had been denounced by some. Haussmann had also put through an ordinance in 1852 requiring property owners to provide connection with the public sewer for the evacuation of rainwater and household wastewater. The prefect Poubelle, who held office between 1883 and 1896, attempted to augment this sanitary provision in 1894 by requiring proprietors on streets provided with a public sewer to evacuate sewage by this means. This, to our eyes, reasonable demand for *tout à l'égout* aroused vigorous protests from many property owners. The application of the regulation did not begin until 1897, and no attempt was made to impose it on all landlords at once. As a result, compliance made such slow progress that as late as 1925 almost one-third of the houses in Paris had not yet made the required sewer connection.[9]

Poubelle also attempted to regulate the disposal of garbage. Until 1870, every evening between eight and nine o'clock all household garbage would be thrown into the street, where it lay until it was picked up the following morning. In 1870 regulations were passed requiring that the garbage be put out only in the morning. Poubelle attempted to improve this rather messy system in 1884 by requiring each householder to provide a covered container for garbage. This regulation, needless to say, was denounced by landlords, who derisively applied the name "Poubelle" to garbage bins, thus providing a form of immortality for the well-intended prefect.

In addition to being hampered by the recalcitrance of landlords, improvements in housing conditions were naturally limited by prevailing standards. Even idealistic reformers were unsure as to what might reasonably be provided in low-cost housing. A physician in 1883 expressed the desire that each dwelling unit have its own toilet,

9. New Legislation in 1926 enabled the city to advance money to property owners to make the sewer connection, and in 1928 the law was extended to include private streets and passages. By 1928 the number of buildings without a sewer connection had been reduced to 18 percent.

but he admitted that this proposition was "radical and completely revolutionary."[10] New legislation for *garnis,* promulgated in 1883, required one toilet for twenty people. For a long time the provision of water for each dwelling unit was regarded as a luxury, and even in the twentieth century, the question of baths for workers was debated. In 1906 a housing official stated that "neither a bathtub nor a shower is indispensable for assuring cleanliness for those who care for it; it suffices for them to have recourse to the simple and economical use of a zinc tub. . . . Bathtubs and showers, with their complications of hot-water heaters, mixing taps, etc., . . . are luxury devices."[11]

The evolution of housing reform reflected a growing conviction that housing conditions were inextricably linked to social stability. According to a reformer in 1906, it was generally acknowledged that bad housing was "insanitary and produces a considerable increase in sickness and death. . . . It only remains to prove that it is one of the causes of the increase in immorality, and the cause of many of the vices that afflict our present-day civilization." Attempting to make vivid the human aspects of poor housing conditions, he described the day-to-day difficulties of a family living in cramped and squalid quarters. The children, lacking space to play, would seek the streets at an early age, spending their days without supervision and exposed to temptation and crime. Within the dwelling, forced promiscuity would inevitably take its toll on human decency. "When father, mother, girls and boys must every day accomplish under the eyes of one another all the necessities of life, however intimate they may be, all dignity, all deference disappears." Without adequate utilities, cleanliness would become virtually impossible, for if all water needed to be carried from a street or courtyard, its use would be sparing. Lacking adequate facilities for cooking and laundry, unable to make any headway against the dirt and dilapidation of her surroundings, the mother would become increasingly despairing or indifferent. The father, seeking calm and repose after his day's work, would find only noise, crowding, and filth. It was not unnatural that he should seek relaxation elsewhere, and if he frequented cabarets it was because, "at the present time, there is no other meeting place for workers but the cabaret." It was essentially through the impossibility of finding adequate housing that the worker would "develop a feeling of hatred against the organization of society and against society itself. . . . Can we blame him if from time to time a sentiment of revolt and hatred manifests itself in him, and he blames his landlord, and with him the concept of property, for all evil."[12]

The same sentiment was more succinctly expressed in 1872 by Paul Leroy-Beaulieu, who stated: "If family life does not exist among the working classes, it is linked to the smallness and filth of the dwellings. The cabaret thus becomes a place

---

10. Guerrand, *Les origines du logement social,* p. 205.
11. Louis Houdeville, *Pour une civilisation de l'habitat* (Paris: Éditions Ouvrières, 1969), p. 188.
12. Ferrand, *Habitation à bon marché,* pp. 85, 88–89.

of meeting and relaxation: one becomes there at the same time envious, greedy, revolutionary, skeptical, and finally a communist."[13]

For most bourgeois reformers, housing improvement embodied the ideal of individual home ownership. Through becoming the proprietor of his own house, the worker would presumably acquire a stake in society, abandoning thoughts of revolution and vain dreams of utopia. The house would become the instrument for a new morality and social tranquility, for, it was believed: "A worker-homeowner will rarely frequent cafés and cabarets. He will hasten, as soon as his work is over, to return home, and he will consecrate all his free time to the maintenance and improvement of his house and garden; he will devote all his leisure to the care of his family and property."[14] The ownership of property would of necessity encourage habits of economy, reducing wasteful consumption while the garden could be employed to supply food and thus provide an effective wage supplement. The preference of many French housing reformers for the single-family dwelling was to be reinforced by the English Garden City movement. The conceptions of Ebenezer Howard became well publicized in France, and the housing designs of English garden cities eventually served as prototypes of French counterparts.

The question of housing continued to be debated by reformers as the century drew to a close, with the factor of public health becoming highly influential. It had frequently been through physicians reports that both the public and government officials had become aware of slum conditions, and such organizations as the Société Française d'Hygiène and the Société de Médecine Publique et d'Hygiène Professionnelle de Paris, both founded in 1877, provided a continuous sounding board for ideas on improved living conditions.

Gradual improvements in urban sanitation produced an overall decline in the death rate by the turn of the century. Typhoid fever killed 2,121 people in 1881, but only 773 in 1894. One disease, however, had grown in virulence. Tuberculosis remained a major scourge with total deaths rising from 11,023 in 1880 to 12,376 in 1894. Tuberculosis, moreover, was the only major disease directly linked to building. In 1882 Robert Koch identified the tuberculosis bacillus, and subsequent study indicated that this bacillus, ejected by carriers of the disease, could survive for long periods of time in places that were dark and badly ventilated. A book on housing published in 1906 maintained that the tuberculosis bacillus "can subsist for years in a state of somnolence, provided that it is sheltered from sun and fresh air, that it has found refuge in a dark and humid corner, in the back of an alcove, or between the floorboards, in ground contaminated by a drain or privy, or in a heap of garbage deposited by the door of a dwelling."[15] Many of the densely built quarters of

13. Houdeville, *Pour une civilisation de l'habitat,* p. 56. The quotation is from Paul Leroy-Beaulieu, *La question ouvrière au XIXe siècle* (1872).

14. Houdeville, *Pour une civilisation de l'habitat,* p. 210.

15. Ferrand, *Habitation à bon marché,* p. 39.

Paris, with their narrow streets and tall buildings, contained dwellings into which the sun never penetrated, and which could be deemed ideal breeding grounds for the disease.

Efforts to improve urban sanitation were consistently promoted by Poubelle, who created the Commission de l'Assainissement et de la Salubrité de l'Habitation in 1892. In the following year he established the Casier Sanitaire des Maisons de Paris, which attempted a complete survey of houses in terms of disease. Housing studies conducted between 1894 and 1904 disclosed the existence of six specific areas with notably high tuberculosis mortality, and these centers of pestilence were designated *îlots insalubres*. City officials became convinced that the demolition of infected buildings was essential as a public health measure. "We must destroy the house, when it harbours the disease. Any palliative would be an illusion."[16] The belief that a building could remain a center of infection almost indefinitely gave continuous ammunition to advocates of massive slum clearance, and it also inspired in certain modern architects and urbanists an almost obsessive concern for sunlight and fresh air.

In 1913 the Commission d'Extension de Paris supported the conception of large-scale clearance, quoting a report of the municipal Service d'Hygiène. "The quarters where tuberculosis has established its home are the quarters where the dwellings are dark and badly ventilated. . . . *Tuberculosis is the disease of darkness.* To combat it effectively, one must first of all oppose it with its natural enemy, the sun." The commission observed: "To demolish squalid quarters, to reconstruct there healthy dwellings, provide squares, planted spaces: this is a program that will seduce philanthropists, statesmen, and administrators concerned with public health."[17] Although preservationists might be concerned about the demolition of historic districts, it was believed that clearance programs could allow for the preservation of some historic buildings. Such structures, it was suggested, might even be improved in aspect when disengaged from the neighboring buildings and surrounded by gardens.

When Le Corbusier presented his theoretical urban concepts, he made frequent reference to the unhygienic aspects of the congested districts of Paris. *La ville Radieuse,* published in 1935, contained a photograph of a slum courtyard captioned: "History. Historic Paris, tubercular Paris."[18] Attempting to bolster his conception of an open-textured urban pattern, he employed such quotations as: "Once tuberculosis has made its way into unhealthful houses, it's there for good: one after

16. Anthony Sutcliffe, *The Autumn of Central Paris* (London: Edward Arnold, 1970), p. 110. The quotation is taken from the Municipal Council reports of 1906.

17. Commission d'Extension de Paris, Préfecture du Département de la Seine. Vol. 2. *Considérations techniques* (Paris: Chaux, 1913), pp. 82–83.

18. Le Corbusier, *The Radiant City* (New York: Grossman, Orion Press, 1967), p. 100. First published as *La ville radieuse* (Boulogne [Seine]: Éditions de l'Architecture d'Aujourd'hui, 1935.

the other, all of those whom their fate has led into this den will be struck down by tuberculosis."[19]

During the years before the First World War, programs of slum clearance were repeatedly considered. Action was delayed, however, partly because of legal complexities in procedures of expropriation, and also because of inadequate financial allocations. It was clear, moreover, that the destruction of existing buildings would only exacerbate the housing problem unless they could be replaced with improved low-cost housing.

One of the results of the housing reform movement was the creation in 1889 of the Société Française des Habitations à Bon Marché. Privately formed, the Société was to be merely advisory, its purpose "to encourage in all of France the construction, by individuals, industrialists, or local societies, of decent and inexpensive houses, or the improvement of existing housing."[20] As the movement gained force, however, it inspired the creation in 1894 of a law providing government assistance for housing. According to the new legislation, societies for *habitations à bon marché* (known as HBM) could, by constructing housing according to certain specified standards, obtain fiscal exemptions and reduced-interest loans from government sources.

Additional legislation in 1906 required the establishment in each *département* of an organization for low-cost housing. This was followed in 1912 by a law instituting public offices for HBM, which were to be "autonomous, independent, perpetual, disinterested,"[21] and financed by the government. The Paris region was served in this respect by the Office Public des Habitations à Bon Marché du Département de la Seine and by the Office Public des Habitations à Bon Marché de la Ville de Paris. A competition for HBM housing was sponsored in Paris in 1912, with the first prize going to Maurice Payret-Dortail. Although the city had voted the sum of two hundred million francs to construct twenty-six thousand dwellings, the onset of the war prevented realization of the project. Instead the Conseiller Général de la Seine, Henri Sellier, used the money to purchase land for future housing.

While the years preceding the First World War had been marked by a growing awareness of the housing problem and by organizational efforts to bring about both slum clearance and new housing construction, most slum areas remained unaffected. Wartime conditions of course exacerbated the situation. Paris was a center for the armament industry, and population expanded rapidly during the war years. Meanwhile all programs for housing construction were postponed, and the dwelling shortage became acute. In 1920 Henri Sellier observed that "in the Département de la Seine as a whole, half of the population is badly housed." He also noted that the

19. Ibid., p. 208.
20. Gurerrand, *Les origines du logement social,* 290.
21. Jean Bastié, *La croissance de la banlieue parisienne* (Paris: Presses Universitaires de France, 1964), p. 192.

"proportion of tubercular mortality and morbidity has increased during the last five years."[22]

A presentation of the day-to-day problems of Parisian workers, including detailed descriptions of housing conditions, could be found in *La vie ouvrière,* published by Jacques Valdour in 1921. Although the modern machine age was transforming Paris in many ways, with the brightly lit Champs Élysées becoming crowded with motor cars, the new nightclubs resounding with jazz, and the cinemas attracting ever-increasing audiences, working-class dwellings seemed to have changed little since the previous century. Room sizes were still minuscule, typically 1.50 by 2 meters, and the rooms were generally without water, heat, or adequate light and ventilation. A worker described the difficulty involved in simply washing his hands in such surroundings. When he got home from work, his hands were covered with grease, and he needed warm water to get them really clean. In his room were a basin and a metal pitcher which contained his water ration for twenty-four hours. "I possess," he admitted, "a little stove; but I'm alone, I would have to find water, buy a pot, some coal, light the fire, wait until the water is warm; and besides coal is expensive and I don't have any place but my room to store fuel." There were, of course, public baths, but these were costly and time-consuming. Once you were clean, moreover, you wanted your clothes to be clean, and laundry cost a lot. Summing up, he observed: "Work makes you dirty; the room is dirty, and also the linen. The worker stays dirty."[23]

Immediately following the war, in 1919, the Municipal Council instituted a survey of buildings which in the previous twenty-five years had evidenced a high level of tuberculosis mortality. The result was a demarcation of seventeen *îlots insalubres,* which included the six areas previously designated (figure 147). Of the seventeen districts, which comprised a total area of 257 hectares, thirteen were located in densely occupied parts of the peripheral arrondissements. Others were in the historic center of the city. The *îlots,* continuing the previous system of designation, were numbered in descending order according to mortality figures. The worst district of all, Îlot 1, retained its position from the original listing. This area was located in the heart of Paris, just north of the Hôtel de Ville and east of the Boulevard Sébastopol (figures 148 and 149). Containing in 1920 a population of 12,654 housed in 347 buildings, Îlot 1 had reported an average annual tuberculosis death rate of 10.35 per thousand inhabitants during the war years. Another Îlot, previously number 2 but reclassified as number 16, comprised the Right Bank district opposite the Île Saint Louis, while Îlot 3 occupied a riverfront quarter on the Left Bank directly opposite Notre Dame Cathedral. Viewing the Boulevard

22. Nils Hammarstrand, "The Housing Problem in Paris," *Journal of the American Institute of Architects,* February 1920, p. 88.
23. Jacques Valdour, *La vie ouvrière* (Paris: Rousseau, 1921), pp. 132, 134.

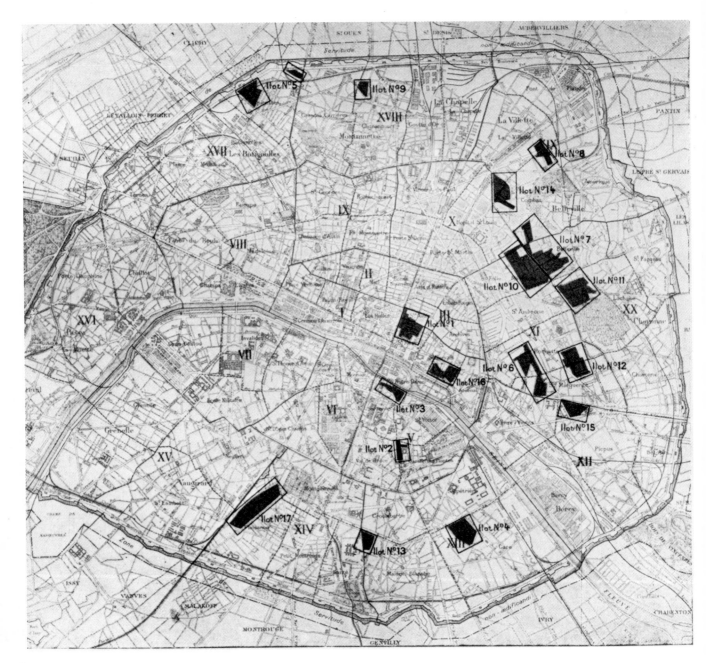

147. The *îlots insalubres*.

148. Rue Saint Merri in Îlot 1. Buildings were demolished during the 1930s.

149. Rue du Maure in Îlot 1.

Sébastopol as marking the north-south axis of the *grande croisée,* it was evident that almost all of the *îlots insalubres* lay in the eastern half of Paris. The overall population of the seventeen districts totalled 186,597, housed in 4,290 buildings.

The renovation of the *îlots insalubres* was to remain for many years an unachieved aim of Parisian officials. It was opined in 1923 that it was "useless to vote funds for the establishment of hospitals and sanitariums, of sport grounds for the creation of reservoirs of fresh air, if, in the populous quarters of Paris, as in the very heart of the capital, murderous districts persist."[24]

For financial reasons, progress was generally slow. It had been decided to begin renovation in the most urgent sector, Îlot 1. Preliminary studies were scarcely begun, however, when, in 1921 bubonic plague developed in Îlot 9, in the district of Clingnancourt. The outbreak of the disease was attributed to rats infesting the quarter, and fear of an epidemic led city officials to begin an immediate redevelopment of the area. Of the 85 buildings in the *îlot,* 47 were demolished, and the site replanned to include three new streets. The HBM office of the city of Paris then constructed housing on the site, providing for 4,000 inhabitants.

Returning to the problem of Îlot 1, city officials found it financially impossible to carry through the operation as planned, and the area to be initially cleared was reduced to the blocks between the Rue des Étuves–Saint Martin and the Rues Simon le Franc, Saint Martin, and Beaubourg. The area of clearance was gradually extended south to the Rue Saint Merri between 1930 and 1936. This open emplacement was used as truck parking for the nearby wholesale market of Les Halles, and later became the site of the Pompidou National Center of Art and Culture.

Although the difficulties of massive expropriations hindered the immediate renovation of many slum districts, the HBM office of Paris constructed a number of new housing complexes during the 1920s and 1930s. All of these were located in peripheral arrondissements, many of them on new sites made available by the demolition of the fortifications that had surrounded Paris since 1845. Generally HBM housing took the form of multi-story apartment blocks using reinforced concrete framing, with exterior walls of red- or yellow-brick infilling. Although the housing succeeded in providing solidly built structures supplied with modern utilities, the design did not always satisfy architectural critics. Some buildings embodied attempts at picturesqueness through the use of pitched roofs and irregular massing, while others reflected the geometric simplicities of the International Style. The siting of the new housing complexes, while intended to improve on the excessive densities of the Paris slums, often showed no radical departure from prevailing building patterns. In the view of some, an opportunity for truly innovative urban design had been ignored (figures 150 and 151).

24. Louis Lacroix, "Les îlots insalubres de Paris," *Urbanisme,* September-October 1932, p. 181.

150. HBM housing built on the site of the fortifications in the Eighteenth Arrondissement.

151. HBM housing on the Boulevard Ney in the Eighteenth Arrondissement, built on the site of the fortifications.

In establishing norms for design, several housing types were created. At the bottom of the scale was the "rudimentary" dwelling. This type of apartment was intended for families distinguished not only by their extreme poverty but by apparent anti-social tendencies. It was thought that "the social education of a family is not made only through the possession of a decent dwelling, and it is to be feared that the presence of several undesirable families would be, for the others, a source of trouble and moral danger. . . . It is necessary to avoid the physical and moral contamination of healthy families, and at the same time not to treat the doubtful families as undesirables incapable of improving. It is necessary, in their regard, to take some precautions in permitting them to begin an elementary social education. That is why a special type of dwelling has been envisaged, in which certain things which make a normal dwelling more comfortable and agreeable to live in (parquet floors, wood paneling, wallpaper, closets) have to be eliminated as facilitating the multiplication of parasites and germs of contamination." It was also considered desirable to reduce the possibilities of conflict among neighbors by eliminating any shared facilities, such as toilets, sinks, or galeries giving access to several dwellings, of which "experience has shown the impossibility of normal usage."[25] In plan, the rudimentary apartments contained a single kitchen-living-dining room, into which the other rooms opened directly.

The next step up the HBM dwelling-scale was the HBM "normal" or "ordinary" unit. An attempt to provide government-supported middle-class housing came through the establishment in 1928 of the Société pour les Immeubles à Loyer Moyen, or ILM. At this time, housing officials became aware that there were many people ineligible for normal HBM housing yet unable to afford ILM dwellings, and to accommodate this *petite classe moyenne* an "ameliorated" or "intermediate" type of HBM housing was created in 1930. The HBM and ILM offices were eventually united as the Office Public d'Habitations à Loyer Modéré, or HLM.

To guide the design and construction of public housing, a series of dwelling types were established, with minimum physical standards assigned to each category. At the same time, maximum rentals for each type were designated. Public housing standards have, naturally, varied over the years, responding to the building economy and changing concepts of housing amenity.

By 1930, HBM "normal" housing included seven basic dwelling types, ranging from a single room, with or without a toilet, having a total floor area of 15 square meters, to an apartment of six rooms, plus a kitchen and toilet, with a total floor area of 72 square meters (figure 152). Although such apartments were equipped with water, gas, and electricity, they usually lacked central heating. "Intermediate" housing was designed to provide the same range of dwelling types as "normal" housing, but with an increase in floor space of 12 square meters per unit. In addition,

25. Claude Berson, "L'Action de l'Office Public d'Habitations à Bon Marché de la Ville de Paris dans le domaine de la construction," *La vie urbaine,* no. 18, November 15, 1933, pp. 358–59.

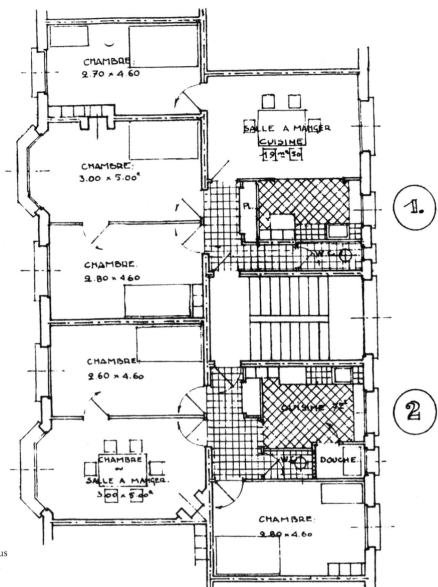

152. Plan of HBM "normal" housing,
1933. One apartment has three rooms plus
kitchen and the other three rooms plus a
dining-kitchen.

dwellings were to be supplied with a shower and a bathroom large enough to permit
the installation of a bathtub. Buildings might have limited central heating and the
possibility of elevators. The ILM housing was assigned the same minimum space
standards as the intermediate HBM units, but with improvements in comfort and
utilities. These would include central heating, together with elevators and
bathrooms equipped with tubs.

Between 1921 and 1940, government-supported housing in the city of Paris
comprised a total of 26,818 dwelling units, including 20,272 HBM "ordinary" units,
3,070 of the "ameliorated" type, and 3,476 ILM dwellings. In spite of earnest
efforts, however, public-housing programs were far too modest to have a noticeable
impact on the extensive Parisian slums. Moreover, the high cost of land and scarcity
of available sites in Paris led many officials to conclude that the future of low-cost
housing lay in the suburbs rather than within the city itself.

The Cités Jardins

The evolution of nineteenth-century Paris had been accompanied by a continuous movement of residential population outward from the center. Constantly increasing land values in the inner districts inexorably drove the poorer classes toward the less densely built peripheral arrondissements. Because the fortified boundaries of the city provided a tax-collecting point for goods entering Paris, prices of food and other products were usually cheaper in the suburbs than in the city. For this reason, the suburbs immediately surrounding the city sometimes became more populous than neighborhoods directly inside the walls.

In general, the prosperous sectors of Parisian society chose to live in the central city, and although a few upper-class enclaves were developed outside Paris, the large-scale settlement of the suburbs was primarily a working-class phenomenon. In addition to providing an area of cheap housing, the suburbs also contained major industrial establishments, and in general they had expanded haphazardly, with unregulated mixtures of factories and housing. Living standards in outlying districts were usually worse than within Paris, and in 1908 a government commission deplored such settlements, "where the population, driven from Paris by misery and also by the exportation of industry to the suburbs, is piled up in small, unhygienic dwellings." It was noted:

> The suburbs are not sufficiently prepared to receive such a large and a rapid addition of new inhabitants; old villages, scattered here and there, have become in a few years large centers of population, which in an uninterruped chain meet to form a disorderly mass like a single city spreading continuously from the center, of which they form an extension, and from which they are only distinguished by their individual activity. Neither the street system, nor the sewers are in a condition to meet the new and growing needs; municipal budgets, meagerly fed by the poor and needy populations, have only minor resources to ameliorate a sanitary situation which can become agonizing for the center itself, closely linked with the suburbs, from the viewpoint of public sanitation, and from the almost fatal repercussions of epidemics and contagious diseases. Old country houses, lacking almost everything from the hygienic standpoint (drinking water, toilets, drainage, paving and maintenance of common courtyards) have received a number of occupants never foreseen in their original accommodations; a quantity of new housing has been constructed in complete freedom, without any regulation, and is no better from the standpoint of sanitation than the old houses of the villages now transformed into cities.[26]

26. Henri Sellier, "Les aspects nouveaux du problème de l'habitation dans les agglomérations urbaines," *La vie urbaine*, no. 19, 1923, pp. 90–91.

Although overall densities in the suburbs might be lower than in Paris, the degree of overcrowding in dwellings was often higher, and tuberculosis rates frequently exceeded those of the central city.

In the Parisian scale of misery, the lowest level appeared to be found in the suburban shack districts. As described by a health inspector in Saint Ouen, in such quarters "the houses are disgusting cabins of wood or pieces of plaster, lighted only by the door, dark even in the month of July, and the nauseating smells defy all description. . . In these miserable huts, there is neither water, nor drainage, nor sewers; there are, on the other hand, plenty of rats. The doctor of the bureau of hygiene recently observed in one of these shacks a child of three or four years, gnawing at a bone on which there remained several bits of putrid meat, while beside him, on the same box, a rat gnawed another bone. Fifteen hundred people live in these conditions, on this land which, rented to the inhabitants, has for fifteen years brought to the proprietor an average of five francs per year per occupied meter."[27]

By 1901, Paris had attained a population of 2,714,000, with a suburban population of 955,000. The central city was to achieve its maximum population in 1921, with a total of 2,906,000, while the suburban area recorded 1,505,000. At this time the city of Paris would begin to decline in residential population, while the surrounding suburbs would expand at an accelerating rate. By 1931 the two areas were more or less equal in population, with the city reporting 2,891,000 and the suburbs 2,016,000.

The rapid expansion of the suburbs following the First World War may be attributed to several factors. The war had greatly augmented the industrial development of Paris, with an accompanying increase in population and an inevitable worsening of the housing problem. The eight-hour day, which became law in 1919, made long-distance commuting feasible for the first time for large numbers of people. At the same time, improvements in rail transport and low-cost commuter fares encouraged travel.

The thinking of housing reformers had been strongly influenced by the decentralist ideals of the Garden City movement. A Société des Cités Jardins was created in France in 1903, and the Garden City concept was publicized and supported by many French urbanists, most notably Georges Benoît-Lévy. The design concepts associated with the movement, in their emphasis on low-density and domestic scale, coincided with the ideals of those French housing reformers who advocated the single-family dwelling as the most desirable housing type, and the term *cité jardin* was to be applied to a number of suburban housing developments in which the designers attempted to reflect the ideals of the movement.

On the eve of the First World War, the Société des Cités Jardins de la Banlieue Parisienne attempted to organize support for a garden city in the Paris region. It was

27. Ibid., p. 98.

not proposed to create a self-sufficient community, however, or one which would embody a varied social range, but rather a model working-class housing settlement, with rapid and inexpensive commuting facilities to Paris. In design it was hoped to "rival the beautiful creations which England offers us as models. If our neighbors have got ahead of us, it's up to us to catch up with them and to do as well as they." Describing the future form of the settlement, it was noted that "nature collaborates here with the architect; the great trees of the neighboring forest live beside the little gardens which surround the home and enliven with flowers the charming dwellings."[28]

Although the war interrupted efforts to establish a *cité jardin* near Paris, the garden city ideal was to have considerable influence on postwar government housing programs. The creation of new towns, however, seemed too ambitious to be undertaken. In 1919 Henri Sellier, who directed the HBM office of the Département de la Seine, submitted a statement in which he outlined the intentions of the office. He indicated that no attempt would be made to "elaborate plans for true garden cities, in the absolute sense of the word. Garden cities, according to Howard and the experiment of Letchworth, constitute a complete town, self-sufficient, independent of all urban agglomerations. . . . The département office has not been created to promote a social experiment of this nature; . . . it has one very limited and well-defined object, which consists of building ensembles suitable to assure the decongestion of the city of Paris and of its suburbs, to serve as an example to developers, who for thirty years have literally sabotaged the suburbs, and to show that, . . . it is possible to assure the working population, manual and intellectual, a dwelling presenting the maximum of material comfort, natural hygienic conditions, . . . and styles of æsthetic amenity notably contrasting with the hideousness of the formulas previously employed." He observed that the HBM office of the city of Paris was compelled to "satisfy the housing problem by building decent dwellings on very expensive land, by consequence concentrating the maximum of population in the buildings it erects. The Office of the Département de la Seine adds to this objective a fundamental preoccupation with urbanism."[29]

In the period between the wars, the Département de la Seine constructed sixteen *cités jardins,* of which the most important were Plessis-Robinson, with a site of 104 hectares and 5,500 dwelling units; Drancy, on a site of 15 hectares with 1,060 dwellings; Châtenay-Malabry, with a 56-hectare site and 1,573 dwellings; Champigny-sur-Marne, with a site of 12 hectares and 1,197 dwellings; Suresnes, on a site of 42 hectares with 2,735 dwellings; Le Pré–Saint Gervais, with a 12 hectare site and 1,040 dwellings; and Stains, with 28 hectares and 1,655 dwellings (figure

28. Société des Cités Jardins de la Banlieue Parisienne. No publisher given. Date appears to be 1914. The statement is contained in a letter written by Ribot to the society; pp. 10, 12.

29. Henri Sellier, "L'Oeuvre de l'Office Public d'Habitations à Bon Marché du Département de la Seine," *Architecture d'aujourd'hui,* nos. 5–6, June 1937, p. 44.

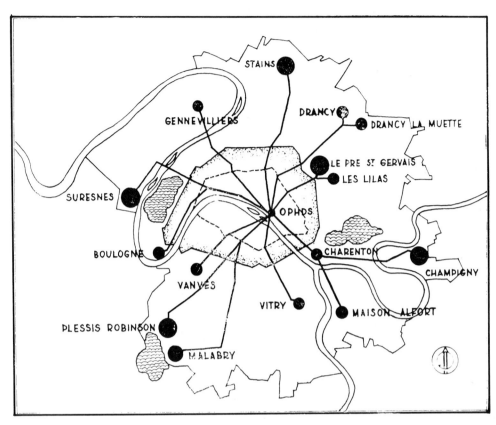

153. Paris and its surroundings, showing the location of the *cités jardins* developed by 1937.

153). Although these settlements were not complete towns, they embodied an attempt to combine housing with community services and abundant open space.

As might have been expected in a type of settlement inspired by the British Garden City Movement, the site planning was, according to Sellier, "directly influenced by the formulas which Raymond Unwin, with Letchworth or Hampstead, and the architects of Bournville and Port Sunlight have made fashionable." This influence was most apparent in those settlements begun shortly after the First World War where it could be observed that: "On the curving streets, the houses, aligned so as to avoid all monotony, and set back from the pathways, display the most picturesque aspects. With the possibilities of sun and light dictating the orientation, with steeply pitched tile roofs, with many angles and breaks, they tend to resemble an Anglo-Norman architecture" (figures 154 and 155).[30] The type of housing favored was a cottage-style dwelling, frequently employing row houses, although small apartment blocks of three to four storeys might also be included.

30. Ibid.

154, 155. Views of the *cité jardin* of Drancy.

As the *cités jardins* were public-housing projects, the social range was limited to those families eligible for subsidized dwellings. Each *cité* would usually include a range of housing types, extending from HBM "normal", through "ameliorated," to HLM *(loyer moyen)* units. In general, the difference in housing type was reflected in the size of rooms and the type of kitchen and bathing equipment provided.

Although the initial conception of the *cité jardin* was based on the single-family house, the HBM office soon decided to abandon this dwelling type in favor of apartments, for reasons that were largely economic (figure 156). The cost of construction had doubled between 1919 and 1926 and had almost tripled by 1930. The multiple-unit building, with its concentration of services and reduction in ground area and street access, seemed a logical building type for low-cost housing. At the same time the stylistic orientation changed, and it was observed that "this necessity, which has produced an effort at standardization, makes it practically impossible to maintain the English picturesque and romantic conceptions and imposes an ordering of terrain and a building æsthetic in rectilinear formulas, the harmony being realized by the play of lines and surfaces, with, in certain circumstances, the use of color." The decision, it was stressed, "was not due exclusively to the propaganda of architects and modern builders in favor of conceptions which, to tell the truth, still run counter to public taste."[31]

31. Sellier, "L'Oeuvre de l'Office Public d'Habitations à Bon Marché," pp. 45–46.

156. Apartment housing in the *cité jardin* of Plessis-Robinson.

The introduction of apartment housing and an architecture dominated by the concepts of the International Style did not completely vitiate the desire for a relatively low density, and apartment buildings generally did not exceed four to five stories (figure 157). It was perhaps inevitable, however, that the designers of *cités jardins* would wish to include that favored building type of modern architects, the tower. The first such apartment tower was to appear in Châtenay-Malabry in 1931. Although the predominant building type was an apartment block of three to five stories, one eleven-story tower was included (figure 158).

Once the decision had been made to provide high-rise housing, the tall apartment building was seen to possess positive virtues. Le Corbusier had envisioned such building for the center of Paris. Although this conception had been far from popular, Henri Sellier suggested: "Why not take what is good in his idea and apply it to the vast terrain, still empty, in the suburbs?" He observed: "There was no group of houses, not a city, not a village, so humble that it did not have, in the past, its clock tower, its belfry, its watchtower, of which the architecture was the identifying sign of the city. . . . An assemblage of low houses, without accent point, without architectural spirit, without an elevation which would be like a rallying center, will remain a housing complex without character or soul."[32]

If one tower was good, presumably several would be better, and the new æsthetic conception of the *cité jardin* was to be epitomized in the Cité de la Muette at Drancy, begun in 1932. Here the picturesqueness characterizing early *cité-jardin* complexes gave way to a strict geometric alignment of three-to-five-story apartment blocks, punctuated by five identical and regularly spaced sixteen-story towers. Advocates of the apartment tower reiterated the view, familiar to admirers of Le Corbusier, that such housing provided sunlight, air, and sweeping views, while preserving large areas of ground surface.

The Mal-Lotis

Although the *cités jardins,* and other housing projects sponsored by government bodies resulted from a well-intended effort to improve working-class living conditions, the scale of accomplishment was relatively modest, and the projects had little impact on the overall development of the suburbs. The extraordinary growth of this region following the First World War was to be found not in planned housing complexes, but in a wave of small privately built houses.

While some housing reformers had considered the single-family house to be the ideal dwelling type, it came to be regarded by HBM officials as too costly to provide an extensive basis for subsidized housing. Judging from events, however, this type of dwelling held a strong attraction, and large numbers of working-class people seemed

---

32. Henri Sellier, "L'habitation en hauteur," *Urbanisme,* no. 16, July 1933, p. 204.

157. Apartment house in the *cité jardin* of Châtenay-Malabry.

158. Châtenay-Malabry.

willing to make considerable sacrifices to obtain it. The pressures of the chronic housing shortage within Paris, the noise, dirt, and overcrowding of the urban slums, accompanied by the constant threat of rising rents and evictions, led many to seek the security of home ownership and a more salubrious way of living, outside the city. The continuance of a period of relative prosperity following the war, moreover, provided many workers with the means and optimism to undertake land purchase.

Facilitating the movement were enterprising speculators, who acquired large tracts of cheap land in outlying areas, parceled it into small lots, and sold the lots for modest weekly payments. Systematic advertising campaigns covered Paris with posters lauding the advantages of home ownership, the wholesomeness of open-air life, and the pleasures of hunting and fishing. Promoters often sponsored excursions to their sites, where persuasive salesmen encouraged purchasers to secure their lots with a down payment of as little as ten francs, an average day's wage for a worker. Lot sizes might range from 100 to 450 square meters and be priced at from two to ten francs a square meter. Although the suburban dwellers were dependent on rail transport for their daily commuting, the new allotments were often far from stations, and the journey to work might involve a one-hour walk before boarding the train.

159. Suburban settlement during the 1920s.

160. Settlement in La Courneuve. The street has served as a garbage dump, with the result that it is a meter higher than the surrounding land.

The purchasers of these small suburban lots were usually too poor to employ commercial builders to construct their houses, and in most cases they built their own small dwellings from materials at hand (figure 159). Often they made do with the most minimal temporary shelter, hoping that eventually their resources would permit a permanent house. The new allotments quickly filled up with an assortment of constructions, including shanties of wood, plasterboard, tar paper, and corrugated metal, accompanied by dwellings adapted from old trucks and wagons. Although during the summer months settlement in these suburban tracts may have had some of the charms of camping out, the onset of winter rains dramatized both the inadequacy of the shelters and the lack of drainage. Then too, as more and more lots were built up, the salubrious country atmosphere which the inhabitants had sought was transformed by a congestion and squalor as bad in its way as the urban slums from which most had fled.

A visitor to a surburban allotment in 1922 described the scene as follows: "We enter the principal street of such a settlement, if one can imagine an irregular path, pitted with ruts, where wastewater stagnates with a repugnant stench, and where the inhabitants make every effort to fill it up by throwing cans and broken bottles, and even garbage (figure 160). This artery is bordered with lattice fences over which one can perceive denuded yards where hordes of dirty children are running around. The yard itself often preserves but little trace of vegetation, encumbered as it is by a disorder of tools and a heap of diverse appendages: sheds, doghouses, rabbit hutches, chicken houses, latrines, etc., which crowd around the principal building, a low structure, insufficiently dimensioned itself; everything constructed of light materials, infinitely varied and often of the most unexpected sort."[33] A similarity in appearance between the suburban allotments and the notorious squatter settlements of the fortified zone was frequently remarked.

33. M. Bonnefond, "Les colonies de bicoques de la région parisienne," *Le vie urbaine*, no. 25, April 15, 1925, p. 526.

Poor housing conditions in the suburban allotments were exacerbated by a lack of urban utilities. Existing legal provisions were inadequate to regulate the new developments, and punitive sanctions for developers were virtually nonexistent. Having no compulsion to do otherwise, land speculators sold the lots without streets, sewers, water supplies, proper drainage, or gas and electrical installations.

Although in some cases advertising posters had announced the provision of utilities and salesmen had assured purchasers of speedy installations, it soon became clear that such promises were not legally binding. Instead of roads, settlements were often served only by rough pathways. Streets, when provided, were left unpaved and without drainage. Occasionally the bill of sale would be written so that the purchaser would be given title to half the road in front of his property, thus assigning him the responsibility for maintenance. During rainy weather, the roadways leading to the stations became such quagmires that commuting workers often wrapped layers of newspaper around their shoes, discarding the muddy wrappings before boarding the train.

Water sources were inadequate and often located far from the allotments. A walk of fifty to a hundred meters and a wait in line might be required to obtain this daily necessity. Some people were able to get water from wells on their land, but the proximity of latrines resulted in frequent pollution and threats of epidemics.

The glaring contrast between the magnificence of Paris and the squalor of its outlying settlements was a subject of frequent comment. A senator observed: "When one admires passionately the severe and grand lines of the architectural beauty of Paris, the spectacle of incoherence, anarchy, and ugliness presented by the greater part of the Parisian suburbs cannot but afflict us. Yes, the Parisian suburbs are a great stain of ugliness on the beautiful face of France."[34]

The æsthetic quality of the allotments was, of course, the aspect most noticeable to outsiders. For the inhabitants of these impoverished districts, there were also serious social consequences. In the opinion of one observer: "It is from the moral point of view, above all, that such colonies present the gravest dangers. The overcrowding, the habitation of entire families in the same room, have the most unfortunate results, and the old inhabitants of the country look with contempt (often exaggerated by hatred) on the immigrants, whom they frankly deem as undesirables. They attribute to them the worst infamies. But one may assume that vice, even if it is more apparent in full sunlight than in the obscure depths of the urban slums from which the inhabitants come, is certainly not a consequence of the exodus to the country. On the contrary. Nevertheless the moral danger of the colonies is immense in the sense that they are schools of discouragement."[35]

A politician advised in 1928: "Let us combat the communists by making property

34. Jean Bastié, *La croissance de la banlieue parisienne,* p. 285. The statement was made by Senator Muller from Bas-Rhin, during discussions of housing legislation in the 1920s.
35. Bonnefond, "Les colonies de bicoques," p. 554.

owners of them."[36] This idea, it may be recalled, was one that had long been promoted by certain reformers. It was assumed that the working classes, secure in the proprietorship of their dwellings, would acquire a stake in the existing social and political order and provide a bulwark against revolution. It became clear, however, that in the Paris suburbs it was precisely the struggle to own their own homes that was leading many toward socialism. The inhabitants of the new settlements found themselves socially isolated, exploited by the land proprietors, and often unable to obtain assistance and support from local governments. The local communes, in turn, saw themselves as caught between the indifference of the land developers and the overwhelming demands of the hordes of new immigrants for urban services that the communes did not feel financially able to support.

The long struggle for improved conditions served to create a new political awareness among the settlers, and they began to organize and consolidate their efforts in such organizations as the Fédération des Groupements de Défense des Petits Acquéreurs de Terrains and the Fédération des Travailleurs Mal-Lotis. As the Communist party began to gain strength during the 1920s, the consistent support of the suburban voters gave the name "red belt" to a circle of communities around Paris. The struggle for improvement of the suburban allotments succeeded gradually, although in some instances as much as ten years passed before all urban services were provided.

The sorry condition of the working-class suburbs and the difficulties of their inhabitants, the *mal-lotis,* received wide publicity and were regarded as major problems of the Paris region during the 1920s. The evident failure of the suburban allotment districts to achieve comfortable or hygienic living standards strongly influenced the thinking of architects and planners concerned with questions of housing. Many concluded that the single-family house, however attractive as an ideal, would be an impossible dream for most people and could never provide a suitable model for housing large numbers. The division of the countryside into small plots came to be looked on as an inefficient use of land, and sprawling tracts of closely set dwellings seemed to vitiate the rural atmosphere. The small suburban houses were judged to provide neither convenience nor adequate space, and the necessity for constructing lengthy street networks and strung-out utility lines considered an excessive financial burden for the community. Many housing officials concluded that satisfactory large-scale housing could be provided only through comprehensively planned apartment projects. It was this view, needless to say, which influenced the thinking of HBM officials when they abandoned the concept of single-family houses in *cités jardins* in favor of apartments.

36. Senator Chastenet, quoted in Bastié, *La croissance de la banlieue*, p. 278.

Postwar Trends

Although some well-intended efforts at housing improvement appeared in the years between the wars, the economic crisis of the 1930s tended to slow construction. In general, building in France remained sluggish compared to that of other European countries, and only one-fifth of what would have been needed for normal replacement of housing stock was built. The Second World War, of course, brought housing construction to a standstill, and the end of the war found the country with a generally backward building industry and a shortage of materials, tools, and skilled labor. In rebuilding, initial priority was given to major aspects of the infrastructure such as bridges, roads, port facilities, factories, and airports, rather than to housing. Just as France lagged behind some other countries in housing construction, Paris lagged behind other cities in France. A decentralist policy in the Ministry of Construction momentarily opposed Parisian expansion, under the assumption that a lack of housing in Paris would deflect population to other centers. By the mid 1950s, the housing shortage in the Paris region had become a well-publicized scandal.

A survey conducted in 1954 revealed that 36 percent of the families begun in 1948 were not yet housed by 1952, and 29 percent of married couples under the age of twenty-five were still living with their parents. In the Département de la Seine, it was found that 213,000 families (430,000 people) were housed in *meublé* accommodations, and by 1956 the central record of the Département listed 240,000 families as *mal logés*. In addition to being overcrowded, much of the housing stock was antiquated. The 1954 study indicated that 34.6 percent of all dwellings in the city of Paris had been constructed before 1871, and 80 percent predated 1914. A significant lack of services was also observed. The most widely distributed utility was electricity, available in 94 percent of all dwellings, while for other services the figures were: gas connection, 77.8 percent; water 77.2 percent; toilet, 48.2 percent; bathtub or shower, 19.2 percent; and central heating, 26.1 percent.

Population density within the city was 328 inhabitants per hectare, with the greatest concentration in the central districts of the city. Dwelling units were found to be generally small, and 65.8 percent of all units had one or two rooms. Only 6 percent of apartments had over four rooms, and these were located mostly in the fashionable Seventh, Eighth, and Sixteenth Arrondissements. Of the available housing, small units were in excess of population need, but there was an acute shortage of units large enough for average-size families.[37]

The infamous *îlots insalubres* were still largely intact, and the president of the Municipal Council observed in 1954 that if the previous rate of slum clearance were to continue in Paris, it would take more than two hundred years to demolish the 2,715 buildings remaining in the *îlots*. Urging more energetic programs of

37. The foregoing statistics are from Michel Bertrand, "Le Confort des Logements à Paris en 1954," *La vie urbaine*, no. 3, January–March 1964, pp. 23–71, and July–September 1964, pp. 273–314.

161. The Passage Lesage Bullourde in Îlot 6, Eleventh Arrondissement, photographed in 1955.

162. The "Impasse des Hautes Formes" in Îlot 6.

163. Eighty-eight Rue de la Roquette in Îlot 6.

renovation, he observed, "More than 100,000 people cannot continue to live in such conditions (figures 161, 162, and 163).[38] It was noted, however, that tuberculosis mortality, which had initially characterized the *îlots insalubres,* had ceased to be a problem. In the years following the Second World War, vaccination and improved methods of treatment had caused the virtual disappearance of the disease, not only in Paris as a whole, where the mortality between 1946 and 1952 had dropped to .49 per thousand, but also in the *îlots,* where the rate for the same period was .72. It was decided to take other factors into account in the definition of slum areas, including overcrowding, dilapidation, lack of services, and excessive ground coverage.

The antiquated housing structure of Paris, which had been far from adequate before the war, was subject to unprecedented pressures as the population of the region mounted. Although the redevelopment of the fortifications had been undertaken before the war and an energetic program for clearing the *zone* pursued during the occupation, shack colonies were by no means a thing of the past.

38. Bernard Lafay, *Problèmes de Paris* (Paris: Conseil Municipal, 1954), p. 114

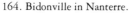
164. Bidonville in Nanterre.

165. Vitry sur Seine in the 1950s. Suburban houses with shanty dwellings in the foreground.

The most extensive of the shanty settlements by this time, however, were in the suburbs (figures 164 and 165). Such districts came to be called *bidonvilles,* the name deriving from the metal oil drums, or *bidons,* which were sometimes used to provide building material. Conspicuous among the slum dwellers of postwar Paris were large numbers of foreigners, especially North Africans. Victims of both poverty and prejudice, the dark-skinned immigrants became the most characteristic inhabitants in the *bidonvilles* and the worst *meublé* accommodations. A newspaper observed in 1972: "The most exploited, the least protected, those whom no one wants, but who are indispensable to the French economy—the immigrant workers—are also the worst housed."[39]

In 1966, in the Département de la Seine alone, a survey disclosed a total of 40,000 foreign workers and their families living in 89 *bidonvilles,* including 25,000 single people, 2,500 couples, and 9,500 children. Local governments were often hostile to the immigrants, and *Le Monde* observed in 1967 that "there have been, in the Parisian region, municipal councils which threatened to resign in a body because it was proposed that housing for foreign workers be constructed in the commune."[40]

39. *France Soir,* November 18, 1972.
40. *Le Monde,* February 15, 1967. Additional information regarding the *bidonvilles,* especially with regard to their social aspects, may be found in Monique Hervo and Marie-Ange Charras, *Bidonvilles* (Paris: Maspero, 1971) and Jean Labbens, *Le quart-monde–la pauvreté dans la société industrielle: Étude sur le sous-proletariat français dans la région parisienne* (Paris: Pierrelaye, 1969).

The large *bidonvilles* were subject to a program of gradual demolition, and by the end of 1972 they were officially declared to be nonexistent. It was noted, however, that a number of *mini-bidonvilles* continued to spring up.

Extensive publicity was given to the housing crisis in 1954 through the efforts of a priest, the Reverend Henri de Grouès, who called attention to the large numbers of people in Paris who were virtually without shelter. The unusually severe winter of 1953–54 dramatized the plight of those whose only protection was a flimsy tent or unheated shack, or who, lacking even this, spent their nights in the streets. One morning in February, following a bitterly cold night, a total of seventeen Parisians were found frozen to death. As an emergency measure, the city created a series of temporary shelters and also allowed certain Métro stations to be used as overnight refuges.[41]

The mid-1950s, when the postwar housing crisis appeared at its most acute, marked a turning point in Parisian building activity. With the economy recovering, the pace of urban redevelopment accelerated, and between 1954 and 1974 the city was to evidence a high volume of new construction, including a large amount of housing. In the period between 1945 and 1950, housing occupied 51.1 percent of the floor area of Paris. By 1974 this had increased to 71.2 percent. The evolution of housing stock between 1954 and 1974 had involved the demolition of 60,000 dwelling units and the construction of 269,400 new units, a gain of 209,400 units, with a yearly average of 10,400 new dwellings. The new dwellings, moreover, were larger than the old, and for each 100 square meters of dwelling space destroyed, 740 square meters of new dwelling space were created, thus providing a substantial increase in overall floor area. Dwelling units now averaged 59 square meters instead of 36 square meters. By 1974 approximately one dwelling in five in Paris was less than twenty years old.

Meanwhile, as housing stock increased, the residential population diminished by 9 percent, providing an increase in dwelling space per inhabitant from 29 square meters to 38 square meters. Thus overall housing conditions in terms of age and size of dwelling might be seen to be improving. Such improvements, however, were accompanied by a social transformation within the city, reflecting an accelerated migration of working-class population to the suburbs. Of the housing constructed between 1954 and 1974, 77 percent of the dwelling units and 79 percent of the floor space represented relatively expensive private building. Subsidized government-sponsored housing accounted for only 22 percent of the dwellings and 21 percent of newly constructed floor space.[42] HLM housing by this time reflected improvements

41. The Reverend Henri de Grouès adopted the name Abbé Pierre while a member of the French underground during the German occupation, and he is still popularly known by that name. Accounts of his activities may be found in Boris Simon, *Abbé Pierre and the Ragpickers of Emmaus* (New York: P. J. Kennedy, 1955), and *Ragman's City* (New York: Coward-McCann, 1957).

42. The statistics are from *20 Ans de Transformations de Paris, 1954–1974* (Paris: Ville de Paris, 1974). This summary of urban development was prepared by the Association Universitaire de Recherches Géographiques et

166. Wall poster in a neighborhood undergoing renovation: Tenants are urged to unite against eviction.

in both equipment and space standards, and in fact public housing was only slightly inferior in space per unit to private housing. (This was in part because a large amount of new "luxury" housing took the form of studio apartments.) The quantity of public housing, however, was far below needs. Between 1947 and 1962, the HLM office had built 16,258 new dwelling units, during which time 40,000 families with housing priority had requested accommodation. In 1961 2,500 units were constructed, for which there were 14,705 applications.[43]

As population expanded during the postwar years, it became increasingly difficult for people with modest means to find housing inside Paris. The city was densely built, and sites for new construction were few. The economic boom had prompted increasing demands for office space, and business enterprises began to move into many buildings previously used for residence. Property values and rents, always high in Paris, soared even higher, and former servants' rooms were often occupied by middle-class tenants. It became profitable for developers to purchase old buildings for renovation, evicting the tenants and replacing what were often small, dilapidated, but inexpensive dwellings with luxury apartments or offices. The tragedy of eviction began to provide a recurrent theme in the Parisian press, with human-interest stories frequently involving elderly people forced out of homes in which they had been long-time residents (figure 166).

Cartographiques. The accompanying text is by Jean Bastié. The study revealed that in spite of the improvements in Parisian housing standards, in 1974 45 percent of all dwellings were without a toilet, 37 percent without a bathroom, and only two dwellings out of five had more than two rooms.

43. Statistical information from Bertrand, *Le confort des logements*, pp. 46–47.

In some instances the transformation of old buildings was linked to government-sponsored programs of preservation and restoration. A conspicuous example was the historic district of the Marais, which was rapidly regaining its fashionable cachet and undergoing a social as well as a physical renovation. In addition to the alteration of housing stock which accompanied the renovation of historic districts, there were also government-directed programs of urban renewal, involving the total demolition and reconstruction of large areas. In some cases the removal of an old *îlot insalubre* would be involved, while in others the program would be justified as an effort to revitalize a decaying district. New construction generally involved relatively expensive housing or commercial space. Thus both economic forces and government planning policies produced a reduction in the amount of low-cost housing in Paris and served to promote the working-class exodus.

In general, those hardest hit by the housing shortage were young families, and it is this group that made up the bulk of the growing suburban population. Although the city of Paris and the suburban region were more or less equal in population in 1931, the balance was to shift dramatically in the postwar period. By 1970 the population of Paris was reduced to 2,600,000, while that of the suburbs had reached 5,600,000. Between 1968 and 1975, the city lost 500,000 people, and in the First Arrondissement, a center for renovation, the population was reduced by 33 percent.

The Grands Ensembles

To Parisian officials, the suburbs appeared a logical site for new large-scale housing. Land was cheaper and more readily available than within the city, and a movement of population outward had long been a trend. Stimulated by the urgency of the housing crisis in the 1950s, government policy began to encourage and promote the rapid construction of suburban apartment projects, and as financing systems were perfected, the building industry developed increasingly standardized methods of construction applicable to multiple-unit buildings. Transportation policies acknowledged the growing volume of large-scale commuting through expanded highway construction and an extended suburban rail system, the Réseau Express Régional.

The pattern of housing established during the 1950s was characterized by the *grand ensemble,* a term officially used to describe a project containing from 8,000 to 10,000 dwelling units and a population of 30,000 to 40,000. The design of the *grands ensembles* often combined towers and high-rise slabs with five- or six-story buildings, usually including some park space, together with schools and shopping facilities (figures 167 and 168). While some projects were largely middle-class, the *grands ensembles* characteristically encompassed subsidized low-cost housing. So rapid was their growth that by 1969 it was estimated that one person in six in the Paris region lived in a *grand ensemble.*

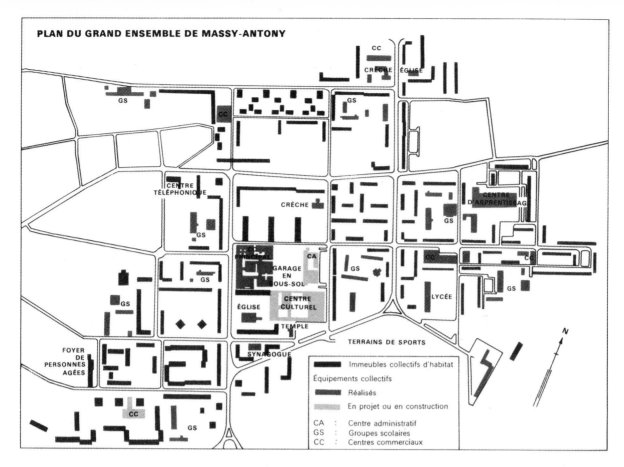

PLAN DU GRAND ENSEMBLE DE MASSY-ANTONY

Legend:
■ Immeubles collectifs d'habitat
Équipements collectifs
■ Réalisés
▨ En projet ou en construction
CA : Centre administratif
GS : Groupes scolaires
CC : Centres commerciaux

167, 168. The *grand ensemble* of Massy-Antony. Planned for 40,000 people, it is located south of Paris and includes part of the communes of Massy, in Essonne, and Antony, in Hauts de Seine.

The building pattern of the *grands ensembles* differed from the pattern of most earlier suburban housing in that it related to automobile rather than exclusively to rail transport. Older settlements of necessity followed the rail lines; the *grands ensembles* tended to fill in the spaces between the existing tracts of small single-family houses.

Although the Parisian concept of commuting is similar to that of many North American cities, the architectural components of the urban region seem virtually reversed. The North American suburbanite generally lives in a single-family house and travels to the city, where he is likely to work in a modern skyscraper. The Parisian suburbanite is likely to live in a modern high-rise building and may commute to the city to work in an eighteenth-century mansion or renovated nineteenth-century dwelling. Common to both is an increasing need to travel by car for shopping and other daily needs. A phenomenon of recent years has been the appearance around Paris of suburban shopping centers whose mammoth parking lots are indistinguishable from their American counterparts.

As the *grands ensembles* became increasingly dominant in the Paris region, they provided a source of continuing controversy. They were a visible manifestation of the population explosion; the size of the complexes was often overwhelming and the architecture monotonous. It was easy to interpret the *grands ensembles* as a distillation of the worst of modern urban life—to recoil from an environment that seemed to bespeak regimentation and inhuman scale (figure 169).

Although it was unlikely that æsthetes would ever become reconciled to the *grands ensembles,* their inhabitants often appeared to take a relatively sanguine view of their surroundings. In an opinion survey made within the *grands ensembles* and published in 1967, it was found that of those questioned 51 percent believed the

169. Apartment buildings in a *grand ensemble.*

construction of *grands ensembles* to be generally a good thing, and 61 percent claimed that the advantages of living in such complexes overrode the disadvantages. When asked to rate their conditions of housing, 14 percent rated it "very satisfactory," 40 percent "satisfactory," and 34 percent "acceptable." Thus 88 percent of the respondents considered their dwellings acceptable or better. When asked to list the advantages of their housing, 23 percent made specific reference to the qualities of the site—to the fresh air and countryside, while the apartment itself was cited by 23 percent. Most respondents considered themselves better housed than they had been previously with regard to comfort, light and air, and size and number of rooms.[44]

If the *grands ensembles* represented a problem, as some believed, they were a problem of prosperity. While they were often viewed as a blight on the countryside and as a mechanical and unimaginative method of providing housing, they reflected a relatively high living standard and a period of booming economic development. Their inhabitants embodied a working class which has been termed the "affluent poor."

A literary view of life within a *grand ensemble* can be found in Christianne Rochfort's novel *Les petits enfants du siècle*, published in 1961. Although fictional, this popular book soon achieved the status of a social document. The story takes the form of a first-person narrative by a young girl, Josyane, the eldest child of a large working-class family, whose utterances reflect a somewhat cool and mocking view of proletarian life. The reader is introduced to a life-style inspired by a system of government family allowances, in which breeding is closely allied to material progress. In one episode a pregnant woman pats her belly, exclaiming, "This one is my refrigerator," and adding, "I'll keep going till I get a washing machine."[45]

Viewing the uniform building facades of the *grand ensemble* in which she lives, Josyane muses on the equally uniform lives of the inhabitants. "At night the windows would light up and inside there were only happy families, happy families, happy families. Going by you could see them beneath the ceiling bulbs, through the big windows. One happiness after another, all alike as twins, or a nightmare. The happinesses facing west could look out of their houses and see the happinesses that faced east as if they were seeing themselves in a mirror. Eating noodles from the co-op. Happinesses heaped one on top of the other, I could have figured out the volume in cubic feet or in yards or in barrels. . . . The wind blew over the Avron plateau, it blew between the apartment buildings as in the Colorado canyons, which could never be such a wilderness. Instead of coyotes at nightfall, speakers howled the word on how everyone could have white teeth and shining hair, how everyone could be beautiful, clean, healthy and happy."[46]

44. Paul Clerc, *Grands ensembles, banlieues nouvelles: Enquête démographique et psycho-sociologique* (Paris: Presses Universitaires de France, 1967), pp. 187–201.

45. Christianne Rochfort, *Les petits enfants du siècle*. This book appears in an English translation as *Children of Heaven* (New York: David McKay Co., 1962). The quotation is found in the English edition on p. 61.

46. Rochfort, *Children of Heaven*, pp. 58–59.

A notable exception to the dullness of most of the *grands ensembles* was found in the work of the architect Émile Aillaud. Within the restriction of low-cost construction, he attempted to create environments of humane scale and varied, imaginative design. The best known and most remarkable of Aillaud's *grands ensembles* was constructed between 1967 and 1970 on a site twenty-five kilometers south of Paris at Grigny and carried the name La Grande Borne (figure 170). The complex was designed for 15,000 inhabitants, with 3,479 low-cost units and 206 unsubsidized houses. The triangular site was bounded on one side by a motor freeway leading to Paris, but there was no rail connection.

A nearby radio station prevented the use of tower blocks and limited building height to not more than five stories. The building construction used standardized elements—a uniform load-bearing panel 2.7 meters square—and it employed three window types, a square window, a small door-window, and a large door-window. These elements were embodied in three basic building types: curving and rectilinear apartment blocks and single-story patio houses (figure 171).

Speaking of such large compositions as La Grande Borne, Aillaud stressed the need to develop a sense of intimate scale. He pointed out that "the principal aim of this new urbanism is to substitute for the eye of God who sees all and surveys the ensemble, the eye of a man who moves about within a city of which the total image always escapes him. . . . Make an urbanism to be walked in, not one to be viewed from above."[47]

The compositional intent in La Grande Borne was to create a series of small ensembles, each with a distinct character and sense of place, in the hope that inhabitants would achieve a strong sense of identity with their own dwellings and experience a visual richness and variety as they moved through the complex as a whole. The site was designed to exclude vehicles. Parking was provided at the periphery, permitting interior motor circulation only for temporary service, and the maximum walking distance from dwelling to automobile parking was calculated at 150 meters. The restriction of the area to pedestrian circulation was a major factor in permitting the creation of intimate scale.

The aspects of La Grande Borne that attracted the most attention, in addition to the spatial variety of the composition, were the generous use of color on building facades and the imaginative distribution of art works throughout. The building panels were surfaced with small glass and ceramic tiles in a vivid range of hues. In addition to creating colorful walls, these tiles provided the tesserae for decorative mosaics varying widely in subject matter and including fanciful animals and landscapes as well as portraits of Rimbaud and Kafka (figure 172). Sculptural objects ranged from surrealistically overscaled fruit and giant pigeons to imaginative abstractions of human and animal forms (figure 173).

47. Gérald Cassio-Talabot and Alain Devy, *La grande borne* (Paris: Hachette, 1972), p. 37.

170. Grigny, La Grande Borne, shown under
construction. A motor expressway to Paris
is at left, bordered by a parking strip serving
the residents of the housing complex.

171. Housing in La Grande Borne.

172. Housing in La Grande Borne.

173. Housing and shops in La Grande Borne.

While La Grande Borne provided perhaps the most favorable image of the *grand ensemble,* the most notorious of these settlements was Sarcelles (figure 174). As the biggest and thus most conspicuous of the projects, Sarcelles soon came to stand for all the flaws, both physical and social, of the *grands ensembles.*

The name "Sarcelles" was borrowed from a nearby town, a settlement about twelve kilometers from the Porte de la Chapelle entrance into Paris. In 1954 a group of employees in the Paris Prefecture of Police formed a building society and located a tract of inexpensive land near Sarcelles which seemed suitable for their purposes. In order to obtain government financial assistance for their housing project, they approached the Caisse des Dépôts et Consignations. The director of this organization was at that moment urgently seeking suitable sites for new housing, and he quickly realized that the police employees had discovered what seemed to be the largest available tract of unbuilt land in the vicinity of Paris. The site was both cheap and conveniently located; it had a major highway on one side and a rail line on the other, connecting with the Gare du Nord. Although the police housing was included in Sarcelles, it was destined to be only a small part of a giant and rapidly growing settlement.

174. The *grand ensemble* of Sarcelles.

175. Sarcelles.

Although government sponsored, Sarcelles embodied a complex collaboration of private and governmental agencies. Most important of these, and serving as a supervisory and coordinating body, was the SCIC, the Société Centrale Immobilière de la Caisse des Dépôts. Construction began in 1959, the original plan calling for 850 units. By 1968 the census reported a population of 51,674, and 1973 estimates predicted a growth to at least 80,000 in the next ten years.

Sarcelles, with its overwhelming and constantly expanding array of new apartment buildings and its massive concentration of people, became a focus of continual criticism. A guide to new Paris architecture published in 1970 commented: "The ensemble of Sarcelles will be, for archæologists of the year 3000, a masterpiece of the disorder—cultural, political, architectural, and civic—of the postwar period. It is already serving as a lesson to the young architects, administrators, and politicians, so that they will never conceive of or commit such mistakes" (figure 175).[48]

Descriptive commentary deemed Sarcelles a "vertigo of technology," a "human silo," and a "termite heap." It was decried as "this dormitory city, this great barracks, this concentration camp where we are locked in rabbit cages," while the inhabitants were pitied as "guinea pigs thrust into one of the worst catastrophes our society has ever invented" (figures 176 and 177).[49]

48. I. Schein, *Paris construit* (Paris: Vincent, Fréal et Cie, 1970), p. 228.
49. Jean Duquesne, *Vivre à Sarcelles?* (Paris: Éditions Cujas, 1966), pp. 100–01.

176, 177. Apartment housing in Sarcelles.

As its physical immensity promoted a vision of nameless, faceless human hordes, Sarcelles became a symbol of the emptiness and depersonalization of modern life. Journalistic accounts made frequent reference to a malady called "la Sarcellite" which presumably afflicted the settlement's inhabitants. The symptoms of "Sarcellite" were especially to be found among young women. "How does Sarcellite begin? First the women cease to be interested in their housework. You visit them at five in the afternoon and the beds aren't made yet. From indifference they pass to disgust, from disgust to hatred. . . . The sick ones are conscious of their state, which doesn't help anything. 'I'm well housed, but when I go outside I can't stand it. This uniformity frightens me like a concentration camp.'. . . Sarcellite, total disenchantment, indifference to social life, insurmountable boredom, ending in nervous depression in benign cases, and suicide in acute cases."[50]

A description of Sarcelles, as it might have been viewed by an inhabitant of a more modest *grand ensemble,* appears in *Les petits enfants du siècle,* as Josyane catches her first glimpse of the settlement. "You get to Sarcelles over a bridge, and all of a sudden, from a little bit above you see the whole thing. Oh gosh! and I thought I lived in a development! This was Project, this was the real Project of the Future! Buildings and buildings and buildings for miles and miles and miles [figure 178]. All alike. In rows. White. And more buildings. Buildings buildings buildings buildings buildings

50. Ibid.

178. The Avenue du 8 Mai, the principal street of Sarcelles.

buildings buildings buildings buildings buildings. Buildings. Buildings. And sky—an enormous sky. Sun. The buildings filled with sun, shining through them, coming out the other side. Enormous Park Areas, clean, gorgeous carpets, each one with its sign saying Respect and encourage Respect for the Lawns and Trees, which incidentally seemed to make more of an impression here than where we lived; people themselves were probably making progress along with architecture."[51]

Reflecting on life in Sarcelles, Josyane concludes, "A person could do no evil here; any kid who played hooky, they would spot him right off, the only one his age outside at the wrong time; a robber would show from miles away with the loot; anybody dirty, people would send him off to wash."[52]

Sarcelles clearly came to exist both as reality and as myth. The myth, as might be expected, exaggerated and embroidered the reality, and the term "Sarcelles" came to symbolize the concept of the *grand ensemble* as such. People who had never themselves visited the complex often considered Sarcelles the exemplar of

51. Rochfort, *Children of Heaven*, pp. 91–92.
52. Ibid., p. 92.

everything deplorable in modern Paris. In spite of the highly dramatized journalistic accounts, however, Sarcelles seems to present no unique or spectacular social problems. Its inhabitants have generally been ordinary working-class citizens, no better or worse than their counterparts still inhabiting picturesque cellars and attics in historically significant slums.

The aversion with which the *grands ensembles* were often regarded went deeper than a simple dislike of large buildings. The *grands ensembles* represented the failure of an idea. Although the design quality varied, these projects embodied certain concepts of the *cités jardins* of the 1920s and 1930s. At a time when suburban slums frequently consisted of flimsy shacks on tiny plots of land, large, comprehensively planned apartment projects, solidly built and equipped with modern utilities, seemed a welcome solution to the housing problem. When the decision was made to base the design of the *cités jardins* on apartment housing, including the use of tower blocks, as in Châtenay-Malabry and the Cité de la Muette at Drancy, the pattern was being initiated for the postwar *grands ensembles*. The difference in conception was essentially one of scale. Humanitarian intellectuals had admired the *cités jardins* constructed between the wars, yet when confronted with the *grands ensembles* spoke of dehumanization, concentration camps, and alienation.

Some of the faults of the *grands ensembles* were faults of planning. Often projects were erected without sufficient regard to proximity of employment and transportation. A project might lack adequate schools, shops, or recreational facilities. Other weaknesses might lie in the physical design of the ensemble: the architecture might be drab and monotonous, open spaces badly conceived, and construction and maintenance poor. Yet even with such faults corrected, with every project well located, amply provided with amenities, and graced with distinguished architecture, the *grands ensembles* would still be big. They daily obliterated more and more of the existing countryside, towering over the pavilions of the older suburbs and pushing the urbanized edge of the city farther and farther from the historic core.

As the *grands ensembles* drew increasing criticism, a certain tolerance developed among housing officials for the single-family dwelling (figures 179 and 180). In the period between the wars, the sprawling suburban tracts had drawn the scorn of many planners and architects. At worst, such developments had been slums, haphazardly constructed and lacking adequate services; at best, even with decent houses and standard urban amenities, they were often deplored for their banality of design. Most modern urbanists had remained convinced that the single-family house had little place in the contemporary city. In the period following the Second World War, moreover, the urbanistic results of the uncontrolled proliferation of detached houses in the United States tended to reconfirm the preference of French planners for collective housing.

It was a predilection not necessarily shared by the public, however. In 1906 a French housing reformer stated that "in France, everyone wants to have his own

179, 180. Suburban houses south of Paris

house, and this sentiment is all the more intense as the moral and intellectual worth of the individual is elevated."[53] This highly intuitive opinion has, to a degree, been supported by opinion surveys.

Immediately after the war, in 1945, the Institut National d'Études Démographiques conducted a survey in which 72 percent of the respondents expressed a preference for the single-family dwelling, 28 percent indicating a willingness to add half an hour to the journey to work in order to obtain it. In Paris, however, the preference was expressed by only 56 percent.[54]

Succeeding inquiries were to reveal a continuing bias toward the individual house. In a survey made in the Paris region in 1964, when asked: "Would you prefer to live in an apartment building not too far from the center of greater Paris, or in a house far from the center?", 68 percent of the respondents replied that they would prefer the house. It was concluded that the preferences of the inhabitants of the Paris region were decidedly oriented toward "a city à l'Américaine. Individual houses, widely dispersed in an urbanized zone which will stretch as far as Chartres, Mantes, Senlis, ... with a belt of apartments in the inner suburbs, and, naturally, ample communication facilities. This extension of the agglomeration over a considerable area appears as 'conceivable' to two-thirds, and 'reasonable' to half of the population of the region; 41 percent find this prospect 'agreeable.' " Among those who found the idea of an extended low-density city "agreeable," 33 percent indicated that it was because they believed "in modernism, in science, in progress," while an additional 33 percent believed that "the agglomeration would become dispersed, which will permit better living."[55]

Government housing policies had, of course, centered on the creation of the *grands ensembles,* and a survey conducted in these complexes, published in 1967, indicated that the inhabitants considered their housing to be generally acceptable. When the same survey, however, asked the question: "Supposing that the cost of housing were the same, would you prefer to live in an apartment or in a single-family house?", 82 percent stated a preference for the house.[56] In 1970 a government survey indicated that in the Paris region 24 percent of the respondents would consider no other type of housing but a house, and in a study of young families, 45 percent insisted that it was the only type of dwelling they wanted. There was apparently also a strong preference for an individually designed house, and 53 percent of a survey group said that they would prefer this type of dwelling even if it cost 50 percent more than a standardized tract house. The report concluded: "It

53. Ferrand, *Habitation à bon marché,* p. 1.
54. A. Suquet-Bonnaud, "L'habitation," *Urbanisme,* no. 2, April 1947, pp. 251–56.
55. "Les Enquêtes d'Opinion et les Problèmes d'Urbanisme," *La vie urbaine,* April–June 1964, pp. 92–93.
56. Clerc, *Grands ensembles,* pp. 189, 387–89.

seems, indeed, that the individual house corresponds with the deep desires of the French with regard to housing."[57]

Although the French had shown a desire for individual houses, it could also be observed that the production of this type of dwelling was particularly low in France. A United Nations survey in 1961 indicated that 78 percent of the dwellings built in Great Britain were single-family houses, 76 percent in the United States, 70 percent in Belgium, 56 percent in Holland, and 49 percent in West Germany. The figure for France for the same year was 32 percent (based on requests for building permits, rather than completed houses).[58] In the Paris region single-family houses accounted for only 20.3 percent of all housing and for 20.2 percent of the dwellings completed between 1949 and 1968.[59]

57. Institut d'Aménagement et d'Urbanisme de la Région Parisienne (IAURP), *L'habitat individuel en région parisienne*, December 1970, p. 26. Opponents of single-family housing have often questioned the results of opinion surveys, claiming that responses are based on a biased phrasing of the questions. Although the house represents an ideal, it is claimed, many people who say they want one do not fully understand the problems of home ownership. A presentation of this point of view may be found in Michel Ragon, *Les erreurs monumentales* (Paris: Hachette, pp. 73–77).
58. "Maisons individuelles et logements collectifs," *La vie urbaine*, no. 3, July–September 1963.
59. IAURP, *L'habitat individuel*.

181. Suburban house. The construction is usually of concrete blocks or hollow bricks, with a surface finish of stucco. A pitched roof is preferred, generally covered with tile.

Individual houses in the Paris region were notably expensive. Land values, financing charges, and the high cost of building materials and construction made this form of housing a luxury only a few could afford. The building industry was geared to large-scale apartment construction, and modernized techniques and industrialized production were not applied to single-family dwellings, for which preferences had generally favored both traditional styling and masonry construction (figure 181). A government report considering the question of house costs remarked on the lightness of construction common in some other countries, and it stated that in order to make individual houses more easily obtainable the French would need to change their attitudes, to consider the house as "a consumer item."[60]

In 1964 the District of Paris sponsored two competitions for the design of single-family houses, based on the conception of large-scale groupings. One embodied an ensemble of two hundred dwellings, and the other one thousand units accompanied by shopping and other community facilities. Similarly, in 1969 the Ministère de l'Équipement et du Logement promoted a housing exhibition called "Villagexpo," constructed in Saint Michel sur Orge, south of Paris. It consisted of various models of single-family houses embodying attempts at industrialized construction and had as its purpose "to acquaint the public with the possibilities of living in an individual house at a price accessible to all."[61]

The feasibility of individual houses was increased by the political unification of the Paris region in 1964, and the development of a regional plan which included the creation of a series of outlying urban centers. In the new poles of development, which were intended to include centers of employment, a pattern of relatively low density could be established (figures 182 and 183). Describing a housing ensemble begun in 1968 near the town of Trappes, a critic stated that the composition, based on single-family row houses, represented "a new stage in the development of a recent style of urbanism, which we have called 'Provincial Urbanism.'" The design embodied traditional style and picturesque groupings similar to those that had governed the earliest *cités jardins,* an image which "differs profoundly from the conceptions which have governed urban development in the last twenty years," and which could be criticized as "a return to the past." The single-family house, it was maintained, was justified not by "arbitrary æsthetic considerations, but by psychology and even biology, and an understanding of the desires of the people for whom it is destined." As to the *grands ensembles,* it had to be remembered that "they are not to everyone's taste; it should also be remembered, contrary to what is sometimes claimed, that this system of urbanism 'en domino' is less the inevitable result of financial, technical, or economic restraints than the expression of a fashion and the manifestation of the æsthetic conceptions of certain professionals."[62]

60. Ibid.
61. La Documentation Française, *Logement et urbanisme en France*, dossier 5–298 (Paris: 1969), p. 37.
62. Jacques Riboud, "Un mode d'urbanisme nouveau," *Urbanisme*, no. 106, 1966, pp. 35–36.

182. Single-family houses in the new town of Saint Quentin en Yvelines.

183. Single-family houses in the new town of Cergy-Pontoise.

A French urbanist once observed that "two life-styles are juxtaposed in France: the Mediterranean type lives willingly outside his dwelling, in the street; the Germanic type loves his home, where he is obliged to remain because of the dampness and cold of the climate." Paris, as the "crossroads of all the provinces,"[63] was seen to embody both temperaments. Certainly the Parisian climate is Germanic, yet the most pervasive image of Parisian life has been essentially Mediterranean. One need never have set foot in Paris to bring this to mind; it has become part of popular mythology. One imagines a relatively self-contained working-class quarter. One pictures a street in early evening, animated with shoppers, strollers, and peddlers. People stop and greet one another, laughing and joking. The cafés are filling up, and workers, still in their blues, are standing at the bar exchanging cheerful badinage with the friendly bartender. Someone is playing an accordion. Inside the many small shops, the proprietors, who know their clientele intimately, join in the gossip. Everyone seems to know everyone else in the quarter; the neighborhood is like a village, a family. Of course it is also a slum, and housing conditions are very bad. But perhaps the definition of housing is too narrow if it is applied only to an individual dwelling unit. If one expands the concept of home to include not merely a private place, walled-in and occupied by a single family or individual, but the total physical and social environment in which one passes one's life, then many slum neighborhoods may be seen to have provided a well-loved home for their inhabitants. For the popular image of the Parisian quarter is not entirely the product of sentimental fiction and films. Such neighborhoods exist and have long provided a measure of social compensation for the physical inconveniences of overcrowded, dilapidated, and badly serviced dwellings. The rapid redevelopment of contemporary Paris has embodied a social transformation fully as drastic as the physical renovation, and as many slum districts are cleared, a certain type of neighborhood life may be headed for extinction.

An extensive account of the wide-ranging social effects of slum clearance may be found in a study by Henri Coing of the renovation of Îlot 4, a working-class neighborhood near the Place d'Italie in the Thirteenth Arrondissement, which had been designated part of a redevelopment area. In contrast to certain run-down districts, in which ancient mansions had deteriorated into slums, Îlot 4 had been from the beginning a dingy, lower-class neighborhood, notably lacking in picturesqueness or remnants of faded grandeur (figure 184). Four buildings out of seven had been constructed between the Commune and the First World War, "a time of rapid and disorderly building."[64] Observing the quarter in the 1960s, a visitor was

---

63. Bertrand, *Le confort des logements*, p. 273.

64. Henri Coing, *Rénovation urbaine et changement social* (Paris: Éditions Ouvrières, 1966.) All subsequent quotations in this chapter are from pp. 31–79 of this work, unless otherwise indicated.

184. Îlot 4 prior to redevelopment. View from number 135 Rue du Château des Rentiers.

"immediately struck by the dilapidated aspect of the Îlot," noting that "the leprous exteriors . . . augur badly for the interior comfort of the buildings." A 1954 survey disclosed that 46 percent of the units consisted of only one room, and 12 percent of two rooms. With regard to utilities, it was found that 9.7 percent of the dwellings were without electricity, 50 percent had no water, 86 percent no toilet, and 98 percent no bath or shower. Housing was characterized by "narrow windows giving on to dark walls, moisture dripping from the walls, filthy, shaky staircases, and lack of sound insulation."

Adding to the problems of defective building were the conditions of chronic overcrowding in which most of the district's inhabitants lived. Sizable families, often including three generations, might live in a single room, with the inevitable physical and psychological tensions. The poorest housed inhabitants were the North Africans, most of whom lived in cheap hotels. Here the room sizes would be minuscule, and investigations of overcrowding disclosed such cases as eight people in a room of fourteen square meters and six people in a space of eight square meters. In view of the prevailing conditions, it was not surprising that the city government would designate Îlot 4 for clearance. In 1956 the Municipal Council approved the directing principles for renovating the Îlot, and between 1958 and 1960 the first relodging of the inhabitants was begun.

While the process of renovation was underway, a study was made of the attitudes of the inhabitants of Îlot 4 toward the transformation of their old neighborhood. It appeared that, in spite of the poor housing conditions of the district, many residents felt a deep attachment to the area. The proximity of employment in or near the Thirteenth Arrondissement, together with the abundance of neighborhood commerce, made the district relatively self-contained, and many of the inhabitants seldom visited other parts of Paris. One young resident reported: "For me, France is the Thirteenth Arrondissement; it's my corner, it's my fief." To some, leaving the quarter was "going to Paris," and it was remarked with regard to those who sought amusement in other parts of the city, "You don't have to expatriate yourself to see a film." It was found that one family employed in the district did not ordinarily cross to the other side of the Seine more than once or twice a year, and an aging man commented: "Paris? Oh, you know, I don't travel very much; I've worked all my life; Sundays I took care of the house: I don't know what a vacation is; my life, it's the quarter." According to a woman of thirty, "To leave the quarter, for me, it's like someone who has to leave his country."

Although the neighborhood had received its share of recent immigrants, it was generally characterized by strong social stability. One resident noted: "In our building, everyone knows everyone else. For us, it's a relationship of two or three years, but many have always known each other, they went through the war together, they are tied together by long-lived friendship. . . . I can speak to them about anyone, and they know him, they know where he came from, they know everything about him." A forty-year-old worker observed, "All my schoolmates are still here; we were raised together, we have the same friends, the same amusements."

The relative social uniformity of Îlot 4, with its heavy concentration of manual workers, was undoubtedly a factor in its strong social cohesion. Newcomers of the same social class as the older inhabitants seemed to fit in easily, and it was observed that "here, wherever you come from, you are accepted, you are adopted." The vocabulary of the family was frequently employed to describe human relations in a neighborhood where people were "like brothers and sisters."

Living in close quarters made it necessary for neighbors to maintain good relations. According to many of the district's inhabitants, however, neighborly assistance often went far beyond the minimum. "In case of trouble, our building becomes a real community: I really saw this when my father died, and when my wife was confined; . . . everyone did his best, even those of whom you wouldn't have expected it." Relations among housewives became particularly intimate, with the common courtyard becoming a place of frequent encounter (figure 185). Naturally, with shared toilets and water taps, with windows closely overlooking neighbors, with children playing together in the court, frequent meetings were inevitable. Even the hotels, for all their crowding and squalor, seemed to engender a certain affection on the part of their residents. A taxi driver noted of his hotel: "It's sympathetic here

185. Courtyard in Îlot 4.

because it's familiar; I know everybody, I have friends; no problems, no thefts (I don't even lock my door)—we often drink a glass together; we live squeezed on top of each other, it encourages relationships."

In spite of the bad condition of the buildings, many residents bitterly regretted the demolitions. A fifty-five-year-old worker stated: "It makes me feel terrible that they're tearing down my building. Because of living there, I have almost the feeling of being the owner. It would make be furious to see them touch it." One could frequently hear in the cafés such remarks as: "Why tear down all this? It was beautiful before, our Rue Nationale."

It was the Rue Nationale, the principal commercial street, which, with its shops and cafés, provided much of the social animation of the district (figure 186). The scene became particularly lively in the evenings, and also on Saturdays, when the sidewalks were filled with peddlers and the street itself taken over by pedestrians.

For the women of the quarter, daily shopping provided a major social event. A young housewife indicated: "For me, shopping is an agreeable time, a relaxation. I make it last two hours, for I'm in no hurry to get back home." Another woman reported, "I spend a lot of time making my purchases; I always meet someone I know; I hold a real reception in the street."

The shopkeepers themselves provided an important part of the social fabric of the quarter. Intimately acquainted with most of their customers, they habitually extended credit and sought to satisfy individual requirements. At the same time, the customers maintained strong loyalty to their customary merchants, seldom even asking the prices of items before a purchase was made. The personal nature of the transaction was highly valued, and a shopper commented, "Here they know you, you are considered."

186. The Rue Nationale.

187. Café on the Rue Harvey, Îlot 4.

Although social life was heavily dependent on street encounters, the primary social center of the quarter was the café (figure 187). For the inhabitants of Îlot 4, as for other slum dwellers, the café provided a salon and a club, an escape from tiny and overcrowded dwellings. Without the safety valve of the café, life in the quarter might well have been insupportable, and the Îlot contained one café for every 130 people. (In 1923 it had been one for every 94 people.) In contrast to the other commercial enterprises, which served the quarter as a whole, each café tended to attract a habitual clientele. The café owner might be seen as a host, entertaining a selected group of guests, and his personality was an important element in creating the atmosphere. Certain cafés provided rendezvous for specific ethnic groups. There were, for example, fourteen cafés that catered to Algerians, where the jukebox played only Arab music. Other cafés would provide a center for the Italians or Bretons. Some cafés drew their clients primarily from specific groups of workers. The twenty employees of a printing plant ate lunch in the same café every day, while the deliverymen from department stores patronized two restaurants on the Place Nationale. Certain cafés would attract adolescents, while others would be patronized primarily by middle-aged or elderly residents. In addition to providing an informal gathering place, the café might serve as headquarters for local organizations. Included in the groups that met in the cafés of Îlot 4 were a cell of the Communist party and certain trade unions.

In examining Îlot 4, a social investigator concluded that "if the population is so attached to this disinherited quarter, it is because they have found a truly human way of living in an inhuman place." In spite of its poor housing conditions, the district embodied a balanced environment, providing for a variety of needs in a reasonably satisfactory way. Praising the integrated totality of the neighborhood, a resident remarked, "I like this quarter . . . you're at home everywhere; there's no barrier between the street, the factory, the house; you go from one to the other *without changing your personality.*"

As demolitions began, many of the residents experienced a sense of helplessness before the powers of the government. None had been unaware of the faults of the district, yet few regarded the passing of the old neighborhood with anything but regret (figures 188 and 189).

The government renovation program gave the dislodged inhabitants of Îlot 4 priority rights in obtaining apartments in the new high-rise buildings slated for the site. In addition, residents who did not wish to move into the new buildings could arrange housing exchanges. Under this system, a resident could transfer his housing rights to someone else and in exchange occupy this person's apartment. In this way, someone who felt he could not afford the new apartments might obtain cheaper housing by taking over an old apartment belonging to someone who wanted to move into a new, more expensive dwelling. Many of the residents, however, simply moved away, presumably finding new housing without government assistance. As the renovation of Îlot 4 formed part of large-scale redevelopment near the Place d'Italie, low-cost replacement housing was virtually impossible to find in the vicinity. Many of those who left the Îlot, therefore, moved out to the suburbs.

Among those who remained in Îlot 4 and came to occupy the new apartments, reactions varied as to the advantages of the change. Some found that their standards rose to match the new facilities, while others considered the new space, comfort, and convenience as waste and extravagance. After years of sharing toilets and water taps, cooking on makeshift equipment, and patronizing the municipal baths, many begrudged the added expenditure necessary to pay for private baths, toilets, central heating, and modern kitchens. In addition to the higher rents, the new apartments necessitated heavy expenditures on furnishings. One suddenly needed curtains, rugs, chairs, sofas, and lamps. Many families had previously lived in minimal quarters, paying a very low rent and spending much of the day outside in the streets, the cafés, and the cinemas. Now, for the first time, these families were compelled to spend a large part of their income on housing, and, unable to afford outside amusements, they found themselves increasingly confined to home and television. Thus the "Mediterranean" life of the street was supplanted by the "Germanic" life of the foyer.

Just as the nature of housing in Îlot 4 was altered through redevelopment, so commerce was transformed. The old Rue Nationale, with its multitude of small

188. Îlot 4 after redevelopment. In
the foreground is the intersection of the
Rue du Château des Rentiers and the
Rue Nationale.

189. Intersection of the Rue du
Château des Rentiers and the Rue
Nationale.

shops, was completely demolished, and new shopping areas were designed to provide for fewer and larger establishments (figure 190). In place of the forty-eight cafés, the new plan provided for one. Ten bakeries were to be replaced by two, twenty-six butcher shops by eight, and twenty-nine general grocery stores by five. The old intimate shop was clearly intended to give way to the *supermarché*.

As the area around the Place d'Italie underwent increasing alteration, it was subject to a social transformation. Before the renovations, a resident of Îlot 4 had commented: "It's curious, when people speak of the Thirteenth they look down their noses, but those who live there don't want to leave." With the old slums disappearing, however, and a growing volume of new apartment construction, the Thirteenth Arrondissement was becoming an acceptable address, and the area of redevelopment received a sizable influx of middle-class residents (figure 191). No longer a predominantly working-class district, the renovated quarter came to reflect an occupational pattern similar to that of Paris as a whole.

190. The Rue Nationale after redevelopment.

191. Middle-class apartments in the Place d'Italie redevelopment area.

In the course of its social evolution, the district lost its old insularity. Instead of working in nearby factories, many of the residents commuted to the center and sought recreation in the city as a whole. Feeling equally at home anywhere in modern Paris, the new inhabitants of Îlot 4 were not dependent on the social warmth of a self-contained, homogeneous neighborhood. Automobile ownership made it easy to leave the city altogether on weekends, and for many even the attractions of Paris could not compete with the quiet and isolation of a *maison secondaire* in the country.

The social focus of the neighborhood, which had been like a family, had in a manner of speaking both expanded and contracted. Its inhabitants were now citizens of greater Paris. At the same time the closely knit intimacy of the quarter had given way to the even tighter intimacy of the nuclear family.

This seems to have been what the housing reformers had always wanted. It had often been maintained that poor housing was detrimental to working-class family life. Yet there had apparently been no recognition of the social value of the family-like neighborhood. The café had been viewed as a center of sedition, and the street as a theater of immorality. The motivation for housing reform had been the image of mother, father, and children, snug behind closed doors, keeping themselves to themselves, thank you, and supporting a social order dedicated to the perpetuation of families securely and comfortably walled in. The image is not altogether unappealing, and certainly few would advocate the perpetuation of slums on the grounds that they engender animated street life. Many of those interviewed by Coing viewed the changes in Îlot 4 as inescapable manifestations of modern life, resignedly reflecting that "old Paris is finished."

As residential population, especially working-class population, has continued to leave Paris, a certain deadness is observed in many quarters. As a result, the image of the traditional neighborhood has gained in appeal as the reality disappears. Beginning in 1961, an industrial working-class quarter bordering the Seine in the Fifteenth Arrondissement was demolished and transformed into an expensive district of high-rise offices, hotels, and apartments. Curiously, the advertising for this new quarter often stressed, not its modernity and luxury, but its purported friendliness and intimacy. Potential occupants of the skyscraper apartment buildings, presumably among the most affluent citizens of Paris, were assured in an advertisement published in 1976 that "in the towers, a social life is often created. People greet each other, they recognize each other, they issue invitations, they meet again." The olympic swimming pool was described as a place where "you meet your neighbors," and the variety of commerce was stressed. Even within the costly confines of the ensemble, one would reportedly find "little bistros where the chef will talk to you himself about the menu."[65] Thus a way of life which, for the poor, seemed in the process of dissolution, might presumably be perpetuated by the rich.

65. Advertisement, *Le Monde*, winter of 1976.

6 THE CITY: PLANS AND PROJECTS

In the years following Haussmann's retirement, controversy about the nature and extent of his planning efforts continued among urbanists. To some critics, the sweeping renovations he had directed appeared insensitive and excessive, the reflection of a megalomaniacal and authoritarian regime. Many would continue to maintain a nostalgic and romantic image of the old pre-Haussmann Paris. In the view of others, however, the weakness of Haussmann's work lay in its insufficient comprehensiveness, inasmuch as it had dealt only with alterations in the physical fabric of the city. As the concept of large-scale planning gained acceptance among urbanists, Haussmann's vision was criticized as too limited. He had not developed a thoroughgoing regional plan, nor had he shown an adequate awareness of the city as a social and economic totality. Some modern theorists would eventually become convinced that all aspects of urban evolution could be subjected to planning, and that a physical design should be developed only in relation to a long-range economic and social plan. Such views, however, reflected largely unattainable goals. With regard to the actual development of Paris, the program of Haussmann, limited as it may have been, would, as it continued, make more than sufficient demands on the resources of the city.

The 1913 report of the Commission d'Extension de Paris described the city at the time of Haussmann's retirement as "a vast *chantier* of demolitions momentarily abandoned, which it was necessary to continue. There were everywhere dead-end streets to open up, projections of boulevards to prolong, a chaos of obstacles to disperse, and pestilential lanes to demolish. The immense impetus given before 1870 has been continued through the uninterrupted effort of forty years, without, moreover, the end being near to attainment." The works carried out by the city in the period since Haussmann were seen to "depend on the same conceptions and, one could say, the same plan."[1]

1. Commission d'Extension de Paris, Préfecture du Département de la Seine. Vol. 2. *Considérations techniques* (Paris: Chaux, 1913), p. 37.

Although Parisian officials continued to be dominated by the vision of Haussmann, a strong interest in the broad aspects of urbanism began to develop in France in the years preceding the First World War. In 1907 the Musée Social in Paris established the Section d'Hygiène Sociale, dedicated to the study of urban legislation, and in 1911 a group from this section, most of them architects, created a new professional association called the Société Française des Urbanistes. The term, *urbanisme,* referring to the multifaceted study of cities and their rational planning, had come into use around 1910.

To promote higher standards of urban design, in 1915 the Musée Social sponsored the creation of the École d'Art Public, while at the Institut d'Histoire, de Géographie et d'Économie Urbaine de Paris, Marcel Poëte directed a comprehensive documentation of varying aspects of urbanism, including the evolution of cities, demography, and urban morphology. Poëte was also instrumental in establishing, in 1919, the École des Hautes Études Urbaines, which was attached to the University of Paris as the Institut d'Urbanisme in 1924. In terms of research, publication, conferences, exhibitions, and design competitions, Paris provided a major center for urban study and the dissemination of planning concepts. It is, perhaps, this plethora of theory which made many observers so impatient with the level of real accomplishment in the French capital.

As Paris grew from the walled city it had been in the era of the horse and the railroad into a metropolis in the age of the automobile and the airplane, governmental planning centered on piecemeal efforts involving street works, transportation, building controls, slum clearance, and public housing. Decision-making depended on a varied assemblage of government agencies, complicated by the division of authority between the city and the national government. Moreover, although the urbanized areas of Paris included the suburbs, there was until the 1960s no political unification of the city and its surroundings, and no effective organization for regional planning control.

In the years after Haussmann, the growth and development of Paris was determined in part by government policies, but also in part by economic forces and by that complex welter of private decisions which often defies analysis, but which, in the long run, may be the primary determinant of urban destiny. Whether or not present-day Paris would be a better city if it had at some point in the past one hundred years been comprehensively "planned" is not certain. While one can find numerous complaints about the timidity and indecisiveness of past Paris administrations, one can find an equal number of complaints regarding the all-too-visible achievements of more decisive recent administrations. Paris has been the canvas on which many urbanists have painted their dreams, and in surveying the multitude of proposals that have been made for the redevelopment of the city, one does not always regret that they remained unrealized.

In spite of limited opportunities for achievement, comprehensive planning

continued to be strongly advocated by many Parisian urbanists. When Eugène
Hénard produced his studies for the planning of Paris between 1903 and 1909, he
tended to concentrate his efforts on street circulation, building alignments, and open
space. He believed such provisions should, however, be related to larger
considerations. "It is necessary to imagine what the capital of France will be in a
hundred years and develop a program of works, to be executed in stages, which in
satisfying present needs will prepare also for the future."[2] Warning against
complacency, Hénard pointed out: "It is not enough, in effect, to cry 'Paris, the City
of Light!, the Queen City!', for Paris, by virtue of this proclamation alone, and
without further effort, will never remain the first city of the world."[3]

In addition to his concern with the street system, Hénard devoted part of his
study to a question that would be a continuing obsession of Parisian urbanists: the
provision of open space in a densely built city. It had long been recognized that the
parks of Paris, together with the landscaped boulevards, were essential to the beauty
of the capital (figure 192). In addition to their æsthetic function, moreover, areas of

2. Eugène Hénard, *Études sur les transformations de Paris. Fascicule 5: La percée du Palais Royal. La nouvelle
grande croisée de Paris* (Paris: Librairies-Imprimeries Réunies, 1904), p. 178.
3. Eugène Hénard, *Études sur les transformations de Paris. Fascicule 3: Les grands espaces libres. Les parcs et jardins
de Paris et Londres* (Paris: Librairies-Imprimeries Réunies, 1903), p. 61.

192. The Tuileries Gardens.

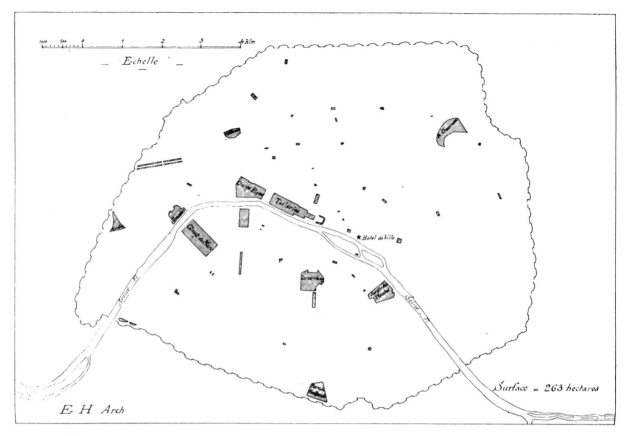

Echelle

Hôtel de Ville

Seine

Surface = 263 hectares

E. H. Arch.

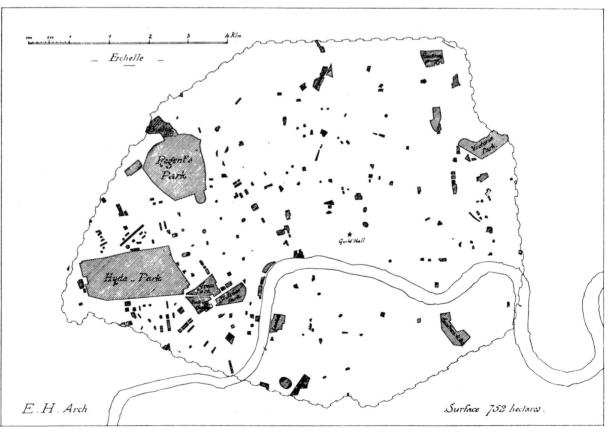

Echelle

Regent's Park

Victoria Park

Hyde Park

Guild Hall

Surface 752 hectares.

E. H. Arch.

greenery were considered important to urban hygiene, providing reservoirs of fresh air as well as space for outdoor recreation. As tuberculosis became linked to a lack of sunlight, the provision of parkland was seen as a major contribution to disease prevention. It was noted by many that, although Paris possessed some gardens of renowned beauty, the distribution of parkland throughout the city was unbalanced, and large districts had virtually no open space at all (figure 193). It was discovered, moreover, that in terms of hygiene park areas had a salutary effect only on their immediate borders. The river Seine, for example, provided a large reservoir of fresh air, yet some of the most pestilential quarters of the city could be found a block from its quays. In order to be beneficial in providing air and sunlight to the city, park areas needed to be created in an intimate relation to housing.

Contained in a study by Hénard in 1903 was the suggestion that a series of nine new parks be created within the city fabric, together with a number of small gardens. He established the goal that no inhabitant of Paris should be more than one kilometer from a large park, and no more than five hundred meters from a garden or square. Hénard had also been among those opposed to the decision of the Municipal Council to sell part of the Champ de Mars for building sites. Following the 1900 Exposition, the Champ de Mars had been left vacant and undeveloped, and as no large expositions were contemplated for the future, many officials regarded the site as useless and a burden to the city. Some advocated sale of the entire site, leaving only a street in the center, while others suggested selling one-quarter of the area. Hénard made a proposal, published in 1904, which would have retained the entire site as open space, although his suggested use for the area embodied a notable departure from traditional park use (figure 194). He suggested that a large portion of the space be used as a landing field for dirigibles, with the still-standing Galerie des Machines to be employed as a hangar.[4] The periphery of the site would embody an eighteen-meter-wide track for automobiles and cyclists, as well as a foot-racing track ten meters wide. Other sport facilities on the site would include gymnasiums, tennis courts, and playing fields.

In spite of public efforts to preserve the Champ de Mars in its entirety, the city sold a ninety-meter-wide strip of land along each side to private builders in 1910. The central portion, however, was developed as a park embodying an open vista toward the facade of the École Militaire.

Although Hénard's planning efforts were to remain largely in project form, his

4. The Galerie des Machines, one of the most notable constructions of the 1889 Exposition, was demolished in 1909. Although many, including Hénard, believed that it should have been preserved, municipal officials insisted that it blocked the view of the facade of the eighteenth-century École Militaire. As a historic monument, the École presumably took precedence over a nineteenth-century metal and glass structure. Hénard's inspiration for the conception of the Galerie as a hangar may have come from the fact that in November 1903 a balloon dirigible did, in fact, land on the Champ de Mars and was temporarily sheltered in the Galerie. His proposal for the Champ de Mars was published in *Études sur les transformations de Paris. Fascicule 4: Le Champ de Mars et la galerie des machines. Le parc des sports et les grands dirigeables* (Paris: Librairies-Imprimeries Réunies, 1904).

193. OPPOSITE. Drawings by Eugène Hénard comparing the park area of Paris with that of London. *Above*: Park space existing within the boundaries of Paris in 1900. *Below*: The amount of park space existing in London within an area the equivalent of Paris.

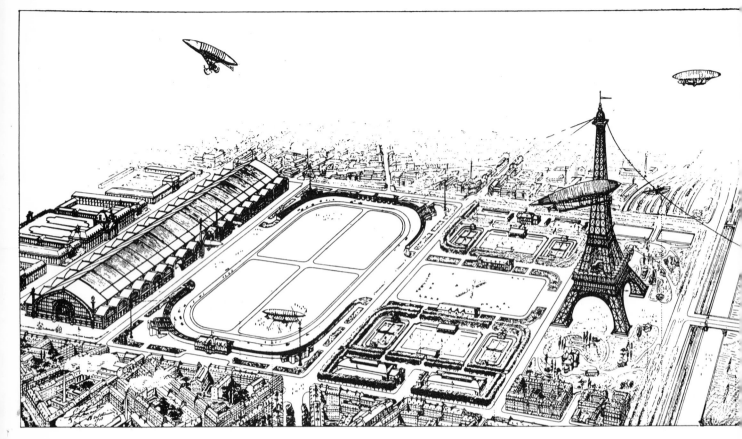

194. Hénard's proposal for the redevelopment of the Champ de Mars.

ideas were well known to contemporary urbanists and often influential. When the Commission d'Extension de Paris made its report in 1913, Hénard's work was acknowledged, even though the commission believed that his proposals advocated street construction that was unnecessary and impractical. With regard to street works, the commission had felt restrained by financial realities as well as by the æsthetic undesirability of massive demolitions. The commission was in agreement with Hénard, however, on the desirability of increasing park space within the city, and it quoted from his writings the statement that: "One must guard against considering parks and gardens as a superfluous luxury. Much to the contrary, *large areas planted with trees and shrubs* in the middle of urban agglomerations are as indispensable to public hygiene as water and light."[5]

Included in the commission report was an analysis of the open space then existing in Paris. Noting that the city possessed 223 hectares of public gardens and parks, the commission confirmed observations that parkland was poorly distributed. The Bois de Boulogne and the Bois de Vincennes, outside the city boundaries, provided

5. Commission d'Extension de Paris, Préfecture du Département de la Seine. Vol. 2. *Considérations techniques,* p. 63.

1,840 hectares of greenery, but they were not easily accessible from the central areas of Paris and were generally usable by large numbers of people only on weekends. It was noted that the Thirteenth Arrondissement, with a population of 142,071 people, had no park other than the one-half-hectare Place d'Italie. The Tenth Arrondissement had only the minuscule Square Saint Laurent and the planting along the Canal Saint Martin for 153,000 people, and the Eleventh Arrondissement a square of 1 hectare for a population of 239,335. Paris was observed to have the highest population density in Europe, with an average density of 370 inhabitants per hectare, as compared with 265 in Berlin and 161 in London. In comparison with Paris, both Berlin and London were considered to possess a better distribution of open space. London, it was noted, was characterized by a pattern of low-rise housing interspersed with numerous small squares, while Berlin was considered "a model city with respect to hygiene and open space."[6]

In the view of the commission, Paris had need of a series of neighborhood parks distributed throughout the city. The problem was how to obtain land within the congested urban fabric. It was theoretically possible for the city to expropriate land, but the likelihood of high indemnities in densely built areas made this unfeasible. The best solution, it was believed, lay in the utilization of land already owned by the government. It was proposed that certain large establishments—markets, barracks, and so forth—be moved to outlying sites, possibly to the emplacement of the fortifications, in this way making land available in the interior of the city. Land freed by the demolition of the *îlots insalubres* might also be used for parks.

Seen in relation to the growing interest in urbanism which characterized the period of its creation, the Commission d'Extension report was in many ways timid and unimaginative. At a time when many theorists were beginning to view the city as a complex economic and social organism, the commission chose to concentrate primarily on street widening and the creation of park space. The commission proposals were governed by their assessment of what was realistically possible, given the limited financial resources of the city, and their suggestions were guided by the desire to keep expropriations to a minimum. They suggested no drastic renovation of the urban fabric and made no proposals regarding guidance or control of the overall development of Paris.

Acknowledging its limitations, the report observed, "It is not within the scope of this study to examine the problems posed at the present time by the incessant growth of Paris and the actively increasing population of the suburban communes." It was recognized, however, that much more comprehensive planning might be needed in the future, and the report noted: "In our country of political, industrial, commercial, and artistic centralization, where everything converges on the capital, the public powers, for fifty years, have not been able to foresee the consequences of

6. Ibid., p. 69.

the limited growth of Paris: who can say what the consequences will be for the present city, in which the population has doubled in that period, and in which the radius of influence extends day by day over a considerable territory."[7]

Although there seemed no immediate likelihood of a political consolidation of Paris and the surrounding region, the commission believed that, for planning purposes, Paris should be considered to include the Département de la Seine, which, with 47,389 hectares of territory, "could provide the natural framework for a plan of extension."[8]

The Wall Surrounding Paris

Although the densely built city of Paris seemed to offer little occasion for large-scale renovation, a major opportunity for comprehensive planning appeared with the redevelopment of the fortifications surrounding Paris. This line of masonry defenses had been completed in 1845 and served to mark the city boundaries as extended by Haussmann. The fortifications themselves, with their walls and bastions, formed a ring 35 kilometers long and 130 to 135 meters wide. Beyond this lay a military zone averaging from 250 to 300 meters in depth, and subject to a regulation of *non ædificandi,* prohibiting permanent building. The purpose of the zone was to insure that nothing blocked the training of artillery placed on the ramparts and to provide a clear view of enemy approaches. Although owners of land in the zone might erect low wooden structures, they would be compelled to demolish them whenever requested by military authorities. Together the fortifications and zone encompassed an area of 1,200 hectares, equivalent to one quarter of Paris (figure 195). During the Franco-Prussian War, the fortifications had proved an ineffective defense, and the long-range artillery of the invaders had easily directed shells over the bastioned walls. Beginning in the 1880s proposals were made for the demolition of the obsolete fortifications and the annexation of the emplacement by the city.[9]

While discussion and negotiations proceeded over several decades, the Parisian press consistently reflected the view that the soon-to-be-acquired land should be employed as park space, a campaign which was supported by the Association des Cités-Jardins de France, the Touring Club, the Ligue pour les Espaces Libres, and, above all, the Section d'Hygiène of the Musée Social. Beginning in 1903, Eugène Hénard began publishing studies for the redevelopment of the fortifications, the

7. Ibid., p. 239.
8. Ibid., p. 47.
9. This first proposal for the elimination of the fortified zone was made in the Municipal Council in 1882. In 1891 the Ministry of War proposed to cede a portion of the forts, intending to construct a second line forming a circuit west of the city between the Porte de Saint Ouen and the southern limit of the Bois de Boulogne. This plan was rejected by the Municipal Council in 1893 in favor of a request for annexation of the complete fortified area. A willingness to cede the entire site was finally expressed by the minister of war in 1904.

195. The fortifications of Paris.

first of which proposed the inclusion of a circular landscaped *boulevard à redans,*
accompanied by twelve new parks.[10] A later scheme, proposed in 1909, would have
eliminated the boulevard and expanded the park areas to include portions of the
zone. The extensive employment of the site as parkland was also urged by a member
of the Chamber of Deputies, Jules Siegfried, who pointed out in 1908 that the line
of fortifications marked the "last reserve of fresh air in our capital." Reminding his
fellow deputies that many foreign cities had recently been subjected to energetic
programs of civic beautification, he observed that if Paris were to continue to attract
foreign visitors, similar efforts would be necessary. "France and the city of Paris owe
it to themselves to catch up immediately the advance which has been lost."[11]

Although the city had initially negotiated only for the site of the fortifications, it
seemed reasonable that the military zone should also be annexed to Paris and the
two areas planned as an ensemble. Acquisition of the fortifications was simply a
matter of purchasing the site from the military authorities. Acquiring the zone,
however, would be more difficult. The land surrounding the fortifications was
divided among thousands of private owners, and portions of it fell within the
jurisdiction of surrounding communes. A convention between the city and the

10. A description of the *boulevard à redans* projected for the fortification site may be found in chap. 1, above,
and also in Eugène Hénard, *Études sur les transformations de Paris. Fascicule 2: Les alignements brisés—la question
des fortifications et le Boulevard de Grande-Ceinture* (Paris: Librairies-Imprimeries Réunies, 1903).

11. Eugène Hénard, *Les espaces libres à Paris* (Paris: Musée Social, Mémoires et Documents, 1908, no. 7), pp.
74–75.

national government regarding the fortifications was reached in 1912, although final legislative approval was delayed until after the First World War.

Negotiations for the acquisition of the fortifications by the city coincided with the planning studies of the Commission d'Extension de Paris. In its 1913 report, the commission foresaw the defensive emplacement as providing sites for new housing and also for such institutions as hospitals, schools, barracks, and so forth. The zone was projected as a band of parkland with the ensemble to be designed in such a way as to include a series of grandly scaled monumental entrances into the city. It was observed: "An equal opportunity to create grandly and beautifully will perhaps never be presented. It has become increasingly difficult to contruct decorative architectural plazas inside Paris. But here, the space is unconfined. . . . We have the ability to lay out on the terrain of the fortifications triumphal entrances, grandiose portals, which will immediately announce the universal city, the capital of the artistic world."[12] Designs were included for a monumental circular plaza at the Porte de Vincennes, and for a similarly ornamental composition, including three linked plazas, at the Porte Maillot.

The legal acquisition of the fortifications in 1919 coincided with the creation of the first national planning law in France. The extensive damages of war convinced officials that coordinated planning activity would be necessary to effect reconstruction, while postwar optimism inspired a determination to improve urban conditions through controlled development. According to the provisions of the new law, every town with a population of 10,000 or more was required to establish a plan for long-range urban growth.[13]

In acknowledgment of the new regulation, the Département de la Seine and the city of Paris sponsored a design competition for a plan for the extension of Paris. It was noted in the competition program that, "Paris being surrounded by a belt of heavily populated communities, the extension of Paris, in the strict sense, can only be considered with regard to the ring of declassified fortifications and the zone *non aedificandi* which surrounds it." At the same time, contestants were urged to keep in mind that Paris and its surroundings "have a community of relations, such that practically no economic or social problem can be envisaged or solved for Paris alone."[14] Just as the entrants were encouraged to think in broad territorial terms, they were also to envisage the long-term evolution of the Paris region.

12. Commission d'Extension de Paris, Préfecture du Département de la Seine. Vol. 2. *Considérations techniques*, p. 97.

13. The creation of the law had been stimulated by studies of the Musée Social in which Eugène Hénard, Alfred Agache, and Henri Prost participated in 1911. This work involved the drawing up of a regional plan for Paris, and it was accompanied by legislative proposals requiring comprehensive plans for all towns with a population of 10,000 or over. In 1914 a government Commission de l'Administration Général Départementale et Communale prepared the legislative framework for the planning law of 1919, which was sometimes known as the Loi Cornudet, after the commission chairman.

14. Préfecture du Département de la Seine et la Ville de Paris, *Programme du concours ouvert pour l'établissement du plan d'aménagement et d'extension de Paris* (Paris: Chaix, 1919), p. 4.

The competition embodied four design categories, the first involving regional schemes, the second, plans for the city alone, the third, designs for the redevelopment of the fortifications and zone, while a fourth category included spot projects of various types. In its intent, the competition was a *concours d'idées*, designed to stimulate suggestions and proposals that might be used as a basis for future study and planning efforts, for there was no immediate likelihood of either a regional plan or a major renovation of Paris being effected. In terms of achievement, the only category of the competition in which plans had a chance of realization was the project for the fortifications and zone. Contestants in this area were asked to bear in mind that the city intended to use some of the fortified site for low-cost housing and for the relocation of barracks. It was also expected that some of the land would be sold to private developers in order to recover costs of land acquisition. The zone was projected as an area that would include parks, sports grounds, and an exposition palace, for which a site had already been selected.

The first-prize project for the fortifications and zone was produced by the architect Jacques Greber. Employing classical design predilections, he projected the fortified site as an area of housing embellished with formal landscaping and the zone as an area of parks and sports grounds. The Porte Maillot was envisioned as the site of a monumental circular plaza.

The demolition of the fortifications was a slow process, not completed until 1932. Contrary to hopes, the emplacement was not developed according to a comprehensive and unified plan. The land was built upon in piecemeal fashion, with results singularly lacking in architectural distinction. Part of the area was given over to institutional use, and part to low-cost apartment housing. Large segments were sold to speculators. By 1937 a total of 38,750 new dwelling units had been erected, mostly in the form of seven-story apartment buildings, housing a population of 120,000. By this time it was clear that what many had anticipated as a well-planned residential district, embodying abundant greenery and reflecting enlightened design concepts, had evolved into a dense wall of mediocrity encircling the city (figures 37, 150, and 151).

The development of the fortifications would long be invoked as a major planning failure in Paris. The Inspecteur Général des Beaux-Arts observed in 1937 that "our generation will have on its conscience the belt of HBM 1920–1930."[15] Complaining bitterly in *The Radiant City,* Le Corbusier observed of the area: "Profit prevailed. Nothing, absolutely nothing was done in the public interest. No kind of advance for architecture, no kind of advance for city planning. This is a wasted adventure, but no one protests!"[16]

---

15. Albert Laprade, "Beauté de Paris, beauté fragile," *Architecture d'aujourd'hui,* June 1937, p. 24. He was referring to the HBM government housing built on the site of the fortifications during the 1920s and 1930s.

16. Le Corbusier, *The Radiant City* (New York: Grossman, Orion Press, 1967), p. 13. First published in 1935 as *La ville radieuse.*

While the site of the fortifications was being redeveloped, the city began to annex the surrounding zone, proceeding gradually, commune by commune. Although the area had been designated *non ædificandi,* the regulations had never been strictly applied, and the zone supported a chaotic jumble of structures, including in its numerous shack colonies some of the most notorious slums of Paris (figures 145 and 146). There were also, however, more substantial structures, and even industrial establishments. The population of the zone included 125,000 people in 15,000 houses. There were also 879 factories supporting 180,000 workers. The annexation of the zone was accompanied by skillful organized protests by the inhabitants, and as expropriation proceeded the zone became, according to an official, "the paradise of speculators and blackmail."[17] It was not unknown, apparently, for occupants, having received one indemnity, to move to another part of the zone, anticipating a second indemnity. It was reported that "large industries install themselves without limiting their development in any way, assured that the city will never be able to pay for their expropriation. . . . The politics of the city consists, as almost always, in valorizing as highly as possible the land it wishes to buy."[18] On the eve of the Second World War, after twenty years of effort, the acquisition of the zone by the city was still incomplete.

Slow Progress

In the years between the wars, the failure of the city to develop the fortification site according to a comprehensive scheme underlined what seemed to be a chronic paralysis of the municipality with regard to planning. Although one could not accuse the city government of total inaction, the financial facts of life seemed continually to contradict the desire of urbanists for far-reaching decisions. Acquisition of the zone had progressed at a slow pace, hampered by lengthy expropriation proceedings. Within the city, where seventeen *îlots insalubres* had been designated in 1919 as needing immediate renovation, the cost of clearance operations sufficed to inhibit governmental action. Although various plans were produced for the redevelopment of the *îlots insalubres,* only minor clearance operations were attempted, and by the end of the Second World War the *îlots* rested virtually intact.

The difficulties inherent in planning achievement were underlined in 1929 by the Directeur de l'Extension de Paris, Pierre Doumerc, as he recalled the planning competition for Paris held ten years previously.

Must I speak of the disappointment, the heartbreak which an administrator feels, who, having studied these projects, having lived during several weeks among mirages of a greater Paris, ordered, regulated, ventilated, sanitized,

17. Jean Giraudoux, "Siège et Reddition de Paris," *Urbanisme,* no. 16, July 1933, p. 232.
18. Ibid.

beautified, regains contact with reality and is confronted by the difficulties of the everyday and the down-to-earth? How he envies the artists-become-poets who have shown him the vision of an ideal city, unaware that they have made even more bitter his disappointing task! . . . And when he sets to work, he finds himself faced with two insurmountable obstacles: shortage of money, crisis of housing. As to the financial difficulty, I shall limit myself to citing two figures: . . . from 1854 to 1871, Huassmann, the great model, spent 1,430 million francs on street openings and promenades, or, in round figures, 100 million per year. From 1871 to 1919, the annual expenditure has been on the average less than 14 million, and since 1919, the devaluation of the franc and the financial and economic crisis have not permitted the undertaking of large works, except for the extension of the Boulevard Haussmann.

If, financially, the realization of a vast program of street operations had been possible, how would the city of Paris have been able, without grave troubles, to demolish a considerable number of buildings? It would have been, in this Paris as full as an egg, to throw families out on the street, who, badly housed perhaps, would have been completely without shelter.

Although many of the planning proposals were tempting, Doumerc felt it indispensable to "remember how far it is between the cup and lips, from the dream to the reality, to the hard and cruel reality."[19] The financial problems of the government, of course, reflected a growing crisis in the private sector, and with the economic depression of the 1930s, building activity of all types entered a period of stagnation. Reminiscing about this epoch, a journalist who had been fifteen in 1931 recalled that "someone of my age could have passed his entire youth without ever seeing a building under construction."[20]

Plans, of course, continued to be produced, and the conviction remained that Paris and its surrounding region should be subject to long-range direction. Concern for a coherent regional development inspired a series of government studies, and in 1936 the Municipal Council of Paris approved the preparation of a development plan for the city. The 1937 Exposition provided a focus for new monumental building in Paris, as well as a means for publicizing ideas for redevelopment.

In spite of the crisis of the times, the Architecte Honoraire de la Ville de Paris, Georges Sebille, reiterated the view that planning should be comprehensive. Urbanism was not merely to be seen as a program of public works, but as the "art of making these works in the best place, and even more to foresee the place of works to come, even works which public opinion and the politicians today find useless, absurd, or utopian. And it is also the art of thinking at the same time of hygiene, education,

19. Pierre Doumerc, "Les résultats du concours d'urbanisme de 1920 ont dégagé des principes intéressants pour l'établissement du plan d'aménagement et d'extension de Paris," *L'Europe nouvelle,* June 8, 1929, pp. 733–34.
20. Françoise Giroud, *Si je mens* (Paris: Stock, 1972), p. 57.

social economy, and political economy; of food distribution, transport, and many other things too; and of æsthetics always." He complained that planning activities in Paris were too limited in scope and that: "There seems to be an idea that it is streets and circulation which create a plan. This is as though one wanted to design a building by studying first the corridors and galleries without thinking about the use and the location of the principal rooms, and without thinking of the nature of the materials to be employed." In 1937, one needed to prepare for "the techniques, the legislation, and the sociology of 1987."[21]

Although the 1919 planning law had attempted to instigate long-range urban planning throughout France, it had been largely ineffective. The responsibility for executing projects had been placed on the individual municipalities, which were "frequently impecunious or indifferent, poorly advised during the preparation of studies whose inadequacy retarded approval of proposals."[22] Additional legislation during the 1920s and 1930s also produced little in the way of results.

Looking back on this period, a historian declared in 1965, that "between Haussmann and the most recent works of urbanism . . . there is nothing." He went on to lament the "lost opportunities and wasted talents," observing that "the work of Parisian urbanists resembles a sort of absurd contest where the prize winners will each time be stripped of their dossiers and sent home with the congratulations of the jury. The administration of Paris is like the one in Kafka's *The Castle,* where the urbanist-surveyor, a roll of numbered plans in his hand, searches vainly for someone in authority."[23]

In terms of planning organization, the crisis of the Second World War provided a sudden impetus to legislation and an augmentation of government power. Legislation in 1940 and 1941 created the Commissariat Technique à la Réconstruction Immobilière, charged with the establishment of reconstruction plans for towns suffering war damage. Also in 1941, the Délégation Générale à l'Équipement National was established and charged with coordinating questions of urbanism and housing construction, while the Comité National d'Urbanisme was created to provide advice on urban problems.

It was wartime legislation that facilitated the complete annexation of the zone to Paris. Expropriation had proceeded slowly for twenty years, and on the eve of the war 259 hectares still remained to be acquired. In 1940, however, the law was amended to permit direct requisition without lengthy court delays, and the grim days of the occupation were marked by a steady eviction of the *zoniers.* By the time of the liberation, the zone had been almost entirely freed, and it was observed that, "if one couldn't speak, in a literal sense, of a green belt, at least there were a group of undeveloped spaces available, given over to thistles, heaps of garbage, and poachers,

21. Georges Sebille, "Le Paris de demain," *Architecture d'aujourd'hui,* June 1937, p. 81.
22. "L'organisation administrative," *Urbanisme,* vol. 25, nos. 45–48, 1956, p. 173.
23. Michel Ragon, *Paris, hier, aujourd'hui, demain* (Paris: Hachette, 1965), pp. 12, 16.

but entirely free."[24] The new powers of requisition were also used to hasten acquisition of property in the *îlots insalubres,* although the housing shortage tended to halt demolitions, and relatively high indemnities still hampered action.

The interruption of construction necessitated by the war and the occupation provided time for study and reflection, and the prevailing atmosphere of self-criticism promoted a desire to avoid the errors of the past. A national law of 1943 repeated the intentions of the 1919 urban legislation in requiring that a development plan be produced by all towns with a population of 10,000 or more and by all communes forming part of urban agglomerations. It was considered a matter of particular importance that Paris have such a plan, and the Ministre du Logement et de la Réconstruction created the Comité d'Aménagement de la Région Parisienne to serve as a consultive committee for its preparation.

Having been declared an open city at the time of the German invasion, Paris had been spared immediate physical damage, and the effects of the war were to be computed largely in human terms. It may be recalled that during the Franco-Prussian War the momentary presence of German troops on the Place de l'Étoile had been looked on as a desecration sufficient to inspire a symbolic purification of the site through fire. During the humiliating four-year occupation of the Second World War, the Germans repeated their triumphal march along the Champs Élysées every day at noon, passing in review at the Étoile. Although the physical fabric of the city remained intact, major monuments received an appliqué of swastikas and German victory slogans, streets carried signposts in German to direct military traffic, and about two hundred bronze statues were removed by the Germans and melted down for their metal.

As the tide of battle changed, however, and the Allied forces approached the city in 1944, Paris was seriously threatened with destruction. While he stood at the head of a seemingly invincible state, Hitler sought to emulate and excel the grandeur of the French capital in a monumental renovation of Berlin. Now, with his power collapsing and his army in retreat, he became obsessed with the desire to accompany his own ruin with the ruin of Paris. Occupying troops were ordered to prepare for a last-ditch stand to coincide with the destruction of the city and its monuments. The bridges of the Seine were mined. In addition, explosives were placed in the Luxembourg Palace, the Invalides, the palaces of the Place de la Concorde, the Chamber of Deputies, the Quai d'Orsay, the Eiffel Tower, and Notre Dame Cathedral. Determined that the Allied army should find "nothing but a blackened field of ruins," Hitler contemplated the use of V1 and V2 rockets against the city, and as the liberation proceeded he demanded frantically of his aides, "Is Paris burning?"[25] The city was saved largely through the procrastination of the German commander, who had come to entertain strong doubts about Hitler's sanity and

24. "L'utilisation de l'enceinte de Paris de 1919 à 1939," *Urbanisme,* vol. 23, nos. 35–36, 1954, p. 8.
25. Larry Collins and Dominique Lapierre, *Is Paris Burning?* (New York: Simon & Schuster, 1965), p. 284.

found himself increasingly hesitant to destroy an internationally beloved city in response to the orders of an eroding regime. Although there was some damage to buildings during the fighting that accompanied the Allied entry, the only major monument to suffer severely was the Grand Palais, which was shelled, burned, and gutted by tanks entering the city.

Toward a Master Plan

Although the thinking of urbanists during the war years had favored comprehensive planning, the immediate postwar period reflected only halting progress toward the establishment of a plan for Paris. Numerous studies and proposals were made, and the problem of Parisian development was under almost continual examination by the Municipal Council and the relevant government agencies. In the same period the question of a regional plan was being considered, and the necessity of looking at the city in terms of its surroundings was recognized. The planning studies provided a focus for thinking about the nature of Paris, about its function and its future. Contained in the proposals were attempts to establish guidelines for the development of the city, together with specific suggestions for renovation. As planning proposals were submitted and rejected, a set of common concepts and attitudes evolved toward the development of Paris.

Just as Paris was acknowledged to need consideration in terms of its region, the Paris region itself was currently being questioned with an eye to its place in French national development. Although the primacy of Paris in France had been a source of Parisian pride, the concept of decentralization was gaining acceptance among government officials. There was doubt about the degree to which Paris would, or should, expand. Immediately following the war, moreover, government assistance focused on areas that had experienced heavy war damage, and some believed that Paris would be forced to restrict renovations to a relatively modest level.

In 1950 the Municipal Council approved the first draft of a development plan containing general proposals for zoning, land use, and building regulations. Further study followed, and in 1952 the Commission d'Aménagement de Paris presented a project to the council which was accepted in part. The plan conceived of Paris in terms of four major zones: a zone of business, a zone of government, a university zone, and a zone of industry. The city was also categorized in terms of zones of protection (sites and perspectives that needed to be preserved) and zones of *affectation* (areas in which renovation might preferably take place). The *îlots insalubres* were examined and classified according to the ease with which they might be renovated.

The following year, another commission began studies focusing on street work, the provision of open space, and the renovation of slum areas. Questions of conservation and restoration were also under consideration, together with the problem of Les Halles and the removal of the wine market at Bercy. At this time pressures for increased office space in Paris were mounting, and the possibility was being considered of creating a new business district at La Défense, outside the city boundaries.

The establishment of a development plan for Paris was delayed in part by the lengthy deliberations of the Municipal Council, but also in part because of the need for national government approval. To achieve acceptance, a plan needed the accord of the municipal administration, the Municipal Council, and the minister of reconstruction. Thus final adoption of a plan approved by the council might take years.

By 1959 the Plan d'Urbanisme Directeur de Paris was produced, and after examination by the requisite government bodies it was adopted by the Municipal Council in 1962. This document, like previous plans, attempted to summarize the existing situation in Paris and to suggest general guidelines for future urban development. Within these guidelines, it was thought that it would be necessary to formulate specific, detailed urban projects. "They are the programs of short-term action in a long-term perspective."[26]

Although a policy of decentralization had been favored by some government authorities, the Plan d'Urbanisme was drawn up on the assumption that the essential status of Paris was to remain the same. Paris was, first of all, the capital of France, the product of a long-standing tradition of centralization. Although some planners were currently proposing a dispersal of government functions, it would run counter to tradition to weaken the role of Paris as the center of political power.

Not only did the plan oppose any removal of government functions, it stated that all the multiform activities of Paris should remain in the city. "While recognizing the necessity for a certain dispersal, it is not necessary to destroy an equilibrium between the forces of all kinds—intellectual, æsthetic, economic, industrial—which give to Paris its physiognomy and its harmony, the sources of all the living values which contribute to its radiance. . . . Finally, it is one of the most important points of human assembly . . . it is this extraordinary accumulation of attractions, of activities, and of richness that confers such magnetism on Paris. . . . Paris must remain what it is: a great metropolis and, at the same time, the capital of France, . . . a city of international prestige."[27] The election of Charles de Gaulle to the presidency in 1958 placed at the head of the French government a man whose sense of national grandeur supported the idea of Paris as a great city, while the entry of France into the Common Market in 1957 enhanced prosperity and underlined the function of Paris as an international economic center.

26. Préfecture da la Seine, *Plan d'urbanisme directeur de Paris, 1959* (Paris: Imprimerie Municipale, 1960), p. 16.

27. Ibid., pp. 46–47, 51.

The Plan d'Urbanisme incorporated from previous studies an analysis of the city in terms of zones. It was noted, however, that unlike some American cities Paris did not have a rigid segregation of activities and frequently exhibited mixtures of housing, commerce, institutions, and industry. A flexible conception of zoning was thus considered appropriate.

The business zone was seen to occupy the Right Bank center. In 1951 the Municipal Council had rejected a proposal to create a new business center in the northeast part of the city. Instead, by the late 1950s the business center was found to be spontaneously spreading westward into the Sixteenth and Seventeenth Arrondissements, where many buildings that had previously been residential were being converted into offices. It was feared that the decline in residential population in the central districts would result in dead areas in the evening, and it was to prevent the increasing dominance of business activity in the center of Paris that the new business district at La Défense had been begun in 1958. It had also been considered desirable to create alternate centers of commercial activity within Paris itself and, in an attempt to establish such a *pole d'animation* on the Left Bank, a commercial center incorporating the tallest building in Europe was being contemplated near the Gare Montparnasse.

The administrative zone of Paris appeared to contain two centers, a zone of national administration, including the Left Bank Palais Bourbon and the ministries of the Right Bank, and a local administrative center, beginning at the Hôtel de Ville and extending eastward toward Bastille.

The university zone occupied a large part of the Left Bank. Planning was underway to expand and disperse some of the university facilities, and the plan suggested the creation of an "intellectual axis" extending along the Ligne de Sceaux Métro, with science faculty and laboratories to be established outside the city.

Zones of manufacturing and warehousing were found to be concentrated near transport facilities, in the vicinity of the railroad stations and the canal network. It was considered important that the city retain its artisan activities, which were in danger of being forced out through urban renovation. "It is necessary that our capital conserve this variety which the years have given it. But this variety must be harmonious and not anarchic."[28]

Problems of housing and street renovation were discussed in relation to previous proposals. It may be recalled that the idea of a loop-shaped motorway within Paris had been finally rejected by the Municipal Council in 1959. The plan made no radical proposals for street renovations, suggesting merely that a study be made for a north-south transversal at Bastille. The *îlots insalubres* were still indicated as areas needing renovation, and it was observed that "nearly one-half of Paris is dilapidated."[29] A lack of open space was also cited as a problem, and a steady

28. Ibid., p. 138.
29. Ibid., p. 128.

reduction in the number of private gardens had been observed. It was hoped that slum renovations would include an increase in open areas.

With regard to overall standards, a theoretical study produced by the Centre de Documentation in 1957 was cited. According to this study, each Parisian should have 42 square meters of space in the city, 12 square meters for his dwelling and his car, 14 square meters of neighborhood facilities, and 16 square meters of general urban equipment. On this basis, the city could have an ideal population of no more than 2,300,000.

Although adopted by the Municipal Council in 1962, the Plan d'Urbanisme did not obtain final government sanction until 1967, at which time it was immediately taken up for revision. It was thought that several factors had made a reassessment of the Paris plan necessary: the creation of a new long-range regional plan, recent financial legislation, and evolving planning techniques. The revised plan, produced in 1968, was termed the Schéma Directeur d'Aménagement et d'Urbanisme de la Ville de Paris. The purpose of the Schéma Directeur was to establish the general orientation of planning in Paris. Within these guidelines, specific programs of action were to be developed. It was noted: "Paris and its future must respond to three imperatives: to put to the best use a space that is very dense, old, and small in extent; to respect the complexity of the functions and structures indispensable to the equilibrium of a great metropolis; to maintain the equilibrium between its territory and that of its region and, equally, the ensemble of the national territory." It was considered necessary to analyze the existing situation, to understand the trends of natural evolution, and to "disengage those elements susceptible to encouragement and those it is preferable to correct."[30] The scheme was thus basically conservative. Its intention was not to alter the character of Paris but to plan in accordance with the prevailing evolution of the city.

The Schéma included a statistical summary of population trends, housing conditions, and economic development. In terms of population, Paris was seen to be stabilizing; in 1962 it had a population of 2,750,000, only slightly more than in 1901. Just as population had been declining, a reduction in employment within the city was noted. Although the number of jobs in tertiary activities had increased by 45,000 between 1962 and 1966, the number of industrial jobs had declined by 61,000 as manufacturing moved either to the suburbs or to other regions. Although the Schéma acknowledged the desirability of a social and economic equilibrium in Paris, no proposals were made to halt what has been termed the *embourgeoisement* of the capital.

Planning efforts were to be directed toward a redistribution of dwellings and places of employment, in order to decongest the center and better use the peripheral areas of the city. It was proposed that tertiary activity be shifted eastward to compensate for the reduction of industrial and artisanal employment in this part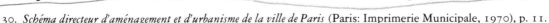

30. *Schéma directeur d'aménagement et d'urbanisme de la ville de Paris* (Paris: Imprimerie Municipale, 1970), p. 11.

of the city, and an improved coordination between employment, dwelling, and transport was sought. It was also considered necessary to respect the historic and architectural qualities of the city, and to "treat differently from the rest of Paris certain quarters of the center where the essence of the archæological heritage is located."[31]

Like the Plan d'Urbanisme, the Schéma Directeur classified the city in terms of zones. The classification included a zone dominated by culture and great spaces (the axes of the grand monumental ensembles), a zone dominated by administration, a zone dominated by the university, a zone dominated by business, and an industrial zone. Open spaces and zones of residence were also listed, although it was observed that, "housing having existed in all the zones of the city, it is not possible to indicate a single residential zone in a specific sense."[32] It was noted, however, that the outer arrondissements had shown the strongest evolution toward residential use.

The future development of the city was to include the creation of poles of employment, similar to the center underway near the Gare Montparnasse, to be established near centers of transport and outside the historic core. The railroad stations were considered to provide natural centers for such poles. Other centers cited included the Place de la Nation, the Place d'Italie, and the Front de Seine. Within the city center, Les Halles and the Gare Saint Lazare area could, it was believed, be redeveloped and modernized. Although the Paris regional plan, which was concurrently being developed, attempted to create outlying settlements combining dwelling and employment, with the intent of reducing the volume of commuting, the Schéma Directeur embodied the assumption that Paris would continue as a focus for daily migrations from the suburbs. By planning the poles of development to be adjacent to railroad stations, the long-established pattern of railroad commuting was used as a basis for projecting the future development of the city.

The planning documents produced by the city of Paris during the 1950s and 1960s served the primary purpose of analyzing the current state of development and providing an opportunity for the study and discussion of Parisian urbanization. But while long-range plans were being formulated, revised, and approved, the redevelopment of Paris proceeded at an accelerating pace. Clearly the renovation of the city was not dependent on acceptance of a master plan, and although few Parisians were aware of the numerous planning studies, reports, and recommendations of the Municipal Council, no one could ignore the rapidly changing face of Paris.

31. Ibid., p. 84.
32. Ibid., p. 97.

The New Urban Scale

As discussion of the postwar planning of Paris began, city officials found themselves in possession of a sizable and largely unbuilt area available for immediate urbanization. This was the wide swath of land provided by the zone, which had been gradually annexed by the city in the years since 1919. It may be recalled that, when the adjacent fortifications had been acquired, many had hoped that the site would be transformed into a belt of parkland. Instead the area had been given over to relatively dense apartment housing. There was a natural desire to prevent a similar development of the zone which, it was hoped, would provide Paris with much-needed open space.

The shortage of building sites within Paris, however, and the intense housing crisis of the 1950s convinced city officials that at least part of the zone should be used for housing. In 1953 the president of the Municipal Council, Bernard Lafay, proposed that the portion of the zone between the Porte de la Plaine and the Porte de Pantin (on the south and east of Paris) be used as a site for 3,800 new dwellings. It was specified, however, that only 20 percent of the site be built over. In compensation for the loss of open space, it was decided that an equal amount of parkland (about twenty-five hectares) should be created within Paris, the most likely sites being the *îlots insalubres*.

In the view of some, the development of the zone should have been linked to a comprehensive plan for Paris. The wall of apartment buildings erected on the fortifications stood as a continuous reproach to Parisian planners and a reminder of their previous failures. Many feared that the decision to build on 20 percent of the new site might create a precedent for a program of relatively dense building. The development of the zone, however, was to be notably different from that of the old fortification site. Reflecting the preferences of many modernists for a relatively loose urban texture, the housing of the zone was characterized by immense, widely spaced high-rise blocks. Thus, while the redevelopment of the forts had been largely a continuation of the existing pattern of Paris, the zone marked a sharp contrast (figures 196, 197, and 198). Accentuating the new scale of Parisian urbanism was the Boulevard Périphérique, following the outer edge of the zone and providing a concrete moat separating Paris from the suburbs. Although many had hoped that the zone might be designed to provide a verdant and serene transition between the city and its surroundings, the circular motorway reinforced the image of Paris as a walled city, replacing the old line of defenses with an impenetrable barrier of high-speed vehicles.

While the redevelopment of the zone was underway, action began on a series of conspicuous renovation projects within the city. Before and during the war, Parisian redevelopment had been relatively restricted in intent, focusing on the demolition and reconstruction of the *îlots insalubres*. Achievement had been modest, involving

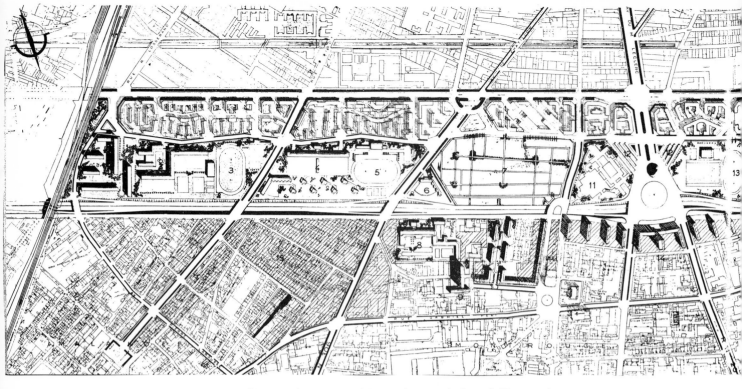

196. Plan produced in 1954 for the redevelopment of the zone between the Porte de Vanves and the Porte d'Orléans on the southern edge of Paris.

197. The northern edge of Paris, looking east from the vicinity of t[...] Porte de Clichy. The Boulevard Périphérique marks the city boun[...] aries, within which lie the paralle[...] bands of the zone and fortificatio[...] sites.

lengthy and expensive expropriations, and often after buildings had been acquired the city could not afford demolition and replacement. Beginning in the 1950s, however, the pace and scale of urban renewal altered dramatically. In the view of some, sweeping changes in Paris were long overdue. A critic wrote in 1957: "That which Paris demands, your task, urbanists, is not little repairs day by day; it is a total reconstruction. It is not a house here and there which it is necessary to demolish, but blocks, I would say even entire quarters."[33]

In 1955 national legislation established the basis for large-scale urban renewal, providing subsidies to local authorities. New organizational methods invited the participation of private capital in government-initiated projects, and in the climate of growing economic prosperity, massive urban renovations were seen as profitable enterprises. Planners and officials spoke optimistically of the "reconquest" of Paris, and urban renewal was seen not merely as the demolition of slums but as a revitalizing process. Sites designated for renovation included not only the *îlots*

33. Albert Guérard, "Urbanisme parisien: servitude de beauté," *Urbanisme,* no. 55, 1957, p. 146.

198. Public housing on the zone.

insalubres, but also districts considered to be *mal utilisés,* areas in which the disposition of land was judged inconsistent with the optimum development of Paris.

In the process of renovation, the Municipal Council would decide on the perimeter of the area to be redeveloped. The Services Techniques of the Préfecture de Paris would then develop a "Plan d'Urbanisme de Détail," which would be submitted to relevant government authorities for approval. Assuming that an acceptable project conformed to the Schéma Directeur, and could be adequately financed, it would be authorized by prefectoral decree. At this point an organization would be created or selected to execute the program. Although a project could be directed and financed entirely by public establishments or by private agencies, a frequently used organizational method involved a *société d'économie mixte,* involving both government and private enterprise.

Included in the new planning powers beginning in 1962 was the right to delineate areas in which long-term urbanization would take place. The purpose was to prevent land speculation, and within such a Zone d'Aménagement Différé (ZAD) land values were controlled and the planning authority given the right of preemption. The ZAD designation could be used to define the perimeter of an area to be redeveloped or it could be used for an area surrounding new development, to control land prices.

Specific redevelopment programs initially embodied the creation of a Zone à Urbaniser par Priorité (ZUP), in which powers of expropriation were established. This classification was later supplanted by the Zone d'Aménagement Concerté (ZAC). The creation of such a redevelopment area in Paris involved the definition of the perimeter by the Municipal Council, following which a preliminary project and financial estimate would be drawn up. Within a ZAC, existing regulations regarding land use and building heights could be supplanted, giving designers the freedom to depart radically from the prevailing urban fabric.

In the period between 1955 and 1960, Parisian renovation included seventeen projects with a total area of 89.7 hectares (figure 199). With the exception of the Montparnasse center, most of these involved clearance of *îlots insalubres.* Between 1960 and 1965, eleven operations were begun, encompassing a total of 116 hectares. Among the most conspicuous of these was the redevelopment of a 25.8 hectare site in the Fifteenth Arrondissement, bordering the river between the Pont Bir-Hakeim and the Pont Mirabeau, and called the Front de Seine (figures 200 and 201). This district, largely occupied by warehouses and factories, was converted, beginning in 1961, into a prestigious ensemble of high-rise office blocks, luxury apartments, and hotels. Because of the high visibility of its location, the scale of its architecture, and the dramatic social change embodied in its redevelopment, the Front de Seine was frequently invoked as a disquieting exemplar of the rapid transformation overtaking Paris (figure 202; see also figures 136 and 137).

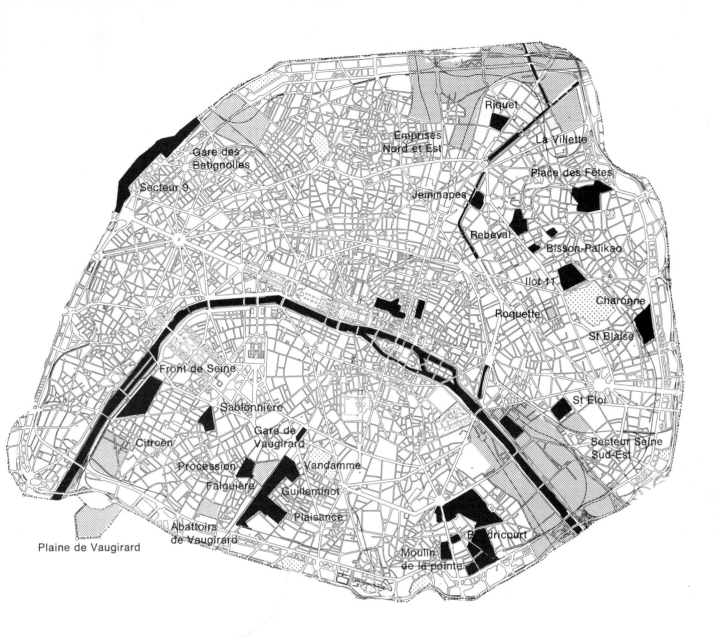

199. Redevelopment areas in Paris shown in 1977.

During the next five years, between 1965 and 1970, urban renewal centered on projects which were relatively few in number, but large in scale, comprising six areas totalling 145 hectares.

The largest single project involved the renovation, beginning in 1966, of an area of 87 hectares extending south and east of the Place d'Italie in the Thirteenth Arrondissement. The importance of the site lay partly in its relationship to a north-south motor route which had been projected as a new transversal for Paris in

200. Air view looking east. The Sixteenth Arrondissement lies on the near side of the river and the Fifteenth on the far side. Visible on the near side of the river is the Maison de l'ORTF. On the opposite bank are the Eiffel Tower and the Front de Seine redevelopment area. The Maine-Montparnasse tower may be seen in the distance.

201. The Front de Seine redevelopment area.

202. Housing in the Front de Seine. The building shown is one of two HLM apartment blocks included in the area.

1962. The first portion of this route was to involve an enlargement of the Avenue d'Italie, leading from the southern edge of the city (figure 203). In making studies for the street renovation, city officials concluded that the surrounding area provided a likely center for renewal, with large industrial emplacements which could be easily acquired and a building fabric of relatively low density. Existing housing included both designated slum areas and run-down working-class districts. Redevelopment involved the participation of both government and private enterprise, and the program included apartment housing, shopping facilities, and offices. Although some HLM housing was provided, many of the new apartments were designed for the affluent classes, and the redevelopment of the Place d'Italie reflected a social transformation similar to that of other renovated districts (figures 184–191).

The desire to reestablish an equilibrium between the east and the west of Paris resulted in an ambitious proposal in 1973 to redevelop a large part of southeast

203. Looking north from the Porte d'Italie at the southern edge of Paris. The Avenue d'Italie is at left, leading toward the Place d'Italie, from which redevelopment extends south and east.

Paris. Included in the contemplated renewal area was the Bercy project, already in progress, which involved the transformation of a 40-hectare industrial site bordering on the Seine into a complex of modern offices (figure 204). Located near the Gare de Lyon, this district was projected as a new pole of commercial activity. The project was begun in 1965 as a long-term effort, with a completion date of 1990. The area considered for renovation in 1973 comprised 280 hectares (one-twentieth of the usable area of Paris), including parts of the Twelfth and Thirteenth Arrondissements, on either side of the Seine (figure 205). This largely industrial district was considered to be "very little, or very badly, utilized: practically empty of inhabitants; free of important structures; occupied by economic activities in decline, or which represent a real waste of space."[34] As projected, the redeveloped area would include

34. "Pourquoi ne pas laisser tout ce secteur tel qu'il est aujourd'hui?", *Paris projet,* no. 12, 1974, p. 22.

204. The Quai de la Rapée, part of the Bercy redevelopment area.

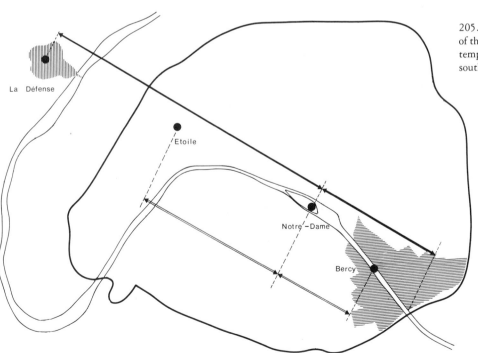

205. Shaded areas show a comparison of the site of La Défense with the contemplated area of redevelopment in southeast Paris.

206. Near the Place d'Italie.

parks, housing, and a pole of activity for offices, absorbing the Bercy center already under reconstruction. The district was considered a likely quarter for renovation because of its ample transport facilities, including the Gare de Lyon and the Gare d'Austerlitz, and its relative centrality (the Pont de Bercy, marking its center, was three kilometers from Notre Dame).

Although different promoters and architects were involved, the renewal areas of Paris tended to reflect similar design sensibilities. What had previously been a relatively dense pattern of masonry building was usually replaced by widely spaced high-rise slabs and towers, characterized by light curtain walls. Such quarters often presented a sharp contrast to their surroundings, and to some observers even the shabbiest of the neighboring streets, with their small shops, narrow pavements, and modest buildings, possessed a humaneness notably absent in the new projects (figure 206).

The social and economic aspects of the redevelopment, needless to say, also brought increasing criticism. Small commerce was disappearing from renovated areas, and artisan activity being forced out. Industrial establishments were increasingly being shifted to the outskirts, together with the working-class population. In the process, Paris was viewed as losing much of its social richness and economic equilibrium.

To supporters of the program, the renovation was essential to the dynamism of Paris. It was frequently observed that Paris was not a museum, and that physical changes were the inevitable accompaniment of economic power and prosperity. Much of the older urban fabric, especially housing, was dilapidated and obsolete. Paris needed new dwellings with improved standards; Paris needed office space; Paris had always been a modern city and should remain one. As to the shift of industry, many believed that the city was not a suitable site for large manufacturing enterprises. Sites were restricted, factory buildings obsolete in terms of modern needs, and transport facilities limited. In the opinion of some urbanists, land in Paris was too valuable to be given over to large-surface industrial use.

The prefect of Paris had observed: "Paris cannot, without irremediably impoverishing itself, dwell in a morose contemplation of its past. This city, on the contrary, knows how to rejuvenate and adapt itself resolutely to its time."[35]

Among the major areas of renovation in postwar Paris, the most ambitious was the new business center of La Défense (figures 128–130). Although the site lay just beyond the city boundaries, the district was closely tied to the center of Paris and reflected the westward spread of office activity. The site, it may be recalled, marked a continuation of the monumental axis of Paris, and the embellishment of the Rond Point de la Défense had been included in the 1931 competition for the development of the Voie Triomphale.

35. Quotation taken from Pierre Lavedon, *Nouvelle histoire de Paris: histoire de l'urbanisme à Paris* (Paris: Hachette, 1975), p. 536.

In 1950 a meeting of the Conseil Général de la Seine proposed that La Défense provide the emplacement for a new business center, for which an architectural project was designed by Charles Nicod. Interest in the development of this site accompanied discussion of a new regional plan, and in 1954 the Direction de l'Aménagement du Territoire selected the site of La Défense for priority development. The initial intention was to reserve the area as a center for government agencies, such as the Ministry of Aeronautics, Ministry of Education, and Office of National Radio and Television. It was also thought that it would provide the headquarters for such international organizations as UNESCO and NATO. A few years earlier, in 1951, a private organization, the Centre National des Industries et des Techniques (CNIT), had shown an interest in La Défense, proposing to build an exposition hall there. The government decision to develop the area as a business center was made in 1956, and in 1958 a public agency was created to direct reconstruction. In contrast to other large redevelopment projects, which frequently employed a *société d'économie mixte,* La Défense remained entirely under

207. La Défense as projected in 1976.

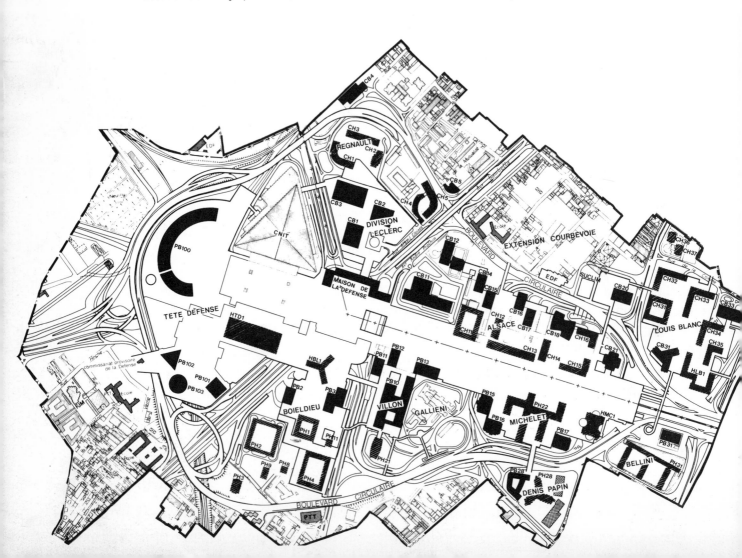

government control, directed by the Établissement Public pour l'Aménagement de la Défense (EPAD).

The overall redevelopment area embodied a site of almost 1,000 hectares, including portions of the communes of Puteaux, Courbevoie, and Nanterre. Renovation of this large district was to include construction of a new prefecture, an educational center, and large complexes of housing. The site for the business center, termed Zone A, occupied a 154-hectare tract beginning at the river Seine opposite the Pont de Neuilly and extending westward beyond the Rond Point (figures 207 and 208).

Site studies began in 1958, while the CNIT exposition hall was under construction. This building was placed just beyond and at one side of the old emplacement of the Rond Point de la Défense. The Avenue de la Défense, leading from the Pont de Neuilly to the Rond Point, would in the new district be replaced by a raised pedestrian platform one kilometer in length, defining the axis of the site and providing access to buildings (figure 209). Although Zone A was planned

208. Air view of La Défense, looking north.

209. The pedestrian platform, or *parvis*, of La Défense, looking east.

primarily as an office complex, apartment housing was also included, reflecting the intent that La Défense contain some of the attributes of a balanced neighborhood (figure 210).[36] A definitive plan for Zone A, embodying an ensemble of twenty-five-story office blocks, was approved in 1964.

La Défense was distinguished from other Parisian renewal areas by the extraordinary size and complexity of its infrastructure. The site was to provide the focus of a large system of transportation, including a new suburban railway station,

36. The housing constructed at La Défense was, needless to say, far too expensive for the average office worker, and a survey in 1975 indicated that 40 percent of the employees journeyed from eastern Paris.

210. The Terrace des Reflets, La Défense. The building at right contains apartments; the others are office buildings.

211. Multilevel subterranean station and shopping complex at La Défense.

an extension of the new Réseau Express Régional (RER), and a terminal for the suburban bus system. An elaborate subterranean interchange of public transport included a mammoth RER station complex and shopping concourse thirty meters below ground (figure 211). Subsurface construction also included a system of motor roads and parking for 32,000 cars, while at ground level the complex was surrounded by a new motor loop connecting with the Boulevard Périphérique.

Government costs in developing La Défense were high, and by 1969 private investment was slower than had been anticipated. At this time the administration of the project was reorganized with a view to forestalling government losses. According to one of the new administrators, Albin Chalandon: "EPAD has taken on

212. La Défense seen from the Seine. At right is the Île de la Grande Jatte.

the construction of an ensemble at once gigantic and excessive. . . . Titanic works have been undertaken below the surface of the ground. They are very, very expensive, and they are not profitable. Why? Because the density of occupation inside the perimeter of La Défense is minimal. This project costs and has cost a lot, and it will still cost the government enormous sums if we are not careful. For a project of this nature must be profitable."[37]

In order to increase revenues from private construction, La Défense was replanned to permit a higher density, allowing for the creation of 1,500,000 square meters of office space instead of the 750,000 originally planned. The number of apartments was increased from 4,500 to 7,500, and the projected working population from 50,000 to 100,000.

It may be recalled that the replanning of La Défense also embodied an increase in height limits, with the result that it became highly controversial on æsthetic grounds.

37. "Tours et détours pour La Défense," *Architecture d'aujourd'hui,* no. 178, March–April 1975, p. 27. The statement first appeared in *L'aurore,* September 29, 1969.

Discussing the change in building controls, the assistant director of architecture, Claude Robin, said: "In the course of the meetings in which I participated, the question was never discussed in a profound manner, probably because the problem of visibility over a long distance was not at that time very well understood. The subjects brought up were of a financial or urban nature, but never æsthetic" (figure 212).[38]

Heart Surgery: The Renovation of Les Halles

One fact that tended to minimize opposition to redevelopment in Paris was that renewal areas were generally restricted to peripheral arrondissements. The historic core and the densely built central districts had remained for the most part intact, and it was possible to justify the extensive renovation of outlying quarters as a means of removing the pressure for redevelopment from the center. In the late 1960s, however, the heart of Paris itself seemed threatened with a drastic transformation. This came about through the decision to transfer the old wholesale food market of Les Halles to the suburbs (figure 213).

In the time of Haussmann the market, located in the First Arrondissement slightly north of the Seine and west of the Boulevard Sébastopol, had been provided with a new set of buildings — a large complex of metal and glass pavilions, designed by Victor Baltard and destined to become a much-admired monument of advanced nineteenth-century design. Located in the center of a densely built area, the market had long presented transport problems, and as the Paris region grew, access became increasingly difficult.

In its 1913 report, the Commission d'Extension included recommendations for shifting the site of Les Halles, "of which the filth and smell are so annoying just a few steps from the Louvre, the Hôtel de Ville, and the stock exchange, and which blocks, for long hours, all the movement on the most important streets. The commission had been concerned with the problem of providing increased open space in the dense fabric of Paris, and it had concluded that the best method of obtaining land would be to move large institutions such as factories, warehouses, hospitals, and markets out of the center. Looking to the future, the report exclaimed, "What a park it will be possible to create in front of the nave of Saint Eustache."[39]

From the time of the First World War, the market facilities themselves had been viewed as needing modernization, and from this time until after the Second World War proposals had been made for rebuilding the market on the same site. The impossibility of expansion, however, and constantly increasing difficulties in

38. *France Soir,* September 9, 1972.
39. Commission d'Extension de Paris, Préfecture du Département de la Seine. Vol. 2. *Considérations techniques* (Paris: Chaux, 1913), p. 90.

213. The quarter of Les Halles, looking west. The open space in the foreground is the Plateau Beaubourg, formerly Îlot Insalubre 1, which was cleared during the 1930s. It is now the site of the Pompidou National Center of Art and Culture. In the background are the market pavilions of Les Halles, now demolished.

214. Les Halles undergoing demolition in 1971.

transport led to the decision in 1961 to create a new produce market south of Paris at Rungis. The Halles quarter was to receive a general renovation, for which detailed preparatory studies were begun in 1963. The removal of market activity from the Baltard pavilions began in 1969.

As proposals for the redevelopment of the Halles district evolved, the transformation of the market site and its surroundings became a focus of continuing and often bitter controversy. Included in the issues were the alteration of the social and physical character of the Halles district, the destruction of the Baltard pavilions, and the nature of the proposed rebuilding on the site (figure 214).

Opposition to the destruction of the market buildings centered on their remarkable æsthetic quality and their importance to the architectural heritage of Paris. Zola had once written that "since the beginning of the century, only one original monument has been built . . . which has arisen naturally in the light of our time. It is Les Halles."[40] In 1969, when the market began moving to its new location, the city did not attempt an immediate demolition of the pavilions. Instead, spaces both in the cellars and aboveground were leased for a variety of uses, including theatrical presentations, concerts, and expositions of various kinds. Thus, while the Municipal Council was contemplating the creation of a new cultural center on the nearby Plateau Beaubourg, it had inadvertently created a notably successful one in the old market complex. Many Parisians evidently hoped that the pavilions might continue to function in their new capacity, and in the summer of 1971, as the time of demolition approached, protests against their destruction intensified.

40. Quoted in Simone Saint Girons, *Les Halles* (Paris: Hachette, 1971), p. 80.

215. Redevelopment of the site of Les Halles. The *chantier* in 1976.

City officials, however, insisted that the removal of the market buildings was necessary to facilitate the construction of a new subterranean station complex linking the city Métro system with the new RER system (figure 215). Les Halles was destined to become a major interchange for public rail transport, and its emplacement was thus potentially one of the most valuable in Paris. Initial plans for the area included the creation of an international trade center intended to provide 90,000 square meters of prestigious office space. A group of design studies prepared for the city in 1967 had outlined the possibilities of an intensive exploitation of the market site, and they served to reinforce apprehension regarding future redevelopment. Not only was a beloved and admired architectural ensemble to be destroyed, but it seemed destined to be replaced by a complex of skyscraper office towers.

To some observers the destruction of Les Halles came to symbolize the threatened destruction of Paris. While demolition of the pavilions was commencing in 1971, a popular magazine commented in an article, entitled "Who Sold Les Halles?": "There was a Paris to which everyone was attached, and within which was born another city, humane, welcoming, tolerable on both the social and urban level. The least one can say is that modern Paris, the Paris of the second half of the twentieth century, is a miserable failure. Look at Maine-Montparnasse. . . .the sector around the Place d'Italie. . . .the lamentable Front de Seine of the Fifteenth Arrondissement. . . and the things we shall see tomorrow. . . .Paris resembles more and more the capital of an undeveloped country, bristling with capitalist symbols and poor counterfeits of an architecture which has some meaning in New York, but which is here an architecture of deception."[41]

City officials had been generally unreceptive to the more radical proposals of the 1967 competition, and subsequent government studies tended to involve reductions in the amount of building projected for the site, together with increases in open space.

While the market emplacement of Les Halles was to be demolished and rebuilt, the surrounding district was to receive a general renovation. It was recognized that the quarter, although deteriorated, possessed æsthetic qualities worthy of preservation, and in preparation extensive analysis was made of the existing urban fabric. It was observed that the number of buildings surviving from the eighteenth century endowed the district with an overall homogeneity. Facades at the time had generally been narrow. The buildings usually had a shop on the ground floor, the first floor being reserved for the proprietor, the attic for servants; and the other floors rented out. Materials of construction included stone and wooden frame, almost all with surface finishes of plaster.

The architectural character of the Halles district had always been dominated by its function as a market center, and it never achieved the fashionable cachet of the Marais to the east. In contrast to the Marais, Les Halles was never a district of mansions, and it was noted that, "with the exception of certain prestigious buildings, Les Halles does not present at first sight monumental ensembles of exceptional architectural quality, of which the need for conservation is indisputable. Its interest resides in characteristics less apparent and more subtle: an ancient urban fabric which determines the prevailing land allotment, street patterns which conform to the historic ways of the capital, sequences of facades filled with fantasy and harmony, forming a refined and elegant urban decor."[42] It was observed that the atmosphere of the district depended on the "narrowness of the street, its sinuosity, the height of the buildings, the silhouettes carved out against the sky by the dormers and the great stumps of the chimneys."[43] Many of the buildings were found to possess detailing of great value, and such elements were cited as "very beautiful stairways in wood with turned balustrades, vaulted basements, a profusion of window supports and balconies in cast iron, porticoes, and mouldings" (figure 216).[44]

41. André Fermigier, "Qui a vendu Les Halles," *Le nouvel observateur,* July 12, 1971, p. 12.
42. "Les Halles: les études de restauration-rehabilitation," *Paris projet,* no. 1, July 1969, p. 35.
43. Unpublished report of the Société Civile d'Études pour l'Aménagement des Halles, Archives of the Atelier Parisien d'Urbanisme (APUR) of the Paris prefecture.
44. "Les Halles," p. 35.

Within these buildings dwelling standards generally reflected slum conditions, and although the renovation of the Halles quarter embodied an intention to preserve the æsthetic qualities of the district, it inevitably produced a social transformation. Closely tied to the function of the market, the surrounding neighborhood was long a boisterous working-class district, famed for its all-night bistros and restaurants. The removal of the market function would in any case have brought changes to the area. The planned redevelopment served to accelerate the process, however, and as buildings were demolished or renovated in accordance with improved standards, their generally impoverished inhabitants were forced out. The resentment felt by many was exemplified in the prophesy on a hand-lettered sign posted in 1971 on a block of buildings slated for reconstruction.

The center of Paris will be beautiful. Luxury will be king. The buildings of the Saint Martin block will be of high standing. But we will not be here. The commercial facilities will be spacious and rational. The parking immense. But we won't work here anymore. The streets will be spacious and the pedestrian ways numerous. But we won't walk here anymore. We won't live here anymore. Only the rich will be here. They have chosen to live in our quarter. The elected officials responding to their wishes have decided. The renovation is not for us. (Figures 217 and 218)

216. OPPOSITE. A street in the Halles quarter.

217, 218. Renovated buildings near the National Center of Art and Culture.

Because of the complexity of the new underground transportation network that was to be built, the redevelopment of the Halles emplacement was of necessity a long-range effort. As the massive excavations began in 1971 and subterranean construction gradually proceeded, the city continued to modify designs for the completed surface installations. The entrance into the transportation complex was to be marked by a sunken concourse, a so-called forum, partially open to the air and containing shops and other commercial facilities. In general the development studies tended to reflect a growing sense of conservatism with regard to new construction. Acknowledging this climate of opinion when he assumed office in 1974, President Giscard d'Estaing, in his public utterances, emphasized the improvement of the "quality of life" in Paris, rather than the pursuit of continuous expansion. The Halles project was taken up for study again, and a new plan was produced in 1976. The previously projected international trade center was eliminated from the scheme, and surface building restricted to the periphery of the site. The central area was envisioned as a formal garden. By the fall of 1978, the deep excavation of Les Halles was at last filling up, and surface constructions began to appear. The first of these was a windowless concrete cube thirty meters high, destined to contain the central

power plant. Although government publicity indicated that its unnerving bulk would eventually be masked by apartment housing (figure 219), the unannounced apparition of this elephantine structure underlined the fact that the city had yet to present an architectural scheme for Les Halles. In the absence of a definitive plan, apprehension about the future exploitation of the site revived. While the mayor of Paris, Jacques Chirac, stressed the desirability of flexible evolution, journalistic comment was pessimistic. As always in modern Paris, one might hope for the best but should probably be prepared for the worst.

The projected park on the Halles site represented the first major landscaped space to be foreseen in Paris in many years. Although the provision of open space in the city had been a chronic concern of planners since the time of Haussmann, little progress had been made in the provision of gardens and parks. The high cost of land and the general shortage of sites had tended to make new open areas virtually unobtainable. There had also been a steady attrition of private gardens as the volume of building intensified. In 1975 Bernard Lafay, former president of the Municipal Council, published *Schéma d'un plan vert pour Paris*.[45] In this study he concluded that Paris, which contained 345 hectares of parkland within its boundaries, was the worst served city in the world in terms of green space. The city had barely 1.40 square meters per inhabitant, compared with 9 in Rome and London, 25 in Vienna, and 50 in Washington, D.C. Like others before him, he deplored the bad distribution of open space in Paris, noting, moreover, that after twenty years the 1953 requirement that the built areas of the zone be counterbalanced by the creation of equivalent open areas in the city had not been met. The number of trees in the city had been steadily declining, and out of the 1,200 kilometers of streets only 330, or 27.5 percent, carried planting. Street widening operations had destroyed many trees and pollution had taken a heavy toll.

Included in Lafay's proposal was the suggestion that the walls surrounding many private and publicly owned gardens be removed, making these areas visible from the street. He also surveyed the city to look for recoverable land, concluding that 101 hectares of land owned by the railroads and the army could be transformed into parks. He believed that in a period of twenty years, the city could add 330 hectares of parkland to the urban fabric, raising the total per inhabitant to 3 square meters. This would still be far short of the norm set by the World Health Organization of 10 to 13 square meters per inhabitant.

The Sacred Polygon

In the mid-1970s, a government survey summarized in statistics what had already become very apparent. In the period between 1954 and 1974, Paris had undergone

45. Bernard Lafay, *Schéma d'un plan vert pour Paris* (Paris: Club Paris 2000, 1975).

219. OPPOSITE. The site of Les Halles, looking north, showing redevelopment proposed in 1978. Part of the area would contain a formal garden. Access to a subterranean transportation complex would be provided by a sunken concourse, or "forum." New building shown adjacent to the concourse is to combine housing with a central power plant. Additional sites for new building are indicated at the eastern and southern edges of the site.

an astonishingly rapid physical redevelopment, with demolition and reconstruction encompassing no less than 1,200 hectares or 24 percent of the buildable surface of the city.

Along with this urban renovation came greater building density, with floor area increasing at a rate of 12.3 percent, or 14.7 million square meters. Thus, for every 100 square meters demolished, 267 square meters had been built. There was also an overall increase in building height, with a gain of about 12 meters in buildings used for housing. The visible evolution of Paris into a major office center was reflected in building statistics. In terms of floor space, between 1954 and 1974 housing increased at a rate of 16.8 percent, government building at 13.3 percent, and offices and commercial building at 21.9 percent. Meanwhile, floor space given over to industrial uses had decreased at a rate of 28.4 percent.

With regard to the future, the report noted that if the same rate of reconstruction were to continue, Paris would be completely rebuilt in eighty years and would experience a 50 percent increase in floor surface. Readers were assured, however, that this involved "a purely theoretical and improbable extrapolation. A period of rapid and relatively anarchic renovation could little by little be succeeded by a period which is characterized primarily by the conservation and maintenance of the building fabric, with a much slower renewal and a reduced densification."[46]

A slower pace of renovation and a greater conservation of the existing urban environment would be, for many Parisians, a highly welcome prospect. That much of the beauty and richness of Paris lies in its architectural heritage has long been taken for granted, and the dismay that has frequently greeted new construction has been matched by bitter regret for what has meanwhile been destroyed. Yet the question of preservation has never been, and likely can never be, satisfactorily resolved. The vitality of Paris has continually inspired growth and change in the urban fabric, and not even the most ardent preservationists have wished to see the city totally static. Nor has there been universal agreement about what should be saved. In the view of some, the residue of the past is more than abundant; to others it has dwindled with appalling rapidity. The situation is also complicated by the constant transformation of the new into the old. The boulevards of Haussmann, so destructive of the existing urban texture when first built, may now be regarded as part of the historic inheritance. Art Nouveau buildings once deplored for their negation of traditional forms, and even International Style structures, may now be deemed worthy of classification. Just as the Baltard pavilions of Les Halles, revolutionary in their day, were later viewed as a precious relic of the past, so it is not inconceivable that one day protest may arise over a threatened demolition of the Pompidou center.

46. 20 *Ans de transformations de Paris 1954–74* (Paris: Ville de Paris, 1974). Prepared by the Association Universitaire de Recherches Géographiques et Cartographiques, with an accompanying text by Jean Bastié. The pages are unnumbered.

As the pace of urban change has accelerated, however, proposals for preservation have corresponded in scope to the scale of destruction. In 1964 the architect Claude Charpentier proposed the complete preservation of what he termed the "sacred polygon," the historic central districts of Paris, which he deemed "the heart of France." This area could be defined by a line which, "leaving Montmartre, would pass near the Étoile, enclose the Champ de Mars, follow the Boulevard du Montparnasse, include the Montagne Sainte Geneviève, and touch the Gare de Lyon, to rejoin Montmartre by way of the Place da la République."[47] Perhaps the most ambitious preservation proposal was made by the writer Albert Guérard, who suggested in 1930 that the entire city of Paris be listed as a monument.[48]

Preservation in Paris has been complicated not only by uncertainty as to what to preserve, but also by legal complexities arising from the rights of property owners. The destruction of historic Paris, although in some instances linked to government programs of renovation, has to a larger extent been the result of private initiative. The demolitions accompanying the street clearance operations of Haussmann were, of course, the focus of much criticism, as they affected the historic core of the city. Haussmann himself, however, remained convinced that he had preserved everything worth saving, and once challenged his critics to "name me just one ancient monument of interest, just one building of artistic value, destroyed by my administrators."[49] By isolating important monuments from their surroundings, he believed he was enhancing their visual impact.

In the years following Haussmann's retirement, interest in ancient buildings continued to mount, although effective legal provisions for preservation were slow to be developed. At the national level, the Commission des Monuments Historiques had the mission of selecting and listing buildings worthy to be preserved and allocating government funds for restoration work. The authority of the commission was, however, somewhat precarious, for although classified buildings were eligible for some government funds, they were not assured permanent protection.

In 1887 a national preservation law specified that no alterations could be made on any classified monument without the authorization of the minister of fine arts. The law was applicable, however, only to publicly owned buildings. No privately owned structure could be classified without the consent of the proprietor, and by 1909 only three such buildings had been listed in Paris. These were the Hôtel Lauzun, the Hôtel Sully, and the Logis à Tourelle on the Rue des Francs-Bourgeois.

Public attention in Paris had been directed toward questions of preservation through the foundation in 1884 of the Société des Amis des Monuments Parisiens, of which Victor Hugo served as honorary president. The Société concerned itself not only with the preservation of existing structures but also with new building, and

47. Claude Charpentier, "Le polygone sacré," *Urbanisme*, no. 84, 1964, p. 32.
48. Albert Guérard, *L'avenir de Paris* (Paris: Payot, 1930), p. 72.
49. Quoted in Anthony Sutcliffe, *The Autumn of Central Paris* (London: Edward Arnold, 1970), p. 181.

it actively opposed construction of an elevated Métro system in Paris. Although it was a private organization, the Société attracted the support of some government officials, and Alfred Lamouroux, an adherent who was a member of the Municipal Council, proposed the creation of a commission for Paris which would have a function similar to that of the Commission des Monuments Historiques for France as a whole. As a result, the Commission du Vieux Paris was created in 1897.

The functions of the commission included historical research, the creation of building inventories, and advising on preservation. As the commission was to retain only an advisory role, it would prove to be somewhat ineffective in opposing the economic powers of the city. Viewing the record of the commission in 1943, an ardent preservationist, Georges Pillement, observed: "It could only express its wishes. These wishes, completely platonic, were simply set aside as soon as a powerful interest came into play. And there were always interests in play. Who didn't have a municipal councillor up his sleeve? There is always profit to be made in demolitions, reconstructions, opening of new streets, realignments, enlargements, and other so-called works of urbanism. How do you think the poor Commission du Vieux Paris can have a project adopted which has no interest but the beauty of Paris, the protection of an ancient monument, of a historic site, when it can offer neither bribes nor any material advantage to its opponents."[50]

In addition to the constant attrition of old buildings resulting from economic pressures, there was, following the definition of the *îlots insalubres* in 1904, a continuing threat that certain old quarters would be wiped out as a public health measure. In the view of some, no solution other than complete demolition would suffice to rid the city of these plague spots. Others had considerable doubts, and in the view of one preservationist there was "no conception more false than the one envisaged in Paris, which condemns an entire quarter with the injurious epithet of *îlot insalubre*."[51] Another writer concurred, stating, "An old house is not, on principle, less healthy than a new house. . . . An old house, well maintained and carefully disinfected, is less dangerous than these modern houses built in haste and exposed to the most sinister drafts."[52]

For those modern architects eagerly seeking to recreate the urban environment during the 1920s and 1930s, the *îlots insalubres* provided a focus for many proposals which, like the renovations of Haussmann, would have left historic buildings isolated while razing their surroundings. Projects exhibited at the 1937 fair, according to one observer, "filled the Parisians with stupor: one saw there, in the great empty spaces planted with fusains and tailored shrubs, some of our most beautiful monuments—the Hôtel de Sens, Saint Étienne du Mont, Saint Eustache,

50. Georges Pillement, "Démolitions présentes et futures," *Destinée de Paris* (Paris: Chêne, 1943), p. 80.
51. Ibid., p. 96.
52. Bernard Champigneuille, "Destinée de Paris," *Destinée de Paris,* pp. 13–14.

Saint Séverin, Saint Merri—put in quarantine, separated from the life of the city in which they have ceased to participate."[53]

In 1909 the national government set up an interministerial committee to coordinate the action of the city and the national government with regard to preservation in Paris. The impetus came partly from the controversy surrounding the 1902 building regulations, for as a growing volume of new building began to depart both in height and style from previous norms, the historic fabric seemed increasingly threatened. Shortly afterward, between 1910 and 1911, the city of Paris established the Sous-Commission des Perspectives Monumentales under the direction of Eugène Hénard. The report of this commission in 1911 attempted to list, for purposes of protection, not only individual buildings but entire urban perspectives.[54]

Meanwhile the steady attrition of old buildings continued. In 1911 Auguste Rodin expressed his regret at the increasing disappearance of seventeenth- and eigthteenth-century structures. "Why demolish them?", he asked. "We will never do anything better than that which past ages have bequeathed us. The old Parisian mansions of the Marais, of the Île Saint Louis and the quais of the Seine, are all of an elegance that will never be equaled."[55]

In 1913, on the eve of the First World War, a new national preservation law was promulgated. It provided for the arbitrary classifying of private property, subject to compensation, if such a listing were deemed to be in the public interest. Buildings could either be classified as monuments or included in an *inventaire supplémentaire,* a list of buildings whose demolition was prohibited. All alterations to classified buildings were to be supervised by the administration of the Caisse Nationale des Monuments Historiques. In the view of many Parisian preservationists, however, there were numerous buildings of purely local interest which were unaffected by the new law, and government money was not always easily obtainable for desired preservation efforts. In general, the preservation of any building was best assured through its direct acquisition by the city or the national government.

The ideal of preservation continued to gain ground among officials and urbanists, however. The Commission d'Extension report of 1913, for example, was generally conservative in its proposals for street widenings in the historic center, and it recognized the desirability of maintaining the historic urban fabric intact. The general slowdown in urban renovation between the wars also tended to postpone

53. Pillement, "Démolitions présentes et futures," pp. 98, 103.

54. Eugène Hénard, "Rapports à la Commission des Perspectives Monumentales de la Ville de Paris," *Journal de l'architecture,* March–April 1911, p. 4. Considering monuments not only in individual terms, but also with an eye to their surroundings, Hénard listed thirty-nine sites according to three categories. The first, the *liste de première urgence,* included perspectives and sites he considered currently menaced. The second included places that could be threatened through the application of the 1902 building regulations, while the third included sites not immediately threatened, but which could be marred in the future by private building in the vicinity.

55. Auguste Rodin, "La Beauté de Paris," *La Revue,* July 15, 1911, p. 166.

large-scale projects which might have threatened older districts. Meanwhile, appreciation of such areas as Montmartre, the Marais, the Île Saint Louis, and the Latin Quarter grew.

Reminiscing about her early days in Paris, Gertrude Stein remarked:

We none of us lived in old parts of Paris then. We lived in the rue de Fleurus just a hundred year old quarter, a great many of us lived around there and on the boulevard Raspail which was not even cut through then . . . So from 1900 to 1930 those of us who lived in Paris did not live in picturesque quarters even those who lived in Montmartre like Picasso and Braque did not live in old houses, they lived in fifty year old houses at most and now we all live in the ancient quarter near the river, now that the twentieth century is decided and has its character we all tend to want to live in seventeenth century houses, not barracks of ateliers as we did then. The seventeenth century houses are just as cheap as our barracks of ateliers were then but now we need the picturesque the splendid we need the air and space you get only in old quarters. It was Picasso who said the other day when they were talking about tearing down the insalubrious parts of Paris but it is only in the insalubrious quarters that there is sun and air and space, and it is true, and we are all living there the beginners and the middle ones and the older ones and the old ones we all live in old houses in ramshackle quarters. Well all this is natural enough.[56]

The desirability of urban preservation was reflected in national town-planning legislation in 1919 and 1924, which gave municipalities the power to establish protected zones around historic monuments and to safeguard groups of buildings. In 1927 the preservation law of 1913 was strengthened to permit the inscribing of buildings on the *inventaire supplémentaire* without compensation. Landlords wishing either to demolish or to alter such property were required to give notice in order to allow the property to be considered for the protected list. The ruling could not, however, control the deterioration of buildings, and many landlords, unable to finance repairs or obtain government assistance, simply let properties decay until demolition was unavoidable.

During the 1930s and 1940s legislation relevant to preservation and the listing of monuments and sites continued, although in many cases the laws were not rigidly enforced. Government bodies, moreover, continued to be hesitant to classify buildings against the wishes of property owners. Protection of many buildings was limited to the facade and rooflines, permitting owners to renovate interiors. Between 1928 and 1940, for example, the Place Vendôme, while preserved on the exterior, was largely renovated into commercial office space. The facades of the Place des Vosges and the Palais Royal are similarly protected.

56. Gertrude Stein, *Paris, France* (New York: Scribner, 1940), pp. 15, 17–18.

A national law of 1943 established a perimeter of protection controlling all construction visible within five hundred meters of a scheduled building. Provisions for the compulsory purchase of property necessary to develop the surroundings of a monument were also included. Although urban renovation in Paris was generally halted by the war, planning efforts proceeded, frequently reflecting a conservative view of the Parisian townscape. Projects for the *îlots insalubres* began to display a new willingness to save the existing urban texture and, in contrast to earlier schemes, often suggested only partial demolitions.

In 1962 a new national preservation law, usually called the Malraux law, was promulgated. This law permitted the creation of *secteurs sauvegardés,* areas or ensembles of buildings whose preservation was deemed desirable for either historical or æsthetic reasons. An entire town could be so classified. An official commentary on the law observed: "It can happen sometimes that the architectural value of the houses examined is weak or debatable, but it is in their ensemble that the irreplaceable harmony of these quarters resides, it is in the alignments, the projection of the facades, that the soul of these blocks resides."[57]

Perhaps the most noteworthy example of a protected sector is the Marais. This district, lying east of the center of Paris, was a focus of fashionable residence in the seventeenth century, containing the Place des Vosges as well as a remarkable number of large mansions. As wealth and fashion migrated westward, the Marais evolved into a center of working-class residence, small commerce, and industry (figure 220). Existing buildings were partitioned and altered into cheap lodgings, while courtyards filled up with sheds and workshops, gradually transforming an area of large houses and gardens into one of the most densely built slums of Paris (figure 221).

The Marais occupied an area of 126 hectares, with a population density reported in 1969 to average 900 inhabitants per hectare, compared with 300 for Paris as a whole. Some blocks attained a population of 2,000 per hectare. Ground occupancy by buildings covered 85 percent of the surface, as compared with 55 percent for Paris as a whole, and green space was only 1.7 percent, compared with 3.3 percent for the city. It was reported that 30 percent of the dwellings were without running water, 60 percent without individual toilets, and 10 percent without electricity.[58]

The southern part of the Marais bordering the Seine had previously been designated an *îlot insalubre* (Îlot 16), and in 1941 the city had envisaged a program of renovation that would have razed the entire sector. Opponents of the demolitions protested strenuously, with the result that a somewhat more conservative surgery was undertaken following the war. The renovation of Îlot 16, while embodying

57. "Le plan de sauvegarde du Marais," *Paris projet,* no. 2, p. 51.
58. The foregoing statistics are from "Le plan de sauvegarde du Marais," p. 47. This article was based on a report made by the architects charged with developing the Marais plan and on a memorandum presented by the prefect of Paris to the Municipal Assembly in October 1969.

220. The Rue Saint Antoine in the Marais. The large building at center is the Hôtel de Mayenne, built in 1605.

221. The Rue du Prévot in the Marais.

222. Houses near the Church of Saint Gervais (at left) before renovation.

223. Houses near the Church of Saint Gervais after renovation.

considerable demolition and street widening, also included the restoration of the Hôtel de Sens and Hôtel d'Aumont. Near the church of Saint Gervais, an ensemble of old houses was restored, and the emplacement between the church and the houses was divested of its industrial sheds and transformed into a garden (figure 222 and 223). While some viewed Îlot 16 as exemplifying a relatively conservative attitude toward urban redevelopment, others cited its renovation as a prime example of wasteful destructiveness. To the preservationist Georges Pillement the district reflected, "a catastrophic operation, absolutely imbecilic."[59]

The controversy over Îlot 16 focused the attention of city officials on the remainder of the Marais, bringing about a desire to avoid the mistakes of earlier redevelopment efforts. Restoration of major monuments began during the 1950s,

59. Georges Pillement, *Paris poubelle* (Paris: Pauvert, 1974), p. 38.

and, with the Malraux law providing official impetus, the Marais was declared a *secteur sauvegardé in* 1964, the first such area in Paris and the largest in all of France.[60]

The Marais plan was not a detailed outline for redevelopment, but rather a "plan of intentions," fixing certain points of orientation for future urbanization. It was hoped "at the same time to conserve the traditional architectural aspect of the Marais, in protecting important buildings and in assuring the homogeneity of their environment, and to create more satisfying conditions for the life of the quarter and of its inhabitants." An architectural inventory resulted in a listing of 56 buildings of "very great quality" (primarily the largest of the mansions), classified in entirety or in part; 121 buildings listed completely or partially in the inventory of historic monuments (and susceptible of being classified); and 526 buildings of "very great interest," neither classified nor listed, but worthy of protection as monuments. In addition there were 1,000 buildings "which belong in the category of buildings of

60. A second *secteur sauvegardé* was created in Paris in 1972 when the historic quarter of the Seventh Arrondissement was so classified.

224. The Rue des Rosiers.

accompaniment or of atmosphere, and which form that environment without which
the monument loses its scale, its harmony, and its significance. Without these humble
dwellings . . . one could not truly speak of a Marais quarter." Such buildings were
often found to possess highly attractive detailing, such as cast-iron balconies, old
wooden staircases and doorways, and so forth (figure 224). It was intended that all
old buildings in the Marais be protected from destruction and subject to long-range
restoration.[61]

In terms of ground coverage, a program of "curettage" was recommended in
which the centers of the densely built blocks would be gradually cleared (figure
225). It was in the centers of blocks that most of the "parasitic" structures—the
sheds, workshops, and new additions—were located. The plan indicated which
buildings it seemed desirable to demolish, but it was stressed that this was a "wish"
rather than an inflexible program. It was assumed that the future evolution of the

61. "Le plan de sauvegarde du Marais"; quotations are from pp. 55, 57–58.

225. Block interior being gutted in the Marais.

Marais would involve a sequence of individual decisions governed by circumstances. Although the plan did not lay down a particular program of demolition, it did specify that the recovered land was to be used as green space. A network of "continuous gardens," open to the public, could thus be created, linked to the streets by passages and arcades and permitting an eventual system of pedestrian circulation through the blocks, independent of the street system. Small retail commerce might also be established in the opened block interiors. As to street widening, it was assumed that the character of the district would prohibit "all spectacular street operations."[62]

It was recognized that the physical renovation of the Marais would inevitably involve changes in the economic life of the quarter. In 1970, the predominant activities included the manufacture of ready-made clothing, knick-knacks, and optical wares. There were also a few producers of chemical products and two metal foundries. The reduction of this type of activity appeared a natural accompaniment to renovation, and it was suggested that some workshops be regrouped at two new poles, one to the northwest, near the Rues Réaumur, de Turbigo, and de Bretagne, the other toward the southeast, near the boulevard Beaumarchais. It was recommended, however, that artisans of high-class goods remain in the quarter, where their activities would be accompanied by new enterprises drawn by the cachet of the Marais, such as bookstores, interior decorators, art galleries, antique dealers, and high-fashion shops. Small commerce was considered desirable in the quarter in order to conserve "its animation and its own life, and to avoid, at all cost, making a museum zone of it."[63]

Although the planners expressed an awareness of the grave problems of uprooting which might be faced by those inhabitants forced out of the Marais, they saw no alternative to a general reduction in population. It was observed that "the maintenance of the present average density of 900 people per hectare, with the dwelling conditions which this implies for certain families, sometimes crowding 8 or 10 people in unhealthy apartments of two rooms and kitchen, deprived of the most elementary comfort, can no longer be conceived in our epoch."[64] In order to achieve the same average density as the rest of Paris, 20,000 people or 25 percent of the total population, would have to leave the quarter.

Although the Marais was to be a district of preservation rather than renewal, the social transformation of the quarter seemed destined to resemble that of working-class districts actually demolished and rebuilt. It was perhaps inevitable that the Marais, with its architectural beauty, its calm ambience, and its relatively central location, would one day revert to its original status as a quarter of fashion and wealth. (figure 226). Although the city plan for the area implied a long-range period of renovation, the pace of transformation has become increasingly rapid as

62. Ibid., p. 63.
63. Ibid., p. 62.
64. Ibid., p. 66.

226. Courtyard of a renovated building in the Marais.

promoters gain possession of old structures and remodel them into luxury apartments. In the process, of course, facades have been refurbished and the process of deterioration halted. Many old mansions that were subjected to years of alteration and neglect have begun to look like mansions again (figures 227–229). Yet one cannot escape the conviction that when the process is completed and there is no one left in the Marais but rich people, the district will have lost much of its interest. A government report on the Marais praised its many "humble dwellings, often ornamented with delicious cast iron."[65] The humble inhabitants of such buildings, one assumes, were deemed insufficiently delicious to warrant preservation.

65. Ibid., p. 56.

227. The Hôtel de Sully before restoration. This mansion, built on the Rue Saint Antoine in 1624, had been subject to extensive alteration. A central portion was added between the side pavilions, and additional floor levels inserted to accommodate a wide range of occupants. Government renovation began in 1951.

229. OPPOSITE. The Hôtel de Lamoignon, built in 1584, has been renovated to serve as the Bibliothèque Historique de la Ville de Paris.

228. The Hôtel de Sully after restoration. It is now the headquarters of the Caisse Nationale des Monuments Historiques.

Predictions

In 1865 the rapidity with which Haussmann's renovations were altering the face of Paris inspired a literary fantasy in which the author, Victor Fournel, imagined himself awakening in the Paris of a century hence. As in most such predictions, contemporary trends were projected into the future, and the Paris of 1965 was envisioned as the product of a hundred years of continuous rebuilding. Thus, by the mid-twentieth century, "as a result of transforming and embellishing itself, the great city had become totally renewed from head to foot. There did not remain a single vestige of the shadowy past which, here and there, had still dishonored its splendor in the year 1865. A century of assiduous effort, directed by a half-dozen prefects, who transmitted like a sacred trust the furious monomania of construction and the delirium tremens of demolition, had made of it the prototypical capital of modern civilization." Not only would all traces of the distant past have been obliterated, but the already observable uniformity of Haussmann's boulevards would have come to dominate the entire city. The streets would be lined with identical, fifty-meter-high buildings. "All these buildings, of which the width equaled the height, formed a long series of gigantic cubes, regularly aligned."[66]

The urban fabric of the new Paris was foreseen as subject to total design control governing every aspect of the city, from the form and placement of monumental structures to the precise and detailed furnishings of shops and restaurants. Thus the variety and visual richness of Paris would have been replaced by a mechanically-ordered uniformity.

Whether or not Fournel would have been gratified to see the real twentieth-century Paris, one cannot say. Although the city was to encompass certain transformations far more radical than Fournel's imaginings, in 1965 the new had not yet obliterated the old, and some parts of the city would have been easily recognizable to a visitor from the previous century. Fournel had been wrong, of course, in predicting the unbroken continuance of the energetic pace of redevelopment that characterized the Second Empire. In succeeding decades, political instability, economic crises, and wars tended to mitigate comprehensive planning power and prohibit large-scale programs of reconstruction. It would not be until after the Second World War that a period of intensive urban renovation returned.

The Paris of 1965 was not unlike the Paris of 1865 in that the city was once again in the midst of a physical upheaval (figure 230). Just as in the time of Haussmann, many were alarmed at the new scale of redevelopment and apprehensive about the future of their beloved city. Just as in Haussmann's time, too, however, opinion was

66. Victor Fournel, *Paris nouveau et Paris futur* (Paris: Lecoffre, 1865), pp. 234, 235. The bulk of the book consists of a critique of Haussmann's renovations.

230. OPPOSITE. Construction site near the Arc de Triomphe, 1967.

divided, and to some the new face of Paris was a sign of vitality. To proponents of growth, to those who saw in the changing cityscape evidence of technical mastery and economic prosperity, twentieth-century Paris was both having her cake and eating it. In a speech given in 1972, the prefect of the Paris region, Maurice Doublet, assured his audience that "when heads of foreign governments come to Paris, they unanimously emphasize the excellence of the results achieved: respect for eternal Paris, renewal of future Paris."[67] Heads of government, however, often receive a somewhat restricted view of the places they visit.

67. Maurice Doublet, *Les transports dans la région parisienne* (Conférence des Ambassadeurs, November 1972), p. 8.

7 THE CAPITAL OF EUROPE: PLANNING THE PARIS REGION

When Victor Fournel made his predictions in 1865 for the Paris of 1965, he correctly assumed that the already visible expansion of the city outside its boundaries would continue (figure 231). In his fantasy he reported that Paris "had successively broken its new walls and spilled out over all parts of its surroundings, absorbing them into its body. It was now more than one hundred kilometers around and in itself filled the Département de la Seine. Versailles was its royal vestibule; Pontoise was proud to form one of its suburbs. Each day the citizens of Meaux climbed the towers of their cathedral to see if the flood of Paris had reached them yet. . . . The Boulevard Sébastopol had pushed its advance to the gates of Senlis, and grandiose blocks of building, sown here and there across the arid and naked plain, in a disorder carefully regulated by the compass of the engineers, like so many surveyor's markers, rapidly extended Paris along the route to Fontainebleau. The monstrous cancer, always expanding, had chewed up all the flesh around it, and, annexation by annexation, all France had become its suburb."[1]

The size of Paris has long been a subject of concern, and as far back as the sixteenth century Henri II had expressed a desire to restrict its growth. Succeeding monarchs, including Louis XIV, attempted with little success to enforce prohibitions against construction beyond the city walls, and a minister of Louis XV warned in 1724 that, "considering the size that Paris has become, one cannot permit a single new addition without exposing the city to ruin."[2] While the city had grown slowly and steadily during the preindustrial age, the nineteenth century brought a sudden upsurge of population, and the rapid physical expansion of Paris was sufficient to alter all preconceptions of urban scale. To Edmondo de Amicis, the Paris of 1878 seemed overwhelming in size. In

1. Victor Fournel, *Paris nouveau et Paris futur* (Paris: Lecoffre, 1865), pp. 232–34.
2. Quoted by Michel Ragon in *Les erreurs monumentales* (Paris: Hachette, 1971), p. 225.

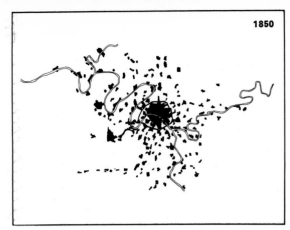

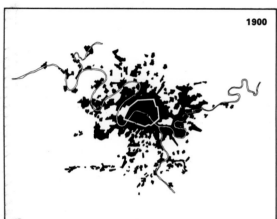

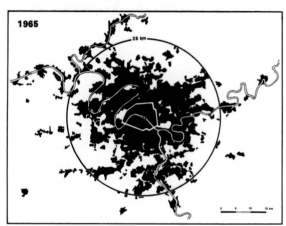

231. The growth of the Paris region.

his words, one scarcely enters the city "when one begins to divine, to feel, to breathe, I was about to say, the immensity of Paris, and one thinks with amazement of those solitary silent little cities, from which we started, called Turin, Milan and Florence, where everyone stands at the shop door, and all seem to live like one great family. Yesterday we were rowing on a small lake, today we are sailing on the ocean."[3]

Paris, together with its surrounding suburbs in the Département de la Seine, had a population of 2,410,000 in 1876 with 1,988,000 people living inside the city walls and 422,000 beyond. (This made Paris the largest city in Europe, with the exception of greater London, which had achieved a population of almost 4 million by 1870 and would reach 4,770,000 by 1880).[4] A century later, in 1976, greater Paris had attained a population of 9,878,524, of which 2,299,830 lived within the boundaries of the city and 7,578,694 in the surrounding area. The French capital had thus grown to four times the size of the metropolis which had seemed so immense to de Amicis.

3. Edmondo de Amicis, *Studies of Paris* (New York: Putnam, 1879), p. 5.
4. Berlin had attained a population of 826,000 by 1870 and would have 1,122,000 by 1880. Similar in size, New York had 942,292 people in 1870 and was to reach 1,206,299 by 1880. An Italian like de Amicis might well have been struck by the comparison in size between Paris and the cities of his own country. Rome had a population of only 244,000 in 1870, growing to 300,000 by 1880, while Milan, with 262,000 people in 1870, would have 322,000 by 1880. In the same period, Turin grew from 208,000 to 254,000.

In his fantasy of the future Paris, Victor Fournel likened the city to a "monstrous cancer." Similar comparisons were inspired by the twentieth-century reality, and an opponent of Parisian expansion was to describe the city in 1947 as a bloated urban parasite, "devouring the national substance."[5] Although advocates of decentralization were often to deplore the effects of untrammeled growth in the Paris region, many government officials and planners came to accept the expansion of the French capital as inevitable. In 1964 Paul Delouvrier, then Délégué Général du District of the newly formed Region of Paris, observed; "The figures of 12 to 16 million inhabitants which we have advanced for the region of Paris in the year 2000 were shocking when they were projected at the beginning of 1963. . . . We don't wish such an increase. . . . No member of the Municipal Council of Paris nor any member of the 1,305 municipal councils of the District of Paris wishes these figures to be attained. . . . But to deny reality, as has been done for too many years, will end in the situation we know: to live in a capital more and more unlivable."[6] As there appeared to be no effective way of arresting the growth of Paris, the only solution, he maintained, lay in the comprehensive planning of the Paris region.

Many problems might have been avoided if regional planning had been instituted sooner. Certainly urbanists had recognized such a need, and as Paris continued its amorphous expansion, numerous proposals were made for consolidating the region and directing its growth. Decisive action, however, was long in arriving, and by the time a regional plan was developed, certain opportunities had been irretrievably lost.

The Concours d'Idées: *1919*

The close of the First World War, it may be recalled, was accompanied by a strong interest in urban planning, resulting in legislation in 1919 which required all cities of 10,000 or more to prepare long-range plans for urban development. In Paris the new law inspired a design competition which included proposals for the Paris region.

Although there seemed to be no immediate likelihood of a political unification between Paris and its surroundings, the entrants were "advised to undertake their study with a large vision, without becoming preoccupied with administrative limitations, and to include in their plans the communes of the Département de la Seine and if they think it necessary, even parts of neighboring *départements*——in a word, everything that, in their conception, constitutes the Parisian agglomeration."[7]

The planning of the region was regarded by some urbanists as an opportunity to

5. Jean-François Gravier, *Paris et le désert Français* (Paris: Flammarion, 1972), p. 60.
6. Paul Delouvrier, "L'avenir de la nebuleuse Parisienne," *Urbanisme*, no. 84, 1964, p. 19.
7. Préfecture du Département de la Seine, Ville de Paris, *Programme du concours ouvert pour l'établissement du plan d'aménagement et d'extension de Paris* (Paris: Chaix, 1919), p. 4.

decongest the city of Paris. An official stressed "the need to reduce energetically the present density of the population, to break through the narrow limits which make Paris the most encumbered of all capitals, to send back into the open air for the greater part of his existence—to nature, to liberty—the anemic, locked-in, suffocated, and febrile Parisian. What is true today for an agglomeration of five million inhabitants will be all the more true for the millions of the future."[8] It was taken for granted that the Paris region was in a state of rapid expansion, and it had been predicted that the population of the city, which had been 2,900,000 in 1911, would reach 6 million by 1961. Assuming the same rate of increase in the suburbs, the population of the Parisian agglomeration would have reached 14 million.

The first prize was awarded to a plan prepared under the direction of Léon Jaussely, a professor at the École des Beaux Arts. In projecting his scheme, Jaussely presupposed a doubling of the Parisian population by the year 1961, at which time, according to his predictions, the region would have attained 8 to 9 million people. (This estimate proved to be reasonably accurate; greater Paris had a population of 7,369,999 by 1962.) He saw the future development of Paris to be closely allied to its position as a port, and he envisioned an augmentation of the existing system of canals, which, together with rail lines, would facilitate the distribution of raw materials and the growth of new industrial zones.

Improved transport was an important element in the Jaussely plan. He observed that within a radius of about 27 kilometers of Paris, rail transport had developed in a series of radial lines about 15 kilometers apart. Settlement patterns had generally followed these lines, leaving the intervening tracts relatively unpopulated, and it was proposed to introduce additional transport lines into these spaces. Modifications of the rail system were also proposed within the city of Paris. A system of tunnels was suggested to enable trains to pass directly through Paris instead of terminating at cul-de-sac stations, thus permitting suburban trains to distribute passengers at numerous points within the city.

Although Jaussely anticipated that rail and water routes would accommodate massive commuting and heavy transport, he included a series of new auto routes in his schemes. These were envisioned as landscaped roads along which parks and garden city communities would be developed. In addition to considering the suburbs as an area for new industry and residence, Jaussely believed they also represented a logical site for large institutions that were outgrowing their Parisian settings. He proposed moving the university science facilities to the vicinity of Sceaux and reestablishing the wholesale market and slaughterhouses outside Paris. A large exposition park was to be created near the Forest of Saint Germain, and aviation fields distributed around the city.

Augmented transportation systems provided the focus of most of the

8. Louis Bonnier, "L'esthétique et l'architecture dans le concours pour le plan d'aménagement et d'extension de Paris," *La vie urbaine,* 1920, p. 30.

prizewinning plans. The second-prize entry, directed by Alfred Agache, included a proposal prophetic of the future Réseau Express Régional (RER), in which a new suburban Métro system would connect with the existing city system. New motor roads, involving both radial and circular routes, characterized many of the plans. At the time of the competition, Ebenezer Howard's garden city concept was well known and highly influential among urbanists. Although none of the competition winners suggested the creation of self-sufficient garden cities, the term *cité jardin* was used to describe new residential satellite communities to be created in the Paris region. The fourth-prize winner, a scheme produced by Faure-Dujarric, Berrington, and Chaurès, proposed a series of loop-shaped rail lines connecting a total of one hundred such satellites.

Although there was no likelihood that the proposals of the 1919 competition would be immediately applied, the contest provided a focus for discussion of the Paris region and its future development. Whatever the virtues of the plans for Parisian extension, not all observers were convinced that growth was in itself a good thing. Analyzing the competition in 1920, a geographer was of the opinion that the Jaussely plan "foresaw for Paris an extension which . . . Paris must not attain and will not attain. That thirty years from now, as the project supposes, the Parisian population would have doubled, that it will rise to 8 or 9 million (a fifth of our total population) . . . this would be, without doubt, a great evil for France, perhaps even a cause of death. In Paris, as in other great urban centers, our race is weakened, diminished, destroyed." She believed that "between the total of our population and the Parisian population, there exists a sort of equilibrium which must not be broken . . . What is it?" She admitted that she was not certain, but maintained that "it appears near to the present relationship."[9] Such opinions would continue to reflect the apprehensions of many about the effects of Parisian growth.

Had the political situation been such as to permit the creation of a viable plan for the Paris region, 1919 would have been an excellent time to institute it, for the succeeding decade was to mark a period of uncontrolled suburban expansion. In 1921 the city of Paris had a population of 2,906,000, while the suburbs housed 1,505,000. A decade later, in 1931, the city population had been reduced slightly to 2,891,000 people, while the suburbs had grown to 2,016,000. This rapid sprawl had taken place spontaneously, unguided by any comprehensive scheme. Most conspicuous in the chaotic pattern of suburban development was the disorderly proliferation of small houses, haphazardly erected on tracts of land that often lacked streets, drainage, and the most rudimentary urban services. Such settlements frequently exhibited a physical squalor equal to that of the poorest squatter slums, and they came to be regarded as a major scandal. At the same time, although transport facilities in the form of suburban rail lines were improved, there was no

9. Myriem Foncin, "Quelques réflexions géographiques à propos du concours (l^re Section) pour le plan d'aménagement et d'extension de Paris," *La vie urbaine,* 1920, p. 80.

coherent transportation plan related to patterns of settlement. Urbanists seeking to demonstrate the hazards of unplanned accretion could find ample support for their arguments in the jungle growth of Paris.

The Prost Plan

It has been reported that on a Sunday in 1928 the president of France, Raymond Poincaré, was returning to Paris from the country when at Chelles, east of the city, his car was halted by an accident that blocked the road. Forced to detour, he received a lengthy exposure to the chaotic squalor of the suburban housing tracts and, thus inspired, sought to promote the establishment of a regional plan.

As an initial step, he created the Comité Supérieur de l'Aménagement et de l'Organisation Générale de la Région Parisienne to begin planning studies. Advising the Comité, the minister of the interior, Albert Sarraut, urged the establishment of strong planning controls. He pointed out that it was "necessary, first of all, to trace around Paris a line, inside of which certain things permitted elsewhere will be forbidden."[10]

The Comité, for which Louis Dausset served as president, included as two of its most active members Raoul Dautry, the director of the national railroads, and Henri Prost, chief architect of the government. These men were charged with the mission of defining the Paris region and organizing the major lines of transport and circulation. The dominant contribution was that of Prost, however, and the resulting regional scheme, initiated in 1932, has generally been termed the "Prost Plan."[11]

As defined by the Prost Plan the Paris region would be contained within a circle with a radius of 35 kilometers measured from Notre Dame Cathedral, with a northern extension to include the areas of Creil and Chantilly (figure 232). Included in the projected region were 656 communes located in the Départements of Seine, Seine et Oise, Seine et Marne, and Oise, comprising 6,418,000 inhabitants and a territory of 512,000 hectares. Although the plan had been prompted by a decade of uncontrolled expansion, its development coincided with the onset of economic depression and a relative slowdown in industrial and population growth. The plan, it

---

10. Albert Sarraut, quoted in "1928 Région parisienne," *Urbanisme*, no. 88, 1965, p. 21.

11. A year after the Comité was formed, Henri Prost wrote an article for *L'Europe nouvelle* (8 June 1929), "La division en zones concentriques" (pp. 734–37), in which he summarized his views on the planning of the Paris region. At this time he favored the immediate construction of satellite towns. He also advocated the creation of "linear cities," having for their principal axis a "super-Métro" line connecting directly with the Paris system. In general he favored a policy of decentralization, believing that many Parisian industries would be better placed in the south-central part of France. The industrial concentration of Paris, he claimed, was a "great danger for national security." His later abandonment of the satellite-town concept probably resulted from the general slowdown of the economic depression. Under such circumstances, concentrating attention on existing communities must have seemed more realistic than making proposals for new towns. The idea of the new Métro system would be taken up following the Second World War, as would the concept of new towns.

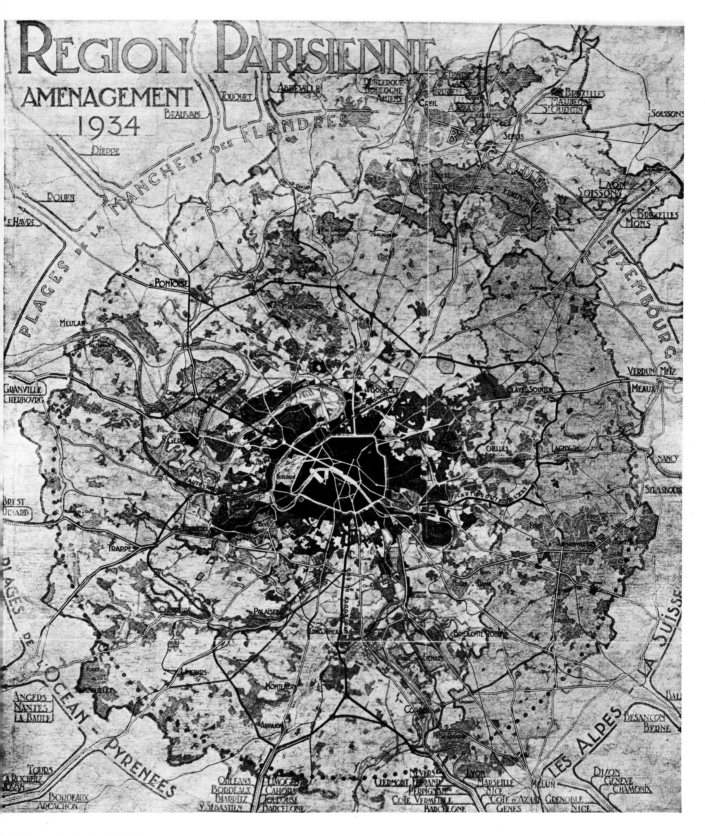

232. The regional plan of 1934.

was hoped, would assist in repairing some of the damage of haphazard development. As Louis Dausset observed: "It is necessary above all to give some order to the existing chaos. The essential thing is to organize greater Paris and not to extend it farther."[12]

It was noted that the untrammeled growth of the previous decade had produced a disequilibrium in urban development. Although the Paris region functioned in many ways as a single urbanized area, wide variations existed among communes and their resources. Certain areas had concentrations of wealth, others of poverty. Many communes were barely able to provide minimal community facilities, and it was anticipated that the creation of a unified region would permit improvements in the distribution of urban amenities.

According to the plan, each municipality was requested to limit its zone of urbanization to the area for which the municipal budget could assure the complete provision of urban services within the next fifteen years. Such services were to include a complete street system; the provision of water, electricity, and sewers; and all administrative services, such as schools, post offices, social services, policing, garbage disposal, and so forth. The intention was to avoid any repetition of the mushrooming and ill-equipped *lotissements* seen during the 1920s. Outside such zones of urbanization, the only building permitted would be individual constructions provided with their own water sources and satisfactory hygienic facilities. Construction in all urbanized areas was to be strictly controlled by zoning ordinances stipulating the density of building and the number of inhabitants each commune would be capable of administering when the zone of urbanization was completely populated. Notably absent from the plan were any proposals for new towns or satellite towns; the intention was not to stimulate expansion, but to control growth in existing centers.

As in the 1919 competition plans, considerable attention was given to transportation. In contrast to the earlier schemes, however, the Prost proposals did not emphasize rail transport. Reflecting the growing dominance of the automobile, the Prost Plan focused on the creation of a series of new regional motor roads. It was proposed to supplement the existing system with five new radial limited-access auto routes. Linking these would be a circular route, or *rocade* intersecting the radials at points 15 to 20 kilometers outside the center.

The planning studies had attempted to analyze the Paris region in terms of recreational areas and open space and to demarcate areas to be preserved from development. Protected areas were specified for sections of the valleys of the Seine, the Oise, and the Marne. Existing forest areas were to be preserved, together with historic sites such as Versailles, Saint Germain, Marly, Meudon, and Sceaux. Altogether 6 percent of the Paris region was to be retained as protected open space.

12. Louis Dausset, "La notion de la plan régional," *Urbanisme,* no. 40, p. 11.

The Prost Plan was presented to the minister of the interior in 1934, and during the following year it was submitted for examination to the communal governments of the Paris region. In urging acceptance of the plan, Louis Dausset stressed the need to adopt a regional plan after so many years of hesitation. He noted that "the late hour when our action seems finally to be reaching its goal only underlines the necessity and urgency . . . and it is the last occasion which offers itself to plan conveniently for greater Paris."[13]

The enthusiasm for planning expressed by Dausset did not, apparently, reflect the mood of many regional officials, and the period of inquiry produced many hostile reactions to the Prost Plan. This had been predicted by one observer when the scheme was first exhibited. "Resistance to urbanism," he said, "is easily explained." Opposition would come from "engineers who believe that urbanism consists in maximum automobile circulation on the roads; lawyers who seek in the law arguments for or against its application; landlords who see a limitation in property rights; merchants who await occasions to speculate in land targeted by the plans; municipal councillors who seek arguments for their reelection; architects who would like to construct the largest buildings possible on the smallest spaces."[14]

As the plan became subject to debate in regional assemblies, it appeared that there was opposition to its local repercussions, although the general concept of regional planning might be acceptable. It was noted: "One encounters everywhere the same arguments: restrictions in building height will diminish the population density, and thus reduce communal resources; the creation of open spaces, reserves, and zones of control will place obstacles in the way of local prosperity." Frequently invoked were the "inalienable rights of small property owners."[15]

To many local governing bodies, the plan represented a usurpation of local prerogatives by outside agencies. It was observed that "there was perhaps a misunderstanding, at the beginning of the studies, of the instinctive hostility of the local communities situated within the orbit of Paris against the encroachments of their big sister. The rural inhabitants of Seine et Oise, those of the communes of the Seine, know full well that if Paris is the past, the territory of their communes constitutes the future of the agglomeration."[16] Although the economic crisis was momentarily restricting urban development, many apparently looked forward to a time of expansion and prosperity. The balance of population between Paris and its surroundings was shifting, with the central city entering a period of decline. While the urbanists of Paris might think in terms of limiting growth, many suburban municipalities were reluctant to hamper what they deemed their future vitality. The Prost Plan was seen not as a plan for growth, but as a plan for nongrowth, and as such

13. Quoted by Henri Sellier and Paul Brasseau in "Le plan d'aménagement de la région parisienne devant les corps élus," *Urbanisme,* no. 40, Oct.–Nov. 1935, p. 2.
14. Ibid., p. 3. Léandre Vaillat is quoted.
15. Ibid., p. 4.
16. Ibid.

it was opposed by those who wished no restrictions on the expansion of individual communities.

As the economic crisis gave way to the graver crisis of war, invasion, and occupation, the Prost Plan gradually gained government approval. It was accepted by decree in 1939, with certain reservations, and finally made law in 1941. Included in the modifications of the plan was a redefinition of the Paris region. Instead of being largely contained within a 35-kilometer radius of Notre Dame, the region was expanded to include all of the Départements of Seine, Seine et Oise, and Seine et Marne, plus five cantons of the Département of Oise. The territory of the region was thus expanded from 512,000 hectares to 1,300,000, with an increase of total population from 6,418,000 to 6,900,000.

Legislative activity continued in 1943, with the creation of the Service d'Aménagement de la Région Parisienne (SARP), placed under the authority of the Délégué Général à l'Équipement National. This organization was to be assisted by a consulting body, the Comité d'Aménagement da la Région Parisienne (CARP). At the time of the liberation in 1944, these two planning agencies were attached to the Ministry of Reconstruction and Urbanism.

The Decentralist Phase

The philosophy governing the planning of the Paris region during the depression and occupation years had been generally conservative with regard to growth, in accordance with the prevailing realities of economic crisis, political uncertainty, and population stability. With the end of the war, however, and the gradual recovery of the French economy, the Paris region regained its potential for expansion. To advocates of decentralization, therefore, it became a matter of national welfare that Parisian development be restrained. One of the most influential opponents of Parisian growth was Jean-François Gravier, a professor at the Conservatoire des Arts et Métiers, who outlined his views in a book, *Paris et le désert français,* published in 1947. This work was to be subsequently reissued and its ideas widely disseminated by those favoring a decentralist policy. Gravier repeated the argument that the city of Paris maintained an abnormal and unhealthy dominance in France and had evolved at the expense of other regions. To redress this imbalance, he urged a comprehensive national policy of decentralization.

It was true that the population of Paris in relation to that of the nation as a whole had been steadily increasing. In 1861 the Paris region had contained 7.5 percent of the French people. By the turn of the century, the figure was 11 percent. Between 1901 and 1946, although the national population had undergone a slight decrease, Paris had expanded by more than 40 percent, and it now represented 16 percent of the total French population.

The postwar French economy reflected a program of government planning based on a series of five-year plans, beginning in 1945. Included in such schemes were efforts to encourage a balanced national development and to give government assistance to areas with high unemployment. Particular effort was made to remedy the economic imbalance between the relatively depressed western part of France and the more prosperous and industrialized east. In an effort to counteract the growing dominance of the Paris region, legislation was enacted in 1955 to restrict new industrial growth in Paris and, in 1958, to limit office construction. In 1964 the program for granting state aid to private industry involved the division of France into five zones, for which varying amounts of assistances were allocated. No assistance whatever was to be given to the Paris region (defined to extend from Rouen in the north to Soissons in the east and Blois in the southwest).

The fifth five-year plan, begun in 1965, included the goal that 40 percent of all new jobs created between 1962 and 1985 be located in western France. A further effort to compensate for the dominance of Paris was the creation of eight *métropoles d'équilibre,* which were designated for preferential assistance in expansion (figure 232). These new urban centers, which involved the linking of some existing cities, included Nantes–Saint Nazarre, Lille-Roubaix-Tourcoing, Nancy-Metz-Thionville, Strasbourg, Lyons–Saint Étienne, Bordeaux, and Marseilles-Aix.

A desire to restrict the growth of Paris dominated the first postwar regional plan. In 1955 the Commissariat à la Construction et à l'Urbanisme was instituted, and in 1958, assisted by SARP, it was charged with the establishment of a new plan for the Paris region. The resulting document, called the Plan d'Aménagement et d'Organisation Générale de la Région Parisienne (PADOG), was approved by decree in 1960. Embodying a general projection for the ten-year period between 1960 and 1970, the PADOG reflected the decentralist views of many government planners. The presentation of the plan observed: For more than a century, industrial expansion—favored by a constantly replenished pool of qualified labor, facilitated by the centralization of the highway and rail system, animated by daring initiative supported by the highest scientific research—has been very much in evidence in Paris and in the Parisian basin, where, however, not a single important natural resource initially justified such an emergence. This development . . . has now made apparent the danger of a critical disequilibrium between a congested capital, around which proliferates a disorganized suburb, . . . and the rest of the country, which is deprived of some of its more active elements.[17]

The intention of the government on the national level was "to favor in the provinces, and in particular in a certain number of regional capitals, the kinds of employment, enterprises, and services that will assure a balanced life in conformity

17. Ministère de la Construction, *Plan d'aménagement et d'organisation générale de la région parisienne, Décret d'approbation,* p. 1.

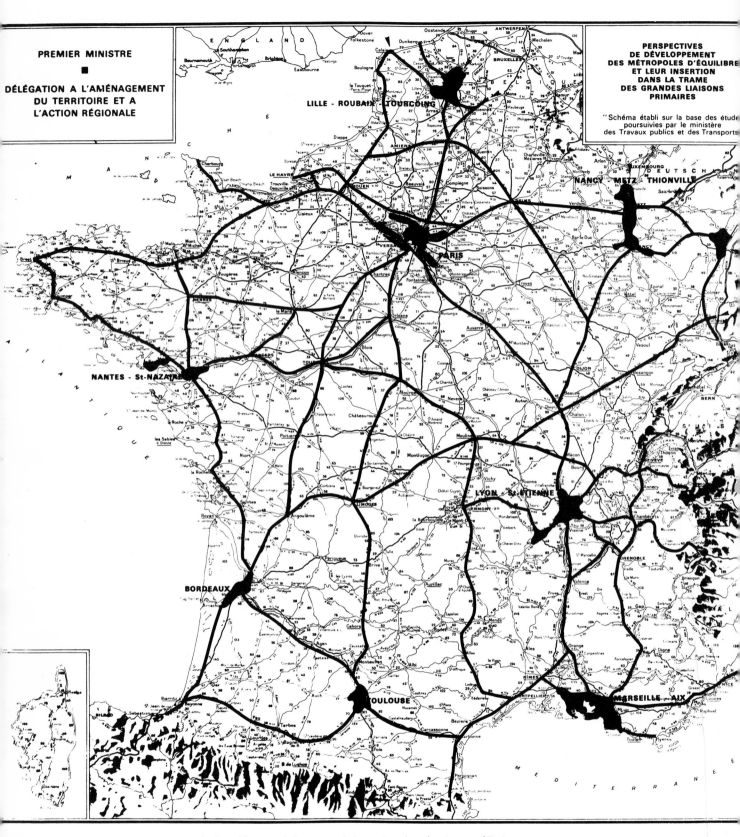

233. The *métropoles d'équilibre* intended to counterbalance the urban dominance of Paris.

with the evolution of modern society and that will be capable of fixing in place a population that otherwise would have a tendency to converge on the capital."[18]

The principles of the PADOG included a determination to stabilize the population of the Paris region, following a 50 percent reduction in the prevailing rate of population growth. It was intended that between 1960 and 1970 the increase not exceed 1 million (of which 500,000 would represent natural increase in the existing population). The development of cities directly outside the Paris region—such as Orléans, Troyes, Reims, Amiens, Rouen, and Le Mans—was to be encouraged as a way of siphoning off and redirecting population in this part of France. Within the Paris region itself, the city of Paris was to be decongested in favor of the suburbs, where urban nodes were to be established, containing centers of employment and housing, and designed to reduce the volume of commuting into the center. The rural zone surrounding Paris was also to be redeveloped, with a moderate expansion permitted to such towns as Mantes, Creil, Meaux, Montereau, Melun, and Étampes.

The District de la Région de Paris, as defined by the PADOG, included the Départements of Seine, Seine et Marne, and Seine et Oise, an area comprising 12,070 square kilometers, 2.2 percent of the territory of France. This district, contained within a general radius 60 kilometers from the center of Paris, was composed of 1,305 separate communes with a total population of 8,500,000. Within the district, the Parisian "agglomeration" was defined, an area of continuous settlement covering a surface of 1,200 square kilometers within a general radius of 20 kilometers from the center. This urbanized area included 80 percent of the total population of the Paris region and about one-tenth of the area. In the center of the agglomeration was the city of Paris, with 104 square kilometers and a population of 2,800,000, one-third of the people in the region.

In 1961, the District de la Région de Paris was placed under the direction of a single planning authority. The previous year had seen the establishment of a large, interdisciplinary organization, the Institut d'Aménagement et d'Urbanisme de la Région Parisienne, which was charged with the creation of regional planning studies.

Although the arguments of the decentralists were in many ways convincing, it was inevitable that there would be opposition to restrictions on Parisian expansion. Included among the proponents of a large, freely evolving Paris was Georges Pilliet, who published his views in *L'avenir de Paris* in 1961. Like many Frenchmen, he regarded Paris as a natural focus of the European Common Market and insisted that efforts to restrict industrial and commercial development would deflect foreign investment to other countries. To attempt to decentralize the multiform activities of the French capital would be to deprive the city of its historic role, for "people from the provinces come to Paris as Europeans used to go to America." Why should Paris

18. Ibid., p. 2.

lose its place as the center of opportunity? As to restrictions on size, it would be "fatal to wish to hold the Paris region at 9 million inhabitants." One needed to consider the importance of Paris in the postwar world, for "if 15 million inhabitants is excessive for Paris, the capital of France, it would be normal, desirable, for Paris, the capital of Europe."[19]

References to Paris as the "capital of Europe" were made frequently by those favoring a policy of expansion. To some, even the role of capital of Europe might be too modest, and Pillier speculated that Paris could be regarded as the "point of equilibrium" for the world.[20] Something of the sort had been anticipated more than a century before by Victor Hugo, who had predicted: "In the twentieth century, there will be an extraordinary nation. . . . This nation will have for its capital Paris, and it will no longer be called France; it will be called Europe. It will be called Europe in the twentieth century, and, in succeeding centuries, even more transfigured, it will be called Humanity."[21]

To proponents of growth, government planning policy seemed designed to deny the greatest city in the world its natural destiny. Sentiments similar to those of Pilliet were published in 1962 by Alain Griotteray in *L'état contre Paris*. Seeking to dramatize the results of decentralization, he included an imaginary conversation with a government planner. Responding to an inquiry about a large white area on a projected land-use map of France, the planner explains: "It's Paris, or more exactly, the emplacement of Paris. For we don't know yet what we're going to put in place of that monster." All that might remain of Paris would be a few architectural monuments isolated "in fields of wheat or clover." As to the population, "One can't permit the Parisians to spoil the landscape . . . we can't leave the Parisians where they are; that would be the negation of urbanism. . . . Halt Paris, empty Paris, after which we can talk about it." Once the planners were finished, "France will have changed its image. No more this monstrous head, but a harmonious sowing of living cities, prosperous and equal. Cholet and Paris will have the same prestige before the universe."[22]

Looking toward the Year 2000

Opinion soon began to grow among government officials that the PADOG scheme had been unrealistic in attempting to restrain the dynamism of the Paris region. In 1963 Paul Delouvrier, who had been appointed Délégué Général to the District of the Paris

19. Georges Pilliet, *L'avenir de Paris* (Paris: Hachette, 1961), pp. 122, 124, 132.
20. Ibid., p. 126.
21. Victor Hugo, *Paris* (Paris: Calmon Lévy, 1879), pp. 3, 10. This book is a reprinting of a Paris guide first published by Hugo in 1867.
22. Alain Griotteray, *L'état contre Paris* (Paris: Hachette, 1962), pp. 7–8.

Region, presented a report in which he acknowledged Parisian expansion as natural and inevitable. He believed that the planning of Paris should be considered in the context of national population growth, increasing urbanization, and general economic development. "All these great movements, which are already underway and going to accelerate, lead one to believe that it would be vain to try to halt Paris in a France in progress."[23]

The fact that one Frenchman in six inhabited the Paris region was, he insisted, not an abnormality, but a reflection of international trends in urbanization. A similar primacy in population was noted in London, Zurich, and the urban nodes of Düsseldorf-Cologne and Rotterdam-Amsterdam. The major difference between France and the other countries lay in the unusually small populations of provincial cities. In France there was not a single city outside Paris of over a million people, and only three cities of over half a million (Lyons with 851,000 inhabitants, Marseilles with 807,000, and Lille-Roubaix with 771,000). The reasons for this, he believed, lay not in the parasitic nature of Paris, but in a generally slow pattern of urbanization in France, the result of demographic stability and a long-standing rural tradition. He noted, however, that the postwar period was evidencing a remarkable trend in French urban growth, and that between 1954 and 1962 many French cities showed rates of increase far exceeding that of Paris. With such trends continuing, it would be difficult to prove that the growth of Paris was detrimental to the development of other centers.[24] Delouvrier concurred with the view that the city should be considered within the context of an economically unified Europe, which placed "Paris and its region in competition with other metropolises. . . . The role of the Paris region in comparison with other regions in France can no longer be the same as before, and it must be defined in new terms."[25] Paris was to be seen as part of a pattern of urbanization comprising a series of great centers forming an arc across northern Europe, from London to Paris to Geneva, by way of Rotterdam, the Ruhr, the Rhine, Basel, and Zurich. Paris was the only French city that could function at the scale of other major European centers, and he argued that the diminishment of its economic importance could only hurt France. In the vitality of Paris lay the vitality of the nation.

As to the future population of the Paris region, it would be reasonable to assume an increase to between 12 and 16 million by the end of the century. To accommodate this, the region would need extensive redevelopment, including improved

---

23. Premier Ministre, Délégation Générale au District de la Région de Paris, *Avant-projet de programme duodécennal pour la région de Paris* (Paris: Imprimerie Municipale, 1963), p. 10. This report has been popularly termed the *livre blanc*.

24. During the period 1954 to 1962, the population of the Paris region had increased 15 percent. For other cities the percentages of increase in the same period were: Grenoble, 45; Cæn, 35.2; Brest, 25.3; Rennes, 24.9; Dijon, 24.3; Toulouse, 21; Nice, 19.1; Lyons, 18.5; Marseilles, 16.4; and Rouen, 16.3.

25. Premier Ministre, Délégation Générale au District de la Région de Paris, *Avant-projet de programme duodécennal*, p. 70.

equipment and transport, and augmented space standards for housing. Of particular importance in determining the formation of the new Paris region would be the increased use of the automobile, for in Delouvrier's view "the city of tomorrow must adapt itself to the automobile, to the democratization of the automobile."[26]

A reconsideration of the PADOG scheme resulted in the development of a new regional plan, published in 1965 and called the Schéma Directeur d'Aménagement et d'Urbanisme de la Région de Paris. Far more ambitious in scope than the PADOG, the Schéma Directeur attempted to project development not for a mere ten years, but until the year 2000. In contrast to the conservatism of the PADOG, the Schéma Directeur did not seek to halt expansion and assumed a population of 14 million by the end of the century. The overall aim was to give order and coherence to future urbanization, seeking a balance of transport, employment, housing, and urban services, and preventing the total obliteration of remaining open areas in the region. Following publication, the Schéma Directeur was submitted for consultation by local and regional government bodies, with a revised scheme produced in 1969. After additional study, a definitive version of the plan received formal government approval in 1971.

The publication of the Schéma Directeur had been preceded in 1964 by a political reorganization of the Paris region, in which the Départements of Seine and Seine et Oise were reapportioned to create six new *départements* (figure 234). These, together with the city of Paris and the existing Département of Seine et Marne, now comprised the District de la Région Parisienne (reconstituted in 1976 as the Région d'Île de France). The city of Paris at the center was ringed by the new Départements of Hauts de Seine, Seine–Saint Denis, and Val de Marne. This inner ring of small, relatively populous districts was surrounded by the much larger, less dense Départements of Seine et Marne, Val d'Oise, Yvelines, and Essonne.[27]

The prospect of a new regional plan had received wide attention, and while official efforts proceeded the press was filled with independent proposals for the reordering of greater Paris. While some, such as the architect Paul Maymont, envisioned the creation of towering megastructures, others suggested patterns of linear expansion or the creation of new towns and satellites.

One of the most publicized suggestions was put forward in 1959 by the journal *Architecture d'aujourd'hui*. The scheme involved, not a series of small satellites, but a large government center, initially containing a million people and providing a virtual twin to Paris. The new city, called Paris Parallèle, was justified as a means of both

26. Ibid., p. 90.
27. The boundaries of the new *départements* were projected on the basis of population estimates for the year 1985, at which time it was assumed all *départements* would be more or less equal in population. The populations in 1962, with their 1985 estimates in parentheses, were as follows: Hauts de Seine, 1,393,126 (1,550,000); Val de Marne, 984,443 (1,350,000); Seine–Saint Denis, 1,089,120 (1,500,000); Essone, 489,188 (1,300,000); Val d'Oise, 556,464 (1,270,000).

234. OPPOSITE. The Paris region before (*above*) and after (*below*) the political reapportionment of 1964.

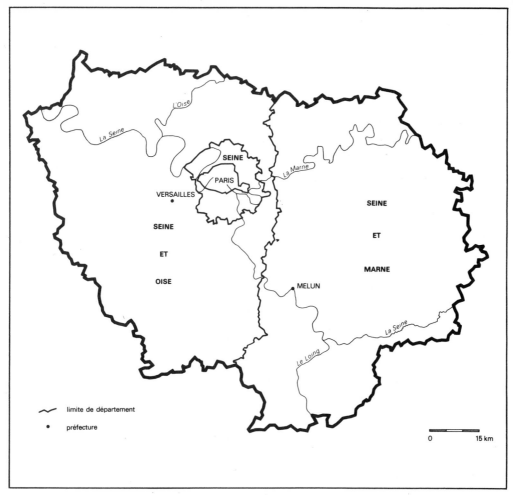

limite de département
préfecture

0   15 km

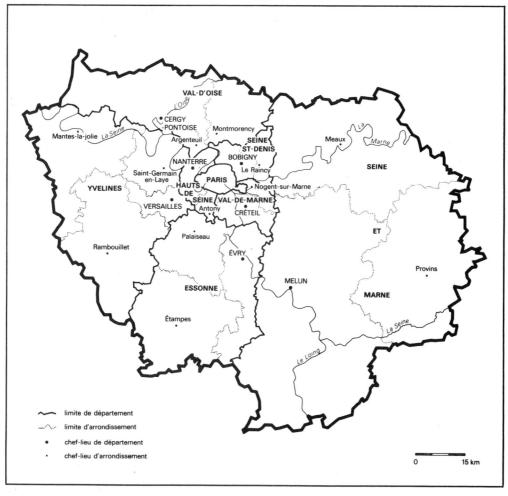

limite de département
limite d'arrondissement
chef-lieu de département
chef-lieu d'arrondissement

0   15 km

preserving the old city of Paris and avoiding excessive redevelopment of the suburban areas. The idea was still being promoted by *Architecture d'aujourd'hui* as late as 1968.[28]

The Schéma Directeur projected the extension of the Parisian agglomeration along two major east-west axes. One of these, lying north of the city, would extend about 75 kilometers, from Pontoise in the west to Meaux on the east, passing through Saint Denis. The other would extend roughly 90 kilometers, from Mantes on the west to Melun on the east, passing south of the city through Palaiseau. The north axis would incorporate the river valleys of Basse Seine and the Marne, while the south axis would extend from the Basse Seine to the Haute Seine. The axes of development were considered to relate logically to lines of transport and industry, serving to extend urbanized development into areas of relatively sparse settlement.

Incorporated in the Schéma Directeur were a series of "new towns" (figure 235). The concept of new towns had, of course, been widely accepted by urban planners as a means of decentralization and regional development. A comprehensive application of the idea could be found in London, where immediately following the war the city had been surrounded by a greenbelt, beyond which a series of new settlements were developed. Reflecting their garden city origins, the first British new towns were conceived of as relatively small, self-contained entities.[29] Although French planners were well aware of the British experience, they decided to use a different approach to the development of the Paris region. Thinking in terms of large-scale urbanization, Parisian planners projected their new towns not as compact settlements modeled on the image of traditional communities, but as urbanized regions; thus a new town might incorporate several already existing towns. The Parisian new towns, moreover, were not conceived of as separate from Paris. Although they were intended to provide centers of employment, they were to be closely tied to the center by motor roads and rail transport. Greater Paris as projected for the year 2000 might thus be considered as a single city of 14 million.

In addition to establishing the new towns, the Schéma Directeur projected the restructuring of a group of existing suburban centers to provide sites for new housing, commerce, and institutional facilities (figures 236–239). Included in these

28. The Paris parallel plan may be seen illustrated in "Paris Parallèle: une solution nouvelle," *Architecture d'aujourd'hui,* no. 88, Feb.–Mar. 1960, p. 10; "Paris Parallèle: cinq hypothèses d'emplacement," *Architecture d'aujourd'hui,* no. 90, June–July 1960; and "Paris Parallèle 1959–1968," *Architecture d'aujourd'hui,* no. 138, June–July 1968, p. 17.

29. The British new towns have reflected an evolution in planning philosophy. The first group of new towns (the Mark I towns) were designed for low densities and populations of about 60,000. Responding to criticism that the new towns lacked urbanity, planners projected the next group (the Mark II towns) for higher densities and larger populations. A third phase of new town design (the Mark III towns), conceived of the settlement, not as a concentrated center, but as a large urbanized district containing a well-developed transport network. The Parisian new towns bear a certain similarity to such Mark III British new towns as Milton Keynes.

235. Regional development plan for the Paris region, showing new towns projected in 1969.

centers were Rosny sous Bois, Rungis, Vélizy-Villacoublay, Le Bourget-Roissy, and Saint Denis. Some of the redeveloped centers were also intended to provide government headquarters for the new *départements* created in 1964. Créteil was to contain the prefecture of Val de Marne, Bobigny that of Seine–Saint Denis, and La Défense the prefecture of Hauts de Seine. Versailles, which had formerly housed the prefecture of Seine et Oise, was to serve as governmental headquarters of Yvelines.

In some instances, the restructured center was the site of a specialized activity. Rungis contained the wholesale market of Paris, while Le Bourget-Roissy was near the new Charles de Gaulle international airport. Both La Défense and Créteil, in

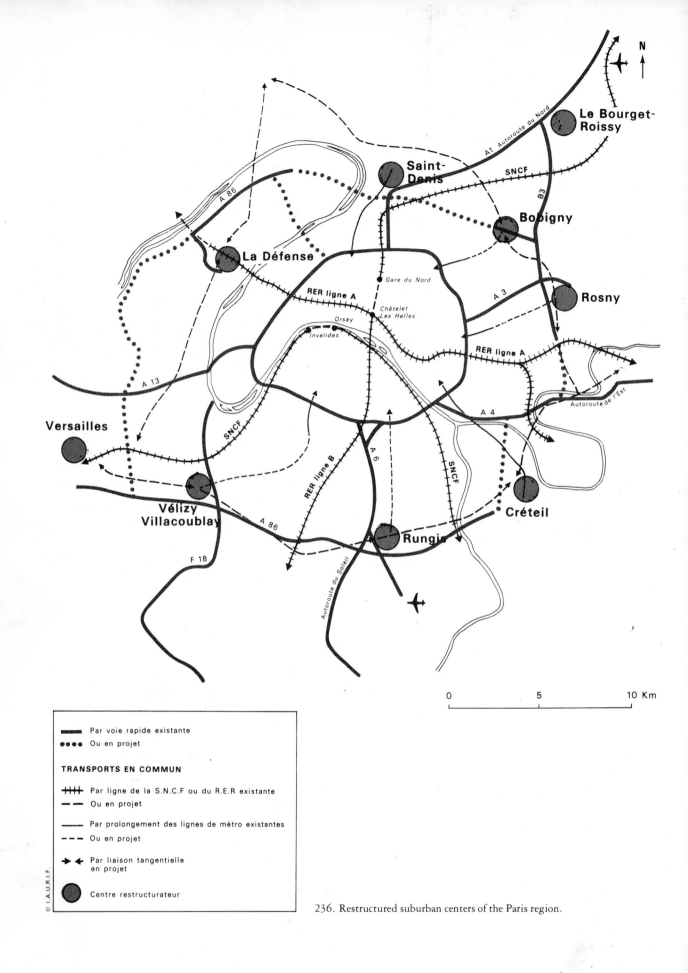

N

Le Bourget-
Roissy

A1 Autoroute du Nord

SNCF

B3

Saint-
Denis

Bobigny

A 86

A 3

La Défense

Gare du Nord

Rosny

RER ligne A

Châtelet
Les Halles

Orsay

Invalides

RER ligne A

Autoroute de l'Est

A 13

A 4

SNCF

Versailles

RER ligne B

A 6

SNCF

Créteil

Vélizy
Villacoublay

A 86

Rungis

F 18

Autoroute du Soleil

| 0 | 5 | 10 Km |

—— Par voie rapide existante

●●●● Ou en projet

TRANSPORTS EN COMMUN

╫╫╫ Par ligne de la S.N.C.F ou du R.E.R existante

– – Ou en projet

—— Par prolongement des lignes de métro existantes

- - - Ou en projet

►◄ Par liaison tangentielle
en projet

● Centre restructurateur

© I.A.U.R.I.F.

236. Restructured suburban centers of the Paris region.

237, 238. Apartment housing in Créteil.

239. The redeveloped center of Bobigny. The prefectural headquarters is on the left, with apartment housing and a covered shopping center on the right.

addition to containing commercial office complexes, provided sites for branches of the university. All restructured centers were intended to be closely linked to the center of Paris and to each other by existing or projected transport lines.

Although, in 1965, eight new towns were projected for the Paris region, in 1969 the number was reduced to five: Cergy-Pontoise, Evry, Saint Quentin en Yvelines, Marne la Vallée, and Melun-Sénart. Because of the large area and the relatively loose structure of the Parisian new towns, they were not intended to receive detailed plans in advance. Government town planning agencies were to provide the overall organization and direction of the towns, the selection and acquisition of the sites, the projection of the land-use pattern, and the preparation of the infrastructure. Tracts of land within the towns could then be developed by private builders. Essential to the creation of the new towns was the ability of the government establishment to designate a *zone d'aménagement différé* (ZAD), in which the price of land could be stabilized and the state given the right of preemption.

The First of the Parisian new towns was Cergy-Pontoise, begun in 1969 and located 25 kilometers northwest of Paris. Initial building operations involved the creation of the Val d'Oise prefecture near the town of Pontoise and the village of Cergy, hence the name of the town. A total of 17 communes, however, were included in the 10,850-hectare site. With a population of 180,000 projected for 1985, Cergy-Pontoise had 88,000 people in 1975 (figures 240–242).

240. The new town of Cergy-Pontoise.

241. Apartments and terrace housing in Cergy-Pontoise.

242. Cergy-Pontoise. The prefecture of Val d'Oise, designed by Henry Bernard in 1968.

In general, because of their distance from Paris, the new towns were projected for relatively low densities (figures 182 and 183). An exception, however, occurred with the town center of Evry, located on a 9,280-hectare site 25 kilometers south of Paris. Although the overall area included 16 communes, it was decided to concentrate initial development in an agglomeration of 6 communes. Within this district, a highly concentrated urban core was to be established, including commercial facilities and offices and providing 7,000 dwelling units to accommodate 25,000 people on 82 hectares. The design of this center was selected through an international competition.

The competition decision in 1973 awarded the construction of the Evry center to an organization called UCY (Union des Constructeurs d'Evry), a group of ten private promoters. Housing was to take the form of large apartment blocks designed like stepped-back pyramids, in which individual apartments and adjacent terraces might achieve a greater physical identity than in conventional units (figures 243 and 244). Bold surface color augmented the dramatic impact of the ensemble. Close to the housing complex a shopping center was created, incorporating a so-called "agora," a large covered space designed to function as an indoor plaza giving access to commerce, restaurants,

243, 244. Apartment housing in the Evry center.

245. The prefecture of Essonne, in Evry, designed by S.E.T.A.P.

theaters, sports facilities, and community services. Elevated walkways for pedestrian circulation were designed to connect the housing, commerce, and agora with the prefecture of Essonne (figure 245). The initial agglomeration of Evry contained 51,000 people in 1975, with 120,000 projected for 1985.

The new town of Saint Quentin en Yvelines, located 30 kilometers southwest of Paris, was begun in 1970. The site of 7,500 hectares included 11 communes, and by 1975 the town had a population of 97,000, with a projection of 220,000 by 1985. The site was considered a desirable one, in the general vicinity of such prestigious centers as Versailles, Rambouillet, and Saint Germain, and the creation of the new town was intended to forestall a spontaneous and disorderly settlement of the region. Initial development included an industrial park near the town of Trappes and residential complexes dispersed among eight different centers (figure 246). Lacking a prefecture or other distinctive focal point, Saint Quentin en Yvelines as yet offers little sense of physical identity.

246. The existing town of Trappes forms part of the new town of Saint Quentin en Yvelines. In the foreground is the pattern of suburban housing typical of the 1920s and 1930s. New apartment housing rises on the outskirts.

Also lacking a dominant focus is Marne la Vallée. This new town, lying to the east of Paris, was projected in a linear formation beginning 10 kilometers beyond the Boulevard Périphérique at Noisy le Grand and extending 20 kilometers eastward to enclose a territory of 15,000 hectares and 26 communes. Having immediate contact with the Paris suburbs at its western end, the new town was intended to augment existing urban facilities, while guiding settlement to correspond with planned rail lines and auto routes. Development of Marne la Vallée has proceeded by means of separated centers, resulting in a series of discrete enclaves, rather than a visually coherent urban entity. The population in 1975 had reached 102,000, with 215,000 projected for 1985 (figures 247 and 248).

The last of the five Parisian new towns to begin construction was Melun-Sénart, projected in 1970 for a 17,000-hectare site 35 kilometers south of Paris, and located between the town of Melun and the Forest of Sénart. Although the initial plan called for the creation of a new town center between the villages of Tigery and de Lieusaint, local officials preferred that this tract of valuable agricultural land be left unbuilt. It was decided, therefore, to redevelop the existing center of Melun. Melun-Sénart was

247, 248. Housing in Marne la Vallée.

projected in terms of three separate settlements: Grand Melun, intended for a population of 150,000; Rougeau-Sénart, projected for 65,000; and Sénart-Villeneuve, designed for 75,000.

The territory of Melun-Sénart lies south and east of Evry, the two sharing a boundary along the banks of the Seine. The two towns thus appear on a map as essentially a single area. This concentration of planned urbanization was intended to counterbalance the heavier development of other parts of the Paris region and to encourage settlement in an area of relatively low density. Because of its distance from Paris and its agricultural surroundings Melun-Sénart was foreseen as a low-density environment including a large proportion of single-family detached houses. Containing 18 communes, Melun-Sénart had a population of 92,000 in 1975, with projections of 180,000 for 1985.

249. The restructured suburban center of Créteil. A covered shopping center with its parking lot is at left. The Métro station straddles the tracks. Apartment housing is at right.

Although the Parisian new towns and suburban centers include some pedestrian-oriented complexes, the overall scale embodies a wide dispersal of facilities. The inhabitants of such areas may be able to commute to central Paris by rail, but they seem destined to be largely dependent on the automobile for access to local recreation, shopping centers, and educational and cultural facilities, as well as employment in the new industrial parks (figures 249 and 250). The design of the new towns implies a way of life similar to that which has developed in many North American suburbs, and such settlements might, in fact, be considered a suburban counterpart to the "Americanization" of Paris already visible in the skyscrapers of the central city.

An American feeling the pangs of homesickness in Paris might be well advised to visit an outlying shopping center (figure 251). Here, after leaving his car in a covered

250. An industrial park in the restructured suburban center of Vélizy-Villacoublay.

251. The new town of Evry. Parking lot and multilevel garage adjacent to the shopping center.

garage or outdoor lot, he could promenade through multilevel shopping arcades lined with chain store outlets, ride the escalators to the accompaniment of piped-in music, and propel his purchases in a familiar metal cart. Should he seek refreshment, he would likely find a Marriott cafeteria or McDonald's *restaurant familial,* where, through a miracle of modern quality control, authentic transatlantic standards of cuisine are maintained (figure 252).

The architecture of the new towns embodies a range of housing types, including apartments and both terrace and detached houses. Because construction has been the province of large developers, variety at small scale, such as may be found in traditional towns, has been lacking. Changes in style and building type occur only between different tracts, rather than between individual structures. Although much of the housing has been designed to appeal to conservative tastes and thus reflects traditional styles, some complexes employ striking and innovative forms. Among

252. A *restaurant familial* next to the Créteil shopping center.

the most visually arresting structures in the new regional centers are the prefectures (figures 253 and 254). As these buildings were intended to stimulate a sense of community, they were consciously projected as dramatic focal points. Schools, too, have often provided the opportunity for unconventional design.

Because of their decentralization, the new towns are difficult to evaluate in traditional terms. They show a conscious avoidance of familiar urban forms, reflecting the assumption of Parisian planners that urbanized regions incorporating large amounts of low-density settlement and based on a high degree of automobile ownership would accord with both economic reality and contemporary preferences in living. The towns were projected, of course, before the present energy crisis, at a time when their dispersed form seemed to reflect widespread trends. It is possible that, while still in their inception, the new towns embody an urban concept that is already becoming obsolete.

253. The prefecture of Val de Marne at Créteil, designed by Badani and Roux-Dorlut, 1970.

254. The prefecture of Seine–Saint Denis at Bobigny, designed by Binoux and Folliasson, 1970.

At best the new towns reveal a serious attempt to guide the development of the Paris region and to forestall a continuation of totally amorphous expansion. Should the new towns eventually reach their projected populations, it may be possible to evaluate the effectiveness with which urban elements are coordinated. As to the intended purpose of the new towns in promoting a balanced distribution of population within the Paris region, a degree of success was indicated in a 1975 census. In the previous twenty years the city of Paris had lost 500,000 people, a population equivalent to the city of Lyons. The surrounding *départements,* while still expanding, were experiencing a drop in the rate of growth. The outer *départements,* however, reported a notable increase, with an annual growth rate of 7.1 percent in the new towns.

The Schéma Directeur was formulated in response to an apparently unending economic boom and a relentless increase in population. Ten years later the future was becoming difficult to predict, and whereas in 1965 the PADOG seemed too modest in scope, by 1975 the Schéma Directeur was deemed overly ambitious. Population growth was slowing down, and the regional population anticipated by Parisian planners for the year 2000 was reduced from 14 million to 12 million, with predicted future expansion based on natural increase, rather than immigration.

Meanwhile the economy was entering a period of uncertainty, and a general slowdown in building activity could be foreseen. While continuing to support the concept of the new towns, Parisian planners agreed that development was likely to take longer than anticipated. Business organizations were hesitant to undertake new construction, and a halt in private investment became dramatically evident in such commercial centers as La Défense. By the mid-1970s, after twenty years of continuing expansion, a period of relative stability seemed at hand.

No Remembering

In 1865, when Victor Fournel imagined the Paris of a century later, he projected the most conspicuous trends of his own time into the future. Would anyone risk a similar prediction today? Fournel doubtless intended his story as a warning; he described the Paris which might exist if a certain type of development were to continue unabated. Thus one might in our own time imagine a future Paris transformed into a cluster of glass-walled skyscrapers, its suburbs endlessly extended by *grands ensembles,* industrial parks, shopping centers, and motor expressways. Just as Fournel was partly right and partly wrong in his imaginings, we too might miss the mark somewhat. The future remains unpredictable. Problems which loom large at the moment may dissipate, or cease to be regarded as problems, while the cloud today no bigger than a man's hand may fill the sky with unexpected menace. One can only be certain that Paris will change.

What is meant by "Paris", of course, may be variously defined. There will be, as always, the constant ebb and flow of human life, creating a city that is a sum of individual experiences. There is also the inanimate physical fabric, the city of steel and stone and concrete. Potentially more resilient than its human content, the physical city, too, is vulnerable to destruction, decay, and renewal. Then there is the city as an idea, the image evoked by the word *Paris,* which is not the city at any given moment, but the sum of everything Paris has been. The city becomes a composite of all the people who have lived and died there, and all the streets and buildings that have existed there. Actively collaborating in the creation of the Parisian image have been the artists and writers who, through the years, have invented a Paris perhaps more vivid and haunting than the city itself. We see Paris through the eyes of Hugo and Zola, Monet and Degas, Stein and Sartre. Paris has become a myth; it is perceived not merely as a place, but as a living presence. To be part of this presence, to graft one's individual life to this collective life, may be a form of immortality.

The myth of Paris has, of course, been highly romanticized, and it may be borne in mind that many quite normal people have led eminently satisfactory lives without ever setting foot within its boundaries. There are, after all, other great cities. Rome is older and has a richer architectural heritage. London has more parks and better housing. New York is more dynamic and culturally innovative. Rio de Janeiro has a more dramatic site and a milder climate. Venice has more charm. Stockholm is cleaner. Certainly, all the criticisms of Paris voiced in the past century have been valid. Traffic was terrible when the streets were crowded with horses, and it is even worse now that the horses have been replaced with motor vehicles. Public transport from the time of the omnibus to the present has been crowded and inadequate. There has been much bad building, and for the past century the visual harmony of the city has been continually marred. Housing conditions have been scandalous, whether one contemplates the crowded and decaying slums of the old city, or the hygienic barracks of the *grands ensembles.* The size of Paris, and its unmanageable growth, have been a source of continual dismay. As to planning, Paris has had too little, too much, or the wrong kind, and, depending on one's taste in rhetoric, exemplifies the evils of laissez-faire capitalism, or authoritarian government control, or a sinister combination of both.

All in all, it might be difficult to explain to, let us say, a visitor from outer space, just why this congested accretion of masonry has been so deeply loved, and why merely being in Paris, standing on a noisy street in a cold winter rain, breathing exhaust fumes and jostled by the crowds, can lift one's heart. But then, "le cœur a ses raisons."

The problems of Paris have had their counterparts in every city since Babylon. People do not live in cities to escape problems. Paris has offered its inhabitants neither physical comfort nor spiritual serenity, but rather a richness of experience and a quickening of life. Those who have attempted to analyze the attraction of Paris have often made reference to a unique equilibrium and completeness. Thinking of Paris brings to mind Alberti's definition of beauty as "a harmony of all the parts" such that "nothing could be added, diminished, or altered, but for the worse." Resistance to change within the city has reflected the assumption that Paris embodies a type of social and physical perfection. And yet for any city perfection is death. In a living city the balance is never held, and for better or worse, things are always added, diminished, and altered. The image blurs and clarifies, the form dissolves and reemerges.

Many people love Paris, and to contemplate the evolution of the city is to be reminded that each man does, indeed, kill the thing he loves. Paris is being killed every day, and every day being born. For as the city alters, memory, too, is transformed. Recalling her own days in the French capital, Gertrude Stein observed, "They always told me that America changed but it really did not change as much as Paris did in those years that is the Paris one can see, but then there is no remembering what it looked like before and even no remembering what it looks like now."[30]

30. Gertrude Stein, *Paris, France* (New York: Scribner, 1940), p. 15.

GLOSSARY

Arrondissement. Ordinarily a subdivision of a *département.* The average arrondissement contains approximately one hundred and fifty communes. Within the city of Paris, an arrondissement serves as the equivalent of a city ward. The administrative headquarters is called the *mairie,* and the chief administrative official the *maire,* (mayor). Since 1860, when Haussmann extended the city boundaries, Paris has contained twenty arrondissements. Arrondissements One through Four lie within the *grands boulevards* on the Right Bank. Encircling this inner core, the Eighth through Eleventh Arrondissements lie between the *grands boulevards* and the exterior boulevards. On the Left Bank, the Fifth through Seventh Arrondissements extend from the river almost to the exterior boulevards. Arrondissements Twelve through Twenty constitute the outer ring of the city, lying for the most part on land annexed by Haussmann. In Paris, reference to the arrondissement is made frequently in locating addresses within the city.

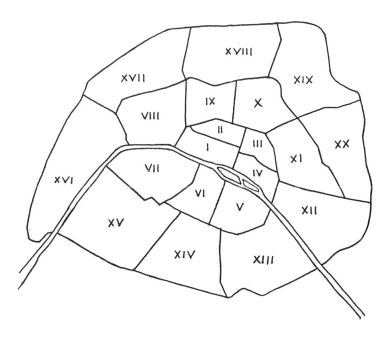

Canton. A territorial subdivision of an arrondissement, used primarily as an election district for departmental councils. Needless to say, because of their small size, the arrondissements of the city of Paris are not subdivided.

Commune. The smallest territorial subdivision in France, corresponding to a municipality. During the Middle Ages, the term referred to a town administered by its citizens and independent of a feudal lord. A commune has a mayor and an elected municipal council. The new towns presently being developed for the Paris region each contain between eleven and twenty-one separate communes.

Département. The basic administrative unit of France. There are at present ninety-four *départements,* of which seven are contained within the Paris region. The chief administrative official of a *département* is the *préfect,* and the government headquarters is called a *préfecture.* Each *département* has an elected council.

Left Bank. The part of Paris lying to the left side of the river Seine as one faces downstream. This is generally the southern half of the city.

Région. An administrative grouping of several *départements,* intended to facilitate regional planning. The District de la Région Parisienne, created in 1961, represented the first such area in France. The chief officer at this time was the *Délégué générale,* who served as representative of the national government and adviser to the prime minister on policy for the region. In 1966, the chief officer became a *préfect,* and a prefectural government was established for the region. The District de la Région Parisienne was reorganized as the Région d'Île de France in 1976.

Right Bank. The part of Paris lying to the right side of the river Seine as one faces downstream. This is generally the northern half of the city.

SELECTED BIBLIOGRAPHY

This study of the urban renovation of Paris has been heavily dependent on the great volume of periodical literature that has appeared during the past century. Included in the publications that have regularly dealt with Parisian architecture and urbanism are *L'architecte, L'architecture, Architecture d'aujourd'hui, Architecture française, Architecture et urbanisme, L'art décoratif, Art de France, L'art vivant, Connaissance de Paris et de France, La construction moderne, Gazette des beaux-arts, Habitation, Habiter, Le logement, Logez-vous, Revue générale de l'architecture et les travaux publiques, Revue de l'art, Revue des arts décoratifs, Techniques et architecture, Urbanisme,* and *La vie urbaine* (known as *Urbanisme et habitation* between 1953 and 1955). Among the foregoing, the most consistently useful with regard to Parisian urbanism have been *Architecture d'aujourd'hui, Urbanisme,* and *La vie urbaine.* It may be noted that *Urbanisme* published an index of its principal articles between 1932 and 1957 in no. 57, 1958, pp. 255–58. An analytical index covering the period between 1932 and 1971 may be found in no. 127–28, 1972, pp. 89–104.

Ongoing developments in Parisian planning are chronicled in periodicals issued by government planning organizations. Among these are the *Bulletin d'information de la région parisienne,* edited by the Institut d'Aménagement et d'Urbanisme de la Région Parisienne (IAURP), for which publication began in 1970. The same organization also published the *Cahiers de l'institute d'aménagement et d'urbanisme de la région parisienne,* beginning in 1964. The name of the sponsoring agency was changed to the Institut d'Aménagement et d'Urbanisme de la Région d'Île de France in 1976, with a corresponding change in the title of its publications. Information specifically related to the city of Paris may be found in *Paris Projet,* published by the Atelier Parisien d'Urbanisme (APUR), a service of the Paris Prefecture. Publication began in 1969. In addition to producing *Paris Projet,* APUR continually prepares studies relevant to the planning of Paris, some of which are available to the public. A list of APUR publications may be obtained from the Paris Prefecture, 17 Boulevard Morland.

Specialized government organizations sometimes issue periodicals relating to their work. The Régie Autonome des Transports Parisiens edits a publication called *RATP Documentation Information* and the organization constructing La Défense produces the *Bulletin d'information de l'établissement public pour l'aménagement de La Défense.*

Another continuing source of publications on the planning of Paris is a national government service, the Documentation Française of the Secretariat Général du

Gouvernement. Of particular interest is the series *Notes et études documentaires: les grandes villes du monde,* which includes an ongoing series of studies relating to Paris.

The following works are grouped according to general subject and listed in order of publication.

General works

de Amicis, Edmondo. *Studies of Paris.* New York: Putnam, 1882.
Paris as it Is. New York: Brentano, 1892.
Smith, Edward Robinson. "The Topographical Evolution of the City of Paris." *House and Garden* 6 (1904): 49–59, 129–42, 190–203, 227–39, 275–89.
Abercrombie, Patrick. "Paris: Some Influences that have Shaped its Growth." *Town Planning Review* 2 (1911–12): 113–23, 216–24, 309–20.
Poëte, Marcel. *Une vie de cité: Paris de sa naissance à nos jours* (3 vols.). Paris: Picard, 1924–31.
Guérard, Albert. *L'avenir de Paris.* Paris: Payot, 1929.
Warnod, André. *Visages de Paris.* Paris: Firmin-Didot, 1930.
Morizet, André. *Du vieux Paris au Paris moderne.* Paris: Hachette, 1932.
Poëte, Marcel. "Paris: son évolution créatrice." *La vie urbaine* 14 (July–December 1937): 195–220, 274, 275–318, 359–74; 15 (January–April 1938): 21–43, 79–109.
Champigneulle, Bernard, Lavedon, Pierre, et al. *Destinée de Paris.* Paris: Les Éditions du Chêne, 1943.
Héron de Villefosse, René. *Histoire de Paris.* Paris: Éditions Littéraires et Artistiques, 1946, and Union Bibliophile de France, 1948.
Lavedon, Pierre. *Histoire de Paris.* Paris: Presses Universitaires de France, 1960.
Bonnome, Camille et al. *L'Urbanisation Française.* Paris: Centre de Recherche d'Urbanisme, 1964.
Christ, Yvan, et al. *La belle histoire de Paris.* Preface by André Chastel. Paris: Perrin, 1964.
Institit Pédagogique National. *Paris: présent et avenir d'une capitale.* Paris: Denoël, 1964.
Larousse. *Dictionnaire de Paris.* Paris: Librairie Larousse, 1964.
Paris d'hier et de demain. Paris: Bibliothèque Nationale, 1966.
Association Universitaire de Recherches Géographiques et Cartographiques. *Atlas de Paris et de la région Parisienne.* Paris: Berger-Levrault, 1967.
Couperie, Pierre. *Paris au fil du temps, atlas historique d'urbanisme et d'architecture.* Paris: Éditions Cuenot, 1968.
Champigneulle, Bernard. *Paris de Napoléon à nos jours.* Paris: Hachette, 1969.
Christ, Yvan. *Paris des Utopies.* Paris: Balland, 1970.
———. *Les métamorphoses de Paris.* Paris: Balland, 1971.
Mollat, Michel. *Histoire de l'Île-de-France et de Paris.* Paris: Privat, 1971.
Hautecœur, Louis. *Paris de 1715 à nos jours.* Paris: F. Nathan, 1972.
Lavedon, Pierre. *Nouvelle histoire de Paris: histoire de l'urbanisme à Paris.* Paris: Hachette, 1975.
Pons, Alain. *2000 Ans de Paris.* Paris: Arthaud, 1975.

The Street Pattern

Hénard, Eugène. *Études sur les transformations de Paris. Fascicule 1: Projet de prolongement de la rue de Rennes avec pont-en-X sur la Seine.* Paris: Librairies-Imprimeries Réunies, 1903.
———. *Études sur les transformations de Paris. Fascicule 2: Les alignements brisés. La question des fortifications et le boulevard de Grande-Ceinture.* Paris: Librairies-Imprimeries Réunies, 1903.
Schopfer, Jean. "The Furnishing of a City." *Architectural Record* 13 (January 1903): 43–48.

Hénard, Eugène. *Études sur les transformations de Paris. Fascicule 5: La percée du Palais Royal. La nouvelle grande croisée de Paris.* Paris: Librairies-Imprimeries Réunies, 1904.

———. *Études sur les transformations de Paris. Fascicule 6: La circulation dans les villes modernes. L'automobilisme et les voies rayonnantes de Paris.* Paris: Librairies-Imprimeries Réunies, 1905.

Magne, Émile. "L'esthétique de la rue." *Mercure de France,* July 16, 1905, pp. 161–81.

Hénard, Eugène. *Études sur les transformations de Paris. Fascicule 7: Les voitures et les passants. Carrefours libres et carrefours à giration.* Paris: Librairies-Imprimeries Réunies, 1906.

Bournon, Fernand. *La voie publique et son décor.* Paris: H. Laurens, 1909.

Hénard, Eugène. *Études sur les transformations de Paris. Fascicule 8: Les places publiques.* Paris: Librairies Imprimeries Réunies, 1909.

Halbwachs, Maurice. *La population et les tracés de voies à Paris depuis un siècle.* Paris: Presses Universitaires de France, 1928.

Ville de Paris et Département de la Seine. *Concours pour l'aménagement de la voie allant de la Place de l'Étoile à la Place au Ront-Point de la Défense.* Paris: Éditions d'Art Charles Moreau, 1931.

"Le concours d'idées pour l'aménagement de l'avenue entre l'Étoile et la Place de la Défense." *Urbanisme,* no. 2, May 1932.

Dervaux, Adolphe. "Le concours de la Préfecture de la Seine 1931. Aménagement de la voie entre l'Étoile et le Rond-Point de la Défense." *La vie urbaine,* no. 9, May 15, 1932, pp. 163–78.

de Souza, Robert. "Les fausses idées d'un concours d'idées." *Urbanisme,* no. 3, June 1932, pp. 91–101; no. 4, July 1932, pp. 132–34; no. 5, August 1932, pp. 166–68; and nos. 8–9, November–December 1932, pp. 255–59.

Ménabréa, André. "Les Enseignements du vieux Pont Neuf." *Urbanisme,* nos. 8–9, November–December 1932.

Prost, Henri. "Le concours d'idées pour l'aménagement de l'avenue entre l'Étoile et la Place de la Défense." *Urbanisme,* no. 1, April 1932, pp. 11–60.

de Souza, Robert. "Le Rond-Point de la Défense et ses transformations en Place de la Victoire." *Urbanisme,* no. 11, February 1933, pp. 69–74, and nos. 17–18, August–September 1933, pp. 257–65.

Meyer-Lévy, Paul. "À propos de la réconstruction du Pont du Carrousel." *Urbanisme,* no. 15, June 1933.

Bardet, Gaston. "Paris, le centre d'échange et les autoroutes souterraines." *Urbanisme,* no. 35, April 1935.

Gutton, André. "Aménagement du Quartier Saint-Germain-des-Prés." *Architecture française,* no. 1, November 1940, pp. 11–18.

Léon, Paul. *Histoire de la rue.* Paris: La Taille Douce, 1947.

L'aménagement routier de la région parisienne. Paris: Union Routière de France, 1952.

Urbanisme et circulation. Paris: Union Routière de France, 1952.

le Cœur, Claude. "Les Quatre Champs Élysées." *Urbanisme* 23, nos. 37–38, 1954, pp. 80–95.

Lafay, Bernard. *Urbanisme et circulation, Paris,* Paris: Union Routière de France, 1955.

Limouzen, Pierre. "Le Boulevard Haussmann." *La vie urbaine,* no. 1, January–March 1957, pp. 51–72; no. 2, April–June 1957, pp. 140–60; no. 4, October–December 1957, pp. 280–85.

Ville de Paris. *Boulevard Périphérique, premier tronçon.* Paris: April 12, 1960.

Gutton, Andre. "L'aménagement de l'Institut de France et le Quartier de Saint Germain des Prés." *La vie urbaine,* no. 2, April–June 1963, pp. 113–48.

Hillairet, Jacques. *Dictionnaire historique des rues de Paris.* Paris: Éditions de Minuit, 1963.

Papon, Maurice. *Paris et l'automobile,* Conférence des Ambassadeurs, January 1965.

Rouleau, Bernard. *Le tracé des rues de Paris, formation, typologie, fonctions.* Paris: Éditions du Centre National de la Recherche Scientifique, 1967.

Gallienne, Georges. *Paris 2000 ou Paris 1900?* Paris: Conférence des Ambassadeurs, October 1968.

Grimaud, Maurice. *La circulation à Paris.* Paris: Conférence des Ambassadeurs, March 1968.

Merlin, Pierre. *Analyse de l'équipement en automobile.* Paris: Institit d'Aménagement de la Région Parisienne, 1968.

Atelier Parisien d'Urbanisme (APUR). "Le sous-sol de Paris et l'urbanisme." *Paris projet,* no. 3, 1970, pp. 9–67.
———. "Les Champs-Élysées: propositions pour un aménagement." *Paris projet,* no. 3, 1970, pp. 86–96.
Knecht, François. *Circulation et stationnement dans la région parisienne.* Paris: Conférence des Ambassadeurs, October 13, 1970.
Lévy, Bertrand, and Pernelle, Jacques. "Espaces centraux et animation urbaine." *Urbanisme,* no. 129, 1972, pp. 39–46.
Rouge, Maurice-François. "Paris sur Seine ou Paris sur autoroute?" *Urbanisme,* no. 130, 1972, pp. 55–61.
APUR. "La voie express Rive Gauche: le tronçon Notre Dame." *Paris projet,* no. 9, 1973, pp. 6–63.
———. "Une zone pour les piétons à l'Opéra." *Paris projet,* nos. 13–14, 1975, pp. 126–37.
———. "Les passages couverts dans Paris." *Paris projet,* nos. 15–16, 1976, pp. 111–51.
de Thézy, Marie. *Paris, la rue.* Paris: Société des Amis de la Bibliothèque Historique, 1976.
APUR. "Á propos des Passages." *Paris projet,* no. 17, 1977, pp. 108–19.

The Transportation System

Arsène-Olivier de Landreville. *Chemins de fer dans Paris et dans les grandes villes.* Paris: Auguste Lemoine, 1868, 1872.
Vautier, Louis Léger. *Chemin de fer circulaire intérieur.* Paris: Blot et Fils, 1872.
Letellier, A. E. *Les chemins de fer projetés dans Paris.* Paris: Vignon, 1875.
Le Masson, E. *Chemins de fer de Paris et de la banlieue.* Paris: Chaix, 1876.
Heuzé, Louis. *Des chemins de fer dans Paris projetés en tunnels; contre-projet.* Paris: Broise et Courtier, 1877.
———. *Paris, chemin de fer transversal à air libre.* Paris: Lapirot and Boullay, 1878–82.
———. *Paris, chemin de fer transversal à air libre dans une rue spéciale, passage couvert pour piétons.* Paris: A. Lévy, 1878 and 1879.
———. *Paris, chemin de fer métropolitain à air libre dans une voie spéciale, avec passage couvert pour piétons.* Paris: A. Lévy, 1879.
———. *Paris, chemins de fer métropolitains en élevation à air libre dans une voie privée, avec passage couvert pour piétons.* Paris: Lapirot and Boullay, n. d.
Chrétien, Jean. *Chemin de fer électrique des boulevards à Paris.* Paris: Baudry, 1881.
———. *Chemin de fer électrique aérien sur les Boulevards Voltaire, de Magenta, Richard-Lenoir, de la Contrescarpe et le Pont d'Austerlitz. Demande de concession.* Paris: Hennuyer, 1882.
———. *Tramway électrique aérien.* Paris: Capiomont et Renault, 1882.
Haag, Paul. *Le Métropolitain de Paris et l'élargissement de la Rue Montmartre.* Paris: A. Lemerre, 1883.
Angéley, A. *Chemin de fer à voie suspendue.* Paris: Chaix, 1884.
Garnier, Jules. *Avant-Projet d'un chemin de fer aérien.* Paris: Chaix, 1884.
———. *Projet comparé d'un chemin de fer aérien.* Paris: Capiomont et Renault, 1885.
Haag, Paul. *Note sur le chemin de fer métropolitain de Paris.* Paris: Capiomont et Renault, 1885.
Tellier, Charles. *Le véritable métropolitain.* Paris: Schlæber, 1885. A second, slightly modified edition was published by Michelet in 1891.
Chemin de fer métropolitain de Paris: plans Comparés. Paris: Schiller, 1886.
Panafieu, L., and Fabre, E. *Chemin de fer métropolitain de Paris: réseau aérien à rail unique.* Paris: Bernard, 1886.
Berlier, J. B. *Paris, tramways souterrains.* Paris: Cusset, 1887.
Arsène-Olivier de Landreville. *Les grands travaux de Paris: le métropolitain.* Paris: Baudry, 1887.
———. *Les grands travaux de Paris de la paix: Paris nouveau.* Paris: Baudry et Cie, 1887.
Latigue, Charles. *Projet de voies aériennes dans Paris.* Paris, 1887 (publisher not indicated).
Villain, Paul. *Projet de chemin de fer métropolitain.* Paris: Grand Imprimerie, 1887.

Latigue, Charles. *Monorail ou chemin de fer à rail unique surélevé.* Paris: Bayle, 1888.

Berlier, J. B. *Les tramways tubulaires souterrains de Paris, 1887–1890.* Paris: Berlier, 1890.

Guerbigny, G. *Des lignes métropolitaines dans Paris.* Paris: Exposition Universelle, 1889.

Berlier, J. B. *Tramways tubulaires souterrains de Paris: ligne de la Place de la Concorde au Bois de Boulogne.* Paris: Cusset, 1890.

Haag, Paul. *Le chemin de fer métropolitain de Paris.* Paris: Chaix, 1890.

————. *Le métropolitain Haag à l'exposition de 1889.* Paris: Chaix, 1890.

Berlier, J. B. *Tramways tubulaires souterrains de Paris.* Paris: Dupont, 1891.

Haag, Paul. *Le chemin de fer métropolitain de Paris* and *Le métropolitain qu'on peut faire.* Paris: Grand Imprimerie, 1891.

————. *Un Métropolitain qui ne coute rien et ne trouble rien.* Paris: Grand Imprimerie, 1892.

————. *Les transports en Commun et les métropolitains dans les grandes villes etrangères et à Paris.* Paris: Baudry, 1897.

Gerards, Émile. *Paris Souterrain.* Paris: Garnier, 1909.

Lagarrigue, Louis. *Cent ans de transports en commun dans la région parisienne* (4 vols.). Paris: Éditions RATP, 1956.

Guerrand, Roger H. *Mémoires du Métro.* Paris: La Table Rond, 1960.

————. *Le métro.* Paris: Les Éditions du Temps, 1962.

Verpræt, Georges. *Paris: capitale souterraine.* Paris: Plon, 1964.

Utudjian, Édouard. *Architecture et urbanisme souterrains.* Paris: Laffont, 1966.

Merlin, Pierre. *Les transports parisiens.* Paris: Masson et Cie, 1967.

Robert, Jean. *Notre Métro.* Paris 1967; distributed by the Musée des Transports Urbains.

Merlin, Pierre. *Le problème des transports.* Paris: La Documentation Française, 1968.

Institut d'Aménagement de et d'Urbanisme de la Région Parisienne. "Les transports urbains," *Cahiers* 17–18 (October 1969).

Robert, Jean. *Les tramways parisiens.* Paris: Jean Robert, 1969 (distributed by Imprimerie Omnès et Cie).

Gros, Brigitte. *4 Heures de transport par jour.* Paris: Denoël, 1970.

Knecht, François. *Circulation et stationnement dans la région parisienne.* Paris: Conférence des Ambassadeurs, 1970.

Institut d'Aménagement et d'Urbanisme de la Région Parisieme (IAURP). *Bulletin d'information de la région parisienne.* March 1971 and December 1972 (special issues on transport).

APUR. "Pour les autobus dans Paris." *Paris projet,* no. 8, 1972, pp. 60–79.

Doublet, Maurice. *Les transports dans la région parisienne.* Paris: Conférence des Ambassadeurs, November 1972.

APUR. "La Seine pour un transport en Commun?" *Paris projet,* no. 9, 1973, pp. 77–99.

Régie Autonome des Transports Parisiens. *Documentation information,* no. 74, April 1974 (special issue on the RER regional system).

Robert, Jean. *Histoire des transports dans les villes de France.* Paris: Robert, 1974.

Régie Autonome des Transports Parisiens. "Les 75 ans du Métro." *Documentation information,* no. 75, 1975.

Architecture

Magne, Lucien. *L'architecture française du Siècle.* Paris: Firmin-Didot, 1889.

Doumic, Max. *L'architecture d'aujourd'hui.* Paris: Perrin, 1897.

Marcou, P. Frantz. "Corner Houses in Paris." *Architectural Record* (January–March 1897): 310–22.

de Olivares, Jose. *Parisian Dream City.* St. Louis: N. D. Thompson, 1900.

Schyler, Montgomery. "Nouveautés de Paris." *Architectural Record.* 10 (1900–01): 361–97.

Schopfer, Jean. "Art in the City." *Architectural Record* 12 (November 1902): 573–83.

Bonnier, Louis. *Les règlements de voirie.* Paris: Schmid, 1903.

Ville de Paris. *Les concours de façades de la ville de Paris 1898–1905.* Paris: Librairie de la Construction Moderne, 1905.

Mallet-Stevens, Robert, and Rœderer, Jacques. "Notes from Paris." *Architectural Review* 22 (July 1907): 18–22.

David, A. C. "Innovations in the Street Architecture of Paris." *Architectural Record* 24 (1908): 109–28.

Léon, Paul. "La beauté de Paris." *Revue de Paris,* November 15, 1909, pp. 280–302.

Léon, Paul. "Maisons et rues de Paris." *Revue de Paris,* August 15, 1910.

Hénard, Eugène. *Rapports à la commission des perspectives monumentales de la ville de Paris.* Paris: Imprimerie de L. Marétheux, 1911. Reprinted in *Journal de l'architecture,* March–April 1911.

Lortsh, Charles. *La beauté de Paris: conservation des aspects esthétiques.* Paris: Bernard Tignol, 1911.

Magny, Charles. *Des moyens juridiques de sauvegarder les aspects esthétiques de la ville de Paris.* Paris: Bernard Tignol, 1911.

Rodin, Auguste. "La Beauté de Paris." *La Revue,* July 15, 1911.

Ville de Paris. *Les concours de façades de la ville de Paris 1906–1912.* Paris: Librairie de la Construction Moderne, 1912.

Lortsh, Charles. *La beauté de Paris et la loi.* Paris: Recuel Sirey, 1913.

Maisons les plus remarquables construites à Paris de 1905 à 1914. Paris: Librairie Central des Beaux-Arts, 1920.

Magne, Henri-Marcel. *L'art français depuis vingt ans: l'architecture.* Paris: Reider, 1921.

Bibliothèque de la Vie Artistique. *Les tendences de l'architecture contemporaine.* Paris: Malhiel-Firmounski, 1930.

Commission des Perspectives Monumentales. *Rapport de la sous-commission chargée de la révision du décret du 13 août 1902.* 1930.

"Immeubles de rapport à Paris." *Architecture d'aujourd'hui,* no. 4, April 1935, pp. 5–29.

Mousset, Albert. "L'ancien et le nouveau Trocadéro." *L'architecture* 49 (April 15, 1936) 109–12.

"Paris moderne 1937." (Map showing locations of modern buildings). *Architecture d'aujourd'hui,* nos. 5–6, June 1937.

Pillement, Georges. *Destruction de Paris.* Paris: Grasset, 1941.

———. "Démolitions présentes et futures." *Destinée de Paris.* Paris: Éditions du Chêne, 1943.

Debidour, Elie. *La conservation du vieux-Paris et l'urbanisme.* Paris: Musée Social, 1945.

Léon, Paul. *La vie des monuments français.* Paris: Picard, 1951.

Lopez, Raymond, and Holley, Michel. "Étude d'aménagement architectural du centre de Paris." *Urbanisme,* no. 84, 1964, pp. 49–59.

Minot, Paul. *Faut-il détruire Paris?* Paris: Conférence des Ambassadeurs, 1964.

Pillement, Georges. *Paris disparu.* Paris: Grasset, 1966.

Besset, Maurice. *New French Architecture.* Teufen: Arthur Niggli, 1967.

de Lagarde, Pierre. *Guide des chefs-d'œuvre en péril: Paris et l'Île de France.* Paris: Pauvert, 1967.

Emery, M., and Mataouchek, V. "Paris-Guide." *Architecture d'aujourd'hui,* June–July 1968.

APUR. "Maine-Montparnasse avant la tour." *Paris projet,* no. 4, 1970, pp. 70–87.

APUR. "Le plan de sauvegarde du Marais." *Paris projet,* no. 2, 1970, pp. 42–74.

Besnard-Bernadac, E. and Putatti, J. "Réflexion sur les problèmes des hauteurs et des sites de Paris." *Urbanisme,* no. 117, 1970, pp. 15–18.

Bourget, Pierre. "Essai sur implantation d'immeubles tours de prestige," *Urbanisme,* no. 117, 1970, pp. 28–29.

Minost, Maurice et al. "Le Marais." *Monuments historiques de la France,* vol. 16, no. 2, April–June 1970, pp. 51–98.

Schein, I. *Paris construit.* Paris: Vincent Fréal et Cie, 1970.

"13 Ans, 26 tours à La Défense." *La construction moderne,* no. 5, September–October 1970, pp. 27–31.

Basdevant, Denise. *L'architecture française.* Paris: Hachette, 1971.

Emery, Marc. *Un siècle d'architecture moderne 1850–1950.* Paris: Horizons de France, 1971.

Ragon, Michel. *Histoire mondiale de l'architecture et de l'urbanisme modernes.* (2 vols.). Paris: Casterman, 1971–72.

Amouroux, D.; Crettol, M.; Monnet, and J.P. *Guide d'architecture contemporaine en France.* Paris: Technic-Union, 1972.

APUR. "Le centre Beaubourg." *Paris projet,* no. 7, 1972, pp. 6–61.

————. "La transformation des grands magasins de Paris." *Paris projet,* no. 8, 1972, pp. 80–101.

"Centre du plateau Beaubourg: concours d'idées." *Techniques et architecture,* vol. 34, no. 3, February 1972 (special issue).

Pillement, Georges. *Paris poubelle.* Paris: Pauvert, 1974.

"La polémique sur les immeubles-tours à Paris et sur le Quartier de la Défense." *Urbanisme,* no. 132, 1972, pp. xvii–xx.

Pompidou, Georges. "Le président de la République définit ses conceptions dans les domaines de l'art et de l'architecture." *Le Monde,* October 17, 1972.

————. "Le règlement du POS et le paysage urbain." *Paris projet,* nos. 13–14, 1975, pp. 4–89.

Secrétariat d'État à la Culture et Ministère de la Qualité de la Vie. *Liste des immeubles protégés.* Paris: Imprimerie Nationale, 1976.

Boudon, Françoise et al. *Système de l'architecture urbaine: le quartier des Halles à Paris.* Paris: Éditions du Centre de la Recherche Scientifique, 1977.

Housing

White, William Henry. "On Middle-Class Houses in Paris and Central London." *Royal Institute of British Architects Transactions,* 28 (1877–78): 21–54.

Marjolin, René. *Étude sur les causes et les effets des logements insalubres.* Paris: Masson, 1881.

Picot, Georges. *Un devoir social et les logements d'ouvriers.* Paris: Calmann-Lévy, 1885.

Du Mesnil, Octave. *Des habitations à bon marché au point de vue de la construction et de la salubrité.* Paris: J. B. Ballière, 1889.

————. *L'hygiène à Paris. L'habitation du pauvre.* Paris: J. B. Ballière, 1890.

Ferrand, Lucien. *Habitation à bon marché.* Paris: Rousseau, 1906.

Valdour, Jacques. *La vie ouvrière.* Paris: Giard & Brière, 1909.

Ferrand, Lucien. *L'habitation ouvrière à bon marché.* Paris: Gabalda, 1911.

Société des cités jardins de la banlieue parisienne. Paris: Imprimerie Lahure, 1914.

Office public d'habitations à bon marché. Documents relatifs à sa création, à son organisation et à son fonctionnement. Paris: Ville de Paris, 1917.

Hammarstrand, Nils. "The Housing Problem in Paris." *Journal of the American Institute of Architects* 8 (February 1920): 88–89.

Valdour, Jacques. *La vie ouvrière.* Paris: Rousseau, 1921.

"L'œuvre des offices d'habitations dans le Département de la Seine." *La vie urbaine,* 1922, pp. 223–28.

"Cités-Jardins et groupes d'habitations de Paris et du Département de la Seine." *La vie urbaine,* 1923, pp. 326–79.

Klaber, E. H. "The Housing Crisis in Paris." *Journal of the American Institute of Architects* 11 (1923): 19–24.

Sellier, Henri. "Les aspects nouveaux du problème de l'habitation dans les agglomérations urbaines." *La vie urbaine,* no. 18, 1923, pp. 81–109.

Bonnefond, M. "Les colonies de bicoques de la région parisienne." *La vie urbaine,* no. 25, 1925, pp. 525–60; no. 26, 1925, pp. 597–626.

Sellier; Henri. *Le problème du logement, son influence sur les conditions de l'habitation et l'aménagement des villes.* Paris: Presses Universitaires de France, 1927.

Lacroix, Louis. "Les îlots insalubres de Paris." *Urbanisme,* nos. 6–7, September–October 1932, pp. 175–81.

Sebille, Georges. "Les aménagements d'îlots." *Urbanisme,* nos. 6–7, September–October 1932, pp. 172–74.

Bonnaud, A. "La cité-jardins de Plessis-Robinson." *Urbanisme,* nos. 6–7, September–October 1932, pp. 189–96.

Berson, Claude. "L'action de l'office public d'habitations à bon marché de la ville de Paris dans le domaine de la construction." *La vie urbaine* 9–10 (May 1933): 177–93: 18 (November 1933): 356–75.

Sellier, Henri. *Réalisations de l'office public d'habitations du Département de la Seine.* Strasbourg: EDARI, 1933.

————. "L'habitation en hauteur." *Urbanisme,* no. 16, July 1933, pp. 202–10.

"La Cité Jardins." *Urbanisme,* no. 32, January 1935, pp. 23–26.

Fender, Emile Xavier. *La crise du bâtiment dans la région parisienne.* Paris: Sirey, 1936.

Cité-jardins de Châtenay-Malabry. Paris: Office public d'habitations du Département de la Seine, 1937.

Sellier, Henri. "L'œuvre de l'Office Public d'Habitations à Bon Marché du Département de la Seine." *Architecture d'aujourd'hui,* nos. 5–6, June 1937, pp. 43–46.

"Relogement de Paris et de la Seine." *Architecture française,* April 1946 (special issue).

Suquet-Bonnaud, A. "L'habitation." *Urbanisme,* no. 2, April 1947, pp. 251–56.

Lemoine, Jean. "La crise du logement." *La vie urbaine,* no. 57, July–September 1950, pp. 172–90.

Logez-vous. (special issue on housing constructed on the zone). May 1955.

Simon, Boris. *Abbé Pierre and the Ragpickers of Emmaus,* New York: P. J. Kennedy, 1955.

Urbanisme et habitation, July-December 1955 (special issue on housing).

Simon, Boris. *Ragman's City.* New York: Coward-McCann, 1957.

de Quirielle, L. *Les nouveaux ensembles immobiliers.* Paris: Berger-Lerault, 1960.

Rochfort, Christianne. *Les petits enfants du siècle.* Paris: Grasset, 1961. English translation, *Children of Heaven.* New York: David McKay, 1962.

Kaës, René. *Vivre dans les grands ensembles.* Paris: Éditions Ouvrières, 1963.

Bertrand, Michel. "Le confort des logements à Paris en 1954." *Le vie urbaine,* no. 3, January–March 1964, pp. 23–71; July–September 1964, pp. 273–314.

Margot-Duclot, Jean. "Les enquêtes d'opinion et les problèmes d'urbanisme." *La vie urbaine,* no. 2, April–June 1964, pp. 81–97.

Taupin, Jean-Louis, "Architecture et urbanisme des groupes d'habitations: 50 ans d'évolution." In *Urbanisation française.* Paris: Centre de Recherche d'Urbanisme, 1964.

District de la Région de Paris. *Étude des besoins en logements dans la région de Paris 1966–1975.* Paris: S.I., April 1965.

Duquesne, Jean. *Vivre à Sarcelles?* Paris: Éditions Cujas, 1966.

Habitations à loyer modéré du Département de la Seine. Paris: Imprimerie Municipale, 1966.

Taisne-Plantevin, Catherine and Bamas, François. "Les logements en région de Paris." IAURP *Cahiers,* no. 6, November 1966.

Clerc, Paul. *Grands ensembles, banlieues nouvelles: enquête démographique et psycho-sociologique.* Paris: Presses Universitaires de France, 1967.

Guerrand, Roger H. *Les origines du logement social en France.* Paris: Éditions Ouvrières, 1967.

La Documentation Française. *Logement et urbanisme en France.* Dossier 5–298, Paris, 1969.

Houdeville, Louis. *Pour une civilisation de l'habitat.* Paris: Éditions Ouvrières, 1969.

Labbens, Jean. *Le quart-monde–la pauvreté dans la société industrielle: étude sur le sous-proletariat français dans la région parisienne,* Paris: Pierrelaye, 1969.

Chailleux, Jean-Yves. *L'habitat individuel en région parisienne.* Paris: Service Régional de l'Équipement de la Région Parisienne, 1970.

Institut d'Aménagement et d'Urbanisme de la Région Parisienne (IAURP). *Cahiers,* vol. 19, 1970 (special issue on housing in the Paris region).

————. *L'habitat individuel en région parisienne,* December 1970.

Mervo, Monique, and Charras, Marie-Ange. *Bidonvilles.* Paris: Maspero, 1971.

Simon, Boris. *Les chiffonniers d'Emaüs.* Paris: Le Seuil, 1971.

Cassio-Talabot, Gérald, and Devy, Alain. *La grande borne.* Paris: Hachette, 1972.

IAURP. "Le Logement." *Bulletin d'information de la région parisienne,* no. 8, December 1972.

_____. "Grands ensembles et habitat individuel." *Bulletin d'information de la région parisienne,* no. 13, August 1974 (special issue).

Paris as a Whole: Large-Scale Redevelopment

Chrétien, Jean. *Les odeurs de Paris.* Paris: Baudry, 1881.

Schopfer, Jean. "The Plan of a City." *Architectural Record* 12 (1902): 693–703.

Hénard, Eugène. *Études sur les transformations de Paris. Fascicule 3: Les grands espaces libres. Les parcs et jardins de Paris et Londres.* Paris: Librairies-Imprimeries Réunies, 1903.

Schopfer, Jean. "Open-Air Life in a Great City." *Architectural Record* 12 (1903): 157–68.

Hénard, Eugène. *Études sur les transformations de Paris. Fascicule 4: Le Champ de Mars et la Galerie des Machines. Les parc des sports et les grands dirigeables.* Paris: Librairies-Imprimeries Réunies, 1904.

_____. "A Description of the Development of Paris." *Proceedings of the American Institute of Architects* 39 (1905–06): 109–13.

_____. *Les espaces libres à Paris.* Paris: Musée Social, Mémoires et Documents, no.7, 1908.

Planet, Paul. "Transformations de Paris." *Construction moderne* 24 (1908–09): 469–72.

Benoit-Lévy, Georges. "La beauté de Paris." *La revue,* October 15, 1909, pp. 525–32.

Hénard, Eugène. *Les espaces libres à Paris: les fortifications remplacées par une ceinture de parcs.* Paris: A. Rousseau, 1909.

Dausset, Louis. "The Maintenance of the Fortifications and of the Zone Subject to Military Regulations at Paris." *Royal Institute of British Architects: Transactions of the Town Planning Conference,* October 1910, pp. 633–35.

Commission d'Extension de Paris, Préfecture du Département de la Seine. Vol. 1, *Aperçu historique.* Vol. 2, *Considérations techniques.* Paris: Chaux, 1913.

Hammarstrand, Nils. "The Plan of Paris." *Journal of the American Institute of Architects* 6 (May 1918): 291–98; 8 (February 1920): 67–86.

Préfecture du Département de la Seine et la Ville de Paris. *Programme du concours ouvert pour l'établissement du plan d'aménagement et d'extension de Paris.* Paris: Chaix, 1919.

Greber, Jacques. "The New Plans for Paris." *Architectural Record* 49 (January 1921): 71–78.

Le Corbusier. *Urbanisme.* Paris: Éditions Crés et Cie, 1925. English translation, *The City of Tomorrow,* London: Architectural Press, 1947.

Guérard, Albert. *L'avenir de Paris.* Paris: Payot, 1929.

Le Corbusier. *La ville radieuse.* Boulogne (Seine): Éditions de l'Architecture d'Aujourd'hui, 1935, English translation, *The Radiant City,* New York: Grossman, Orion Press, 1967.

Architecture d'aujourd'hui, nos. 5–6, June 1937 (special issue on the planning of Paris).

Les Architectes Indépendants Réunis. "Projet d'aménagement de l'îlot insalubre no. XVI." *Architecture française,* no. 2, 1940, pp. 5–21.

Le Corbusier. *Destin de Paris.* Paris: Éditions Fernand Sorlot, 1941.

B. Champigneulle, et al. *Destinée de Paris.* Paris: Éditions du Chêne, 1943.

Debidour, Elie. *La conservation du Vieux-Paris et l'urbanisme.* Paris: Musée Social, 1945.

Conseil Municipal (Paris). *Délibération du conseil municipal en date du 14 décembre 1950 portant approbation du programme d'aménagement da la ville de Paris.* Paris: Imprimerie Municipale, 1951.

Joffet, Robert. "Le point de vue du conservateur des jardins de Paris." *Urbanisme,* nos. 3–4, 1952, pp. 109–24.

"L'aménagement de la ceinture vert de Paris." *Urbanisme,* vol. 23, nos. 35–36, 1954, pp. 4–16.

Lafay, Bernard. *Problèmes de Paris: esquisse d'un plan directeur et d'un programme d'action.* Paris: Conseil Municipal de Paris, 1954.

Le Corbusier. *Les plans Le Corbusier de Paris.* Paris: Éditions de Minuit, 1956.

"Propos sur Paris." *Urbanisme,* vol. 25, no. 55, 1957 (special issue).

Kerhervé, Jacqueline. "Le quartier des Halles à Paris." *La vie urbaine,* no. 2, April–June 1959, pp. 111–50.

Préfecture da la Seine. *Plan d'urbanisme directeur de Paris.* Paris: Imprimerie Municipale, 1960–63.

Holley, Michel. *L'espace parisien.* Paris: Centre de Documentation de d'Urbanisme de la Ville de Paris, 1961.

Conseil Municipal (Paris). *Enquête publique sur le plan d'urbanisme directeur de Paris.* Paris: Imprimerie Municipale, 1962.

"Paris." *Urbanisme,* vol. 31, no. 74, 1962 (special issue), pp. 2–21.

de Lauwe, Chombert. "Aspects sociologique de l'évolution de Paris." *La vie urbaine,* no. 4, October–December 1963, pp. 271–82.

"Les Halles et le Quartier des Halles à Paris." *La vie urbaine,* no. 4, October–December 1963, pp. 303–14.

"Destin de Paris."*Urbanisme,* vol. 33, no. 84, 1964 (special issue).

Mazé, Jean. *Paris à l'heure du choix.* Paris: Flammarion, 1965.

Ragon, Michel. *Paris, hier, aujourd'hui, demain.* Paris: Hachette, 1965.

Ministère d'État, Affaires Culturelles, Direction de l'Architecture. *Paris, propositions pour le cœur historique.* Paris: Imprimerie Nationale, 1965.

Techniques et Architecture. Vol. 25, no. 6, September 1965; vol. 29, no. 1, February 1968 ; and vol. 34, no. 2, December 1971 (special issues on La Défense).

Beaujeu-Garnier, J. "Aspects et problèmes de la rénovation parisienne." *La vie urbaine,* no 3, July–September 1966, pp. 169–80.

Coing, Henri. *Rénovation Urbaine et Changement Social.* Paris: Éditions Ouvrières, 1966.

"Paris: les Halles." *Architecture d'aujourd'hui,* no. 132, June–July 1967, pp. 23–28.

Atelier Parisien d'Urbanisme. *Projet de schéma directeur d'aménagement et d'urbanisation de la ville de Paris.* Paris: 1968.

Architecture d'aujourd'hui. no. 138, June–July 1968 (special issue on Paris).

"Projets pour Paris au Conseil de Paris." *La vie urbaine,* no. 1, January–March 1968, pp.39–76.

Wolf, Peter. *Eugène Hénard and the Beginning of Urbanism in Paris 1900–1914.* The Hague: International Federation for Housing and Planning,1968; Paris: Centre de Recherche d'Urbanisme, 1968.

APUR. *Paris projet,* no. 1, July 1969 (special issue on Les Halles).

Paris. Inspection Principale des Halles. *Halles centrales de Paris.* Paris: Imprimerie Municipale, 1969.

Préfecture de Paris. *Aménagement du quartier des Halles.* Paris: Imprimerie Municipale, 1969.

APUR. "Espaces verts dans Paris." *Paris projet,* no. 4, 1970, pp. 8–39.

Auzelle, Robert. "L'intéret expérimental du projet da la Défense." *Urbanisme,* no. 120–21, 1970, pp. 57–60.

"Espace parisien." *Urbanisme,* vol. 39, no. 117, 1970, pp. 12–32.

Meau, Yves. *Aménagement du quartier de la Défense.* Extrait du Moniteur des Travaux Publics et du Bâtiment, September 1970.

Millier, Jean. "Le quartier d'affaires de la Défense." *Urbanisme,* no. 120–21, 1970, pp. 52–56.

Schéma directeur d'aménagement et d'urbanisme de la Ville de Paris (Paris: Imprimerie Municipale, 1970).

Sutcliffe, Anthony. *The Autumn of Central Paris.* London: Edward Arnold, 1970.

APUR. "Paris 71–75: le 6ᵉ plan." *Paris projet,* no. 5, 1971, pp. 6–39.

————. "Le 7ᵉ arrondissement." *Paris projet,* no. 6, 1971, pp. 2–29.

Godard, Francis. "La rénovation urbaine à Paris: l'opération 'Italie 13.' " *Espaces et Sociétés,* no. 2, March 1971, pp. 149–68.

Herbert, Jacques. *Sauver les Halles: Cœur de Paris.* Paris: Denoël, 1971.

Préfecture de Paris. *Espaces verts parisiens.* Paris: Imprimerie Municipal, 1971.

APUR. "Le forum des Halles." *Paris projet,* no. 8, 1972, pp. 8–59.

"Urbanisme parisien." *Académie d'Architecture Bulletin,* vol. 61, 1972, pp. 40–91.

Archer, B. "La rénovation urbaine pervertie." *Architecture d'aujourd'hui,* no. 169, September–October 1973, pp. 70–75.

Evenson, Norma. "The Assassination of Les Halles." *Journal of the Society of Architectural Historians,* vol. 32, no. 4, December 1973, pp. 308–15.

Godard, Francis. *La Rénovation urbaine à Paris: structure urbaine et logique de classe.* Paris: Mouton, 1973.

APUR. *Paris projet,* "L'avenir de Paris," nos. 10–11, 1974 (special issue).

———. "Le schéma directeur Seine sud-est." *Paris projet,* no.12, 1974, pp. 8–85.

"Paris/Londres." *Architecture d'aujourd'hui,* no. 156, November–December 1974, pp. 1–72.

Ville de Paris. *20 Ans de transformations de Paris, 1954–1974.* Paris: Association Universitaire de Recherches Géographiques et Cartographiques, 1974.

Lafay, Bernard. *Schéma d'un plan vert pour Paris.* Paris: Club Paris 2000, 1975.

"Paris" *Revue de l'art,* no. 29, 1975 (special issue).

"Paris: urbanisme, classes, pouvoir." *Espaces et sociétés,* nos. 13–14, October 1974–January 1975 (special issue).

Viguier, Jean-Michel, and Gangneux, Marie-Christine. "Tours et détours pour la Défense." *Architecture d'aujourd'hui,* no. 178, March–April 1975, pp. 26–44.

APUR. "La Villette: aménagement des anciens abattoirs et les abords du bassin." *Paris projet,* nos. 15–16, 1976, pp. 4–109.

———. "L'aménagement du Canal Saint-Martin." *Paris projet,* no. 17, 1977, pp. 4–63.

———. "L'aménagement des terrains Citroën." *Paris projet,* no. 17, 1977, pp. 64–107.

The Region

Bonnier, Louis. "La population de Paris en movement 1800–1961." *La vie urbaine,* nos. 1–2, 1919, pp. 7–21.

Préfecture du Département de la Seine. Ville de Paris. *Programme du concours ouvert pour l'établissement du plan d'aménagement et d'extension de Paris.* Paris: Chaix, 1919.

La vie urbaine, 1920 (special issue on the 1919 regional planning competition).

Hammarstrand, Nils. "The Programme for the Greater Paris Competition." *Journal of the American Institute of Architects* 8 (January 1920): 27–36.

Honoré, F. "Paris dans Cinquante Ans." *L'illustration,* April 3, 1920, pp. 196–98, and May 1, 1920, pp. 269–72.

Sellier, Henri. *Les Banlieues Urbaines.* Paris: Rivière et Cie, 1920.

L'Europe nouvelle, June 8, 1929 (issue on the extension of Paris.)

"La loi sur l'aménagement de la région parisienne." *Urbanisme,* no. 2, May 1932, pp. 73–74.

Minvielle, Georges. *L'aménagement de la région parisienne.* Paris: Sirey, 1932.

Morizet, André. *Vers le grand Paris.* Paris: Hachette, 1932.

Rosier, Camille. "La loi et l'urbanisme en France." *Urbanisme,* no. 4, July 1932, pp. 124–30.

Patoud, Japy, and Defrasse. *L'urbanisme de la région parisienne 1937.* Paris: Mouillot, 1933.

Descoutures, M. J. "L'évolution de la banlieue nord-est de Paris." *Urbanisme,* no. 29, October 1934, pp. 278–301.

Dausset, Louis. "La notion de la plan régional." *Urbanisme,* no. 40, October–November, 1935.

Sellier, Henri, and Brasseau, Paul. "Le plan d'aménagement de la région parisienne devant les corps élus." *Urbanisme,* no. 40, October–November 1935, pp. 2–11.

"L'urbanisme et les décrets-lois." *Urbanisme,* no. 40, October–November 1935, pp. 2–55.

Latour, François. *Paris 1937 et le grand Paris.* Paris: Imprimerie Municipale, 1936.

"La région parisienne." *Urbanisme.* no. 41, January 1936 (special issue).

Architecture d'aujourd'hui, nos. 5–6, June 1937 (special issue on the planning of Paris).

Gravier, Jean-François. *Paris et le désert français.* Paris: Le Portulan, 1947; revised edition, Paris: Flammarion, 1972.

Gibel, P. "La région parisienne." *La vie urbaine,* no. 58, April–June 1950, pp. 114–54.

"L'aménagement du territoire national français." *La vie urbaine,* no. 61, July–September 1951, pp. 241–54.

Bricet, André. *Population et habitat dans la région parisienne.* Paris: Imprimerie Nationale, 1956.

Poisson, Georges. *Évocation du grand Paris.* Paris: Éditions de Minuit, 1956–60.

"Paris et sa région." *Urbanisme,* vol. 25, no. 51, 1956 (special issue).

Berrurier, Raymond. "Reconquête de l'agglomeration parisienne." *Urbanisme,* no. 55, 1957, pp. 170–76.

Construction et urbanisme dans la région parisienne. Paris: Imprimerie Municipale, 1957.

Pottier, Henry, et al. "Projet pour une capitale fédérale au nord de Paris." *Architecture d'aujourd'hui,* no. 80, October–November 1958, p. 20.

George, Pierre; Randet, Pierre; and Bastié, Jean. *La région parisienne.* Paris: Presses Universitaires de France, 1959 and 1964.

"Aménagement de la région parisienne." *Urbanisme,* no. 68, 1960 (special issue).

Délimitation de l'agglomération parisienne. Paris: Direction Régionale de l'Institut National de la Statistique et les Études Économiques, 1960.

Ministère de la Construction. *Plan d'aménagement et d'organisation générale de la région parisienne,* 1960 and 1962.

"Paris et sa Région." *Architecture d'aujourd'hui,* no. 88, February–March 1960, pp. 3–11, no. 90, June–July 1960, pp. 70–81.

Lavedan, Pierre. "Le plan d'aménagement de la région parisienne." *La vie urbaine,* no. 4, October–December 1961, pp. 281–310.

Pilliet, Georges. *L'avenir de Paris.* Paris: Hachette, 1961.

Griotteray, Alain. *L'état contre Paris.* Paris: Hachette, 1962.

District de la Région de Paris. *Avant-projet de programme duodécennal pour la région de Paris.* Paris: Imprimerie Municipale, 1963.

Premier Ministre. Délégation Générale au District de la Région de Paris. *Avant-projet de programme duodécennal pour la région de Paris.* Paris: Imprimerie Municipale, 1963.

Bastié, Jean. *La croissance de la banlieue parisienne.* Paris: Presses Universitaires de France, 1964.

————. *Paris en l'an 2000.* Paris: SEDIMO, 1964.

Boutet de Monvel, Noël. *Les demains de Paris.* Paris: Denoël, 1964.

Delouvrier, Paul. "L'avenir de la nébuleuse Parisienne." *Urbanisme,* no. 84, 1964 pp. 19–23.

Margot–Duclot, Jean. "Les enquêtes d'opinion et les problèmes d'urbanisme. Quelques resultats pour la région de Paris." *La vie urbaine,* no. 2, April–June 1964, pp. 81–97.

"Destin de Paris."*Urbanisme,* vol. 33, no. 84, 1964 (special issue).

Cornuau, C. et al. *L'attraction de Paris sur sa banlieue.* Paris: Éditions Ouvrières, 1965.

Délégation Générale au District de la Région de Paris. *Schéma directeur d'aménagement et d'urbanisme de la région de Paris* (3 vols.). Paris: 1965–66.

Ragon, Michel. *Paris, hier, aujourd'hui, demain.* Paris: Hachette, 1965.

Sarraut, Albert. "1928 Région parisienne." *Urbanisme,* no. 88, 1965, p. 21.

Bastié, Jean. "Les problèmes d'aménagement et d'urbanisme de l'agglomération parisienne: Le schéma directeur." *La vie urbaine,* no. 1, January–March 1966, pp. 1–31.

Delouvrier, Paul. *L'aménagement de la région de Paris.* Paris: Imprimerie Moderne de la Presse, 1966.

"Rapport d'avis de la société française des urbanistes sur le schéma directeur d'aménagement et d'urbanisme de la région de Paris." *Urbanisme,* vol. 35, no. 93, 1966, pp. 75–84.

"Paris." *Architecture d'aujourd'hui,* no. 138, June–July 1968 (special issue).

Walsh, Annamarie Hauck. *Urban Government in the Paris Region.* New York: Præger, 1968.

Christ, Yvan. *Les métamorphoses de la banlieue parisienne.* Paris: Balland, 1969.

Merlin, Pierre. *Les villes nouvelles.* Paris: Presses Universitaires de France, 1969. English translation: *New Towns,* London: Methuen, 1971. Chapter 4, "New Towns Policy in France," includes a discussion of the Paris region.

"Villes nouvelles françaises." *Urbanisme,* no. 114, 1969 (special issue).

Kessler, Marie-Christine, and Bodiguel, Jean-Luc (editors). *L'expérience française des villes nouvelles.* Paris: A. Colin, 1970.

Vaujour, Jean. *Le plus grand Paris.* Paris: Presses Universitaires de France, 1970.

"Code pratique de l'urbanisme: rubrique région parisienne." *Urbanisme,* nos. 69–70, 1971 (special issue).

Doublet, Maurice. "Paris, capitale européenne." *La nouvelle revue des deux mondes,* August 1971, pp. 278–83.

IAURP. "Les villes nouvelles." *Bulletin d'information de la région parisienne,* no. 3, June 1971.

Merlin, Pierre. *Vivre à Paris 1980.* Paris: Hachette, 1971.

Ragon, Michel. *Les erreurs monumentales.* Paris: Hachette, 1971.

Préfecture de la Région Parisienne. *La région parisienne 1969–1972: Quatre années d'aménagement et d'équipement.* Paris, 1973.

Beaujeu-Garnier, Jacqueline. *Place, vocation et avenir de Paris et sa région.* Paris: Documentation Française, 1974.

Chatin, Catherine. 9 *Villes nouvelles.* Paris: Dunod, 1975.

IAURP. "Accueil en région parisienne." *Bulletin d'information de la région parisienne,* no. 15, 1975 (special issue).

————. "Paris-Province." *Bulletin d'information de la région parisienne,* no. 9, August 1975.

————. "Le schéma directeur d'aménagement et d'urbanisme de la région parisienne." *Bulletin d'information de la région parisienne,* no. 17, May 1975.

————. "La mise en œuvre de la réforme régionale." *Bulletin d'information de la région parisienne,* no. 23, October 1976.

Préfecture de la Région d'Île de France. *Schéma directeur d'aménagement et d'urbanisme de la région d'Île de France. Rapport.* Paris: July 1976.

INDEX